WATCH AND CLOCK MAKING
AND REPAIRING

By the same author

Clock and Watch Escapements

WATCH AND CLOCK MAKING AND REPAIRING

Dealing with the Construction and Repair of
Watches, Clocks and Chronometers

W. J. GAZELEY, F.B.H.I.

ROBERT HALE · LONDON

© W. J. Gazeley 1953, 1958 and 1993
First edition 1953
Second edition 1958
Reprinted 1965
Reprinted 1971
Reprinted 1973
Reprinted 1975
This revised edition 1993
Reprinted 1994

ISBN 0 7090 4995 1

Robert Hale Limited
Clerkenwell House
Clerkenwell Green
London EC1R 0HT

WARNING

Most of the cleaning agents mentioned in this book e.g. benzine, methylated spirit, ether, etc give off highly flammable fumes. Use only in a well-ventilated room and always away from a naked flame or any incandescent material. It is safer to use a cleaning machine (*see* page 377) wherever possible.

Mercury is a deadly poison and its use is not recommended. Where a thermometer, barometer or a compensated pendulum requires repair the work must be entrusted to a specialist.

Printed in Great Britain by
St Edmundsbury Press Limited, Bury St Edmunds, Suffolk
Bound by WBC Bookbinders Limited

PREFACE

THIS book was written by my father in response to the interest shown in his series of articles in the *Watchmaker, Jeweller and Silversmith* and the continued demand for it over forty years indicates the value of a work which explains the principles and construction of watches, clocks and chronometers in a simple manner. Included, too, is a wealth of practical information on the important subjects of cleaning and repairing. The student, the man who is taking up the craft as a career and indeed the practising repairer have all found this book an invaluable source of information.

The book opens with a description of the various tools and materials essential for good work; details are then given concerning the construction and repair of the various types of movement, trains, motion work and gearing, the various forms of escapement, keyless mechanisms, balances and balance-springs, pendulums, striking and repeating mechanisms, calendars, chronograph work and chronometers. The subject of cleaning is given careful consideration, while filing and turning, the two most important operations in watch and clock making, are given special attention.

Very often in repair work a certain operation can be simplified and carried out more quickly by means of a tool designed specially for the job. Tools which the author found extremely useful in such circumstances are described and instructions are given as to how they may be made. In addition, an appendix lists the various causes of failure and bad time-keeping in watches and clocks.

The information given is as valid today as it was on first publication in 1953 but it should be noted that some terminology has changed. In particular, when the author was taught his trade a balance wheel was the escape wheel of a verge watch rather than the balance proper. However balance wheel has now become the accepted alternative to balance. Also many of the old makers, the author included, refer to the escape wheel as the 'scape wheel. Escape wheel is now the accepted term. A clock was a timepiece with a striking, chiming or alarm mechanism otherwise it was just a timepiece. Nowadays any timepiece may be referred to as a 'clock'. However a watch which strikes the hours 'on passing' as well as when the 'repeat button' is pressed is still referred to as a clock-watch.

J. R. Gazeley
1992

CHAPTER 1

TOOLS AND EQUIPMENT

WITH both watch and clock work it is most essential to have a good kit of tools, also a suitable bench on which to work. The watchmaker, to use his skill to the best advantage, should work in suitable conditions and in a comfortable position, so that he can concentrate on his work and not be distracted or suffer from aches or cramp.

Benches

The height of the bench is an important consideration and this must be decided by the individual according to his size. The bench should be high enough to prevent cramping the stomach, and just low enough for the craftsman to be able to place both arms on the bench when carrying out a careful examination of a watch or clock movement. Some watchmakers like to stand at their benches at times. The bench should therefore be high enough for the craftsman to be able to stand in comfort at work, and a stool of suitable height should be available for use when required. The stool should be fitted with a footrest.

The clockmaker should keep the height of his bench constant as it helps him to file flat. A change of height means a change of style. He has to get used to the height of his vice, otherwise the tendency is to file the back of the work too much if the bench is low, and the front of the work if the bench is too high. Often when changing his place of employment, the bench is different, with the result that he has to accommodate himself to the changed conditions.

Bench Lighting

The bench should be equipped with an adjustable lighting fitting, in addition to the normal workshop lighting. It is bad practice, however, to work with a light that is too powerful, and a 40-watt lamp is suitable for most work, with a 60-watt lamp available as a substitute for use when examining small mechanisms closely. The light should not be concentrated, but should give the minimum amount of shadow. Daylight is obviously the best light of all and perfect if from the north. It is almost impossible, in London anyway, for every watch- and clockmaker to work by daylight, so the best available lighting has to be accepted.

1

The Watchmaker's Eyeglass

The next item to be considered is the watchmaker's eyeglass, and this also is very important. A watchmaker is dependent upon his eyesight for his living, and the longer his sight lasts the longer he can work. It must be emphasized that the use of too strong an eyeglass is definitely harmful. It is better to dispense with an eyeglass if one can see comfortably without its aid, but if this is not the case, it is advisable to use the weakest glass one needs, remembering always to avoid all strain. In other words, use an eyeglass of necessity, but not to magnify. As one gets older a stronger glass will become necessary, and if one has used an eyeglass unnecessarily strong, a microscope will eventually be necessary.

In passing, as the care of the eyes is so important to the watchmaker, it is worth mentioning that when turning in the lathe, especially if the lathe is power-driven, it is advisable to screen the eyes, as pieces of hot metal may fly off and stick to the eyeball, making a visit to the hospital necessary.

Files

With the kit of tools, undoubtedly files are the most important items. Files are of many types and sizes, and all should be fitted into handles, both for safety and efficiency. It is awkward to file using the tang of a file as the handle, because there is no feeling of balance.

The correct way to put a file into a handle is illustrated.

First make the tang of the file red hot, and push it into the hole in the handle, until about half an inch stands out. Remove the tang and shorten it by about half an inch. Then place the shortened tang in the hole, and by holding the handle in the hand, with the file perpendicular, hit the handle on the bench sharply ; the file will then drive into the handle firmly. Finally, check up to see that the handle and the file are quite straight. This is very important, as will be found from experience.

To take a file out of its handle, hold the file by its edges in the vice, with the brass ferrule and handle standing proud. Give the handle a sharp tap at the ferrule end, and the handle will come off cleanly and without damage.

Types of File Required

A clockmaker needs an eight-inch " bastard cut " file, a smooth cut, and a dead smooth, in addition to the files used by a watchmaker. Most will be on a larger scale, but some clockwork is quite small and needs small files. A watchmaker's files are innumerable, but such files as the pillar, pottance, 3-square, square, rat-tail, ridgeback, crossings, rounding-up, fast-cutting and smooth are common to both jobs. Many watchmakers' files have to be made as required because they cannot be bought. With watchmakers, small crossings or oval files are used for making small drills, etc.

3

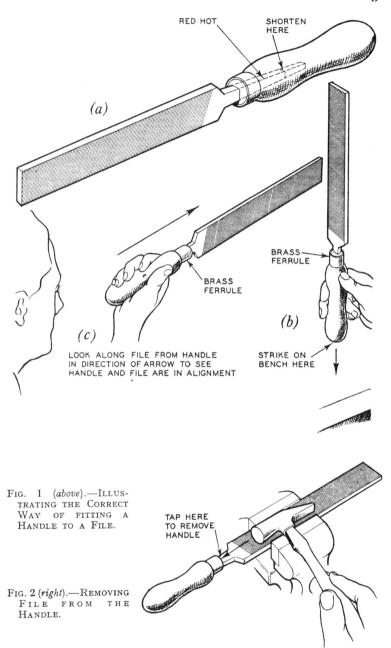

RED HOT

SHORTEN HERE

(a)

BRASS FERRULE

(c)

LOOK ALONG FILE FROM HANDLE IN DIRECTION OF ARROW TO SEE HANDLE AND FILE ARE IN ALIGNMENT

BRASS FERRULE

(b)

STRIKE ON BENCH HERE

FIG. 1 (above).—ILLUSTRATING THE CORRECT WAY OF FITTING A HANDLE TO A FILE.

TAP HERE TO REMOVE HANDLE

FIG. 2 (right).—REMOVING FILE FROM THE HANDLE.

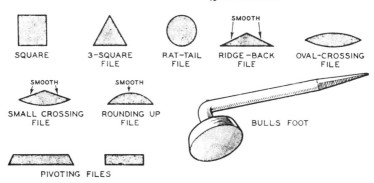

FIG. 3.—TYPES OF FILE USEFUL TO WATCH- AND CLOCKMAKERS.

Another useful file is a very smooth No. 8 cut, about 2 inches long and about $\frac{1}{8}$ inch broad. This is useful for recentring balance staffs and pinions, etc., when they have been cut to length. (Its use will be described later.)

Cleaning and Care of Files

When files become clogged and fail to cut, they can be cleaned by first washing in benzine to clean off any grease, and then, with a piece of sheet brass used edgewise and rubbed across the cut of the file and between the teeth (not against the cut), all the metal clogging the file can be removed. (See Fig. 4.) A file treated in this manner will be almost as good as new and give further useful service. On no account use a steel scratch brush as it will ruin the file.

Never use a new file on steel; keep it for brass only, until the sharp cut has been worn off. If a new file is used on steel, the teeth get chipped and broken, and the file is useless for any metal. If treated in the proper way, a file will last for many years. A craftsman gets used to a particular file; there seems to be a certain "feel" about it.

When purchasing a new file, always see that the teeth are up, in other words, the tops are quite sharp. Some modern files have nice flats on the top and thus will not cut. Another fault with some new files is the burrs on the edge. They should be quite square and sharp at the corners. If they have burrs a square corner

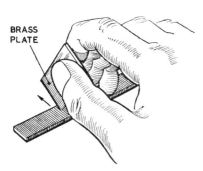

FIG. 4.—CLEARING CUT OF FILE, USING BRASS PLATE.

cannot be cut. The safe edge can be trimmed up, but not the cutting edge.

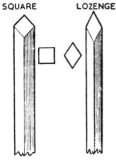

Fig. 5.—Square and Lozenge Gravers.

Uses for Worn-out Files

When a file is worn out do not throw it away, as it is generally made of very good steel, which is extremely useful for making other tools. It has to be annealed, however; that is, softened. It is not sufficient to make the old file red hot and then let it cool. The best method is to place the file in the fire when the fire is red, but dying down, and leave it there to get red hot and then allow it to cool down with the fire as it dies out. After this treatment the steel will be found easy to work. Steel treated in this way is admirable for new keyless wheels, small tools and special cutters, but is not suitable for springs.

Gravers

The most useful graver for a clockmaker is a square one about $\frac{3}{16}$ inch square. For a watchmaker suitable gravers are a No. 3 or about $\frac{3}{32}$ inch square, and a No. 3 lozenge. A clockmaker does not need a lozenge graver so much as a watchmaker, but he must have one to turn a deep undercut for riveting wheels on to pinions, etc. All gravers are best purchased from the materials dealer, as they are difficult to make with the equipment available in most workshops.

On no account use a graver which is too small, as it will not be rigid, will chatter, and tend to turn the work oval instead of truly round, apart from being very rough. On the other hand, a graver which is unduly large is unsatisfactory and wastes time, because it takes longer to keep in condition. Always use a graver of the correct size in relation to the size of the work in hand.

Square-nosed Tool

Some craftsmen use what is termed a square-nosed tool, that is, a graver sharpened like a chisel. It is very useful for fast cutting, especially hardened and tempered steel. The square-nosed tool is followed by an ordinary graver to clean up the square shoulders.

When purchasing a graver, make sure it is quite hard and cannot be touched with a file. If too brittle, the temper can be drawn to suit the particular job. Drawing of the temper is carried out as follows. If the sides are quite bright, wash the graver in benzine to remove any grease, then place the graver in brass filings on a tin plate and heat over the gas. If the graver is watched carefully it will be seen gradually to change colour, and as soon as this happens

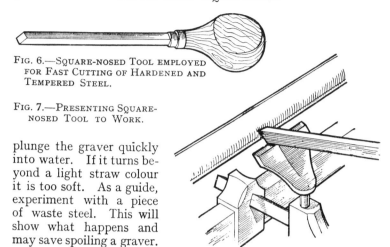

FIG. 6.—SQUARE-NOSED TOOL EMPLOYED
for FAST CUTTING OF HARDENED AND
TEMPERED STEEL.

FIG. 7.—PRESENTING SQUARE-
NOSED TOOL TO WORK.

plunge the graver quickly
into water. If it turns beyond a light straw colour
it is too soft. As a guide,
experiment with a piece
of waste steel. This will
show what happens and
may save spoiling a graver.

Preparing Graver for Use

To prepare for use, grind the graver from corner to corner at an
angle of 45°, as shown in Fig. 8a. Make sure it is quite flat. It
will then look diamond shaped and the cutting angles will be correct.
If a longer point is required, use a lozenge graver. After being
ground, finish up on a smooth oilstone, Arkansas if possible ; if not
available, a smooth India stone is quite in order. Do not use the
oilstone dry, always put thin oil on it. If used dry, it will not only
get hot and soften the cutting edges, but will leave the graver very
rough and coarse. Apart from the bad effects on the graver, the
stone itself will become pitted and therefore useless. An oilstone
can always be washed in benzine if the stone becomes clogged or
fails to cut.

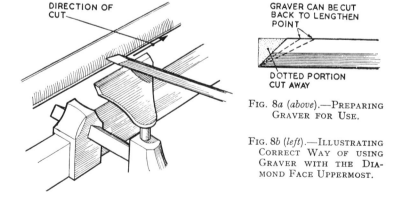

DIRECTION OF
CUT

GRAVER CAN BE CUT
BACK TO LENGTHEN
POINT

DOTTED PORTION
CUT AWAY

FIG. 8a (above).—PREPARING
GRAVER FOR USE.

FIG. 8b (left).—ILLUSTRATING
CORRECT WAY OF USING
GRAVER WITH THE DIA-
MOND FACE UPPERMOST.

If brass is to be turned, the face of the graver should be polished on a zinc block. This will enable brass to be turned very smoothly, and with practice an almost polished finish can be obtained. We will deal with polishing in a later chapter.

How to Use the Graver

Only use a lozenge graver when a deep undercut is required. The lozenge graver is not meant for ordinary turning as the point is too delicate. A series of lozenge gravers, each ground back a little more than the other—in other words, a longer point to each —is essential if a very deep undercut is required. The use of each graver to cut out a little more metal is far less strain than if one tries to take a deep undercut with one graver only, apart from it being almost impossible even if one has unlimited time. Always use the graver with the diamond face uppermost. (See Fig. 8b.) In this position the cutting and clearance angles are correct and the work will turn out round and smooth.

Some watchmakers use their gravers with the side uppermost, especially when using the lathe. This is bad practice, as the great tendency is for the work to become oval. When using a graver do not force the point to do the work ; it is not strong enough and it will break off. Use the point as a feeler and cut with the side of the graver near the point. The point should follow, not lead. A sharp-pointed graver is essential if a square shoulder is required.

Lathes

Most people are under the false impression that the turns are superseded by the lathe and thus old fashioned. The lathe is a useful addition, capable of turning between dead centres, but by the time the lathe is fixed up for the job it can be done twice as quickly and more conveniently in the turns. In these days the turns and lathe are an essential part of a watch- and clockmaker's kit. If a watchmaker cannot afford or have access to a lathe the turns will be sufficient for his purpose. We shall deal with this point later.

Examining a Lathe before Purchase

When purchasing a lathe, examine the bearings and see if they are replaceable, or if there is some means of taking up for wear, etc. See that the lathe runs perfectly smooth and free without any shake in the bearings. Examine the thread on the collets and see that it is a well-cut deep thread and not just a scratch. Take out the draw in spindle, and screw it about three or four turns on the collet, or split chuck, and if there is any play reject it. If the slots in the collets are very wide they may not close properly, so watch this point carefully.

Examine the tailstock to see if it is correctly lined up. The easiest way is to put a small collet in the lathe head and screw it

8

FIG. 9a.—SPLIT CHUCK OR COLLET.

The thread should be well cut and there should be no play in the draw-in spindle.

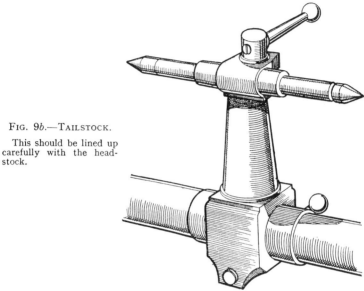

FIG. 9b.—TAILSTOCK.

This should be lined up carefully with the head-stock.

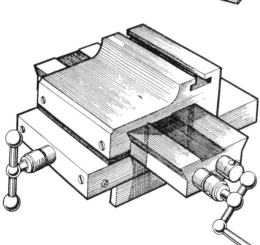

FIG. 9c.—SLIDE REST.

The slides should fit without shake and the lead screws should be a good fit.

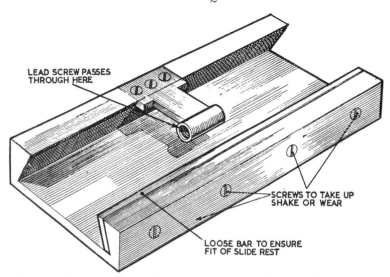

LEAD SCREW PASSES THROUGH HERE

SCREWS TO TAKE UP SHAKE OR WEAR

LOOSE BAR TO ENSURE FIT OF SLIDE REST

FIG. 9d.—SLIDE OF SLIDE REST, SHOWING LOOSE BAR FOR ADJUSTMENT.

up lightly. Put the tailstock on very close to the headstock. Now put a runner, with a male centre, through the tailstock and notice whether the point enters the collet. Then move the tailstock slightly further away and try the point again. If it does this all the way it is nicely lined up.

Try the slide rest very carefully. Make sure the lead screws are fully up and have a clean, deeply cut thread ; also it must fit the slide without any shake, and yet turn smoothly. A good lathe will have some means to take up shake which will develop as regards wear, etc. Test the slides and dovetails. All slide rests, if they are any good at all, have some means of adjustment. It is usually a supplementary strip of steel, specially ground in to fit, and lies down one side of the dovetail. There are three or four screws which engage with this strip and can be pushed in if the slide flops about, or eased if too tight. The strip should lie close to the outside dovetail with no visible gap in between. If there is a gap, reject it, as it will be a constant source of trouble. It will never be firm unless fitting very tightly and will damage the lead screws.

Another point : make sure that replacements are obtainable for the collets or split chucks and other accessories. A lathe is almost useless without true collets.

A good new lathe is very difficult to obtain these days, so do not reject a second-hand one providing, of course, that it is in first-class condition. Lorch, Boley and Wolf Jahn lathes are of German manufacture and are extremely good. The Webster Whitcomb is a very good American lathe. Collets for these are available in this country.

Fig. 10a. — Lorch Lathe with Revolving Head, also Slide Rest and Mandrel Face Plate.

A. Mandrel face plate.
B. Slide rest.
C. Cutter holder, clamp, etc.
D. Draw-in spindle.
E. External pulleys.
F. Index for slide rest adjustment.
G. Drilled head to rod securing slide rest.
H. Winged screw to secure slide rest to the bed of the lathe.

Fig. 10b.—Lorch Lathe fitted with Hand Wheel fixed to the Bench.

This lathe may be adjusted to any height that is required.

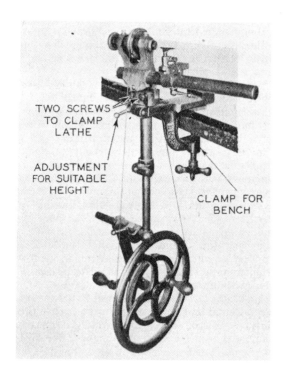

TWO SCREWS TO CLAMP LATHE

ADJUSTMENT FOR SUITABLE HEIGHT

CLAMP FOR BENCH

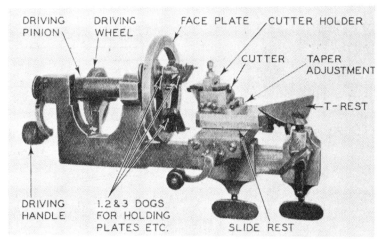

DRIVING   DRIVING   FACE PLATE   CUTTER HOLDER
PINION   WHEEL

                                                  CUTTER   TAPER
                                                              ADJUSTMENT

                                                              ←T-REST

DRIVING   1.2&3 DOGS
HANDLE   FOR HOLDING
                 PLATES ETC.   SLIDE REST

FIG. 11.—SWISS HAND MANDREL.

The Lathe Drive

The lathe can be driven by hand-wheel, treadle or electric motor, depending upon the type of work to be done on the lathe. In any case it is certainly very convenient to have a hand-wheel.

If pivoting of hard steel is to be carried out the lathe can be driven very slowly with a hand-wheel, and, in fact, it is difficult any other way. It is also convenient to be able to bring the lathe to the bench at will. Where electric current is not available there is no alternative but a treadle or hand-wheel.

When buying an electric motor, do not obtain a very fast one. An induction motor is the best type, operating at about 1,435 revolutions per minute. It can always be stepped up by pulleys if a higher speed is required, but to cut down a high-speed motor is a noisy operation, and also there is excessive vibration.

Mandrels

A mandrel. or mandrel face plate, is a very useful and, one may say, essential accessory to the lathe. Failing this, an English or Swiss hand mandrel is called for.

The unit termed the loose-pulley attachment is another very useful accessory. It converts a lathe into a throw, and thus enables work to be done between dead centres. (See Fig. 12a.) Small carriers form part of this unit and they can be bought or made to suit particular jobs.

Wax chucks also must not be forgotten. These chucks have innumerable uses and more will be said about them later.

The Turns

The turns, a small dead-centre lathe used by watchmakers, is a fairly simple piece of equipment which may be bought or made

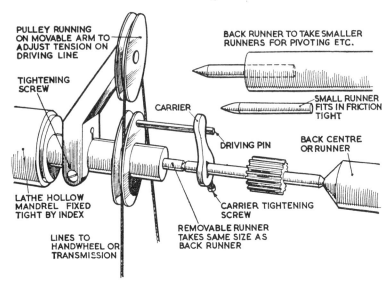

PULLEY RUNNING ON MOVABLE ARM TO ADJUST TENSION ON DRIVING LINE

TIGHTENING SCREW

CARRIER

DRIVING PIN

LATHE HOLLOW MANDREL FIXED TIGHT BY INDEX

LINES TO HANDWHEEL OR TRANSMISSION

BACK RUNNER TO TAKE SMALLER RUNNERS FOR PIVOTING ETC.

SMALL RUNNER FITS IN FRICTION TIGHT

BACK CENTRE OR RUNNER

CARRIER TIGHTENING SCREW

REMOVABLE RUNNER TAKES SAME SIZE AS BACK RUNNER

FIG. 12a.—SMALL TURNING BETWEEN CENTRES, USING LOOSE PULLEY ATTACHMENT IN LATHE.

fairly easily. The price to-day suggests making the equipment oneself. It need not be elaborate ; in fact, the simpler the better. The old English pattern is the most convenient. The runners are about ¼ inch in diameter, and if one does not possess a lathe the runners can easily be drilled and attachments made to enable any work to be carried out that is normally done in a lathe. A bow made of whalebone, cane or hardened and tempered steel, with a piece of horsehair or nylon stretched between the ends, provides the motive power. (See Fig. 13c.) It is surprising the speed that can be obtained with this arrangement, especially with practice. Before the advent of nylon, human hair was a good medium for very small turning.

The turns has an advantage over the lathe for true turning and is ideal for the very small turning jobs. The author would strongly advise young watchmakers to make themselves proficient in the use of the turns. For polishing or burnishing pivots and other round steelwork it is a very quick and convenient means, owing to the backward and forward motion. A watchmaker who is proficient with the turns will be much more particular when using

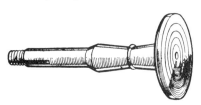

FIG. 12b.—WAX CHUCK.

FIG. 13a.—OLD-PATTERN ENGLISH TURNS HAVING ¼-IN. RUNNERS AND
SUITABLE FOR GENERAL WORK.

a lathe, and will turn out a better job as he will know whether the
work is true or not.

Some lathe work is anything but truly round and often ridgy as
well. In fact, some balance staffs turned in a lathe look like nails.
Another advantage of working in the turns is that the work can
be closely examined and measured with accuracy and certainty.

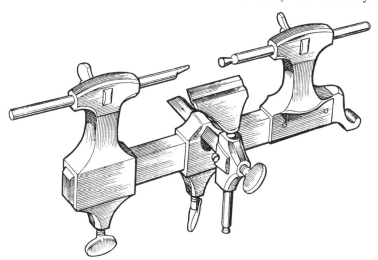

FIG. 13b.—SWISS TURNS.

This is of a lighter pattern than the English type and is suitable for most watch
work.

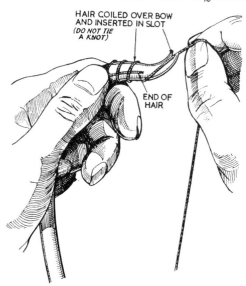

FIG. 13c.—PUTTING NYLON OR HORSEHAIR ON
Bow.

It can also be taken out and put back easily without the work going out of true.

The work is carried, or driven, through the medium of screw ferrules, or solid ferrules made of brass or steel. The former are screwed on to the work and the latter are fitted on friction tight, not driven on, but pushed on with the fingers. They can be quickly removed and changed over, and by this means one has full control over the speed of the work.

The runners must always be in good condition, and if once properly prepared last a very long time without renewal. Runners for specific jobs will be described later. The runners are used quite hard, with the exception of the back eccentric, which is hard at its acting end but soft at the back, as it can then be bent for centring, etc.

Tweezers

Tweezers should be of the very best quality obtainable, and made of good steel, properly hardened and tempered. They do not want to be too strong, but must be quite firm and without any tendency to twist. The acting or pointed ends should be long and thin, and for ordinary work need not have sharp points ; in fact, they are often better if they are not sharp. The inside should be slightly roughened and not polished or smooth. This lessens the tendency for pieces to fly out of the tweezers when gripped tightly.

Do not use steel tweezers on

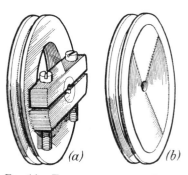

FIG. 14.—FERRULES, SHOWING SCREW
FERRULE (a) AND SOLID TYPE (b).

highly polished steel or brass pieces, as they are likely to mark and scratch the metal ; also do not grip pinion leaves with steel tweezers, but use those made of brass or German silver. When made in brass or German silver they must be heavier, but not too strong in the spring parts.

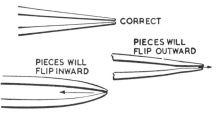

FIG. 15.—ILLUSTRATING CORRECT AND INCORRECT TYPE OF TWEEZER POINT.

Always keep tweezers in first-class condition. Make sure the points do not part company when the tweezers are squeezed hard together ; at the same time there must not be too great a gap behind the points as they are just as likely to flip backwards as forwards. The flat inside surfaces of the tweezers therefore want to meet for some distance behind the points. (See Fig. 15). There are numerous types of tweezers, and they will be discussed separately when dealing with the various jobs for which they are used.

Screwdrivers

Screwdrivers are more important than generally realized. The general tendency of any old screwdriver will do is all wrong and is very bad practice. It is inexcusably bad workmanship to slip

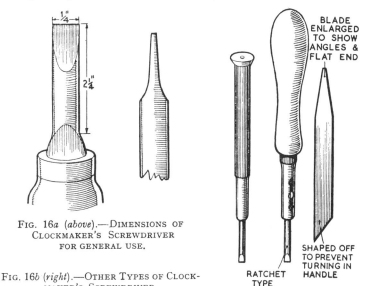

FIG. 16a (above).—DIMENSIONS OF CLOCKMAKER'S SCREWDRIVER FOR GENERAL USE.

FIG. 16b (right).—OTHER TYPES OF CLOCKMAKER'S SCREWDRIVER.

on a screw-head. Apart from spoiling the head of the screw, such items as bars, plates and cocks, as well as cases, etc., get badly scored and marked and often cannot be rectified ; thus the general appearance of the watch or clock is marred. A screwdriver, with a blade about ¼ inch across, is an absolute necessity to a clock-maker. It must be of good-quality steel, properly hardened and tempered to a dark blue. Many mild-steel bladed screwdrivers are available, but they are unsuitable. The total length, including the handle, should be about seven inches. Another of the same blade, but about twelve inches long, is necessary for deep cases. Larger screwdrivers are necessary for bigger clocks.

The ratchet type is another useful screwdriver. This enables one to work in awkward corners with a reasonable amount of comfort. It is fitted with a three-position knob, which can be manipulated by the thumb. The first position screws up ; the neutral converts to an ordinary screwdriver by fixing solid ; and the third changes to unscrew. Some good-quality ratchet screw-drivers are available.

Another point : always have a suitable handle, one that does not easily slide round in the hand. Some have skimpy little handles and are useless.

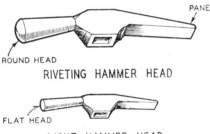

PANE

ROUND HEAD

RIVETING HAMMER HEAD

FLAT HEAD

LIGHT HAMMER HEAD

Fig. 17.—Hammer Heads.
The face of the riveting hammer should be rounded and polished. The light hammer head should be about ½ oz. in weight.

A clockmaker requires most of the screwdrivers used by a watch-maker. A watchmaker needs about eight screwdrivers in graduated sizes. In other words, a screwdriver is necessary for each size of screw-head. Do not use too small a screwdriver, it will spoil the slot of the screw ; also, do not use one too large, as it will overlap and scrape and score the plate or bar. The blade should not be filed to a knife-edge but should have a definite flat end. It should be filed with a smooth file across the blade, not lengthwise ; this prevents the screwdriver sliding out of the slot. On no account finish a screwdriver blade on an oilstone ; otherwise it is certain to slide and slip in use. The two sides of the blade should form an angle of about 20° to each other.

Always keep screwdrivers in first-class condition ; it saves an endless amount of time. However tight a screw may be, it can be moved with the right screwdriver.

Hammers

A watchmaker needs four hammers. These are: a flat-faced steel hammer with a weight of about 1½ to 2 oz. ; a brass hammer of the same weight ; and a small steel hammer about ½ oz. in weight. The faces of these hammers should be quite smooth and flat, while the pane should be thin but not sharp. Often small steel pieces get worn and have to be stretched. This job can be nicely carried out by using the indispensable small steel hammer. The fourth is, of course, the round-faced riveting hammer. The face should be well rounded and polished. For riveting solid bushes, etc., it is a necessity.

A boxwood or hide mallet is another almost indispensable tool. It can be shaped to suit any requirement. It is often worth while to have one or two mallets. Some clockmakers prefer a lead hammer, as it has weight but does not mark steel.

Burnishers

Burnishers of several types are required. A clockmaker needs a 6-inch flat and an 8-inch flat, also an oval burnisher for crossings, etc. A watchmaker requires, for general work, a 4-inch flat, an oval, and what is termed a flat oval, that is, one just off the flat with thin edges.

Burnishers are used for finishing winding and set hand-squares, screw-heads, etc. The oval and oval flat are used for finishing edges of steel springs and inside slots and crossings, and for putting final finishes on polished arbors, etc. The various types will be dealt with later when describing the jobs for which they are used.

Burnishers can be bought, but it is better to make them, and most craftsmen prefer to do this. To make a burnisher, select an old worn-out file and rub all the cut away on a flat wood block on which coarse emery cloth has been stuck firmly and flat, or on emery sticks purchased from the material dealers. When all the cut has been removed, finish up on a No. 2 emery buff and then give a light rub on a No. 1 to take away any sharpness.

Keep burnishers well away from damp to prevent rusting. If one is inclined to perspire, always rub the burnisher with a dry duster after use, and smear a little oil on it. Some watchmakers use a flat lead strip and cover it with emery powder to give cut.

Pin Tongs and Pin Vices

Watch- and clockmakers cannot manage without pin vices, as they are so extremely useful. When choosing a pair of pin vices always see that the jaws meet properly ; also make certain that they are hardened and tempered. After a time they get worn and will fail to grip small pin wire and must be replaced. Thus one acquires a collection over a period of years, all with different-sized holes. Therefore, if the jaws gape at first, all advantage of a new pin vice is lost. Another point, do not force them by inserting

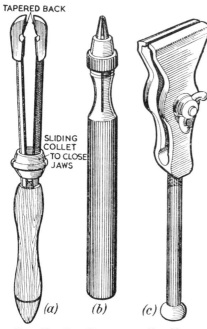

FIG. 18.—PIN TONGS AND PIN VICES.

larger wire than they are intended to hold, as this will distort them badly and they will be useless for good work. The best pin vices will take a lathe collet.

Pin tongs are useful for holding small pieces for rounding up the ends. They are called pin tongs because they are chiefly used for gripping pins, and although they are shaped like a vice are referred to as tongs. However, they have many uses, such as holding small pieces to file them up to shape, especially when too small to hold in the bench vice. They are also useful for chronometer work, and their use for this purpose will be described later.

When purchasing pin tongs make sure the jaws grip in the front and taper off at the back, otherwise when attempting to file a piece held in the pin vice it will suddenly twist round and damage will be done, or the piece will fly out and may be lost. Again, see the jaws are parallel in front and do not grip just at one end. Both watch- and clockmakers need a good assortment of pin tongs and pin vices.

Filing Blocks

When discussing pin tongs, one naturally thinks of a filing block, which is part and parcel of the combination. The best filing blocks

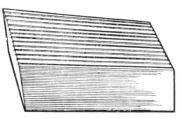

FIG. 19.—FILING BLOCK, SHOWING GROOVES.

are of boxwood, shaped like a rhombus. They are shaped like this to make the edge stand away from the lower part, thus giving greater freedom to work.

An ivory block is more useful for some work, but for filing up pins, etc., it is too slippery. The ivory blocks last longer than the boxwood type, and this is probably their only advantage.

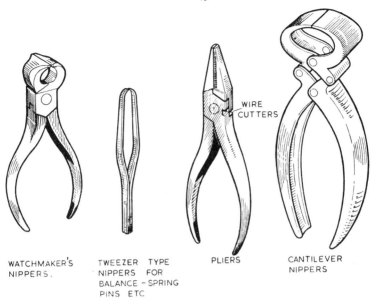

WATCHMAKER'S NIPPERS. TWEEZER TYPE NIPPERS FOR BALANCE - SPRING PINS ETC WIRE CUTTERS PLIERS CANTILEVER NIPPERS

FIG. 20.—VARIOUS TYPES OF NIPPERS AND PLIERS.

Nippers and Pliers

Nippers and pliers are another set of very necessary tools, but are very difficult to obtain these days. A watchmaker's nippers should be of the very best quality obtainable. On no account use, or allow anyone else to use, the nippers on anything but the very thinnest of soft steel, or brass up to about 0·050 inch. They are not intended for larger metal and will only chip or break if treated thus. If one wishes to cut steel wire of larger dimensions, cut the steel partly through with a file and break it, or else use a pair of pliers which have a wire-cutting side. If nippers are used correctly one needs only one pair during a lifetime.

Clockmakers require a more powerful pair of nippers capable of cutting iron or steel wire up to ·one-tenth part of an inch in diameter. They are used for pulling out pins, shortening pins and for any reasonable levering job. Do not overstrain them. Always make sure that both watch- and clockmakers' nippers are almost dead hard and cannot be filed. In both cases always keep one pair with a very sharp edge for cutting very small brass pins, but keep them for this one purpose only.

A pair of cantilever nippers should be in a clockmaker's kit, if such a tool can be obtained. They have a double joint and, owing to the principle on which they are made, have tremendous power.

Pliers

All clockmakers need a large pair of pliers with a couple of notches cut on the side for wire-cutting. This type is very satisfactory and seldom gets broken. Also required is a pair of pliers with a good grip, having the inside of the jaws roughened like the jaws of a vice. Always make certain that the jaws meet nicely at the ends and are made of hardened and tempered steel. There are many about made only of mild steel, or very poor-quality steel at most.

Round-nosed and bending pliers are almost a necessity. The latter have a convex and a concave jaw which fit into one another. They are very useful for bending shaped wire springs and other pieces without leaving nasty kinks, and, as the bend can be taken gradually, they reduce the tendency to breakage.

A very long-nosed pair of pliers, with jaws about $3\frac{1}{2}$ inches long, is very convenient for working between the plates of a clock, or for putting a screw into position in a deep clock-case.

Watchmakers require several pairs of pliers. The pliers are generally made of very good-quality steel and each pair is adapted for a particular job, which will be fully explained later. However, all watchmakers need a small pair of pliers with softened jaws, tempered to a green-white colour, or almost soft, softer than the usual balance staff pivot. The outside of the jaws must be filed back, leaving the edge of the nose almost sharp. The inside of the jaws must be quite smooth and flat, almost polished. They are used for straightening pivots and are much better than tweezers for this job. The smallest of pivots can be straightened without damage or risk of breakage and with the minimum amount of marking. When straightening a pivot they can be made hot and will retain their heat for some time.

Callipers

Callipers of various types are required. There are the usual types for inside and outside measurement, and the double-ended, that is, the inside and outside measure combined.

The average engineer's callipers are useful to clockmakers, and we must not forget dividers, which are almost indispensable. A pair of dividers to span 12 inches is required, as well as small stiff ones for scribing small circles on steel, for pallet making, hand making and for other small parts.

The watchmaker's requirements are the same, but on a smaller scale. His callipers are specialized and of various types. Callipers for truing, etc., and callipers for poising will both be described fully in the chapters dealing with their particular uses.

Two types which a watchmaker must possess are figure-of-eight callipers and cross-over callipers. The latter is pivoted at one end and the arms cross over each other ; thus when the back is pressed the jaws in the front open. Never change from one

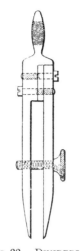

FIG. 21.—INSIDE AND OUTSIDE CALLIPERS.

FIG. 22.—DIVIDERS OR SCRIBING COMPASSES FOR WATCH PALLET MAKING.

FIG. 23.—DIVIDERS.

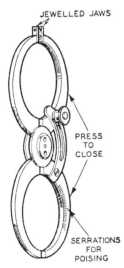

JEWELLED JAWS

PRESS TO CLOSE

SERRATIONS FOR POISING

FIG. 24.—FIGURE-OF-EIGHT CALLIPERS.

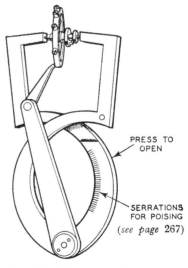

PRESS TO OPEN

SERRATIONS FOR POISING (*see page* 267)

FIG. 25.—CROSS-OVER CALLIPERS ADAPTED FOR POISING.

type to the other when renewing, as one gets used to a particular kind and a change will be certain to cause damage. In other words, with the figure-of-eight callipers, pressure on the front or back will close the jaws. With the type pivoted at one end and crossing over, pressure on the back opens the jaws and pressure on the front closes them. If one gets used to this type it will be automatic to put pressure on the back to open. If one has changed to figure-of-eight, one will be sure to put pressure on the back and instead of opening they will close and crush whatever is between the jaws.

If callipers are used for poising, use them for this sole purpose and put them away when not in use.

Punches and Staking Tools

The ordinary punch has almost been superseded by the staking tool. When purchasing a staking tool careful examination is necessary. First of all, see that the punches are held quite upright to the stake. Some have an adjustment for centring the punches with the holes in the stake, but this does not make them upright. If the tool is not upright when new it never will be.

The staking tool is bought complete with punches, stakes and other useful tools, and is well worth acquiring. However, some of the older craftsmen still prefer to hold the punches in the hand. For clockwork, punches held in the hand are a necessity. For riveting large pinions to wheels and other jobs, it is by far the easier and more accurate method. Of course, it requires skill to use a punch properly. A number of special punches cannot be bought and must be made. We will leave this subject until a later chapter, when the various punches required for particular jobs will be described.

The staking tool can be used for other purposes, such as sinking holes in cocks or bars, to fit screw-heads, etc., as fitted in jewelling, and it can be used to push in friction-held jewel holes, sinking screw-heads into springs, and so on. It is a tool well worth taking care of. Rust, as usual, has to be guarded against, so keep it clear of damp and be careful if the hands perspire much. Dust and dirt can also be a nuisance and, therefore, it is advisable to keep it under cover.

Mainspring Winders

The mainspring winder is used for winding mainsprings into barrels and is an essential tool for a watch- or clockmaker. On no account should a mainspring be wound in by hand; it will absolutely ruin a mainspring, whether watch or clock.

We will consider a watch mainspring winder because a clock spring winder is essentially the same, but on a larger scale. There are two kinds, and one is as efficient as the other. In one type, the mainspring is wound into a barrel, which is part of the tool, and then transferred into its proper barrel. In the other, the spring is wound direct into its own barrel. Where, as with some English pocket chronometers having a fusee, the mainspring is fitted with a square or round hook instead of an eye, the barrel incorporated with the winder is the better and easier type to use. The same applies to the very small baguette type of watch where the mainspring is very low.

In the normal way, the first and commoner type is better because it is quicker in use. The winder consists of a bar of brass or steel pivoted between two uprights and controlled by a ratchet wheel and double-ended click which is pivoted or screwed in the centre to the upright. The click can be made to act in two directions according to whichever way the spring has to be wound in. The click is controlled in the usual manner by a spring. A handle is fitted to one end of the rod, the other end is drilled to take various types and

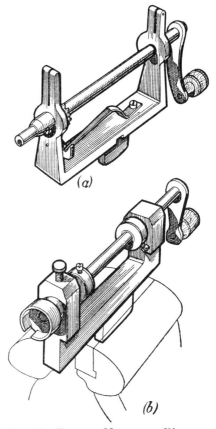

FIG. 26.—TYPES OF MAINSPRING WINDER.
(a) Standard type of winder.
(b) Fitted with supplementary barrel.

sizes of arbors, and a screw is positioned through the side of the rod to make them secure.

The eye of the spring is put on a suitable arbor, the handle is turned and the spring wound right up. The barrel is slipped over the wound-up spring, the click is pushed out and the mainspring let down slowly. The eye is slipped off the arbor, leaving the spring wound in the barrel. If properly carried out, there will be no distortion or damage to the mainspring.

If a mainspring is in any way distorted, reject it and put in another. A distorted spring is likely to break, or at least will not give its full power.

Brushes

The clockmaker needs various brushes, depending upon the method of cleaning adopted. If a cleaning solution is used, a brush of medium stiffness about $1\frac{1}{4}$ inches wide is required to brush the plates and brasswork when they are removed from the solution. If an abrasive is employed, such as rottenstone or pumice powder, a stiffer brush is essential.

For small clocks, such as French carriage clocks, soft brushes should always be used, both for cleaning and polishing. A round paint brush, about $1\frac{1}{2}$ inches in diameter and as soft as possible, is the best type to use when washing out clocks in benzine. The same type is also suitable for use with gilt clocks which are only passed through the benzine. For bigger clocks, use larger and stiffer brushes accordingly.

Watchmakers should have, for ordinary jobbing, a No. 3 watch brush, generally a four row, of medium stiffness. For new watches a soft fine-haired brush is necessary. A brush made of human hair is, of course, the best, and this is ideal for new gilt watches, especially English watches gilt direct on to the brass, without any other plating between. These plates can easily be scratched and the whole appearance spoilt if a rough brush is used. To keep the brush clean rub it on soft chalk and then on tissue paper to remove the chalk. Under no circumstances clean a watch, whether Swiss or English, with a chalky brush ; it spoils the appearance and makes the plates or bars look scratchy and greasy.

If plates look dull, use burnt bone on the brush and roll the brush with a circular motion on the plates. This will bring the dullest plates up clean and bright.

Even if a cleaning machine is used, a brush is necessary to ensure that nothing is left adhering to the plates or wheels and pinions.

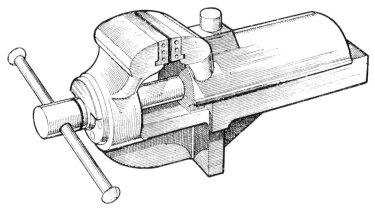

FIG. 27.—PARALLEL TYPE OF BENCH VICE.

To prevent a new brush from scratching, rub the hairs or bristles across a piece of broken glass ; an old watch-glass will do.

Pegwood

Pegwood is a stick of close-grained wood used for cleaning out pivot holes and other parts of watches and clocks. The material can be purchased in three sizes, clock, small clock and watch.

Pith

This is the pith of elderwood used in cleaning watches and clocks, and is useful for cleaning pivots, pallet faces, etc., for examination and for removing polishing material.

Bench Vices

The parallel type of bench vice is the best and forms an essential part of a watchmaker's kit. A $2\frac{1}{2}$-inch jaw is the most serviceable ; the smaller ones have their limitations.

To prepare a new vice for use, take out the steel jaws which are invariably screwed in and, if bright, remove any oil or grease with benzine. Heat them on a brass block, slightly to draw the temper, or until they change to a pale straw colour. They are less likely to chip or break in use if treated in this way.

A large leg vice is very useful to a clockmaker ; if not available, a $3\frac{1}{2}$-inch parallel vice will serve the purpose. Always see that the vice is fixed firmly.

Glass Covers and Trays

Glass covers, trays, etc., are all obtainable from the material dealers, and are essential for quick and satisfactory work.

Glazed white paper is the best material to work on. It is easier to keep clean and is not so slippery as plate glass, although plate glass has advantages for some jobs. Always see that the glazed paper is firmly secured to the bench, otherwise if one happens to catch the edge of the paper anything on it is likely to be upset over the bench. Four drawing-pins, one at each corner, answer the purpose quite well.

A thin sheet of Perspex is a useful substitute for board paper. It must not be too smooth, however. White paper placed underneath helps to throw the light up.

Other tools and accessories will be discussed as and when required.

CHAPTER 2

MATERIALS

THE two metals used mostly in watch and clock work are brass and silver steel. Brass is used for such parts as plates and wheels, and silver steel for pinions and screws. Although silver steel is more difficult to work than mild steel it has the great advantage that it can be hardened and tempered.

Mild Steel

Mild steel is more easily worked, but can only be case-hardened ; it is really a better-quality iron. When mild steel is case-hardened the outside skin is converted into steel and thus hardened.

For making filing templates or jigs, mild steel is the best metal to use. The jig can be filed up to shape and case-hardened. It can then be gripped tightly in the vice without any fear of breakage. If a jig is made of silver steel and hardened, as soon as any pressure is applied it will snap as easily as a piece of glass. The reason, of course, is that the core or inside of the mild steel is soft, whereas silver steel is hard right the way through.

Case-hardening

The case-hardening of mild steel is a simple operation to-day. as many preparations are made for this purpose by specialist firms, The jig or any other article to be hardened is covered by the particular preparation and brought to red heat and is kept at this temperature for a period depending on the depth of hardness required. It is then plunged into water and it will be found to resist being cut by a file or graver. As all the preparations for case-hardening are as good as one another it is unnecessary to recommend any particular make. All the material dealers or tool suppliers stock one or the other.

Hardened and Tempered Steel

For large taps and dies, mild steel is the most suitable metal to use, because they do not snap so readily or chip like those made of silver or cast steel. However, they do not retain their sharpness as long, and for small dies or taps silver steel is by far the best metal.

The same applies to large screws ; they are better in mild steel, but, again, small screws should be made of silver steel hardened and tempered. A small screw, if soft, will get badly torn, and eventually it will be almost impossible to remove it, especially if a small chamfer-headed endpiece screw. The slots of these screws are at most only about four- or five-thousandths of an inch deep. With silver steel such small screws can be hardened and tempered and can be polished flat. They look good, and if handled by a craftsman can be easily removed without marking, and always retain their appearance.

A small pinion or a watch pinion must always be made of silver steel hardened, tempered and polished. The idea of polishing the leaves of a pinion is not to make them look attractive but to reduce friction to a minimum. A pinion is faced or polished at the end of the leaves to ensure the removal of burrs left after the wheel has been riveted on.

All screwdriver blades must be made of silver steel hardened and tempered.

Balance springs (or hairsprings), suspension springs and all the numerous springs and pieces used in complicated watches must be made of a steel which can be hardened and tempered. Sheet steel, that is silver steel which has been rolled flat, is the best metal to use for such purposes.

Steel is made in various shapes for convenience, including square rods or stud steel, click steel for making clicks, etc., and flat steel for polishers and burnishers, etc. It should only be necessary to ask for the particular type required.

Cast Steel

Cast steel is much harder than silver steel and is used for files and other tools. Watchmakers use cast steel for cutters, turning tools and screwplates, etc. Always anneal cast steel before trying to work it as it will spoil the tools, even though it has not been hardened before. This also applies to silver steel, but only when making screws. Silver steel works easier in its original condition as purchased. When cast steel has once been hardened, however, it must be very slowly annealed, as explained in Chapter I.

If keyless wheels are made from an old cast-steel file, after hardening they can be tempered to a light blue colour or even softer, and the wheels will withstand wear much longer and be far stronger.

High Speed Steel

High speed steel is very useful to clockmakers in the form of cutters or lathe tools when carrying out repetition work and also for turning silver steel at high speed. Where an ordinary cast-steel or silver-steel cutter would become soft by the heat caused by turning at high speed, a tool made of high speed steel will become blue and even red hot and yet will still be hard and cut in this condition.

The high speed steel tool will not, however, cut hardened and tempered steel as it lacks the hardness of a cast-steel cutter. For certain applications, however, there are available what are termed "tipped tools", and these are much harder.

Brass

Brass is a soft metal, but it can be hardened by hammering or rolling. For the general run of watch and clock repairing the modern " easy cutting brass " is not entirely suitable. Although it can be turned, drilled and tapped very easily it is very brittle and difficult to rivet satisfactorily ; it cannot be hardened as it splits and cracks, and it cannot be softened.

The old " red brass " is a better metal to use because it can be hardened by hammering or softened by heat. It is, however, very difficult to work as it is inclined to grip or bind up when being drilled or tapped, and oil has to be used freely, otherwise broken drills and taps result. It is generally referred to as " best brass ".

There is a very good brass with a yellow appearance which used to be referred to as " French brass ". This brass is very easy to turn, drill or tap, and was used by the old watch-movement makers. These days it is very scarce, and any stock is well worth looking after and keeping for special jobs. It is readily bent into shape without fracturing, and can be hammered and hardened to a great degree of hardness. It was used for 'scape wheels such as duplex, ratchet and chronometer, and can be highly polished.

For ordinary train wheels and barrels always use a good quality brass as they have to stand up to much wear.

Gold

Gold is another metal which is used fairly extensively in watches and clocks. It is often employed for train wheels in watches, especially when used with nickel plates or bars. It is used for hands and for 'scape pinion collets in best quality watches, also for balance screws, including the mean time screws and nuts. At one time gold balances were quite common, but they are not made now.

The passing spring of a chronometer detent is always made of gold, except, of course, in the older types. One often sees a steel passing spring, but it should be replaced unless, of course, it is an antique piece. The big advantage with gold is that it does not corrode. If an impulse or ruby pin cannot be obtained in a jewel it is in order to substitute a gold one temporarily as it will not harm the lever, but a steel one will cause damage, especially if working in a steel lever.

Hairsprings were at one time made in gold, but this practice has now been discarded as they do not give a good performance.

Non-magnetic escapements, that is lever, pallets and roller, were often made of gold in English hand-made watches. This is, of course, apart from the gold case which was and still is the most popular form of watch-case.

Palladium

Palladium replaced gold as a non-magnetic metal for balance springs, and gives a much better performance ; in fact, it is almost perfect.

" Invar "

" Invar " is one of the nickel-steel group of alloys. It is used for pendulum rods because its coefficient of thermal expansion is very small.

"Elinvar" is a later addition to this useful group of alloys and is used for watch hairsprings. A plain balance requires very little adjustment for temperature when fitted with an "Elinvar" hairspring. A small bimetallic affix is all that is necessary, and very high marks have been earned at the National Physical Laboratory in the past in the form of Kew "A" certificates. The highest has been in the nature of 19·7 marks out of 20 for compensation.

Platinum

Platinum is used only in watchwork in the form of screws, which act as weights to alter the weight of a balance for adjusting compensation errors. Two gold screws can often be replaced by one of platinum as it is a very heavy metal.

It is often used for electrical contacts in galvanic chronometers and clocks.

Silver

Silver is employed only for dials and dial rings ; it is no longer a popular metal for watch cases, being replaced largely by stainless steel, which is particularly suitable for the purpose as it is extremely hard and resistant to tarnish. Silver, on the other hand, is a very soft metal and is easily bent and bruised.

Hard Solders

One of the best hard solders is Easy-flo, which is available in a range of melting points, from 667°C to 800°C and has its own purpose made flux. The flux runs at a slightly lower temperature than the solders, which flow at a dull red heat.

Five kinds of silver solder can normally be obtained from the material dealers: "Extra easy", "Easy", "Medium", "Hard", and "Enamelling". The first variety is best for normal work because of its lower running temperature. Borax is the flux used, and is crushed to powder and mixed with clean water to a smooth paste. The flux is applied, often with a small camel-hair brush, where the solder is required to run.

Gold solder can be purchased in 9 ct. to 22 ct. and in several colours as required. Melting points range from 650°C to 877°C. The flux is the same as for silver solder, namely, borax.

These hard solders require only moderate heat, and the use of a blowpipe held in the mouth is usually sufficient to provide the necessary heat when using a gas flame.   If a large article is to be hard soldered, a continuous-blast bellows connected to a blowpipe is quite satisfactory.

The articles, if small, can be tied with binding wire to a charcoal block, and the heat applied is preserved by the charcoal instead of being wasted.   Do not apply extra heat once the solder glistens as other troubles may arise.

Diamantine

Diamantine is a very fine white powder used for polishing steel, brass, gold and other metals, and should not be confused with diamond powder, which is an entirely different material.

It can be purchased from the material dealers, and two suitable grades are Welter No. 2 and Matthey No. 1.   Both of these give a high polish and are very quick in their action.

Diamantine must be kept scrupulously clean or it will scratch. It should be mixed with good quality oil on a hard steel block to obtain a stiff paste, almost like putty.   When used, it turns black in colour and cuts best when slightly wet, but polishes as it dries. More will be said about this later.

Diamond Powder

Diamond powder is an expensive material used for abrasive purposes and for polishing jewel stones.   It can be obtained from a precious-stone dealer or wholesale jeweller.

Before use, diamond powder has to be " washed ", that is graded. This is carried out by putting the diamond powder, in its original state as purchased, into olive oil and stirring well until the solution appears a milky colour.   Allow it to stand for about three or four minutes, then pour the solution into another jar.   A sediment will remain at the bottom of the jar ; keep this because it cannot be used as it is.   The second jar should be allowed to stand for about ten minutes and then the contents poured into a third jar.   The sediment left in the second jar is useful for grinding stones.

The third jar is allowed to stand for about half an hour, and then the contents of this jar are poured into a fourth jar.   The sediment from the third jar will polish any stone, including a diamond, but it should be covered up, as dust and dirt will render it useless and it is too expensive to waste.

The last jar can be left as long as required ; the longer it is left the more will settle at the bottom.   When another quantity of diamond powder is to be washed, pour the contents of the fourth jar into the first and use it again ; no diamond powder is ever wasted this way, provided that it is always kept clean.   After a time the accumulated rough powder in No. 1 jar can be crushed up and washed again.

Water of Ayr Stone

Water of Ayr Stone is a bluish-grey stone used for smoothing brass when it is to be gilded or polished. There are two varieties: one is referred to as " grey stone "; this is a mottled grey colour and cuts a little faster, but is not so smooth as that which is termed " blue stone ". This blue stone must not be confused with copper-sulphate, which is also called blue stone and has no use in watch and clock work.

A plate can be gilded direct after using blue Water of Ayr Stone. Grey stone is used by clockmakers for curling their plates, and imparts a good appearance.

Mercury

Mercury is a necessity for clockmakers, being used in barometers, thermometers and, of course, in the mercurial compensation pendulum. It must be handled with care, however, and should be kept well away from the work-bench. It has a rare affinity for gold, being attracted to the gold case of a watch or even to the gilding of watch plates, with the result that they are completely ruined if this is allowed to happen. The only way to get rid of it is by evaporation.

Mercury is injurious to health, so it must always be treated carefully.

Shellac

Shellac is employed for fixing or securing pallet stones, ruby or impulse pins, locking stones and various other jewels used in watches and clocks.

It is useful for fixing small pieces to wax chucks in the lathe for turning, such as jewel holes set in brass. Shellac has many other uses and we shall have more to say about this later.

Methylated Spirits

Methylated spirit or spirits of wine is used mainly in the watch- and clockmaker's spirit lamp, but it is used also as a medium to dissolve shellac. When anything has been fixed to the wax chuck a deposit of shellac is left behind after the job has been carried out, and this can be removed by boiling in methylated spirit.

Turpentine

Turpentine is used only to lubricate drills. The use of turpentine, or turps as it is commonly called, helps the drill to bite when drilling very hard steel and the steel does not readily burnish. At the same time it keeps the drill cool. If oil were used it would make the drill slip.

Hydrochloric Acid

Hydrochloric acid or spirits of salts is a powerful corrosive agent and should be handled with care and, like mercury, should be kept well away from the bench or, better still, used outside the workshop.

It is used for cleaning the blue oxidizing off steelwork and for making soft soldering flux, but in the author's opinion it should not be used on watch or clock work. For soldering collets on clock pinions rosin should be used as it does not corrode.

Lubricants

The choice of lubricants for watches and clocks is a difficult one and no expense should be spared to obtain the very best quality of the appropriate grade for the various parts of the movement.

A special pack of "Microtime" lubricants is available containing oil of four viscosities and two greases for watches and clocks.

Another excellent range is that sold under the name of "Moebius", oils and greases, which are creep resistant and remain fluid through a wide range of temperatures.

Benzine

When cleaning watches by hand it is best to use benzine contained always in a glass jar, so that it can be seen if any pieces are left behind.

If they are badly tarnished, especially polished pieces or parts not gilt or lacquered, place them for a short time in a solution of soft soap and water and ammonia, then wash the pieces in benzine and dry them thoroughly in boxwood dust. Make perfectly sure that the parts are dry, as a watch rusts quickly enough.

Cleaning Solution

Most clocks are not gilt or lacquered, so they have to be cleaned in something stronger than benzine. A suitable solution can be made up of four pints of water and two tablespoonfuls of soft soap, which is thoroughly dissolved by boiling, and then adding two tablespoonfuls of full-strength ammonia or a quarter pound of rock ammonia. It can be used for a long time, and when the strength of the solution weakens it can be replenished by the addition of another tablespoonful of ammonia. After a solution has been used for a long time, it can be saved for the very dirty clocks and a fresh solution can be prepared for the better clocks. When this second solution becomes dirty, the first can be thrown away and replaced by the second, and so on.

Always be sure to remove all fluid from the clock pieces by immersing in benzine and drying thoroughly in boxwood dust. It only remains to brush up with a chalky brush and peg out the holes and the clock is ready for assembly ; use a chalky brush only on clockwork, never on watches.

Rottenstone

Rottenstone is a mild abrasive for brass and can be used on clocks when the cleaning solution has failed to brighten them. It leaves a bright but not a polished finish.

Sometimes verdigris eats into the plates, and rottenstone is the best medium to remove it.

Tripoli

Tripoli is a polishing medium for brass and can be used either on a flat bluff or on a revolving one fitted to a lathe.

The material can be purchased in lumps ready for use, or in powder form, when it has to be mixed with oil before use.

Both rottenstone and tripoli can be used on a brush for cleaning wheel teeth and any shaped pieces with odd corners.

Emery

Emery is not a good medium for cleaning clocks unless it is double washed. In the ordinary way the mineral is too coarse and leaves deep lines. It is, however, useful in the form of emery buff sticks for cleaning up steelwork, and as emery paper for use on arbors which are left grey or unpolished. It is also useful for re-surfacing burnishers, and for use with emery blocks for straight graining steel springs or complicated watch levers and jumpers.

These emery blocks are made with shellac and emery mixed and pressed into square-shaped rods, or into flat sticks, often with a handle attached. When the blocks get ridged and worn they can be re-surfaced by rubbing two together with benzine or petrol.

Precious Stones

Diamonds, other than in the powder form described previously, are not used to any great extent in watch and clock work. They are used mostly in the form of chippings or rose diamonds, and are employed for the balance endstone in a marine chronometer and in good-quality hand-made English watches.

Chippings are again mounted into copper or brass as drills for making jewel holes or for turning hard steel when one does not wish to temper it, such as a revolving file for pallet making and other jobs, or for giving a clearance to small circular saws.

Another precious stone having greater use is the sapphire, which is used for jewel holes in best-quality English watches, also for pallet stones, impulse pins, locking stones and impulse and discharging pallets for marine chronometers. It is a very hard stone, and very seldom shows any signs of wear. The Swiss use synthetic sapphires and these give good results.

Rubies are not too popular these days, as a few of the older craftsmen suspect the natural stone of being porous. The Swiss synthetic seems quite in order. Ruby jewel holes were very popular for appearance when set in gold and mounted on nickel plates and cocks, which in turn were polished and spotted.

Polishing powder, under the heading of Rubitine, has no relation whatever with the ruby except its colour.

The garnet is used for jewelling in the cheaper grades of watch. The stone is very soft, however, and is not used much these days.

The agate is a very popular stone for jewelling regulator pallets and other jewelled surfaces in clocks. It is inclined to be soft, but does not readily chip and will stand fairly rough usage, which makes it popular for clockwork.

Boxwood Dust

There are still a few watchmakers who like a final dry-out in boxwood dust—a little old-fashioned perhaps but probably worth while.

Boxwood dust is much finer than ordinary sawdust and dries very quickly, and is used extensively by clockmakers after using soft soap and ammonia solutions.

CHAPTER 3

WATCH MOVEMENTS

WATCHES in general use are of three kinds—pocket, wrist and complicated pocket and wrist. The ladies pocket watch has almost disappeared, a few only being kept in repair. In any case, the ladies watch is only a large wrist watch as far as size and principles are concerned. The wrist watch is now preferred and has about reached its limit as far as smallness of size is concerned.

Pocket Watches

The pocket watch is still extensively worn by people who are particular with regard to close timekeeping, and some wear a wrist watch for convenience and carry a pocket watch as well.

One cannot expect a small watch to keep a good rate ; it cannot be made proportionally. A high-grade pocket watch has balance staff pivots as fine as 0·003 of an inch in diameter. A watch made a quarter the size cannot have pivots in the right proportion and it is extremely doubtful whether they could be machined to that size. The same applies to the rest of the movement.

The most serious fault is in the size of the escapement. It is bound to be very heavy and thus the inertia is great. All these spoil consistency of rate. Also less reserve of power is available, and wheels and pinions, balance, etc., have to run much closer to each other. The pivots have a greater amount of freedom proportionately and any errors are exaggerated.

A number of ladies half-hunter watches were converted to wrist watches by replacing the front cover and bezel by a crystal bezel and adding loops. The pendant shortened and a new button added made an admirable job.

Some pocket watches still in use are keywinds, but most are pocket chronometers and quite good-quality levers, although many have been converted to keyless. The old Geneva bar-movement watches are sometimes met with by repairers, but almost all have disappeared, except for a few chronometer or duplex, or some other quality escapement kept in use for some particular reason.

English Movements

The gent's pocket watch is still being manufactured at home and abroad, but very few English hand-made watches are being produced. Some mass-produced watches are being made, but are of a different style and quality. Present-day English hand-made watches still follow more or less the old pattern which has proved

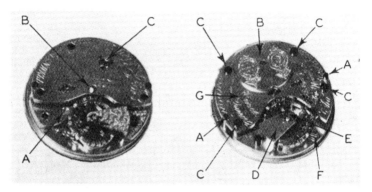

FIG. 28.—ENGLISH HALF-PLATE AND THREE-QUARTER-PLATE MOVEMENTS.

English half-plate, free-sprung movement with screwed barrel piece and centre square retained.

A. Fourth cock.
B. Centre arbor or centre square.
C. Raised bush for barrel arbor pivot.

English three-quarter-plate movement with raised barrel.

A. Case or dog screws.
B. Raised barrel piece.
C. Pillar screws.
D. Balance cock.
E. Diamond-shaped stud.
F. Tuning-fork lever.
G. Top plate.

itself second to none for performance. Modern ideas, of course, have been added.

The hand-made English watch has a style all its own and cannot be confused with the products of any other country. They are made in what are termed half-plate or three-quarter plate (see Fig. 28).

In the half-plate the barrel, centre, and third pivots are carried by the top plate, with the fourth wheel under a separate cock, the 'scape wheel and pallets being under one cock.

In the three-quarter plate the barrel, centre, third and fourth are carried by the top plate, with the 'scape wheel and pallets under one cock. The balance cock in an English watch is totally different from the Continental. The first quality are invariably free sprung, that is, there is no index or regulator on the balance cock.

The Indexed Type

In the index type the index is fitted friction tight on to a raised block which is solid with the balance cock (see Fig. 29). This block is turned back taper and the index snaps on and will not ride up or down. It is tight but can be moved stiffly at will. Two holes are drilled in the index, through which are fitted two brass pins which embrace the overcoil of the hairspring. Generally the pins hold the hairspring about one-eighth of a turn from the stud to give the maximum length of overcoil disengaged. When the index is moved towards the stud it lengthens the acting length of the hairspring, thus the watch goes slower and, of course, when moved in the opposite direction, away from the stud, it shortens the acting length and the watch gains or goes faster.

About a third of the index is cut away to allow clearance for a diamond-shaped stud which is screwed on top of the balance cock (see Fig. 29). The screw hole in the stud has a slot cut to the outside which enables the stud to be removed without completely withdrawing the stud screw.

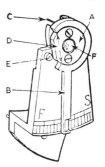

FIG. 29.—ENGLISH BALANCE COCK WITH INDEX.

A. Raised block.
B. Index.
C. Index pins.
D. Index cut away.
E. Stud screw.
F. Endstone.

The Overcoil

The overcoil is thus termed because it is bent, or formed up from the body of the hairspring, and stands over and parallel to the body of the hairspring (see Fig. 30). Its main object is to enable the watch to be made isochronous. That is, to perform all vibrations, whatever their length, in equal time. We will deal with the question of isochronism later, in Chapter 11.

Some English watches have two, three or even four overcoils, or, to use the correct term, terminal curves. They are referred to as double, triple and quadruple overcoils. Some have " duo in uno " hairsprings, that is a flat and helical hairspring combined and formed from one length of wire (see Fig. 31).

Types of Lever

The escapement is under a 'scape cock, and if a lever may be either of the ratchet- or club-tooth form. The ratchet is so termed because the 'scape-wheel teeth are ratchet shaped. It is an extremely good escapement. The club-tooth escapement generally has a steel 'scape wheel. In this form, the impulse to the balance is divided between the wheel teeth and the pallets. If well made it is a better escapement than the ratchet-tooth, but inferior if not. Various types of lever will be met with, such as dog-leg, tuning-

(a)

(b)

FIG. 30.—OVERCOILS.

(a) Double overcoil.   (b) Single overcoil.

FIG. 31.—" DUO IN UNO " HAIRSPRING.

fork, tulip, spring-tail and others. Some have a definite purpose and will be dealt with in their turn.

Jewelling and the Top Plate

The jewelling is neatly fixed in position by two screws for each hole. The top plate is usually engraved with the maker's name and number of the watch. Also on the top plate are the two polished case screws which hold the movement in its case. These have about a third of their heads filed away flat and are known as dog screws. To remove the movement from the case it is only necessary to unscrew them until the flat of the screws coincides with the band of the case. The movement is then free to come clear of the case.

On some of these watches there is a raised part of the plate. This is to enable a higher barrel to be fitted when the watch is made. Others have a bush screwed in with three screws for the top barrel arbor pivot. This is to make a longer hole or bearing for the pivot when the plate has been turned out very thin.

In some $\frac{3}{4}$- or $\frac{1}{2}$-plate English movements, the squares on the barrel arbor and centre arbor are still retained, although on a shortened scale. They are generally well finished and are only for appearance. It is sometimes convenient to have these squares when taking a watch to pieces.

English Movements with Swiss Keyless Work

From the front plate, that is, under the dial, the keyless work and motion work, etc., are again different from the Continental. The English use the rocking-bar keyless mechanism. There are, however, certain types of English watches with Swiss keyless work, and others with Swiss pattern keyless work made in England. The English rocking bar is an extremely strong keyless mechanism ; the only disadvantage is the presence of a set hands push-piece. It is no real disadvantage, except that the average person prefers the action of pulling out the winding button to set the hands.

In English watches the minute wheel is of steel, whereas in most Continental watches it is made of brass. The winding is carried out through the medium of a winding pinion, which is fitted through the pendant of the case and gears into the central wheel of the rocking bar. This is a bevelled wheel specially cut to take drive at one angle and transmit it at another. It will be described later.

Continental Movements

The Continental watch, with the exception of one or two models, is a totally different design. The majority are built up in three sections (see Fig. 32).

The first contains the barrel bar, or bridge, which supports the barrel and arbor with its transmission wheels and click visible on top.

FIG. 32.—FIRST QUALITY
SWISS PART MOVEMENT,
SHOWING THE LAYOUT.

A. Crown wheel.
B. Castle wheel.
C. Barrel.
D. Centre, third and fourth
bridge.
E. Differential up-and-down
mechanism.
F. Pallet cock.
G. Trigger screw.

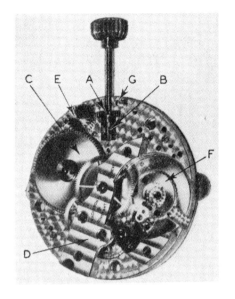

The second section comprises the centre bar, or bridge, which supports the centre, third and fourth wheels and pinions, and often the 'scape wheel and pinion as well.

Finally, the third section is the balance cock which supports the balance staff and the balance, etc.

The Index

The index is fitted differently from the English. The index centre is a separate unit and is often referred to as the top endpiece because the top endstone is set into it. The endpiece is screwed into the balance cock by two small screws. Sometimes the endpiece holes are tapped. The two screws are then screwed from underneath the balance cock, through the cock into the endpiece, and thus hold index and endpiece firmly to the cock. At other times, the balance cock is tapped and the screws pass through the endpiece freely and fit into the balance cock itself. Either way is good. The index is often split, which ensures it being firm and yet still capable of being moved to adjust the rate of the watch.

The index differs from the English counterpart. With the English type the pins are fitted in the index circle and the tail extends to the back of the cock. The Swiss index, however, is fully circular with a tail, but the front protrudes over the edge of the balance cock and carries the index pins, as shown in Fig. 34.

Index Pins and Turnboot

With watches fitted with ordinary flat hairsprings, the index pins may be either two pins and a turnboot, or one pin with the turnboot acting as the other pin. The main purpose

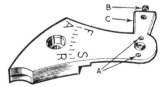

FIG. 33.—SWISS BALANCE COCK.

A. Endpiece screw holes.
B. Stud screw.
C. Projection with hole for stud.

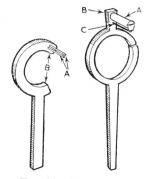

FIG. 34.—ENGLISH AND
SWISS INDEX.

English Index.	Swiss Index.
A. Curb pins.	A. Turnboot.
B. Cut away for stud.	B. Nose of index.
	C. Index or curb pin.

of the turnboot is to cover the index pins and to prevent the other coils of the hairspring jumping in when the watch receives a blow or is shaken violently.

Sometimes the turnboot is slotted so that a screwdriver can be used to release the hairspring when the watch is being taken to pieces. On other occasions the turnboot is drilled through the side, thus enabling it to be turned by means of a piece of steel wire inserted in the hole. The turnboot is pivoted into the index and the end of the pivot is riveted over just enough to make it firm and yet permit it to be turned at will. If, on the other hand, the hairspring has an overcoil there is no turnboot, but just two pins which embrace the overcoil of the

hairspring. In this instance, the turnboot is unnecessary because, if the pins and hairspring are arranged correctly, it is almost impossible for the hairspring to jump into the pins.

The Stud

The stud varies considerably in Swiss and English watches. Studs of various types are illustrated in Fig. 35. Usually the stud passes through a hole in a projection of the balance cock and is locked in position by means of a small stud screw. The stud slides up and down to enable the hairspring to be set flat, and when this is so the stud screw is tightened and the stud is firm. It is most important for the stud to be held quite firmly.

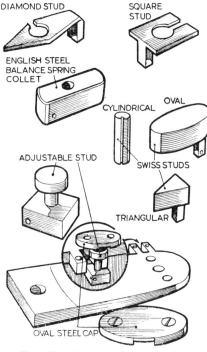

FIG. 35.—VARIOUS TYPES OF STUD.

With studs of round section, a V-shaped slot is cut and the stud screw fits into this and ensures that the stud is always in the same position in relation to the index pins.

Keyless Mechanisms

From the front plate the appearance is again different from the English. The keyless work is of the shifting-sleeve type. It consists of a winding stem which passes from the outside of the movement through the side and is pivoted to work in a hole, half of which is in the plate and half in the underside of the barrel bar.

In some of the more modern watches, however, the hole is fully into the pillar, or front plate, which is a much better arrangement. The stem has a part which is square and this fits into a female square through the castle wheel, so called because of its shape. It has teeth at both ends. One end has ordinary gear teeth and the other ratchet teeth, both of which are set at right angles. The gear teeth engage in the motion work at will.

The castle wheel has a turned slot into which the return lever or spring, as it is called, engages. On the turned part of the stem a crown wheel is fitted. This crown wheel has gear teeth in the ordinary position, but has ratchet teeth at right angles to the body of the wheel. These ratchet teeth are the counterpart of the ratchet teeth in the castle wheel.

The Winding Operation

When the watch is being wound the return lever holds the castle wheel up against the crown wheel and the ratchet teeth interlock. As the winding stem is turned, through the medium of the square section and square hole of the castle wheel, the castle wheel is rotated. The ratchet teeth of both crown and castle wheels being interlocked, the motion is transmitted to the crown wheel and then through the large, or idle, crown on the barrel bar, into which the crown wheel is geared and the watch is wound up.

On turning the winding stem in the opposite direction the ratchet

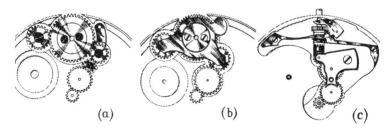

(a) (b) (c)

FIG. 36.—ENGLISH AND SWISS KEYLESS MECHANISMS.

(a) English rocking bar above the wheels.
(b) English rocking bar below the wheels.
(c) Best quality Swiss crown and castle wheel mechanism.

teeth on the crown and castle wheels slide over one another and do not wind. This is called the back action and is partly a safety device.

Hand Setting

When setting the hands the action in Swiss and most Continental watches is to pull out the winding button a certain distance. The mechanism is quite simple, and although varying according to different makers the principle is the same.

Pivoted between the front plate and barrel bar is a shoulder screw which holds the pull-out piece, or trigger as it is known. On one end of this trigger is a drop piece which fits into a turned slot in the winding stem. The other end of the trigger engages in the return piece, or lever. This return lever may have a separate spring to push it into place, or the lever and spring may be one piece, as it often is in the better-quality watches.

The return lever engages in the turned slot in the castle wheel and presses the crown and castle wheels together for winding. Thus, when the winding stem is pulled out by means of the winding button the trigger is partly turned. The end engaging into the return lever pushes this lever down and, with it, the castle wheel. The gear teeth of the castle wheel engage into the minute wheel direct, or through a small intermediate wheel, and thus set the hands.

Sometimes the watch is kept in set hands by a separate spring which acts on the trigger and holds it in place, or the end of the trigger is so shaped and the return lever or spring designed accordingly, that they lock into one another. Either way is sound. This method of set hands dispenses completely with a push-piece, which if badly fitted, as they mostly were, let in dust and dirt and eventually stopped the watch.

There are various other types of keyless work and these are dealt with in Chapter 10.

Dials

In Continental watches dials were fitted and held in position in various ways. Some dials were fitted into silver or brass rings and these rings were snapped on the pillar or front plate of the movement like the lid of a tin. A very good method, but too expensive for the mass-produced watches of to-day. It is still used in good-class and complicated watches, both English and Continental.

The most favoured method uses screws fitted through the edge of the front plate and screwed on to the copper feet of the dial. The only disadvantage is that when the screws become rusty, or if the heads or slots get badly damaged or scored, it is often impossible to get them out and remove the dial.

In another method dial keys are used. These are either flat or

TALL DIAL
KEY

FLAT DIAL
KEY

A→

ENGLISH DIAL
KEY

DIAL KEY WITH
INTERNAL THREAD

FIG. 37.—DIAL KEYS.

" A " on the English dial key indicates the inclined plane which pulls on the
dial foot.

tall, as shown in Fig. 37.   The flat type is better because it usually
fits into a sink in the plate.   The tall type is used when the dial
feet come through the front plate under a bridge or cock.   The
screw head is partly cut away and a slot is made in the dial feet.
When the cut-away part of the head coincides with the dial foot
the dial can be withdrawn, and, conversely, when the dial is put
on, the screws are partly turned until the solid part of the head
enters the slot in the dial foot and holds the dial firmly in position.
The English type is the best, where the head is thick and is sloped
up at an angle.   Thus, when the screw is in position it draws the
dial up tightly and the screw will not work out.   With the Swiss
type, the screw can work out, become lodged in the watch and
stop it.   Breguet used the English type of key.

The pinned-on dial is used only in England these days.   It is
a good method, but takes time.   The dial feet are drilled to take
the pins.   Sometimes the dial is screwed on to the front plate by
two or more screws.   The only objection is that the dial often
gets badly marked by careless jobbers.

Watch Shapes

The modern watch is made in a variety of shapes, chiefly oval,
rectangular, square and tonneau, that is, square at each end but
with the sides curved outwards ; usually they are about twice as
long as they are wide.   (Fig. 38.) Messrs. Smiths Ltd. used to make
one which was $8\frac{1}{2} \times 5\frac{1}{4}$ lignes.

Then there are the baguettes, a very small rectangular shape,
generally about fifteen millimetres long by about eight millimetres
wide.   These movements are distinctive as they have a layout
different from the general run of work.   They are built up in two
planes.

The balance and escapement are on top of the train instead of
in the same plane.   From the front plate, on which are the third
and fourth wheels and pinions, the 'scape pinion, being a long one,
is carried through to the back.   The 'scape wheel is mounted on
the back end of the pinion and the pallets are carried over the
fourth wheel.   The balance is over the third wheel and the jewel
holes are very close together.   It is essential to oil the top third

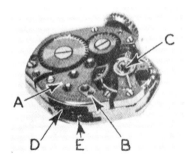

FIG. 38.—5½ LIGNE MOVEMENT WITH "INCABLOC".
A. Bar for centre, third, fourth and 'scape pivots.
B. 'Scape endpiece.
C. "Incabloc" jewelling.
D. Fourth wheel.
E. 'Scape wheel.

and fourth holes before putting the escapement in place. These are very delicate watches and have to be handled with great care.

Layout of Swiss Watches

Most Swiss watches are laid out in bars or bridges. The main one is the barrel bar or bridge. This is generally secured by three screws with threads usually of different lengths, and care is necessary with the correct positioning of each screw. The reason for this is that the keyless springs, that is the return spring or trigger piece, are sunk into the pillar, or front plate, and the screws are shortened to clear these pieces. Thus, if a long screw is used where a short one should be fitted, the return spring, or trigger, may be broken and replacements are sometimes difficult to make.

On the same barrel bridge are the two winding wheels. The smaller of the two is termed the large crown, or transmission crown, wheel to distinguish it from the crown wheel which is between the plates. This is held on usually by a steel collar and a left-hand screw. The reason for using such a screw is obvious. When the watch is being wound up the transmission crown is turning to the left, or anti-clockwise, and would eventually unscrew if a right-hand or ordinary screw were used. Sometimes the collar is screwed by three or four screws ; a very good idea, but the single screw is more favoured as it is quicker.

The transmission crown wheel is geared into the winding ratchet which is fitted on to the barrel arbor by a square on the arbor and a square hole in the wheel. The barrel arbor is drilled and tapped, and a large-headed screw secures the ratchet wheel to the arbor. Some have left-hand screws. This is wrong as a left-hand screw is not an advantage and may be troublesome. If these screws are very tight it is always advisable to try to turn them in both directions before using too much force.

The Click

The next item is the click. This is almost certain to be what is termed a recoil click. The purpose of this type is to allow the ratchet to run back when fully wound to take any false power off the barrel, or to take the extreme strain away, if a barrel without stop-work. Sometimes the click has a screwed-on spring, but the majority of the cheaper grade have a wire spring resting in a milled-out sink underneath the ratchet wheel. It operates on a pin through the click, but sometimes it acts between the fork, or the supplementary part of the click. Underneath the barrel bar and between the plates are the crown and castle wheels described earlier.

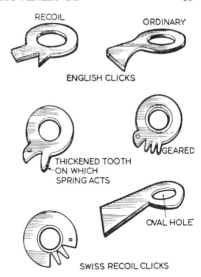

FIG. 39.—ENGLISH AND SWISS CLICKS.

The next bar, that is the centre bar, as it is termed, is really a bridge because it is anchored at both ends. It usually carries the top centre pivot and the top third pivot. It is secured by two screws which often vary in length, so care is necessary when replacing the screws. The fourth and 'scape wheels and pinions may be carried in their top holes by one bar and sometimes in separate bars, or, as they are often termed, cocks. In some instances the centre, third, fourth, and 'scape pinions are all under one bridge.

With some older Swiss watches, the barrel bar is also dispensed with and the whole train, that is, barrel, centre, third, fourth and 'scape pinions, are all under one plate. This is not a convenient arrangement because the watch has almost to be taken to pieces to replace a broken mainspring.

Lever and Pallets

The lever and pallets are usually under a small cock beneath the balance. In nearly all Continental watches of modern manufacture the escapement is a club-tooth, that is, the impulse is divided between the 'scape wheel and pallets. Also they are mostly double roller, as it is easier to obtain a safe guard action, especially when machine made, and this form allows a greater margin of error. Sometimes the pallets or, as it is really, lever and pallets in one piece, have a steel bridge instead of a cock (Fig. 40). The idea is to obtain greater rigidity and reduce thickness. Only in the older models are the lever and pallets encountered as separate pieces. Some of the levers were very elaborate and delicate pieces of work, and if one were broken it required much ingenuity and patience

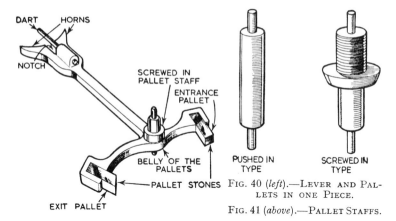

FIG. 40 (*left*).—LEVER AND PALLETS IN ONE PIECE.

FIG. 41 (*above*).—PALLET STAFFS.

to make a replacement. Usually these models were hand finished, but this is now considered very old-fashioned.

Most of the modern pallet staffs are merely pressed into the lever (see Fig. 41), but there are many models which have a screwed-in pallet staff. The screwed-in type is easier to replace as it is more certain to go back into position than the pressed-in type, especially if it has been doctored or faked in any way.

Balances

The balance staffs of to-day are very plain and unfinished in most of the general run of work, and although supposedly interchangeable it does not seem to work out in practice, and there is much faking. In other words, a nice balance may be fitted to an unsuitable staff and sometimes a good watch to an unsuitable staff, with disastrous results to both balance and watch. We will deal with this subject later, in the chapter dealing with turning.

For some time the better-quality wrist watch was fitted with a compensation balance and a steel hairspring, but this has been superseded by the solid balance used in conjunction with an " Elinvar " hairspring, as described in Chapter 11 dealing with balances and balance-springs. For wrist watches this has a distinct advantage as the balance is stronger and is less likely to be damaged in handling.

" Incastar " and " Incabloc "

Another modern arrangement is what is termed the " Incastar ". It was devised to dispense with the index and index pins, the aim being to make them free-sprung.

The hairspring, instead of being pinned to a stud as is usual, is held between rollers. The centre roller is carried through the balance cock and a steel star wheel is mounted on it. The star wheel is turned to regulate the watch. (See Fig. 42.)

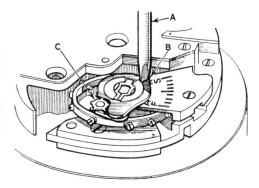

FIG. 42a. — PART MOVEMENT WITH "INCASTAR" AND "INCABLOC".

Putting in beat after adjusting hairspring while unit is turned by screw-driver A in slot at B. C regulates star wheel.

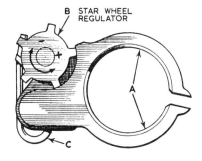

B STAR WHEEL REGULATOR

FIG. 42b.—TOP VIEW OF "INCASTAR" REGULATING UNIT.

A. Connection point to "Incabloc" unit.
B. Regulator.
C. Tension spring.

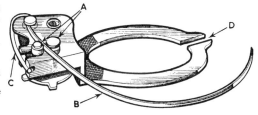

FIG. 42c.—UNDERSIDE VIEW OF "INCA-STAR".

A. Friction rollers hold-ing hairspring.
B. Hairspring.
C. Loading or tension spring.
D. Slot for turning whole unit.

Another modern idea is the "Incabloc". The object of the device, illustrated in Fig. 43, is to make a watch shockproof so that it will withstand a blow or a fall without breaking the balance staff pivots. This was first used by Breguet in 1790.

The jewel hole is mounted, or set in a brass collet, and the collet is bevelled on its edge. The endstone fits on a shelf in the same brass collet and lies just free of the jewel hole. The collet fits into a sink of the same style, or a sink with sloping sides. This sink is in the balance cock itself.

The collet, with jewel hole and endstone, is held in place by a very thin twin spring which is tongued in on one side of the sink and is pressed on to the endstone and then into a reverse

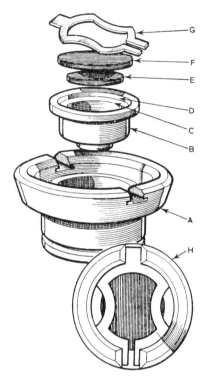

FIG. 43.—" INCABLOC " ARRANGEMENT.

A. Block fitted into balance cock.
B. Brass collet in which jewel hole is set.
C. Jewel-hole seat.
D. Endstone shelf.
E. Jewel hole.
F. Endstone.
G. Spring which holds jewel setting and
   endstone in place.
H. Assembled shock-absorbing unit.

T-slot. The twin spring opens and the two ends are put under the T. This holds the jewelling in place. It is thus a resilient bearing. The lower jewelling is very similar.

Other Types of Resilient Bearing

Other forms of resilient bearing are in use. Instead of the twin spring some types have a spring with three semi-circles of metal projecting from a circular piece of very thin metal. The balance cock has the usual sink to take the jewelling but has a recess cut to take this circular spring. On one side the recess is cut away sufficiently to allow one of the protruding semicircles of metal to pass into the recess. This is pushed around until the next semicircle is over the cutout and this is then pushed in and around until the third one comes into line. When the last semicircle is pushed in and turned around the spring stays in position and holds the jewelling in place.

The lower jewelling is very much the same, with the exception of the spring which is usually of a horseshoe shape and is kept in place by a screw.

There is another type in which the endstones only are on springs.

Sweep-Seconds Watches

Nowadays, of course, we have what are termed sweep-seconds watches. At one time these were referred to as centre-seconds as the seconds hand was in the centre instead of at six o'clock on the dial.

The layout of the movement is very much the same as the ordinary Swiss wrist watch, except that the top pivot of the third pinion is extended and carries a supplementary third wheel which is pressed tightly on to the extended third pivot. The centre pinion is hollow, that is, drilled right through. A pinion with a long arbor is fitted to the hole in this hollow centre pinion and passes through the pinion and the motion work and stands proud of the hands. The supplementary third wheel is geared into this pinion which we will call the supplementary or extra fourth pinion. (See Fig. 44.)

FIG. 44.—SWEEP-SECONDS MOVEMENT WITH SUP-PLEMENTARY THIRD WHEEL AND FOURTH PINION.

A thin spring is screwed to the top plate or bar and the free end of this spring, called a skid, rests on the top of the extra fourth pinion. This holds it in place and pre-vents it from jumping about. A long seconds hand fits on to the end of the pinion arbor which protrudes through the motion work and stands proud of the minute hand.

There are objections to this type of centre-seconds, namely, the extra friction of the skid, etc., which is considerable, and also the drag on the train. In spite of this, however, the movement seems to perform very well. Sometimes the skid is on the side of the extra fourth pinion arbor. In this instance, the pinion has a top pivot and is bridged or has a cock which carries the jewel hole into which the pivot runs.

Again, where the extra fourth pinion is pivoted and runs in a cock or bridge the skid is tongued and is underneath the pinion. This is not a good method, the friction being very heavy. The type with a spring screwed on the side of the small cock and resting on the side of the pivot is much better.

The best type is that having no extra wheels, that is, where the fourth pinion itself is planted in the centre of the watch.

Older Pattern Centre-Seconds

The modern version is better than the old type centre-seconds. In the older models there was a lot of backlash in the motion work. The seconds and minute hands did not always correspond and at times one was unable to ascertain which minute was indicated.

The centre wheel instead of being in the centre of the watch was planted to one side and the fourth wheel and pinion were in the centre. A pipe with a flange was screwed to the plate over the long fourth or seconds pivot. The cannon pinion ran freely on this pipe, being carried through the medium of the minute wheel by a wheel, having the corresponding number of teeth, fitted tightly on the centre arbor. Thus, there was the accumulated shake of all three wheels which amounted to about $1\frac{1}{2}$ minutes in many cases. Any inaccuracies in the wheel teeth and also in the dial were amplified. It was often difficult to get accuracy within half a minute on the best of them.

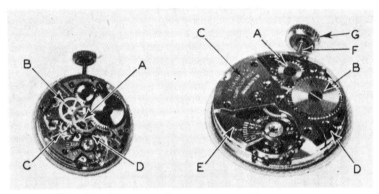

FIG. 45.—SWEEP- OR CENTRE-SECONDS MOVEMENTS.

10½ ligne sweep-seconds movement with bridge removed, showing fourth pinion in the centre and large 'scape pinion.

A. Fourth wheel and pinion.
B. Third wheel and pinion.
C. 'Scape pinion.
D. Centre wheel (just visible under the fourth wheel).

Modern 10½ ligne centre-seconds or sweep-seconds movement.

A. Large crown wheel.
B. Winding ratchet.
C. Bridge spanning third, fourth, and 'scape top pivots.
D. Barrel bar.
E. Balance cock.
F. Winding stem.   G. Winding button.

The modern watch is a better arrangement. The centre and fourth wheels and pinions are both in the centre, one above the other. The layout of the watch is very similar to the normal, except that over the top centre pivot hole is a small plate which carries the lower fourth pivot. The 'scape pinion has an extra long pinion head. (See Fig. 45.)

The centre pinion has a bridge to itself. The third wheel is raised above the level of the centre wheel and gears into the fourth pinion which is pivoted in the plate above the centre hole. The fourth wheel, also above the centre wheel, is geared into the long 'scape pinion. The top third, fourth and 'scape pivots are run in a common bridge. The centre pinion is, of course, hollow but the cannon pinion snaps on in the ordinary way. The long fourth or seconds pivot passes right through the centre pinion and cannon pinion and stands proud of the minute hand. This carries the sweep-seconds hand. As it is continuous drive there is no backlash in the gearing and inaccuracy in the dial only can give trouble.

Self-Winding or Automatic Watches

The automatic or self-winding watch is generally an ordinary caliper movement with the self-winding mechanism added.

The principle of self-winding is certainly not new, only as it applies to wrist watches. A system of self-winding was introduced in the early eighteenth century, but only a few watches were made.

The mechanism is developed from the old pedometer which was

designed to register distances walked. The vibration of walking oscillated a pivoted weight, or pendulum. As the pendulum oscillated, or moved up and down, it gathered up teeth on a ratchet wheel. They were adjustable to the length of the wearer's stride and so many teeth were gathered accordingly, and through a train of wheels the distance was indicated by a hand on a dial.

Three main types of self-winding mechanism are used to-day. In the first, the pendulum is banked on spring buffers, and in the second type, the pendulum can turn a full circle but winds the watch only one way. The third and latest type is so arranged that the pendulum or rotating weight can turn a full circle and wind both ways.

These automatic mechanisms are explained in greater detail in Chapter 10.

Chronographs

The next mechanism to be considered is the chronograph. This watch, besides giving the time by means of the usual hands, has also a sweep-seconds hand and a recording hand to show its number of revolutions. Usually the recording hand shows minutes and the watch is referred to as a minute-recording chronograph. The sweep-seconds mechanism is under the control of the wearer and can be started, stopped, and the hands returned to zero by pressing a separate push-piece or by pressing the winding button.

Another and more complicated design is the split-seconds chronograph. This has an additional sweep-seconds hand fitted either above or below the usual chronograph hand. This hand is carried by the chronograph mechanism in the ordinary way, but by pressing a separate push-piece the split-seconds hand can be stopped and held for observation, and when released it will immediately return and join the chronograph hand with which it proceeds once again. One advantage of this type is that the time of a lap in a race can be measured without losing the total time of the race, but this is only one of its many uses.

The chronograph mechanism can be started or stopped without any interference with the mean time of the watch section. These mechanisms are explained later in Chapter 14.

Complicated Movements

We now come to the more complicated mechanisms which not only include repeaters and clock-watches, but such intricate designs as the perpetual calendar.

A repeater is a watch or clock which will strike the hours and quarters which have just passed when a button or a slide is pushed. With minute repeaters the hours, quarters and minutes are struck in the same way. In addition, there are ordinary hour repeaters, quarter repeaters, giving hours and quarters, five-minute repeaters, giving hours and five-minute intervals between the hours, and

FIG. 46.—" KARRUSEL " REVOLVING
ESCAPEMENT.
The carriage on which the whole escapement is mounted is shown at " A ".

half-quarter repeaters which are sometimes referred to as seven and a half minute repeaters.

Clock-watches, on the other hand, strike the hours and quarters on passing and are not dependent for their operation on the pressure of a button or a slide. They have a mainspring for the striking train which is wound up by the winding button. The button turned the usual way winds the watch and, instead of back action, the reverse direction winds the striking mainspring.

Often, however, these clock-watches are equipped as a minute repeater as well. By pressing a button the striking train is released and strikes the hours, quarters and minutes. Further details are given in Chapter 12.

Some complicated watches have many features in one frame, comprising minute repeater, split-seconds chronograph and perpetual calendar. The perpetual calendar is designed to show hours, minutes and seconds, the date, days of the week, month, and the phases of the moon, the intricate mechanism even providing for leap year when February has 29 days. There are a few watches which give other solar information, such as the equation of time and the position of the larger planets. Details are given in Chapter 14.

Revolving Escapements

Another intricate mechanism is the " Karrusel " which is a revolving escapement performing one revolution every $52\frac{1}{2}$ minutes. Its counterpart, the centre-seconds " Karrusel ", completes one revolution every 34 minutes. The object is to eliminate the positional errors.

Then there is the tourbillon, in which the escapement is mounted on a delicate steel carriage which has the fourth pinion fitted to it. Thus the carriage acts as the fourth pinion and carries the seconds hand on one end, or pivot, and the top pivot is supported by a polished steel bridge. The fourth wheel is a fixture and the carriage revolves round it.

When fitted with a chronometer escapement it is a perfect time-keeper, but is extremely delicate and must be handled with great care. It is described in Chapter 15.

There are other types of watch and these are dealt with later.

CHAPTER 4

CLOCK MOVEMENTS

THE English dial movement, as it is called, is one of the simplest, so it is appropriate to begin this chapter with a description of it. The size of the movements varies, but is generally about 5 inches by 4 across the plates, and about 2 inches between them. This is not a standard size as the movements are generally hand-made, or partly machined. They are usually fitted to a 12- or 14-inch dial. The movements are made appropriately larger for bigger dials, but on the same principle.

Dial Movement with Fusee

The movements are chiefly fusee (see Fig. 47), but a going barrel is often substituted for cheapness. The better-quality movements had fusee chains, but the majority were fitted to take gut lines. Many have had the gut changed for steel lines, which is much better providing the lines are fitted with care and are of the right size. Some were badly fitted and were too thick, with the result that the first groove was badly damaged and, as the line always has the tendency to run up the grooves or jump the first turns, further damage often resulted to the other grooves.

Maintaining Power

Some good movements were also fitted with maintaining power, that is a supplementary spring fitted inside the fusee which is wound up by the mainspring and held by a click, termed the maintaining detent (see Fig. 48).

As the clock is being wound the power is taken off the fusee and the set-up maintaining spring keeps the clock going. Without maintaining power the train has a tendency to run back and, in any case, the train stops running and the clock is that much slow as a result. It is really a luxury in a dial, but a necessity in a good clock.

Fusee Stop-work

The fusee is turned sixteen times in eight days, that is one turn every twelve hours. The fusee is prevented from winding more than sixteen turns by " stop-work ". This mechanism consists of an arm, about an inch and a half long, which fits freely into a slot cut in a brass block screwed to the front plate. The screw usually passes from the outside of the plate and through it into the block, thus enabling the stop-work to be removed for alterations without

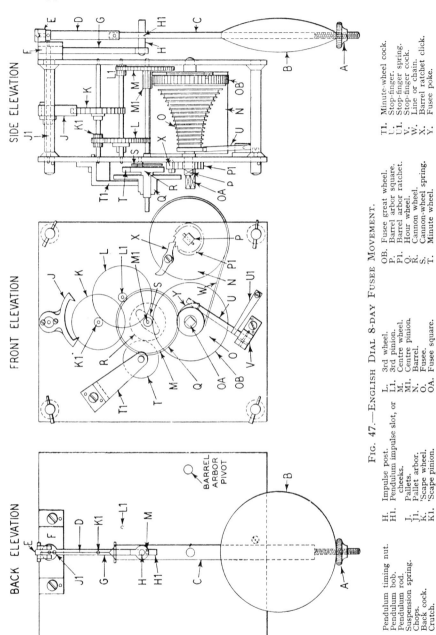

SIDE ELEVATION

FRONT ELEVATION

BACK ELEVATION

BARREL ARBOR PIVOT

FIG. 47.—ENGLISH DIAL 8-DAY FUSEE MOVEMENT.

A. Pendulum timing nut.
B. Pendulum bob.
C. Pendulum rod.
D. Suspension spring.
E. Chops.
F. Back cock.
G. Crutch.

H. Impulse post.
H1. Pendulum impulse slot, or cheeks.
J. Pallets.
J1. Pallet arbor.
K. 'Scape wheel.
K1. 'Scape pinion.

L. 3rd wheel.
L1. 3rd pinion.
M. Centre wheel.
M1. Centre pinion.
N. Barrel.
O. Fusee.
OA. Fusee square.

OB. Fusee great wheel.
P. Barrel arbor square.
P1. Barrel arbor ratchet.
Q. Hour wheel.
R. Cannon wheel.
S. Cannon-wheel spring.
T. Minute wheel.

T1. Minute-wheel cock.
U. Stop-finger.
U1. Stop-finger spring.
W. Stop-finger cock.
W. Line or chain.
X. Barrel ratchet click.
Y. Fusee poke.

taking the clock to pieces. A hole is drilled in the arm to corre-spond with a similar hole drilled in the brass block. A pin holds the arm in place, but allows it to move to and from the front plate.

The free end of the arm has a shelf or hook. A brass spring holds the arm away from the plate. The smaller end of the fusee has a snail-shaped piece termed the " fusee poke ". The stop-work is positioned in direct line with the fusee chain or gut line and, as the clock is wound up, the line engages with the arm of the stop-work and lifts it towards the front plate into the path of the fusee poke. As soon as the chain or line reaches its last turn the poke engages with the shelf or hook on the stop-work arm and the fusee cannot be turned. Without this stop-work the chain or line would overrun the fusee and be broken.

Care has to be taken to see that the line on the barrel is in its correct position with regard to the stop-arm. In other words, the line must lift the stop-arm the correct height to engage with the poke. Also care must be taken to ensure that the poke does not foul the stop-arm on the first turn running down ; if it does, it will probably stop the clock. Some-times the barrel is so placed that this cannot be prevented. In this case, the engaging part of the stop-arm must be bent to engage earlier or later, whichever is re-quired.

FIG. 48.—MAINTAINING POWER.

Other forms of stop-work are used with this type of movement, but do not warrant description as they are so simple and should present no difficulty.

Drop Dials

As stated previously, the fusee is turned sixteen times for eight days, that is one turn every twelve hours. Most dial movements have a centre pinion of eight leaves, so the great wheel, that is the wheel mounted on the fusee, must have 96 teeth.

The other part of the train, that is the centre wheel, third wheel and pinion, 'scape wheel and pinion, have numbers in accordance with the length of the pendulum. Thus with a $9\frac{3}{4}$-inch pendulum which beats half-seconds, that is, 120 beats per minute, the train would be : centre wheel 84 teeth, the third pinion of seven leaves, the third wheel 70 teeth, the 'scape pinion seven leaves and the 'scape wheel 30 teeth.

This type of movement would be applied to a drop dial, or one with the case extended downwards to take the longer pendulum, sometimes referred to as a trunk dial.

Round Dials

The round dial has a pendulum about 6 inches long, and the train varies accordingly. This is a fairly common train, centre wheel 84 teeth, third pinion of seven leaves, third wheel 78 teeth, 'scape pinion of seven leaves and a 'scape wheel of 34 teeth. This train would require a pendulum approximately six inches in length. (The formula for determining lengths of pendulums is given in Chapter 12. A list of clock trains in common use is also included in that chapter.)

Escapements used in Dial Movements

A few of the movements in drop dials have a dead-beat escapement, but it is really unsuitable. The majority have a recoil escapement which is much better for this type of clock. The dead-beat, to give a good rate, requires ideal conditions, whereas the recoil escapement will perform well under almost any conditions providing, of course, the escapement is in order.

The Pallet Arbor

The pallet arbor, or verge as it is often referred to, carries the pallets in the centre and the crutch at its end. (This will always be referred to as the pallet arbor, as it is only a survival of the time when all clocks were verges.)

The front end is pivoted in the front plate and the crutch end is pivoted in the back cock. The back cock has a post (usually solid with it), which is slotted to take the chops of the suspension spring. The cock is secured to the back plate by two cheese-headed screws, and usually has two steady pins which fit closely into corresponding holes in the back plate. This is to ensure that the cock is replaced correctly each time the clock is taken down for cleaning.

The pallets generally span or embrace seven and a half teeth and this is quite satisfactory. The pallets are usually fixed to the pallet arbor by a brass collet which is soldered on to the pallet arbor and secured by two screws, or riveted to the collet in the cheaper type.

The crutch is fitted to the pallet arbor in the same way. The crutch consists of a brass arm about $2\frac{1}{2}$ inches long, with an upright steel post, at right angles to the plate, or horizontally standing out. This post engages in the slot cut in the pendulum rod and gives or passes on the impulse from the escapement which makes up the losses due to friction in the suspension and from air resistance, and keeps the pendulum vibrating or swinging.

It must be noted that the pendulum is not driven in the real sense of the word ; it is only kept going by the losses being made up.

The plates are invariably pinned together on the front plate, but some dial movements have the pillars screwed into the back plate. Most, however, have the pillars riveted into the back plate. The dial is pinned on in the same way as the front plate.

The Motion Work

The motion work is not complicated. The centre pinion has a long arbor which protrudes about an inch above the front plate. On this arbor and near the front plate is fitted a small brass plate. The hole in this plate fits the centre arbor closely and rests on a shoulder above the front centre pivot. This small plate is bent upwards from the front plate and acts as a spring washer. The cannon wheel fits easily on this same arbor. The minute hand is fitted to a square section on the pipe of the cannon wheel. A brass collet domed underneath fits over the centre of the minute-hand boss, and also over the centre arbor. The centre arbor has a small hole drilled through it to take a pin.

The brass collet over the minute hand stands higher than the hole in the arbor, with the result that the collet, hand and cannon wheel have to be pushed against the small plate or spring washer before the hole is visible and the pin can be pushed in. Thus the cannon wheel is under pressure against the centre pinion and is carried round by it. The whole being on a spring allows the hand to be moved at will, and is certain of being carried by the turning of the centre wheel. This system is typically English.

The cannon wheel is geared into the minute wheel of the same size and number, generally 30 teeth, which is mounted on a pinion of six leaves. This minute wheel and pinion is pivoted into the front plate and the other end is carried by a cock, screwed and steady-pinned to the front plate.

The hour wheel runs either on the pipe of the cannon wheel itself, or the cannon wheel has a bridge over it with a pipe on which the hour wheel runs. This bridge is also screwed and steady-pinned to the front plate. There is no advantage in having a bridge, but it is not uncommon.

The Motive Power

The motive power is provided by a mainspring which is enclosed in a barrel. The outside end is anchored on a hook screwed inside the barrel, and the inside end of the spring is held on a hook on the side of the barrel arbor. The barrel arbor is pivoted in the bottom of the barrel and also in the barrel cover which is snapped into a groove turned in the body of the barrel. Both barrel and barrel-cover holes have a raised boss to make the length of barrel arbor bearings longer ; without these bosses the holes would wear very quickly.

The barrel arbor is again pivoted between the two plates and has a square section to the arbor on the front end. On this square section is fitted a ratchet wheel which is held in place by a pin fitted through the same square section of the barrel arbor.

Screwed on to the front plate is a click which engages into this same ratchet and keeps the ratchet in place when the spring is set up. Once the mainspring is set up the click and ratchet are a fixture.

The power from the mainspring is transferred through the fusee chain or gut line to the fusee, the only function of which is to equalize the power. The fusee is really a series of different-sized pulleys. The small ones require more power and the strongest part (or when the mainspring is wound right up) acts on these. When the power is least, or when the mainspring is running down, it acts on the largest pulley which requires least power, and so on. A fusee requires a stronger mainspring than a going barrel.

The Going Barrel

A going barrel is one which has the great wheel and barrel combined, in other words, a barrel with teeth cut on it, as against the fusee barrel which is quite plain. The pendulum is generally a simple affair. It consists mainly of a lenticular-shaped bob filled with lead.

Passing through the centre is a flat brass rod which has a thread cut on the bottom end to take a timing or rating nut. The pendulum bob rests on this nut and, as the nut is screwed up, it shortens the pendulum and makes it move faster, and vice versa.

The top end carries the suspension or suspension spring which is usually pinned to a slot in the pendulum rod. This must be pinned firmly and must not wobble. The top of the suspension spring has brass chops which fit precisely into the cheeks or slot in the back cock. On no account must there be any wobble or movement here when the pendulum is swinging ; there is a great loss of power if there is. The chops are sometimes made up of one piece of brass bent over the suspension spring and riveted. The best arrangement, however, is to have two separate pieces of brass which are riveted firmly together.

ENGLISH BRACKET CLOCKS

The next type of movement, which is akin to the dial, is that of the English bracket clock (Fig. 49). This is more or less a dial movement with a striking train added, with the result that there are two fusees and two barrels and, of course, two separate trains of wheels. The bracket clock also has a short pendulum about 5 inches long, depending again on the height of the case. With the popular size bracket clock the pendulum is about as long as the plates.

Many old bracket clocks with verge escapements are still functioning well. Some of them have been converted from verge to recoil

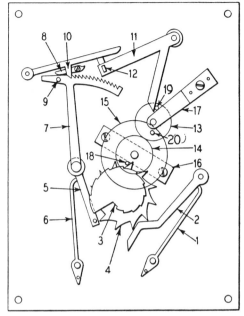

FIG. 49.—ENGLISH
 BRACKET STRIKING
 MECHANISM.

1. Jumper spring.
2. Jumper.
3. Snail.
4. Star wheel.
5. Rack tail.
6. Rack spring.
7. Rack.
8. Gathering pallet.
9. Locking post.
10. Rack hook.
11. Lifting piece.
12. Warning block.
13. Minute wheel.
14. Cannon wheel.
15. Hour wheel.
16. Cannon or hour wheel
    bridge.
17. Minute-wheel cock.
18. Pin for turning star
    wheel.
19. Hour lifting pin.
20. Half-hour lifting pin.

escapements. This is a mistake, as the advantage gained is not worth the trouble and expense. The verge, if in good order, will perform extremely well.

From the back plate the dial and bracket movements are similar, excepting, of course, the older ones just mentioned.

Pendulum of the Bracket Movement

The better-quality bracket movements have a difference in the pendulums : with the dial the rating nut is at the bottom of the bob ; in the bracket movement the rod has a block of brass riveted to it about a third of the way up (see Fig. 50). This block is filed out to provide a close fitting for the rating nut.

A hole is drilled and tapped in the centre of the bob and a flattened steel rod is screwed to it. This rod passes through the block on the pendulum rod and here the steel rod is screwed with a fine thread. The rating nut screws closely on to this thread and, also, as it fits closely into the block, very fine alterations for mean time can be made. With this type of pendulum the errors due to temperature changes are considerably reduced.

The Striking Mechanism

The striking mechanism is all contained on the front plate. The motion work is the same as for a dial, with the exception of a

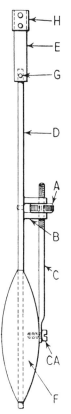

pin fitted through the minute wheel termed the lifting pin. As the motion work turns, this pin lifts up the lifting piece which runs or turns on a stud screwed into the front plate. This lifting piece engages and lifts another piece called the rack hook, which also turns on a stud screwed to the front plate.

The rack hook, as it is lifted, releases the rack and allows the rack to fall until the rack tail engages with a snail-shaped piece which is called the " snail ". This snail controls the distance the rack can fall. The snail is sometimes mounted on the hour wheel itself, but with good-quality bracket clocks it is mounted on a twelve-pointed star wheel and runs on a stud screwed to the plate. It is kept in place by a jumper and spring. The jumper is a piece of metal, usually brass but sometimes steel, mounted on a pipe or collet and run on a stud screwed to the plate. The acting end is filled up to form an obtuse angle and polished on the flat sides to a point ; the cleaner the point, the quicker the star wheel changes from one place to another.

The snail is divided into twelve steps, each step representing the number of teeth that the rack falls. The smallest section, or the section nearest to the centre of the snail, corresponds to the greatest distance the rack can fall, that is twelve hours, and, of course, the largest, or the section furthest from the centre, is the smallest fall, which is one hour. Thus the adjustment of the rack, rack tail and snail control the number of hours that the clock can strike.

The Warning Action

As stated earlier, the minute wheel turns and the pin on the minute wheel lifts the lifting piece, etc. The lifting piece has an attachment where it engages with the rack hook. This attachment is fitted through a slot in the front plate where it can be put into the path of the warning wheel. This warning wheel has a pin fitted securely through its band. As the lifting piece is raised this attachment, called the warning piece, is placed in the path of the warning pin. As soon as it is lifted high enough the rack is dropped and the

FIG. 50.—BRACKET CLOCK PENDULUM.

Rod supported from centre.

A. Rating nut.
B. Brass block riveted to rod.
C. Supporting rod.
CA. Supporting-rod screw.
D. Pendulum rod.
E. Suspension spring.
F. Brass shell filled with lead forming pendulum bob.
G. Suspension spring riveted to rod.
H. Suspension block or chops.

striking train is released, but the warning pin is held by the warning piece and the striking train is held up. The lifting piece and warning piece are lifted a little higher to make certain of clearance and then are dropped by the lifting pin to release the striking train. This whole action is termed the warning.

The Locking Wheel

Geared into the warning-wheel pinion is the locking wheel. The pinion fitted to this locking wheel has a large pivot at its pinion end near the front plate. This is a long pivot and is filed square from where it stands above the plate. Fitted on to this square pivot is the gathering pallet. The name is self-explanatory as its main purpose is to gather up the rack teeth. For each turn of the locking wheel one tooth of the rack is gathered up until all the teeth have been gathered. On the front end of the rack is a steel post which is screwed into the solid part of the rack just below the teeth. The gathering pallet is extended on the opposite side to the actual pallet just enough for it to engage with the post on the rack after it has gathered the last tooth and thus locking the striking train.

The general rule is for the rack to have one extra tooth, that is thirteen instead of twelve, the reason being that the rack-hook is in front of the gathering pallet and must have a tooth to hold when the twelve teeth have been gathered by the gathering pallet.

The rack teeth are usually shaped with one side radial and the other side concave, something like the circle covered by the gathering pallet. The object of this shape is to give clearance to the gathering pallet on one side and to enable the rack-hook to hold the rack by means of the radial side.

The train obviously has to have the right number of teeth in wheels and pinions.

The Hammer Wheel

Geared into the locking wheel, mentioned previously, is a wheel variously termed .the hammer wheel, pin wheel or cam wheel. (The author personally prefers hammer wheel as it is less confusing.) This wheel usually has eight pins fitted into the band of the wheel. Sometimes the number varies, especially with some of the older clocks. These pins lift and drop the hammer which strikes a bell or gong.

Regulating the Speed of Striking

If there are eight pins in the hammer wheel, then the proportion of the hammer wheel to the locking-wheel pinion must be eight to one. The locking wheel gears into the warning-wheel pinion. This must be an even proportion, otherwise the warning wheel would take up different positions each time the striking train was locked. This proportion, with the fly following, controls the speed of the striking or the number of strokes per minute. Thus with a locking wheel of 49, a warning pinion of 7, a warning wheel of 49 and a fly pinion of 7, the fly would turn 49 times for each blow of the hammer.

The weight and size of the fly are, of course, other factors to be considered, and some have an adjustable fly to vary the speed.

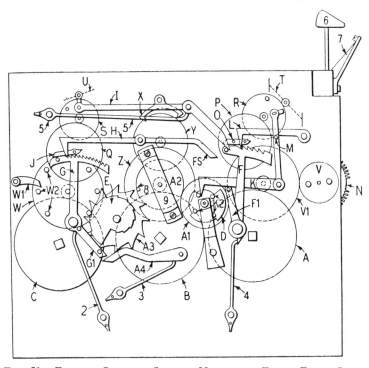

FIG. 51.—ENGLISH QUARTER CHIMING MOVEMENT—THREE TRAIN CLOCK, FULL QUARTER-CHIME MECHANISM.

A. Quarter great wheel.
B. Going great wheel.
C. Striking great wheel.
D. Quarter rack.
F1. Quarter rack tail.
FS. Tail engaged by rack head, to lift rack hook.
G. Hour rack.
G1. Hour rack tail.
H. Hour rack-hook.
I. Hour warning lever.
J. Hour gathering pallet.
K. Lifting piece.
K2. Lifting pins.
L. Quarter rack-hook.
M. Lifting pin.
N. Chiming barrel.

O. Quarter gathering pallet.
P. Quarter locking wheel.
Q. Hour locking wheel.
R. Quarter warning wheel.
S. Hour warning wheel.
T. Quarter fly.
U. Hour fly.
V. Wheel fitted on chiming barrel.
V1. Intermediate wheel driving chiming barrel wheel V.
W. Hour hammer wheel.
W1. Hammer pallet for hour hammer.

W2. Lifting pins for hammer (8 pins).
X. Pallets.
Y. 'Scape wheel.
Z. Centre wheel.
A1. Minute wheel.
A2. Cannon wheel.
A3. Hour snail star wheel.
A4. Jumper.
2. Rack spring.
3. Jumper spring.
4. Quarter rack spring.
5. Hour warning spring.
6. Quarter hammer.
7. Quarter hammer springs.
8. Pin carrying over hour snail.
9. Hour wheel bridge.

The speed can also be altered by changing the number of teeth in the warning wheel or, if a very great alteration is required, by changing the number of the fly pinion leaves.

Some bracket clocks, particularly the older ones, have a bell at the top of the movement, others have one fitted on the back plate, and again some have gongs.

Bracket Clock with Half-hour Striking

We have dealt with the plain dial movement and the bracket clock with hour striking only. Modern clocks strike the half-hour with one blow as well as the hours. This is often carried out by having another lifting pin on the minute wheel situated nearer the centre. As a result it does not lift the lifting piece quite so high. It lifts just enough to release the first tooth on the rack which is

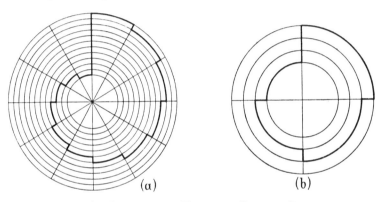

FIG. 52.—CONSTRUCTING HOUR AND QUARTER SNAILS.

(a) Hour snail lines divide blank into 12 parts or sections. Circles are drawn on blank by rack tail and filed to shape.
(b) Quarter snail.

slightly shorter than the others. Sometimes it is carried out only by a snail which, instead of being on the upper side of the minute wheel, is situated below so that it does not contact the lifting piece. It does not release the striking train at all, but just lifts and drops the hammer at the half-hour.

This same principle is adopted for clocks without striking mechanism to strike one blow at each hour.

ENGLISH QUARTER CHIME

The next to be considered is the English quarter chiming movement. There are two kinds. The first is provided with three complete trains of wheels and pinions, and the second with only two trains. The latter are referred to as " three part by two ". As a rule, the three-part-by-two type do not strike the four quarters at the hour, but strike the hours only. There are, however, various types in use to-day which are three part by two, but do strike the full quarters, including the four quarters at the hour.

The Three Train Clock

We will deal with the three train clock first (Fig. 51). Again we have the fusees and chains as in the dial movement, and the going train which is in the centre of the movement is more or less the same.

The hour-striking mechanism is very similar to the bracket movement just described, except that in the bracket movement the striking is released by the minute-wheel lifting pin and in the majority of good-quality chiming clocks it is released by the back of the quarter rack when it falls for the full four quarters at the hour. Thus the striking of the hours has no real connection with the motion work.

The lifting pins on the minute wheel, which, of course, are four in number, engage a lifting piece as in the bracket clock. The lift-

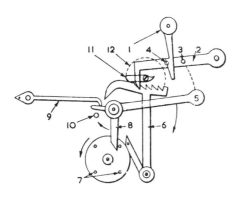

FIG. 53.—ENGLISH CHIME FLIRT ACTION.

1. Locking piece to hold rack-hook.
2. Rack-hook.
3. Post engaged by flirt.
4. Pin on rack-hook which is locked by locking piece (1).
5. Flirt.
6. Quarter rack.
7. Lifting pins on minute wheel.
8. Tail of flirt pulled back by lifting pins.
9. Flirt spring.
10. Banking pin for flirt.
11. Gathering pallet.
12. Dotted line showing path of gathering pallet.

ing piece has the warning piece in a similar way which performs the same operation, only on the quarter or chime train. The gathering pallet is identical and carries out the same function as in the bracket clock. The quarter rack has five teeth, one extra for the rack-hook.

The Quarter Snail

The quarter snail is mounted on the minute wheel itself, the lifting pins are between the snail and the wheel and the snail is mounted on a raised collet. This snail is similar to the hour snail (see Fig. 52), but has only four divisions or steps and, of course, is not mounted on a star wheel.

The Quarter Rack

The hour striking mechanism is released, as stated previously, by the back of the quarter rack. The rack-hook of the striking train runs on a stud and has an extension which is in the path of the quarter rack. As the quarter rack falls for the four quarters it lifts the rack-hook of the striking train, releases the rack and the train and is held by the warning piece. The warning piece runs on a stud and also has an extension which is in the path of the quarter rack as it is being gathered up.

The warning piece is acted upon by a spring which holds it in the path of the warning pin of the striking train. Thus the quarter rack, as it is gathered up, lifts the tail of the warning piece and, as it reaches the end of the quarters, the warning piece is lifted completely out of the path of the warning pin and the striking train runs off.

Chiming Clocks with Flirt Action

There are, however, some chiming clocks which have " flirt action ". In this instance there is no warning in the quarter train. The flirt is held in the path of the lifting pins by a banked spring. As the minute wheel turns it lifts the flirt against the banked spring and thus the spring is " set-up ". As the flirt is released by the lifting pin it flies up and knocks out the rack-hook and at the same time releases the quarter train and the rack, etc. To make sure that the rack will fall another piece is added to hold the rack-hook away from the rack. This piece is termed the " rack-hook locking piece ". As the gathering pallet turns it engages with this locking piece and releases the rack-hook, thus enabling the rack to be gathered up and held. (See Fig. 53.)

The hours are released in the same way with both types, that is by the quarter rack.

Chiming Barrel

The same principle applies to the quarter train, that is the whole train is in proportion, but as four hammers have to be lifted, or even eight as there are often, time must be given to lift them one after the other and not all together. For this reason a chiming barrel is used instead of a pin wheel or hammer wheel.

The barrel, with a brass wheel, is mounted on a steel arbor pivoted to run into the front plate at one end and into a cock which is screwed on to the back plate at the other. This barrel is divided up and brass pins are screwed in at set intervals to act as lifting pins for the hammers. There are ten quarters to be struck during one hour. Thus we may consider the chiming barrel as being a hammer wheel of five pins, but as it revolves twice for a full set we must have a proportion of ten to one. To have ten sets of quarters on one barrel, however, would necessitate an immense barrel and very large power would be required to drive it and lift the hammers.

The second wheel of the chiming train has eighty teeth and the brass wheel fitted on the chiming barrel has forty teeth. So the chiming barrel performs two revolutions to one of the second wheel.

The second wheel also gears into the locking-wheel pinion which is of eight leaves, thus we obtain our ten-to-one proportion. The locking wheel must be proportionate to the warning pinion so that the warning pin will be always in a constant position when the train is locked. Thus a locking wheel of sixty-four teeth needs a warning pinion of eight leaves.

Adjusting the Chimes

Often in chiming clocks the warning wheel has fifty teeth and a fly pinion of eight leaves. The fly is invariably adjustable, so that the speed can be altered to suit the individual.

Some chiming clocks, especially English, have eight-bell chimes and strike the hour on a gong. The eight-bell chime is often adjustable so that it can be altered at will to chime on four bells only. This is accomplished by moving or pumping the barrel out

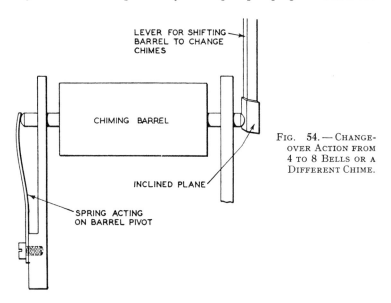

LEVER FOR SHIFTING
BARREL TO CHANGE
CHIMES

CHIMING BARREL

INCLINED PLANE

SPRING ACTING
ON BARREL PIVOT

Fig. 54. — Change-over Action from 4 to 8 Bells or a Different Chime.

of its position so that one set of pins can be put out of action and another set put into action.

Some have eight bells and four gongs. The bells can be disengaged and the gongs brought into action at will. In this instance, the arrangement comprises a double set of hammers and also two chiming barrels fitted on the same arbor. The change-over from one to the other is carried out in the same way by moving the barrel out of the path of one set of hammers and putting another set of pins into action with the other set of hammers.

The Change-over Mechanism

The change-over with all types is usually carried out by means of a hand situated at the top of the dial or positioned to one side of the top of the dial. As this hand is given half a turn it engages and moves a lever which is on a stud screwed to the front plate. One end is engaged by the hand arbor on which is a spring collet, and on the other end is a block with an inclined plane which rests on the extended pivot of the chiming-barrel arbor (Fig. 54).

As the hand is moved the inclined plane is pushed against the chiming arbor, and this arbor is pushed towards the back plate. On the back plate is a flat spring which is pressing against the other end of the chiming-barrel arbor. Thus, as the hand is put back to its original place, the inclined plane goes back and the spring on the back plate pushes the chiming barrel back to its original position.

Sometimes chiming clocks have three different chimes on one barrel. The same principle applies, but the pump piece has two inclined planes, one following the other, and there are three different sets of pins on the chiming barrel.

Constructing a Chime Barrel

A chiming barrel is constructed as shown in Fig. 55. A tube of hard brass, as large as the clock will conveniently take, is cut off to the required length and faced up square. This is mounted on its arbor and made to run perfectly true. It is then placed in the clock and the position of the four hammers (or whatever the number required) is clearly marked. The barrel and its arbor are then put in the lathe and thin grooves are cut with a graver, while the lathe

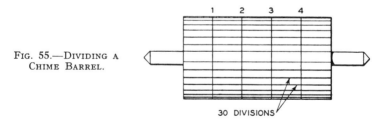

FIG. 55.—DIVIDING A CHIME BARREL.

30 DIVISIONS

is running, to coincide with the positions of the hammer tails. The circumference of the barrel is then divided into thirty equal parts, and lines are drawn from end to end of the barrel to coincide with the thirty divisions. Now we have four circles around the barrel and thirty parallel lines across it.

The next operation is to make the lifting-pin holes. With Westminster chimes the first quarter is quite easy as the hammers are lifted in order 1, 2, 3, 4. Therefore where the first circle crosses the first line a hole is drilled. Next, where No. 2 circle crosses

No. 2 line another hole is drilled, and similarly where No. 3 crosses No. 3 line and again where No. 4 circle crosses No. 4 line.

Before the next quarter is marked two lines rest must be allowed, although some allow only a single space for rest. Thus the next quarter is 3, 1, 2, 4. Therefore the pin holes will be in the following positions : where No. 3 circle crosses No. 8, where No. 1 circle crosses No. 9 line, where No. 2 circle crosses No. 10 line and where No. 4 circle crosses No. 11 line, and so on according to the various chimes.

The reason for thirty lines is that each quarter requires four lines and two lines rest, total six lines. There are five quarters on the barrel, and therefore we need thirty lines.

Musical clock barrels are marked in the same way. Some of the Continental chiming clocks are constructed on the same principle, but most of the modern type incorporate different ideas.

Self-correcting Chime

There is one particular type which has a locking plate controlling the quarters and has rack striking mechanism. This particular model is also made in England. The origin of the idea is not certain, but is generally considered to be English. With the type of English chime just described if the chiming mechanism is stopped

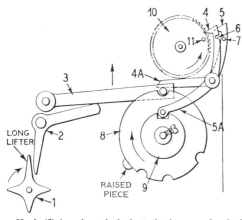

FIG. 56.—SELF-CORRECT-
ING MECHANISM FOR
CHIMING CLOCK.

1. Lifting cams—one longer than the others.
2. Lifting piece.
3. Locking control lever.
4. Locking hook for quarters.
5. Locking hook for hour release.
6. Cut-out for pin (7).
7. Pin lifted out at three-quarters.
8. Locking plate for quarters.
9. Supplementary locking plate.
10. Locking wheel.
11. Locking pin.

Hook (5) is only unlocked at the hour, and only locks at the three-quarters.
Locking hooks out of position to be visible.
Raised piece on locking plate releases the hour train.

intentionally or otherwise the quarters get out of sequence, but with the type now to be described the sequence is corrected automatically, or the chime is what is termed " self-correcting ".

In the first place, a going barrel is used and the movement is not fusee driven. The rest of the mechanism is very similar until it comes to the quarters. These are controlled by a locking plate which has an additional one-section locking plate attached to it. The cannon pinion has four cams instead of pins ; three are the same length and the fourth, which is at the hour, is appreciably longer (see Fig. 56).

As in the English type, the quarters are released, and at the end of the four quarters at the hour the quarters release the hour striking. This is carried out by a raised piece on the last section of the

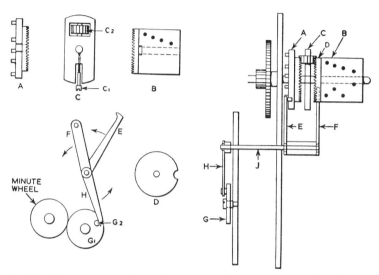

FIG. 57.—MECHANISM FOR FULL CHIME AT THE HOUR WITH ONLY TWO TRAINS.

(*Left*) " Three part by two " with various pieces. (*Right*) " Three part by two " with full chime at the hour, all pieces in position.

A. Hour striking cam.
B. Quarter striking or chiming barrel.
C. Connecting pinion gearing into both A and B.
D. Outside edge of A, showing cut out for locking.

E. Locking piece for hour cam.
F. Locking piece for chiming.
G. Pin on idle wheel which moves F to lock chiming.
H. Spring-connected arbor, pivoted through plate.

locking plate. The lifting piece of the striking train rests on the locking plate. As the raised piece comes round, the striking-train lifting piece is raised and is then dropped as soon as it reaches the end of the quarters. If the quarters get out of sequence the quarters will still run until they reach the three-quarters, when the supplementary locking plate operates. (This is the one-section locking plate mentioned previously.) To release the quarters when they are locked through this supplementary locking plate requires a greater lift. The lifting cam for the hour provides this extra lift, and thus the sequence is corrected.

(a) Rotherham escapement (*left*) from the top, (*right*) underneath.

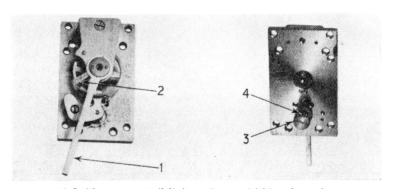

(b) Smith escapement (*left*) from the top, (*right*) underneath.

FIG. 58.—MODERN ENGLISH PLATFORM LEVER ESCAPEMENTS.

1. Tail of index, which is separate from index head, and can be put to either end.
2. Index head, containing index pins.
3. Long drop cock.
4. Long 'scape pinion.

"Three Part by Two" Full Chimes at the Hour

The "three part by two" is a quarter chime with only two trains (see Fig. 57). The English type is very good indeed, although it has been extensively copied abroad in a cheaper version. The principles involved are the same as before, the movement having a mechanism with a rack of sixteen teeth, four for the quarters and twelve for the hours. The chiming barrel is connected to the striking train by a differential gear.

When the quarters are struck, the chiming barrel is carried by the train. When the clock reaches the hour, an extra wheel, having a cam or pin and gearing into the minute wheel, engages into a lever resting on the solid part of the differential which is carried to strike the quarters. As the last quarter is struck a small groove comes into view and as it reaches the position where the lever is resting, the lever drops into the groove and holds the quarter chime barrel.

As a result, the chime barrel is held stationary and the other part of the differential starts to move. On this part of the differential are the lifting pins for the hours, so the hours are struck according to the number of teeth on the rack which remain to be lifted or gathered up.

The Differential Gearing

The principle of this type of differential gearing is as follows. The chiming barrel itself is provided with teeth standing at right angles to its body in a similar manner to a contrate wheel. On the same arbor is a disc with lifting pins on one side and teeth at right angles on the other side.

The teeth of both are geared into a pinion which is pivoted and turns freely on an arm fitted tightly on the arbor on which the chiming barrel and the disc with its pins run freely. As the striking train is running, this arm with its pinion is turned and carries either the disc or the chiming barrel.

If the disc is held, the chiming barrel runs or is carried by the arm, and if the chiming barrel is held, then the disc with its pins runs. It is a clever idea and when made by a craftsman is a simple and trouble-free mechanism.

Use of Platform Escapement

Most of this type are fitted with platform escapements instead of a pendulum. A platform escapement is a large form of watch escapement made up on a platform with the 'scape pinion extended and a long drop 'scape cock to enable it to engage with a wheel on a different plane (Fig. 58).

Sometimes they are planted flat to the back plate, and as such the gearing is straightforward. This is a bad principle, however, as the balance is running on the sides of both pivots with the maximum amount of friction.

When the platform is planted on the top of the clock, it requires a contrate wheel and endpieces for the contrate-wheel pinion to

control its endshake and thus keep the depth or intersection of the
contrate wheel and 'scape pinion constant.   The advantages, however, are so great that it is worth this extra trouble and expense ;
friction is less and the balance gives a better and more constant
vibration, with, of course, better timekeeping.

SYNCHRONOUS CHIMES

Another type of chiming clock is, of course, the electric or synchronous motor type.   There is no need to go into detail as the same
principles are involved.   The great difference is, however, that one
motor drives all three actions or trains.   The drive takes place from
the reverse end, in other words, there is no fly to control the speed.
The motor is the control and it is actually in the same relative
position as the fly in the spring clock, with the result there is enough
power and to spare.

On the rotor is a pinion which drives a fibre wheel.   This fibre
wheel is the connecting link, as this is constant to the time train

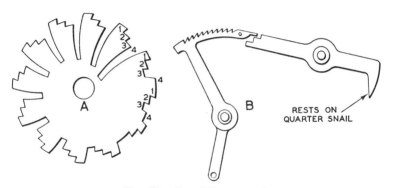

FIG. 59.—THE " TING-TANG ".

A.   Quarter snail imposed on hour snail.   Sometimes found in " three part by two "
quarter chimes.   1, 2 and 3 :   quarter steps.   4 :   hour steps.
B.   Stepped lever controlling fall of rack.   Sometimes the quarter snail is reversed,
that is, the rack falls most when the lever drops least.

and the chiming.   It is constantly in action with the time train,
but is only in action with the chiming at the quarter and the hour.
This connection is made through a rocking bar which is put in and
out of gear by the striking mechanism.   There is no warning and
all actions are instantaneous.

Where these clocks are used for tubular chimes there is usually
a separate motor for the lifting of the hammers, which is switched
on and off by the clock, generally by means of a mercury switch.

The advantage is that the clock can be installed upstairs and the
chimes in the hall.   Like all synchronous electric clocks, they are

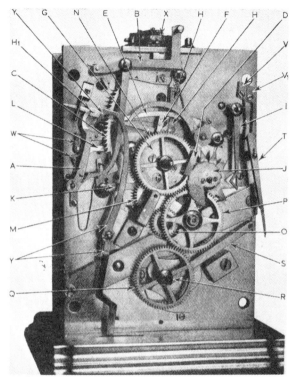

FIG. 60.—FRENCH CARRIAGE QUARTER " TING-TANG ", ALARM OR
" GRANDE SONNERIE ".

A. Rack-hook.
B. Repeating piece.
C. Hour rack.
D. Hour rack tail.
E. Quarter rack.
F. Quarter rack tail.
G. Quarter snail.
H. Flirt (seen below).
H1. Pin in flirt which holds rack-hook.
I. Hour snail jumper.
J. Hour snail.

K. Lever preventing hour rack falling except at the hour.
L. Lever controlling falling of the hammers.
M. Minute wheel.
N. Hour wheel.
O. Set hands wheel.
P. Transmission wheel from hour wheel.
Q. Alarm wheel.
R. Stepped steel collar to control release of alarm.

S. Lever worked by steel collar to hold hammer tail.
T. Alarm hammer tail.
V and V1. Two springs to hold hammer from the gong when at rest.
W. Hammer pallets working on L.
X. Platform escapement.
Y. Strike silent and hour striking control lever.

completely dependent on the electric supply for their operation, and may be unreliable for close timekeeping due to mains frequency variations.

THE " TING-TANG "

The " ting-tang " is so called because it gives only two blows at the quarters on two gongs or bells having different tones. With some of the older types, however, both blows were struck on one bell, with the hour using the same bell.

The majority vary little from the ordinary strike movement. They have two hammers working off the same pin wheel or hammer wheel, and at the hour one is pushed or pumped out clear of the lifting pins. In these types the rack is the same in principle, but the first three teeth are graduated in length and are shorter than the rest. The lifting pins are placed accordingly. The first three pins just release the first three teeth in sequence and, of course, the fourth pin raises the lifting piece to its full height and releases the whole of the rack according to the number of hours.

The snail differs inasmuch as the quarter snail is imposed on the hour step, the other part of the snail being as usual. The best of this type, however, is where a lever with three steps, controlled by a quarter snail, controls the number of rack teeth which is released. This same lever is put out of action at the hour to allow the rack to fall its full distance (Fig. 59).

FRENCH CARRIAGE REPEATERS

The French carriage quarter repeater is a " ting-tang " quarter (see Fig. 60). Generally these are termed " Grande sonnerie " and they strike the quarters on passing and repeat on pressing a button at the top of the case. They are also fitted with an alarm mechanism and are rather complicated, but the mechanism is quite sound and if assembled correctly does not give trouble.

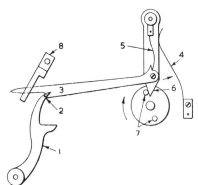

Fig. 61.—French Carriage Repeater Flirt Action.

1. Rack-hook.
2. Pin in rack-hook engaged by step on flirt.
3. Flirt.
4. Spring acting on flirt.
5. Spring forcing flirt downwards.
6. Part of flirt engaged by lifting pins and pulled in direction of arrow.
7. Lifting pins.
8. Cock with tongued slot to hold flirt in place.

The French repeating carriage clock is slightly different in design from the English, but the principle is the same. The striking train of the French clock is locked in a different way ; instead of being locked by the gathering pallet it is locked between the frame. A pin on the locking wheel is held by a lever fitted to an arbor pivoted between the plates. On one end of this arbor is a long pivot, filed square, on which the rack-hook is fitted tightly.

While the rack is dropped the rack-hook is held back and the locking piece is held clear of the locking-wheel pin. When the rack is fully gathered up the rack-hook falls forward and the lever connected to it also falls into the path of the locking pin and stops the striking train running. The gathering pallet only gathers up the rack, and when the striking is finished the gathering pallet is placed clear of the rack and also clear of the flirt.

French Carriage Repeater Flirt Action

The flirt is the method adopted to release the striking train. Again it is different from the English type of flirt (Fig. 53). The French flirt runs on a stud situated in the centre of the front plate and just above the motion work. It is in two parts (Fig. 61). One part engages with lifting pins on the cannon wheel (not on the minute wheel as in English clocks). The other part is secured by a shouldered screw to the first part and has a spring which is screwed to the first part but acts on the second part and keeps it pressed downwards or towards the bottom of the clock.

The second part rests on the rack-hook or, to be more correct,

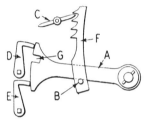

THE DUMMY BLOW AT THE END OF STRIKING THE HOURS

HAMMER STOP LEVER "A" IS LIFTED BY PIN "B" IN END OF HOUR RACK "F" AND GATHERED BY GATHERING PALLET "C" AND PLACED IN PATH OF HAMMER PALLETS "D" AND "E" PREVENTING HAMMERS FALLING.

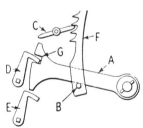

STRIKING THE QUARTERS

HAMMER STOP LEVER "A" IS AGAIN LIFTED AS HOUR RACK "F" IS GATHERED AND HAMMER "D" FALLS INTO SLOT "G" LEAVING PALLET "E" FREE OF STOP LEVER "A"

NOTE:- IN EACH CASE GATHERING PALLET "C" IS AT THE END OF ITS LIFTING AND IS ABOUT TO BE FREE.

FIG. 62.—FRENCH QUARTER " TING-TANG " CARRIAGE REPEATER.

on a pin which is fitted into the rack-hook. It is kept from riding up by a small slotted cock which is screwed to the plate. The action is as follows : The cannon lifting pins engage and draw back the flirt ; the second half of the flirt, which has a step in it, is also drawn back until the little step falls over the pin in the rack-hook. It is then released by the cannon lifting pins and the flirt, by means of a spring which is screwed to the plate pressing against it, jumps forward, pushes the rack-hook back and releases the rack.

As the flirt still holds the rack-hook it must be released to enable the rack-hook to hold the rack as it is being gathered up. This is released by an extended section of the gathering pallet, which lifts the end of the flirt clear of the pin in the rack-hook and allows the rack-hook to engage and hold the rack.

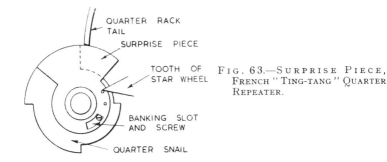

QUARTER RACK
TAIL
SURPRISE PIECE
TOOTH OF
STAR WHEEL
BANKING SLOT
AND SCREW
QUARTER SNAIL

Fig. 63.—Surprise Piece, French " Ting-tang " Quarter Repeater.

The snail is fitted to a star wheel, runs on a stud and has the usual jumper and spring. The snail is carried from one hour to the other by means of a pin on the top of the cannon wheel and is arranged to carry the snail over, as near as possible, dead on the hour. On no account must the snail change over too early, because, if the repeater is released just before the hour, the incorrect time may be given, the next hour being struck.

Arrangement for Striking the Half-hour

The half-hour is struck in exactly the same way. A lever is included to prevent the hours from being struck at the half-hour. This lever runs on a stud and is acted upon by a pin in the minute wheel. The minute wheel has to be put in mesh correctly with the cannon wheel in order that the lever may be in the right position at the half-hour. There is a pin in one end of the lever and at the half-hour this pin is placed immediately under the rack, thus preventing the rack from falling and only one blow is struck.

Arrangement of the Quarters

The quarters are arranged in the following way. There is a quarter rack and a quarter snail. The snail is fitted on the pipe of the cannon wheel. The quarter rack is fitted and sometimes runs on the same stud as the hour rack and the rack-hook acts on both. The part of the rack-hook which acts on the quarter rack is shorter, thus the quarter rack cannot be held until the hour rack is fully gathered up. The two hammers are lifted by the same hammer-wheel pins and, unlike most " ting-tangs ", there is no pumping action to disengage one of the hammers.

The quarters are struck after the hours have been struck. There is a pin at the bottom end of the rack, and this pin engages into a steel lever which runs on a stud. The end of this lever is curved and has a curved slot. On the arbors of the two hammers are two pallets which are engaged by the curved end of the lever. As the hour rack reaches the end of its lift the pin raises the steel lever and puts it into the path of the pallets, thus preventing the hammers from falling and no blow is struck (Fig. 62).

As the rack drops back into place the steel lever is lowered and again raised higher and both hammers fall, one after the other, and repeat this operation according to the number of quarters to be struck.

The " Surprise Piece "

The quarter snail in the quarter " ting-tang " carries over the hour snail instead of the usual pin. This snail has what is termed a " surprise piece " which is free to move back and forth and is banked by a pin, or sometimes two pins spaced apart. Two other pins are fitted to the surprise piece itself. These two pins project

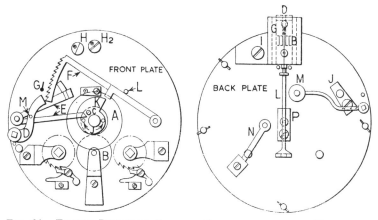

FIG. 64.—FRENCH PENDULUM STRIKING CLOCK, STRIKING THE HOURS AND HALF-HOURS.

FRONT PLATE (*left*).		BACK PLATE (*right*).	
A.	Hour wheel.	B.	Regulating chops of Brocot.
B.	Minute wheel.	D.	Threaded rod with gear wheel
C.	Cannon wheel.		riveted to it.
D.	Rack-hook.	G.	Body of Brocot.
E.	Lifting plate.	I.	Back pallet cock.
F.	Rack.	J.	Hammer wheel cock.
G.	Gathering pallet.	L.	Pendulum crutch.
H.	Striking speed adjustment.	M.	Hammer.
H2.	'Scape depth adjustment.	N.	Bell standard.
J.	Lifting pins.	P.	Centre wheel cock.
K.	Snail screwed to hour wheel.		
L.	Banking pin for rack.		
M.	Lifting pin for rack-hook.		

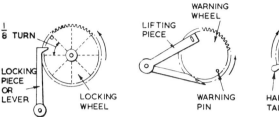

WARNING WHEEL

HAMMER WHEEL

$\frac{1}{8}$ TURN

LIFTING PIECE

LOCKING PIECE OR LEVER

LOCKING WHEEL

WARNING PIN

HAMMER TAIL

HAMMER JUST DROPPED, POSITION OF LOCKING PIN

POSITION OF HAMMER LIFTING TAIL WHEN TRAIN IS LOCKED

1.   2.   3.

Fig. 65*a*.—French 8-day Striking Clock—Relative Position of Wheels when Assembled.

1. Position of locking pin when hammer has fallen.
2. Position of warning pin when train is locked.
3. Position of hammer lifting tail when train is locked.

and are used to carry over the hour snail. The object of the surprise piece is safety. It prevents the clock being stopped if the repeater is brought into action too close to the change-over.

As the cannon wheel approaches the hour, the first pin on the surprise piece engages the star wheel and starts to change it over. As soon as the star wheel reaches the apex or point of the star wheel jumper it jumps to the next hour. The following tooth on the star wheel engages with the second pin on the surprise piece, pushes it forward about half-way and covers the last step of the quarter snail; thus preventing the quarters from being struck.

These clocks are usually provided with a long lever, which acts as a strike-silent piece and also as a means of adjustment either to prevent the hours from being struck at each quarter or to prevent the quarters from being struck on passing.

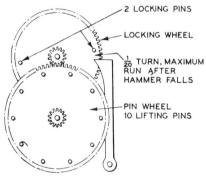

2 LOCKING PINS

LOCKING WHEEL

$\frac{1}{20}$ TURN, MAXIMUM RUN AFTER HAMMER FALLS

PIN WHEEL 10 LIFTING PINS

Fig. 65*b*.—French Carriage Clock, Quarter Repeater "Ting-tang".

Position of locking pin when hammer is dropped.

The lever is generally found protruding from the bottom of the case, and there is nothing elaborate or complicated about the mechanism. There are three or four positions in a slot cut through the bottom of the case. This slot has steps cut in one side, the lever snaps into the step required and is kept in position by the lever spring. All that happens is the lever is positioned to obstruct the quarter rack, hour rack or flirt, whichever is required.

French Alarm Mechanism

The alarm mechanism is plain and straightforward. An arbor is pivoted between the plates and has a fairly strong brass spring washer or plate between the shoulder of the arbor and the plate. This prevents the arbor from being moved easily. The arbor is extended on the front plate end, and on this is a wheel which has a sloped back pin or small post projecting about one sixty-fourth of an inch. Above this wheel, the arbor is squared and a steel collet is fitted and pinned on tightly. The steel collet is slotted to allow the sloped pin or post to drop in easily. One side of this slot is perfectly square and the other side is sloped to allow the pin to ride up.

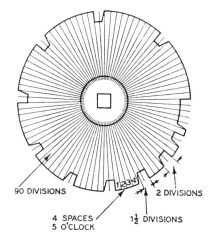

90 DIVISIONS   2 DIVISIONS

4 SPACES   1½ DIVISIONS
5 O'CLOCK

FIG. 66a.—CONSTRUCTING A FRENCH LOCKING PLATE.

Underneath the wheel, which has the sloped pin, is a brass or steel lever which is pressed against the centre of the wheel, forcing it against the slotted steel collet. This lever is on a stud which is screwed to a cock fitted to the front plate. At the opposite end of this same lever is a tightly fitting screw, and the thread showing through is turned to a long tapered point. This point engages with a lever which is fitted on the hammer arbor of the alarm hammer.

When the sloped pin is in the slot of the steel collet this lever is clear of the alarm hammer lever, but when the sloped pin is resting on the solid part of the collet the lever holds the alarm hammer lever and the alarm cannot run. The wheel with the sloped pin is geared through an intermediate wheel to the hour wheel. The arbor, carrying the wheel with the sloped pin and steel collet, is continued through the dial and carries the alarm hand. Thus this steel collet controls the position where the alarm will be released.

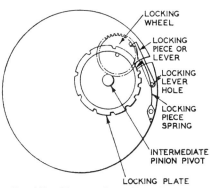

LOCKING WHEEL

LOCKING PIECE OR LEVER

LOCKING LEVER HOLE

LOCKING PIECE SPRING

INTERMEDIATE PINION PIVOT

LOCKING PLATE

FIG. 66b.—FRENCH CLOCK BACK PLATE— LOCKING PLATE STRIKING MECHANISM.

FIG. 67.—TYPICAL ENGLISH 8-DAY REGULATOR MOVEMENT.

A. Crutch.
B. Banking.
C. 'Scape wheel.
D. Maintaining detent.
E. Jewelled pallets.
F. Maintaining ratchet wheel.
G. Great wheel.
H. Barrel.

The alarm hammer lever has a pin fitted nearly central which is banked by two springs. The idea is to keep the alarm hammer clear of the gongs when at rest, otherwise, if the hammer were laid on the gong, the striking would sound unpleasant and chattery.

FRENCH 8-DAY STRIKING CLOCKS

The ordinary French clock has a very similar striking mechanism to the carriage clock, except, of course, that it has a lifting piece and a warning (Fig. 64). The snail is mounted on the hour wheel itself instead of on a star wheel. It should be noted that the motion work must be carefully put together. If the hour wheel is out of position it will stop the clock at a few minutes to one o'clock, owing to the rack tail fouling the step of the snail.

The striking train has to be assembled in a certain way. The locking-wheel pin should have an eighth of a turn left to run to reach the locking piece after the hammer has dropped. Also, the warning pin must be half a turn away from the warning piece when the train is locked. On no account must the hammer be left " on the lift ", nor must the tail of the hammer rest on a lifting pin.

These rules apply to all striking clocks with a lifting piece and warning, and that with regard to the hammer, to all striking clocks. With a flirt action there is no warning, but the locking wheel must have an eighth of a turn left to run before locking after the hammer has dropped.

French 8-Day Strike and Locking Plate

Another type of French striking clock has a locking plate instead of a rack to control the number of hours struck. They are generally older types and are not now made. (Many English clocks had a locking plate.) The locking plate is generally fitted on an extended pivot of the second wheel of the striking train. This extended pivot is filed square to fit tightly into a square hole in the boss of the locking plate where it is pinned firmly (Fig. 66b).

Usually the locking plate does one full turn for the twelve hours, but there are several where the locking plate completes one turn in twenty-four hours. The plate is made from a large wheel blank. Thus, for a twelve-hour locking plate it must be divided into ninety parts, and for a twenty-four hour plate into one hundred and eighty parts (Fig. 66a). This allows for seventy-eight hours to be struck and twelve half-hours and one hundred and fifty-six hours and twenty-four half-hours in the case of a twenty-four hour locking plate.

The slots or sections which are cut out are the stopping places for the striking mechanism. The space usually corresponds to the last stroke of the hour and the half-hour. The raised portions are all preceded by an inclined plane to assist the knife-edged part of the locking piece to rise when it is to strike the hours.

It is important to check the locking plate for truth, also that the second wheel hole has not worn oval or is very wide. The same applies to the pivot holes of the locking piece. The trouble with a locking plate is that as it is progressive it will not necessarily correspond to the correct hour as registered by the hour hand. If for some reason it fails to lock on one particular hour it will run on and strike the next half-hour and will go on striking half an hour out all the time.

The old English type of locking plate did not have the half-hour striking, and the locking plate spaces were quite square. The principle was different. The locking was carried out by a wheel having a hoop riveted on and a small section cut away. The locking piece merely dropped into this space if it corresponded to the slot in the locking plate ; if not, it was held up by the locking plate until both corresponded, then the locking piece dropped in the space and locked the striking train.

WATCHMAN'S RECORDING CLOCK

The watchman's recording clock, or " tell-tale " as it is known, is perfectly straightforward as far as the movement itself is concerned. It is, of course, portable and is fitted with a platform escapement. In some movements the barrel differs from the usual type. It is a resting barrel; in other words, the barrel itself is screwed firmly to the plate and the barrel arbor turns. Fitted on the barrel arbor, which has a square near the pivot, is a ratchet wheel with a square hole. On the extended arbor is fitted the great wheel which has the click and click spring fitted to it. The great wheel receives its motive power through the ratchet on the barrel arbor and on to the click screwed to the great wheel. The barrel arbor ends in a threaded portion on to which is screwed the winding square.

Running on the great wheel, and banked by a screw and spring, is a brass disc which carries a dial, a card and a carbon paper. The clock is provided with keys bearing either a letter or a figure. The keys are pushed into the slot in the front of the case and pressed on to the dial, the carbon paper underneath giving an impression on the dial of the letter or figure at the particular time. By this means a record can be maintained of the time a watchman visits any number of stations.

Another type has a steel post which is screwed to the barrel. The barrel arbor passes through this post and ends in the usual winding square. About half-way down this post a small slot is turned. Fitted on to this hollow post is a brass plate with a pipe. This pipe has a raised pip which fits into the turned slot and thus keeps the brass plate from riding up. The pipe of the disc also has a turned slot over which is fitted a thumb nut having a spring attached which fits into the turned slot. There are also two pointed pins in the disc corresponding to two holes drilled in the thumb nut. A dial fits on this disc, and when the thumb nut is pressed home the two pins pierce the dial and hold it firmly. The clock is set to time by adjusting the thumb nut. This rotates the brass disc which turns stiffly and is kept down by the pip and slot.

The keys are put through the side of the case and according to their shape lift certain levers which mark or prick the dial. With these tell-tales there is generally a piece screwed into the case which will mark the dial if the tell-tale is opened at any time. Other types are in use, but the principle is the same.

Complicated and other clock mechanisms will be dealt with in later chapters.

CHAPTER 5

FILING AND MAKING DRILLS, TAPS AND SCREWS, AND METHODS OF POLISHING

THE various types of file used by watch- and clockmakers having been dealt with in Chapter 1, we can now continue with a description of the correct methods of filing and the making of drills, taps and screws in which the use of files plays an important part.

Filing Flat

The first essential to good work is the ability to file flat, and to do this the craftsman should be able to work in comfort and not be cramped for space. As explained previously, the height of the bench and vice is another important consideration and should be so arranged that the work is held elbow high.

The file should be held firmly by the handle, the palm of the other hand resting on the top of the file at the front. Always take a full length stroke with the file while going forward, and under no circumstances put pressure on the file on the return journey ; it is often the return stroke which spoils the work. Putting extra pressure on the front of the file must be avoided. The object is to apply constant pressure for the whole length of the stroke.

Another important point is not to use a worn-out file ; the teeth must be sharp to do good work. It was often the practice with apprentices or pupils to give them an old file, with the mistaken idea of breaking them in. In actual fact, it spoilt their work and got them into bad habits.

When filing brass, use a new file ; it will last a very long time and there will be no difficulty in keeping the work flat. Alter the direction of the stroke, that is, first push the file front left and then front right ; this will show where one is actually cutting. The grain made by the file intersects and the reflection of the light on the work makes a dark or shadowy line. The aim is to keep this line in the centre of the work, and flat work will result if this is carried out.

If filing, say, the edge of a clock plate, do not attempt to file it from end to end. For one thing it requires great skill to do this and keep it flat and square. The easiest and best way is straight across the plate. The other way, from end to end, is often used to disguise bad workmanship. Another bad practice is straight-graining or draw-filing a plate edge ; it does not make it flat and only misleads the inexperienced.

Filing Square Corners

When filing up to a square shoulder do not make the mistake of resting the file against it, particularly if the cutting edge is towards the shoulder. File the shoulder slowly and carefully, watching the edge of the file to make sure that the file is square to the shoulder and travelling perfectly straight when the file touches it. The aim is to take down the metal and leave the shoulder standing. It is good practice to use the file with the safe edge towards the shoulder, especially with small work.

Similarly, with steel always use a file which cuts but, as stated before, on no account use a new file. Not only will the file be ruined completely, but it will tear the metal and leave deep ridges which will require a lot of work to clean up smoothly. A file which has been used extensively on brass and has the very sharp edges worn off, that is, not broken or chipped off, is the most satisfactory and saves time.

Filing a Square

When filing a square for a drift or a winding square on a barrel arbor a good plan is to put a carrier firmly on the work and use it as a guide, as well as a means of holding the work while filing.

The first side is filed with one end of the carrier uppermost and held perpendicular. When that side has been filed the same end is placed downwards, also making sure that it is perpendicular, and the second side is filed. The carrier is then turned through a quarter of a turn, as shown in Fig. 68a, and the third side is filed. Again the carrier is given half a turn and the fourth and final side is filed. It is a good idea to give the same number of strokes to each side. By this means and with practice a perfect square can be obtained.

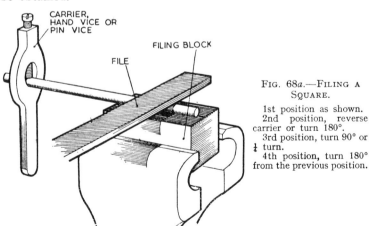

CARRIER, HAND VICE OR PIN VICE

FILING BLOCK

FILE

FIG. 68a.—FILING A SQUARE.

1st position as shown.
2nd position, reverse carrier or turn 180°.
3rd position, turn 90° or ¼ turn.
4th position, turn 180° from the previous position.

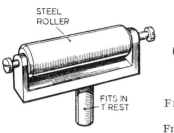

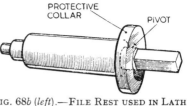

STEEL
ROLLER

FITS IN
T'REST

PROTECTIVE
COLLAR

PIVOT

FIG. 68b (*left*).—FILE REST USED IN LATHE
WHEN CUTTING A SQUARE.
FIG. 68c.—PIVOT PROTECTED BY FERRULE
IN CASE FILE SHOULD SLIP.

If there is a pivot behind the square it can be covered with a brass or steel ferrule of suitable size as a precaution in case the file should slip. (See Fig. 68c.)

Watchmakers' files, being smaller and shorter, are invariably held in one hand without being balanced by the other, but the same procedure applies to both small and large files. The watchmaker usually sits while doing small filing work, whereas the clockmaker stands up as his is usually heavier or larger work.

Some Practical Hints

It is not advisable to file stainless steel or bell metal as they will spoil the file ; they are best ground on the grindstone and finished off with a file.

To file tin and other soft metals it is as well to chalk the file, otherwise it clogs badly. Tin is used only for polishers and needs merely a clean-up with a file. Lead is always cast and, if necessary, is hammered to shape.

Gold and silver are filed with a good cutting file, but a lot can be done by hammering or casting and finishing off with a file.

MAKING DRILLS

Drills most useful to the watch- and clockmaker are the old spear-head type which can be made easily and at little cost.

To make a drill, select a piece of steel as near as possible to the size of drill required, a round rod for preference. Hold the steel rod in a hand vice if a large drill, and if a small one use a pin vice. File a flat face tapering gradually towards the end to a third of its thickness. Next give the rod half a turn, file that side flat and tapering and remove half of the remaining metal. The thickness at the end will remain about a third of the thickness of the rod.

File the edges of the flats to form an arrow-head with the point dead central and the sides making an angle of 90° to each other, that is 45° sides. This applies to brass. With a crossing file make a curve behind the arrow-head for clearance on each side. The curve will be as long as the length of the hole it is required to drill. The drill is now ready for hardening.

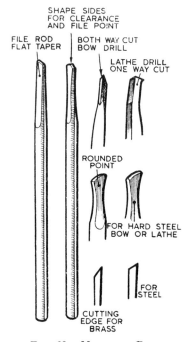

SHAPE SIDES
FOR CLEARANCE
AND FILE POINT

FILE ROD | BOTH WAY CUT
FLAT TAPER | BOW DRILL

LATHE DRILL
ONE WAY CUT

ROUNDED
POINT

FOR HARD STEEL
BOW OR LATHE

FOR
STEEL

CUTTING
EDGE FOR
BRASS

FIG. 69.—MAKING A DRILL.

Hardening Drills

The best way to harden the drill is to heat it until it turns cherry-red in colour, when it can be plunged quickly into oil if to be used on brass, or into water if for steel. Do not overheat the metal, otherwise the drill will disintegrate as soon as it is used.

After hardening, clean off the fire skin or oxidizing with an emery stick until it is bright. Grip the extreme end of the head in a pair of pliers and heat the metal, away from the head, until it starts to colour. The colour will change from pale straw to dark straw and eventually to dark blue. The colour will gradually run towards the head and as it reaches dark blue, near the head, plunge it into water to cool. Rub the flats of the drill on the oil-stone until they are sharp, then rub the edges at an angle of about 20° until the flat and the angle of the edge become sharp. The drill is now ready for use.

Small drills are made in the same way except that they are hardened differently. The best method is to cover the drill with fine iron binding wire as a protection, heat them both until red hot and then plunge into oil.

Commercial types of spear-head drill are available, of course, and can be used if preferred.

The commercial twist drill is a very useful tool and can be bought very cheaply. It is essential where mass production is carried out ; it is then under control but tends to drift from its original setting.

The straight flute drill makes a nice round hole but also has to have some support. Neither the spiral flute nor the straight flute drill will cut hardened and tempered steel, so the use of these drills is limited as far as the repairer is concerned.

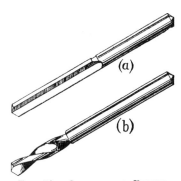

(a)

(b)

FIG. 70.—COMMERCIAL DRILLS.
(a) Straight flute drill.
(b) Spiral flute or ordinary twist drill.

TAPS

The B.A., or British Association, taps, dies and screws are of great assistance to clockmakers, but are not so useful to watchmakers. Unfortunately it is difficult to obtain silver steel screws or screws which can be hardened and tempered, but the dies and taps are worth having as fresh taps and screws can be made in silver steel. The odd numbers of taps and dies are always difficult to obtain these days.

The Whitworth threads are rather coarse and that is the objection to them.

Making a Die

The Swiss screw plates are the best investment when they can be obtained. Most of them, however, are made without cutting edges, but this can be remedied by making small dies for oneself.

A piece of 20-gauge plate steel, prefer-ably that which used to be known as black steel, but silver steel will do, is drilled to the core diameter of the screw required. A tap is made from silver steel and hardened and, of course, left quite hard.

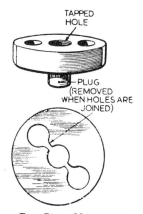

FIG. 71a.—MAKING A SMALL DIE.

The piece of plate steel is tapped and brought up to a full thread. Two holes are drilled on opposite sides as close as possible to the tapped hole. (See Fig. 71a.) A piece of steel is then threaded and left soft and is screwed into the tapped hole. Shorten this piece of steel on one side until it is flush with the piece of plate steel and leave the other end standing out so that the piece of steel can be removed after-wards. This piece of threaded soft steel acts as a plug. File (not broach) the two holes previously drilled until they break well into the tapped hole. This will mean, of course, that the soft steel plug will be filed away as well.

Unscrew the plug and take it right out, and it only remains to harden and clean-up the plate. The idea of using the plug is to prevent the thread from becoming badly burred.

Making a Tap

To make a tap choose a piece of silver steel, a couple of sizes larger than the full diameter of the thread required. If a large tap, hold the steel in a hand vice ; and if a small one, use a pin vice. File one end to a square and, as this is the end to be held, avoid any tendency towards a taper, making it as straight as possible. Change over the steel and hold the square end in the pin or hand vice. Proceed to file the other end to a gradual taper, and as

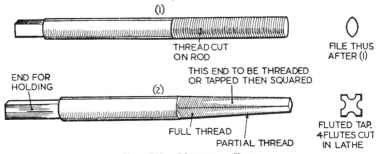

FIG. 71*b*.—MAKING A TAP.

Operations 1 and 2 show stages in the making of a taper tap.

round as possible, until the steel just passes by about its own diameter through the screw plate. Turn it into the screw plate, using a liberal amount of oil, until a full thread is cut.

File the tapped steel square, but retain the taper, and bring the edges up sharp without removing the thread completely, but leaving a half of it at full thread. In other words, if measured across the diagonal of the square the measurement will be the same as when it was round. The four flat sides where they meet form the cutting edges.

Fluted Tap

If a lathe is available with a slide rest and a vertical slide, the sides of the tap can be fluted instead of filed. The tap can be put into the collet and the other end into a centre in the tailstock. A cutter of suitable size in the vertical slide can be run along the tap to cut out three or four grooves in the side. These fluted taps make a very good cutting edge, but the square ones are suitable for most purposes.

When the tap is squared or fluted it can be hardened ; if for brass, draw the temper to a pale straw colour, and if for steel, leave it hard.

Never use too much force with taps as they are difficult to remove if they get broken in a hole. The best way to remove a broken tap is to knock it out.

Plug Tap

If the hole to be tapped is a blocked hole, that is one which is not open at both ends, two taps are needed ; a taper tap, which has just been described, and a plug tap. A plug tap is a straight tap with no taper, or with a thread that is " up " all the way.

When making a plug tap, the steel is not filed to a taper but is left straight.

SCREWS

Screw-making is a large subject, but we will endeavour to confine it to screws for watch and clock work. The B.A. is, of course, the most convenient, especially for clock work.

Select a piece of steel rod of the same size as the head, and turn it down to the full diameter of the thread ; if using a cutting die or a cutting plate, leave the extreme end slightly tapering to give it a lead into the die.

Make sure the die is held firmly in the die-holder, also that it is lying flat. In most die-holders there are two screws to hold the die and another which engages in the slot or split. This third screw controls the size of the die or the full diameter of the screw. These dies have a fairly large adjustment.

The lead into the die is important ; make sure it leads in perfectly straight, otherwise the thread will not be true. When the thread is full, the shape of the head is turned and, if a cheese-headed screw, it only remains to part it off after measuring the height or length of the head.

Parting-off Tool

A parting-off tool is made by filing a piece of square steel about three-sixteenths of an inch wide to a thin blade. The best way is to file the steel from each side so as to form a parallel blade about ·05 in. wide (see Fig. 72), about a quarter of an inch long and the same depth as the steel. File the blade to make the depth taper ; this is for clearance. File across the front to make it flat and cut back underneath to give clearance and to form a cutting edge at the front. Then harden it, being careful not to burn, and draw the

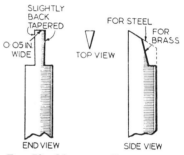

FIG. 72.—MAKING A PARTING-OFF TOOL.

temper to a pale straw colour at the extreme front, and a dark straw at the back or away from the cutting edge.

The blade is held against the steel at the centre ; if too high it will not cut, if too low it will probably break. If held correctly it will cut quickly and save time.

When parting off hand-made screws it is a good idea to leave just a small neck and break it off ; this will indicate the centre of the head and make it easier to slot.

Slotting a Screw

To slot a screw, a slotting or slitting file is used. This is a narrow and tapering, sides and edge cutting file which does not make a straight-sided slot but one which is wider at the top than at the bottom. Another way of slotting is by means of a saw, if it is a large screw.

In factories they are slotted in a small machine. The screw

is placed in a holder and brought up against a circular saw and as the holder is brought back to its starting point the slotted screw is pushed out and another is put in. The operation is carried out very quickly.

Making Small Screws

Very small screws, such as the screws used to fix a dart on a double roller lever, are made in hardened and tempered steel. The steel is hardened and then tempered to a stage beyond light blue. This is hard enough for its purpose and yet soft enough to enable a thread to be cut. It has to be done carefully, however. Jewel screws and endpiece screws can be made in the same way when they are very small.

The best and easiest way with the larger screws is to thread them when the steel is soft, and it is often an advantage to anneal the steel before making the screw.

Gold and platinum screws are difficult to make. These metals have to be worked with care, as they tend to grip or bind and break easily. The best way is to thread the screw in stages, especially if it is a long one such as a quarter screw. Turn the metal down, tapering towards the end and allow it just to pass through the hole in the screw plate. Put some oil on it and screw it into the plate and when the first full thread is obtained turn down the remaining metal to coincide with it. In other words, use the first full thread as a guide to the size ; it will be quite safe to thread the whole length, but make certain it does not taper forwards.

Always have a spare piece of metal through the screw plate in case the screw breaks in the plate. It is useful to be able to remove the broken piece. A blocked hole in a screw plate cannot be cleared.

Matching a Broken Screw-thread

One of the greatest difficulties which the watchmaker has to contend with is the pitch of a screw. Even to-day there is no standard which is universally adopted. If a collection of screw plates is available it may still not be possible to match the thread of a broken screw. The easiest way, where it is possible, is to re-tap the hole to a suitable screw plate, and then a screw can be made accordingly.

The pitch of a screw is the number of complete threads per inch, and again there is the shape of the thread to be considered.

Use of a Screw-cutting Lathe

The pitch and shape of a screw-thread can be matched, of course, in a screw-cutting lathe, but it is a problem with watch screws.

A screw-cutting lathe has a lead screw running generally the whole length of the bed of the lathe. In the larger lathes this thread is four to the inch. This operates a compound slide rest.

The head of the lathe is fitted with various studs on movable arms. The hollow mandrel of the lathe has a small wheel mounted on it which can run freely, or can be fitted tightly to it at will by means of a grub screw.   When a thread is to be cut this pinion runs freely.   This leaves the hollow mandrel and anything in its collet to run free of the pulleys driving the lathe.   The mandrel can be geared up by means of various change wheels or wheels of different numbers to get a definite relationship between the mandrel and the slide rest.

As an example, if it is required to cut a thread forty to the inch the mandrel can be revolved ten times to one of the lead screw. The lead screw is four to the inch, thus forty threads will be cut per inch.

It requires skill, however, to cut a good thread, because it is impossible with small screws to take out all the metal with one cut and the slide rest has to be put back to its starting point for each cut.   The slide rest can be disconnected from the lead screw by a lever, put back to the start of the thread and then fixed with the lever.

Left-hand Threads

The shape of the thread is decided by the shape of the cutter and the depth of cut is controlled by the section of the slide rest which holds the cutter.   This section of the slide rest can be pushed in or out from the centre of the lathe.

In a screw-cutting lathe it is just as easy to cut a left-hand thread as it is to cut a right-hand thread, but with screw plates it is a different matter.   A left-hand screw plate can be obtained occasionally, but even then the pitch may not be suitable, so it is often necessary to improvise or adapt something to do the job.

Find a right-hand screw plate having as nearly as possible the same pitch as the left-hand screw required.   Make an ordinary right-hand tap, but instead of filing the sides square make them oval until the two sides or ovals meet in a sharp knife edge without removing the top of the thread.   At this stage the tap has no direction but has merely a number of teeth spaced equally apart. Harden the tap and make a screw plate or die as described previously, but screw the tap in left-handed and it will form a left-hand thread of the same pitch as the right-hand plate from which it was made.   Harden the plate and it can then be used to make any required number of screws and taps.   After a time a useful collection is acquired and they earn every penny they cost to make.

Chasers

Some of the larger screws were cut with a hand tool called a chaser.   The cutting edge of the tool is serrated to correspond to the profile of a screw-thread.   Skill is required to use the tool, but any size of thread can be cut, although the pitch remains constant according to the pitch of the teeth on the chaser.

Chasers of different pitch were available and with a certain amount of trouble can be obtained now. There were two kinds, an inside and an outside chaser. They were used chiefly for cutting the thread on cases and bezel where they were screwed on. Another important use is in connection with the chronometer, where they are used for the bowls or brass case and the bezel, also for the gymbal screws.

The chaser is used in the same way as a hand graver. The greatest difficulty is to get started, and once a start has been made the rest of the thread can be cut easily. The chaser is held against the work with the lathe revolving slowly. As soon as the chaser reaches the end of the thread it is lifted and placed at the start again, and this is repeated until the complete thread is cut.

POLISHING

In this chapter it is appropriate to mention polishing. If the craftsman has the inclination, polishing can be carried out to impart a finish to an article, although it often seems to be regarded as old-fashioned these days.

The secret of all good polishing is experience. Unless an article polishes quickly there is something wrong either with the method or the material used, and it is generally impossible to obtain a satisfactory finish. To start with, the surface must be smooth and flat before even attempting to polish and, most important of all, everything must be scrupulously clean.

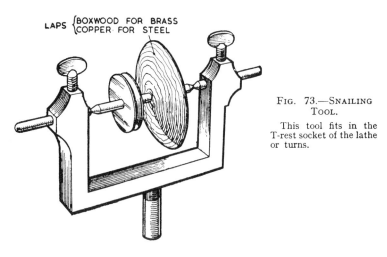

LAPS { BOXWOOD FOR BRASS / COPPER FOR STEEL

Fig. 73.—Snailing Tool.

This tool fits in the T-rest socket of the lathe or turns.

Snailing

Keyless wheels are often highly polished and have a snailed finish. The best way to carry out the snailing is in the turns by using a smaller tool, something like a small turns, which will fit into the T-rest. The snailing tool is really a lap mounted on an arbor with a brass ferrule to provide the motive power. The tool is mounted in the smaller turns in the T-rest and is set at a very slight angle to the piece to be snailed. It is revolved

BELL METAL LAP FOR POLISHING LARGE SHOULDERS AND ARBORS

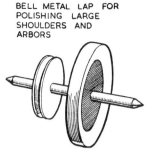

Fig. 74.—Bell Metal Lap.

only in one direction and as it is turned it also revolves the article being snailed.

Polishing in the Turns

The principle can also be used for polishing barrel arbors where there is a large square shoulder. In this case the lap is set dead square to the shoulder to be polished and a bow is used both on the lap and on the barrel arbor so that they revolve in opposite directions. A brilliant polish and a dead square shoulder can be obtained. Diamantine is used on the lap for polishing.

When snailing use oilstone dust and oil for steel, and bluestone or Water of Ayr Stone powder for brass.

The hollows in a keyless wheel can be polished in the same way; it is merely a question of arranging the lap suitably.

The Facing Tool

Narrow undercuts, such as behind a fusee square or an English keyless ratchet, are polished with a facing tool held in the hand, as described in the next chapter under the heading " Facing Pinion Leaves ". A backward and forward motion is necessary to obtain a good finish.

The Bolt Tool

Screw-heads, ends of squares, etc., can be polished in the lathe with a lap, but it is easier if held in what is termed a bolt tool and polished by hand on a zinc block smeared with diamantine. Only a small amount of diamantine is necessary to get a good polish.

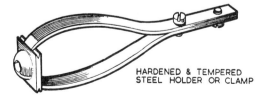

HARDENED & TEMPERED STEEL HOLDER OR CLAMP

Fig. 75.—Tool for Polishing Fusee Hollow.

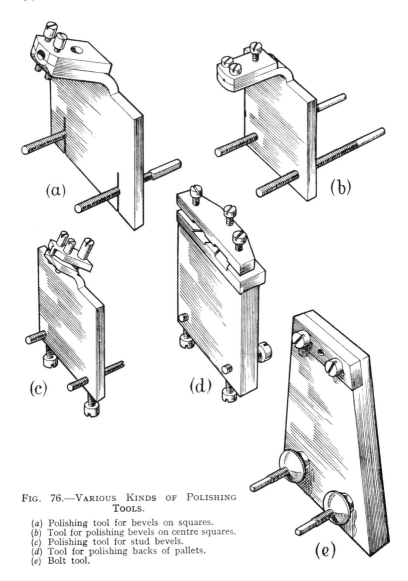

FIG. 76.—VARIOUS KINDS OF POLISHING
TOOLS.

(a) Polishing tool for bevels on squares.
(b) Tool for polishing bevels on centre squares.
(c) Polishing tool for stud bevels.
(d) Tool for polishing backs of pallets.
(e) Bolt tool.

A bolt tool is illustrated in Fig. 76, together with some other useful
polishing tools.

Bevelled edges, such as on a stud or ends of squares, are polished
in a tool which has one part bent at an angle of 45° and is provided
with adjusting screws to obtain the correct bevel. The bevelled

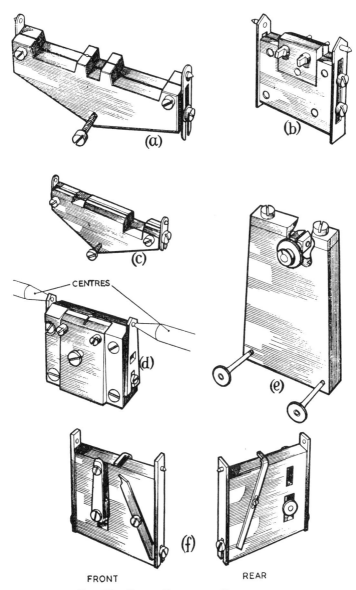

FIG. 77.—SWING TOOLS FOR POLISHING.

(a) Tool for straight sides of chronometer detents.
(b) Tool for edges of levers, etc.
(c) Swing tool for foot of chronometer detent.
(d) Tool for polishing belly of pallets; also showing how a swing tool is used in the turns.
(e) Multiple tool for polishing sides of detent foot, also heads of screws, etc.
(f) Front and rear views of tool for polishing 'scape wheel teeth, showing guard and positioning click and adjustment for height.

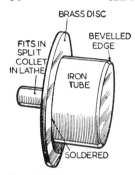

FIG. 78.—LAP FOR POLISH-
ING BEVEL ON THE
CIRCLE OF AN INDEX.

Bevelled edge is smeared
with diamantine.

edges of a diamond stud can be polished in a similar tool, but with a head shaped differently to take the stud so that each section of the stud can be moved into position for polishing.

Swing Tools

There is also a tool for polishing the backs of pallets and another for polishing the belly dead flat and square. These are known as swing tools and are easy to make (see Fig. 77).

The easiest method of polishing the bevels of an index is on a lap in the lathe. The lap comprises a piece of iron piping soldered to a brass plate which has a steel post screwed into it to enable it to be held in the lathe. (See Fig. 78.) The whole is turned true to the post. The index is held in a holder which fits into another holder or rest fitted in the T-rest hole. The circle can be well polished this way. The bevels on the tail are best polished by hand on a willow block using a zinc polisher and diamantine.

The square of a winding stem can be polished easily between centres, using the principle of the swing tool. If using a bell metal or flat iron polisher, it will be found that the polisher will keep the square flat as the stem will follow the polisher owing to it being between centres.

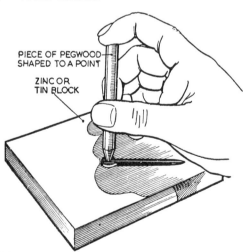

FIG. 79.—POLISHING HAND BOSSES, FLAT FACE OF ROLLERS, STEEL COLLARS, COLLETS AND SIMILAR PIECES.

Polishing Blocks

Some clock plates are polished with tripoli and oil. This gives a bright appearance, but diamantine on a flat tin polisher will give a brilliant polish, and when spotted like marine chronometer plates looks even better.

Watch hands are polished by hand when polishing the bosses. A piece of pegwood is used, as is illustrated in Fig. 79, to press the boss of the hand on to the polishing block. If the hands are of steel a zinc block and diamantine is used; if made of gold, brass or other soft metal, a tin block and diamantine is used.

Zinc will polish steel whether the steel is hard or soft. Iron, steel or bell-metal polishers will polish only hardened and tempered steel. They will not polish softer metals, such as gold, silver or brass. Tin polishers are for the softer metals. A balance rim is polished with a tin block because the tin will polish both brass and steel.

Other methods of polishing employed for specific jobs are dealt with in later chapters.

CHAPTER 6

TURNING

TURNING is equally as important as filing in watch- and clockmaking. No effort should be spared by the young watch-maker to make himself proficient in the art of turning. It brings its reward, if only to make him self-supporting and independent.

Many so-called watch- and clockmakers have to depend on someone else to do all their turning and there are others who attempt turning and make a most unsatisfactory job of it. If fitting a new balance staff to a watch, more often than not they fit the watch to the balance staff to the detriment of the watch. A balance staff should be replaced according to the quality of the one removed, or according to the quality of the watch.

The purpose of turning is to make a body perfectly round and true. In this chapter we will describe how this operation can be carried out.

How to use the Graver

The graver has been dealt with in the first chapter, so we can start with a description of how the tool is used in turning.

Whether turning in the lathe, or in the turns, the graver must be held with the diamond face uppermost and the edge of the graver must be presented to the work on the centre line. For this purpose a hand-rest is necessary or, as we shall refer to it, a T-rest. The graver is held firmly on the T-rest by the forefinger with the forefinger itself also on the rest. The back of the graver is pressed into the work by the palm of the hand and, therefore, a handle is required. If the graver has only a cork or even a lump of sealing-wax fixed to the end it will do the job ; too big a handle is a nuisance. The edge or side of the graver is not presented parallel to the work but at a slight angle with the point lowest and just below the line of centres. When heavy cutting is being carried out the point of the graver is not used as it is too delicate, and this is the reason for using the graver at an angle to the work. Do not allow the graver to follow the work, this is most important when the work is not true when the turning is started. The work will not be true if the graver is not held firmly.

Arrangement of the T-rest

The T-rest must be arranged according to the size of the graver. If an eighth of an inch square graver is used, then the T-rest must be below the centre line by a sixteenth of an inch, and when a larger graver is used the T-rest must be lowered accordingly. That

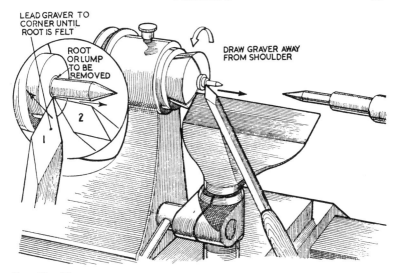

LEAD GRAVER TO CORNER UNTIL ROOT IS FELT

ROOT OR LUMP TO BE REMOVED

DRAW GRAVER AWAY FROM SHOULDER

Fig. 80.—Method of squaring a Shoulder (1) and clearing a Root (2)

is one advantage of adhering to a constant-size graver ; the T-rest need not be moved.

When turning a straight arbor do not attempt to tear it off with the point of the graver ; cut with the side just behind the point and do not lead with it, but move the graver away from the point.

If a deep cut is to be made, lower the point of the graver clear and underneath the work and use the centre of the side of the graver. This means lifting the back of the graver and turning it about a quarter of a turn so that the flat diamond face is almost at right angles to the work. It will stand pressure and will cut quicker this way.

Clearing a Root

To square up the corner of a shoulder use the point of the graver as a guide. Feel the shoulder with the point and lead it towards the corner until the root is felt. Light pressure on the root using the side of the graver is sufficient to start cutting. As the cut is made, draw the graver away from the shoulder and not towards it, otherwise the point will break. If it is only a small root this one cut may clear it ; if not, repeat the operation until the root is removed.

Under no circumstances push the point of the graver into the shoulder in an endeavour to clear the root, as the point will immediately break off and the root will be burnished and worse than before. (See Fig. 80 (2).)

Square Shoulders

It may be found that after clearing the root the shoulder itself is either undercut or back-sloped. The way to square up the shoulder is similar to clearing a root (see Fig. 80 (1)).

Hold the point of the graver square to the arbor or pivot with the diamond face uppermost. Rest the point on the arbor with sufficient pressure to feel that it is there but not enough to cut. Move the graver towards the shoulder until the corner is felt, then with the side of the graver press against the shoulder and at the same time bring the graver upwards towards the top of the shoulder.

The first cut will not show a great deal if the shoulder is back-sloped as the metal removed will only be near the arbor. The second cut, unless the shoulder is very much out of square, will bring up the shoulder dead square. On the other hand, if the shoulder is undercut the top of the shoulder will receive the first cut and the last cut will meet the corner and a square shoulder will result. This sounds a lengthy operation but takes only a few seconds, and if the shoulder is kept square from the start this small difficulty will not arise.

Sometimes the thumbscrew or wing-screw securing the T-rest gets in the way of the graver or the hand when the back of the graver is brought down to square up a shoulder. It is as well to arrange the wings of the screw to stand upright. If the wings

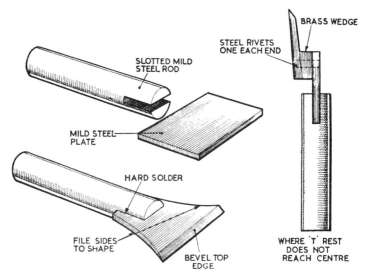

BRASS WEDGE

STEEL RIVETS
ONE EACH END

SLOTTED MILD
STEEL ROD

MILD STEEL
PLATE

HARD SOLDER

FILE SIDES
TO SHAPE

BEVEL TOP
EDGE

WHERE 'T' REST
DOES NOT
REACH CENTRE

Fig. 81.—Making a new T-rest for the Lathe or Turns.

are parallel, file off one of the wings, the obstructing half of course. There must be no obstructions in the way of the graver.

Making a New T-rest

Another point arising here is the T-rest itself.

Some modern lathes and turns have the T-rest too flat. (The rest should stand almost upright and clear of anything at the back, as it is impossible to turn true with a graver fouling the back of the T-rest.) If one of this type is provided it is better to scrap it and make a new T-rest, as shown in Fig. 81.

To make a new rest for either the lathe or turns, first select a piece of mild steel rod which fits closely into the T-rest holder. Next choose a piece of mild steel plate about 18 gauge, $\frac{1}{16}$ in. thick, about an inch long and $\frac{1}{2}$ in. wide. Make a slot in the mild steel rod to fit the plate steel and cut the slot about $\frac{1}{8}$ in. deep and central. Then put the plate steel with the long side into the slot and braze them together. Brazing is by far the best method and the rest will be rigid. This will make a T-rest an inch long. It is as well to make two rests, as a short one is often very convenient for some jobs.

Instead of using a piece of mild steel plate an inch long, use a square piece, say $\frac{1}{2}$ in. square. This will make a T-rest $\frac{1}{2}$ in. long. Cut the end corners back to bring the extreme end of the T-rest almost to a sharp point. It is useful as a toucher for testing the truth of, say, a large balance which is too big to go in the ordinary callipers.

Shortening an Arbor

If requiring to shorten an arbor, do not force the point of the graver into it, but use the side of the graver near the centre. Move the graver in a small circle until reaching almost half-way and then break off the unwanted piece (Fig. 82 (a)). In the lathe the ragged edge can be easily turned clean by means of the graver.

Centring with a V-bed

In the turns the operation is just as simple. Place the end of the arbor on a runner with a V-bed, and have the arbor standing beyond by its own diameter. The size of the V-bed depends, of course, on the size of the arbor. Hold a small, smooth file against the end of the arbor and rest the file on the runner outside the V-bed. The file holds the arbor in place and forces it to run true. The bow is then drawn rapidly up and down with long and short strokes alternately so as to ensure perfect truth until the centre comes up sharp. (See Fig. 82 (b).)

Male and Female Centres

The two sides of the centre should be at an angle of 45°, as illustrated in Fig. 82 (c). This angle is a constant factor with all small

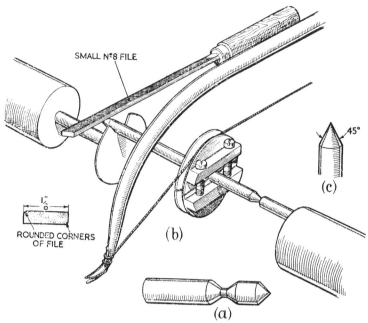

SMALL N°8 FILE

45°

(c)

$1\frac{1}{2}$″

ROUNDED CORNERS OF FILE

(b)

(a)

FIG. 82.—SHORTENING AN ARBOR AND FILING A NEW CENTRE.
(a) Arbor partly cut through. (b) Filing a new centre. (c) Finished centre.

turning, however small, when it is carried out between centres whether in the lathe or turns.

With large turning between centres it is better if the article to be turned has female centres and the runners have male centres. It would be very difficult to drill holes in very small pivots, so male centres on the work is the only possible way.

TURNING IN A PINION

Fitting a pinion into a new watch is very different from replacing a broken or a worn pinion.

In a new watch the holes are jewelled after the pinion is turned in and the jewel holes are adjusted for endshake. If the pivots are run in brass holes the plate is turned for endshakes, heights, etc.

When replacing a pinion the work has to be carried out to precision as the proportions have been determined and no craftsman worthy of the name would interfere with these measurements either by bumping or burring up pieces to accommodate bad workmanship.

Swiss Fourth Pinion

The bottom or lower measurements are the most important as these determine the position of the wheel in relation to other pieces in the watch. We will deal with the fourth or seconds wheel and pinion. The fourth wheel is geared into the 'scape pinion and it must be clear of the 'scape wheel. Sometimes the third wheel is below the 'scape wheel level and, if so, it can be ignored.

The next thing to notice is the position of the balance. Sometimes the balance is so arranged that the outside of the balance overlaps the path of the fourth wheel. In this case the height of the fourth wheel must be midway between the balance and the 'scape wheel.

If the fourth wheel is riveted on to the fourth pinion, notice whether the wheel is above or below the pinion. In most Continental watches the wheel is below the pinion or the

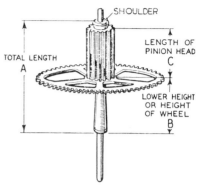

Fig. 83.—Swiss Fourth Pinion ("Pinion Up").

pinion is " up ". We must turn this pinion between centres either in the lathe or in the turns. As it is easier in the turns we will deal with it this way.

Taking Measurements

The distance is measured exactly between the shoulders of the pivots either with a micrometer or a pinion gauge. A douzième gauge is not sufficiently accurate for this work, but there is a gauge of similar shape which measures to a tenth of a millimetre in which a movable arm runs on pivots and in pivot holes. It measures only up to ten millimetres, so it is limited in scope. Some useful gauges are illustrated on the following page.

The idea of measuring the total length at this stage is because it is easier to hold the wheel and pinion than just the pinion unmounted. It is an advantage to have more than one pinion gauge, as each can be set to any individual measurement of the piece and thus save time.

Removing Wheel from Pinion

The next operation is to knock the wheel off the pinion using either a riveting stake or a staking tool. Find a hole which is an easy fit (not loose) on the pinion and put the pinion through the hole with the wheel resting on the stake. Pick out a punch which is free on the pivot but will not pass over the shoulder. If a staking tool is used, turn the stake until the hole required is

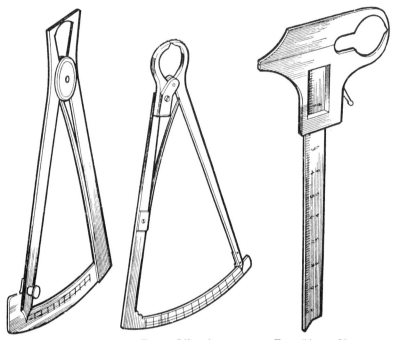

Fig. 84a.—Douzième Gauge for Measuring Pinion Height, etc.

Fig. 84b.—Another Form of Gauge measuring to $\frac{1}{10}$ mm.

Fig. 84c. — Vernier Slide Gauge, sometimes graduated in Thousandths of an Inch.

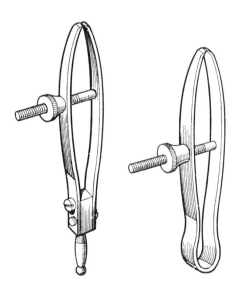

Figs. 85a and b.—Pinion Length Gauges.

The gauge on the right is simpler in construction, and is made from bent steel plate, hardened and tempered. To save time it is an advantage to have more than one pinion gauge.

FIG. 86.—RIVETING STAKE MADE OF STEEL OR BRASS WITH
GRADUATED HOLES.

in line with the punch.   A sharp tap with a hammer will dislodge
the pinion and drive it out.

Next measure the length of the pinion head with a second pinion
gauge.   Then, using a third gauge, measure the distance from where
the wheel is mounted (the wheel seating) to the lower pivot shoulder.
All the measurements have now been taken.

Fit a screw ferrule on the new pinion arbor, or if a screw ferrule
is unobtainable use one made of solid brass.   The solid brass ferrule
is fitted on to the pinion head.   It is necessary, however, to ascertain which way the pinion head tapers, because the ferrule must
be pushed on to the smaller end if it is to remain tightly in place.
Most pinions have a slight taper one way or the other.

The Wheel Seating

Put the bow on the ferrule and place the pinion between centres
using the eccentric runners, and turn the wheel seating making
certain that there is sufficient length at each end of the pinion.
Turn the pinion down until the wheel fits snugly, but do not drive
it on, merely push it on with the finger and thumb.   The shoulder
on which the wheel rests must be perfectly square and flat, if
anything slightly undercut, but only very slightly.   Do not use
tweezers to press the wheel in place, otherwise the wheel will be
scratched and marked.   There will be grooves in the hole in the
wheel where the old pinion fitted ; be sure to place these grooves
corresponding to the leaves of the new pinion.   Do not broach
the hole.

Cut the surplus metal from the wheel seating and leave about
·003 or three-thousandths of an inch standing above the wheel.
Turn this remaining metal undercut and up to a sharp edge, deep
enough so that when it is riveted it will be flat with the wheel.

Riveting Wheel to Pinion

Take the pinion out of the turns and proceed to rivet the pinion
on to the wheel.   If a staking tool is not available, use a steel stake
with a hole into which the pinion arbor fits easily.   Select a hollow
flat punch with a hole into which the pinion arbor also fits easily.
Both should be an easy fit with very little play.   Hold the punch

between the forefinger and thumb, making certain that it is upright, and place it over the arbor and on the undercut wheel seat.

Use a steel hammer and strike the punch once with not too heavy a blow. The pinion is then moved round slightly and given

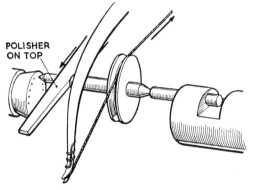

POLISHER ON TOP

FIG. 87a.—METHOD OF POLISHING AN ARBOR IN THE TURNS.

Viewed from back of the bench.

another blow and so on until the undercut seat is flat with the wheel. Do not strike while the pinion is being rotated, otherwise it will burr up.

The wheel should now fit tightly and should lie flat and be perfectly round.

Cutting Pinion Head to Length

Smooth off the excess metal after riveting, using the side of the graver until the face is square.

Place the wheel and pinion in the turns, cut the pinion head to the proper length and leave the end smooth and square. At first it will be difficult to turn the pinion leaves owing to the spaces between them. Keep the graver rigid and do not allow it to jump in and out of the leaves, because a broken leaf may result if it is a small pinion.

When the riveting face and the acting face of the pinion are both square, turn the arbor down to size and undercut the pinion face as near the arbor as possible, without cutting into the arbor to any great extent.

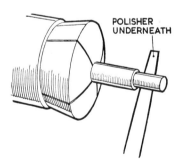

POLISHER UNDERNEATH

Polishing the Arbor

If it is a good-quality watch, polish the arbor. If the arbor has been turned smoothly this will be

FIG. 87b.—METHOD OF POLISHING ARBORS OR PIVOTS IN THE LATHE.

easy. If it is ridged it must be smoothed with oilstone powder mixed with oil on a steel polisher, until all visible lines have been removed. The polisher is then cleaned and re-surfaced and the arbor is polished with diamantine.

The procedure for polishing is exactly the same as for smoothing, except for the dressing on the polisher. The polisher is a piece

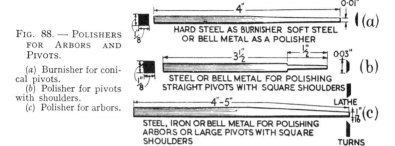

FIG. 88. — POLISHERS FOR ARBORS AND PIVOTS.

(a) Burnisher for conical pivots.
(b) Polisher for pivots with shoulders.
(c) Polisher for arbors.

of flat steel about ⅛ in. wide by 1/16 in. thick and approximately 6 in. long. Naturally it must be made of soft steel, otherwise it would not retain or grip the polishing material. The flat face is filed with a smooth file to make a grain something similar to the cut of a file. One side is cut back to make the corner of the steel stand out and the same side is slightly curved. The idea of the curve is to minimize the rounding effect on the work if the polisher is not kept perfectly straight.

The polisher is used in a similar manner to a file, except that it is essential to use the return stroke as well as the forward stroke, and a sideways movement is also used in conjunction with the back and forward movement.

Facing Pinion Leaves

When the arbor has been polished it is necessary to polish or face up the pinion face.

First a steel facing tool is used with oilstone powder for smoothing and then an iron or bell metal facing tool is used with diamantine for polishing.

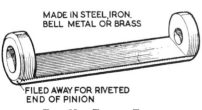

FIG. 89.—FACING TOOL.
One end for face of pinion head ; smaller for riveted face.

The facing tool can be made in several ways, but the best method is to use a piece of steel rod drilled to be an easy fit on the pinion arbor. It can be a double-ended tool and have holes of different size at each end. The middle is filed out flat so that the holes are exposed

clearly. The idea is to remove any obstruction to the free movement of the end of the arbor. These facing tools should be only
about three-quarters of an inch long overall ; if any longer they
are awkward to balance. The flat end of the rod is smoothed and
grained like the polisher
and ˙placed over the
arbor to rest flat on the
face of the pinion leaves.

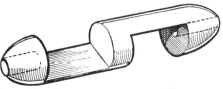

The other end of the
pinion is rested in a
runner either in the
turns or in the vice,

FIG. 90.—TOOL FOR POLISHING UNDERCUT
BETWEEN PINION FACE AND PINION ARBOR. whichever is more convenient. The bow is
held at the top instead of the bottom as is usual, the idea being to
equalize the pull. As the bow is moved up and down, the pinion
face resting against the facing tool not only turns round but moves
up and down and sideways according to the size of hole in the
facing tool. The size of the hole plays an important part in the
success of the job ; if too big, the face of the pinion goes out of
flat, and if too small, circular ridges form on the face. With practice
the job becomes quite simple and takes only a minute or two.

Facing Riveted End

Next reverse the wheel and pinion and face up the riveted end.
The face of the tool for this job must be the same size as the face
to be polished, and must not be larger under any circumstances.
It is important to ensure that the operation is carried out quickly,
otherwise all of the rivet will be cut away and it will be difficult
to polish the brass wheel and the pinion face.

Another important
point is that the work
must be cleaned
thoroughly with a
piece of pith, especi-
ally after using the
oilstone dust ; a
minute fragment ·of
oilstone will render
diamantine useless.

It is usually a sign
that the work is
polished when it
squeaks, and if polish-
ing is continued after
this noise is heard the
work will become
brown or " foxy ".

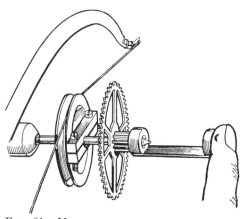

FIG. 91.—METHOD OF FACING OR POLISHING
PINION FACE.

This means that the polisher will have to be cleaned and fresh diamantine used and time will, of course, be wasted.

Polish the arbor and do not forget to protect the polished face of the pinion. Place a small piece of paper between the polisher and the pinion face while the arbor is being polished.

Turning the Seconds Pivot

As the pinion is "up", the lower end of the arbor carries the long seconds pivot. The height has already been taken in the pinion gauge, so if we mark off on the arbor the position of the lower shoulder we can start turning the seconds pivot. It should, of course, be very slightly tapered to obtain a good fitting for the seconds hand, although the part of the pivot which is actually in the hole should be straight.

Turn the pivot its whole length and, most important, keep the shoulder square all the time. As the pivot becomes smaller, square up the shoulder each time with the graver. Let the pivot through the hole : obviously it must be quite smooth at this stage. The next operation is to polish the pivot. It is always as well to obtain the total length of the pivot at this point.

Obtaining Total Length of Pivot

Put on the dial and pass the pivot through the hole, marking it where it comes flush with the dial, with, of course, the shoulder of the pivot resting on the jewel hole or brass hole.

Take the pinion out of the plate and replace it in the turns and turn a circle about a quarter of the way through to indicate where the total length of the pivot ends. This cut into the pivot will be a safety measure, because, if a little extra pressure is put on the pivot when polishing, it will break at the cut rather than at the shoulder.

Polishing the Pivot

Use a polisher just narrower than the pivot's length. As the bow is pulled downwards, the polisher is pushed forwards, and as the bow is pulled or pushed upwards, the polisher is drawn back. Apply constant pressure both backwards and forwards, also keep the polisher flat on the pivot without any extra pressure one side or the other.

Do not keep the edge of the polisher against the shoulder all the time, but keep the polisher moving backwards and forwards with a circular movement. By this means any scratches in one direction will be removed by the reverse movement.

When the pivot has been polished, give about two strokes with a clean small burnisher to harden the surface and impart an attractive bloom, but be careful not to burnish too much otherwise the whole finish will be spoilt.

Turning the Top Pivot

We can now proceed with the top pivot. The distance or length has been taken with the pinion gauge, so mark off the position of the shoulder and proceed to turn the pivot. This is a shorter pivot, so the best way is to have it a little longer than required.

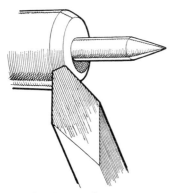

Again turn the pivot until it passes through the hole or jewel hole without any play. The shoulder must be square and the pivot straight and smooth. Cut a circle where the total length of the finished pivot ends and polish the pivot as before. As soon as the pivot is polished, turn off the sharp corner where the arbor and the shoulder meet. Use a graver sharpened in the usual way, but stone the point of the graver flat. It is a fairly simple job and, with care, these corners can be turned without risk of breakage.

FIG. 92.—SHAPED GRAVER USED TO BREAK SHARP CORNER OF PIVOT SHOULDER.

Shorten both pivots to their correct lengths and round them up and burnish, being careful not to rub a burr on the pivots themselves. Bring the burnisher well round and on to the flat pivot.

Taking Lengths of Pinions

There is one point which cannot be emphasized too strongly. Do not allow anything to spare when measuring up a pinion ; measure and turn everything exactly to pattern, providing, of course, that the old pinion used as the pattern is correct.

If the pinion is lost, or if the old pinion is incorrect, the procedure is slightly different. As stated before, the bottom height is the most important. Various gauges are available for taking these measurements, but the author prefers the following simple method using a template.

Put the plates together, or if there is a bar secure it in place. Always remove any burrs underneath and make certain that the bar or bridge is not bent in any way.

Choose a piece of brass or steel rod of about $\frac{3}{64}$ in. diameter. Cut the rod so that its length is equivalent, as nearly as possible, to the distance between the top and bottom jewel-holes. Place in a screw-head tool, or lathe, and smooth and make the ends dead flat.

Try the rod between the holes and shorten it, keeping it flat all the time, until the length corresponds exactly to the distance between the top and bottom jewel-holes, or in other words is the exact length that the pinion must be from shoulder to shoulder. As this will be the fourth pinion, place the 'scape wheel and pinion and the third wheel and pinion in position in the frame, and also any other pieces which may be in the path of the fourth wheel. The position which the fourth wheel must occupy can easily be seen.

Place the gauge for the total length over the lower fourth hole and stand the gauge on its flat end and notice the position that must be occupied by the wheel. Remove the gauge and mark the position with a slight scratch on the side and then replace it to check that the mark has been made accurately. If it is correct, mark it distinctly with a slotting file and make a scratch to denote which is the top or bottom end. Notice the position of the third wheel as this will determine the length of the pinion head.

The job is now straightforward and can be continued as with a pattern. The gauge used, known as a template, is well worth keeping, as it can be employed time and time again.

Turning an English Fourth Pinion

The method of turning a fourth pinion to a Swiss watch has been described previously and we will now deal with an English fourth pinion.

The procedure is the same, but the arbors are finished differently. With the Swiss watch the arbors are straight, terminating into the undercut in the pinion face. The English watch has a back-tapered arbor and ter-minates in a square shoulder, the under-cut being behind the square shoulder. Thus the arbors are easier to polish with-out the risk of slipping on to the polished pinion face.

Another difference is that in the majority of English watches the pinion is "down", that is underneath the wheel, and the seconds pivot shoulder is almost flush with the pinion face. Thus the pinion face has to be deeply undercut to be

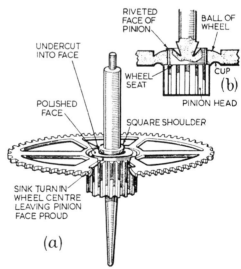

Fig. 93.—English Fourth Pinion ("Pinion Down").

(a) Wheel and pinion. (b) Various sections of wheel and pinion.

able to back-slope the shoulder of the long pivot. The idea of this is to create capillary attraction and keep the oil on the shoulder of the pivot instead of running up into the pinion leaves.

TURNING IN A SWISS 'SCAPE PINION

Some Swiss watches have the 'scape pinion " down ", especially the older models. This is not a good system but invariably the layout or caliper of the watch is such that no alteration can be made. It is invariably a difficult pinion to turn in, particularly if a small watch.

The 'scape wheel is riveted on to the pinion in the same way as the fourth wheel just described. It is better to turn the 'scape pinion in the turns, as truth and accuracy are extremely important. A " rough " or partly finished pinion can be obtained from the material dealer. The leaves of the pinion are polished and ready for use and are generally left longer than required. Thus the first job is to turn them off to length.

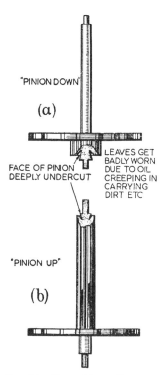

"PINION DOWN"

(a)

FACE OF PINION DEEPLY UNDERCUT

LEAVES GET BADLY WORN DUE TO OIL CREEPING IN CARRYING DIRT ETC

"PINION UP"

(b)

Fig. 94.—Swiss 'Scape Pinions.
(a) " Pinion down", older pattern.
(b) " Pinion up ", modern pattern.

With a small pinion this is a tricky job, because, if too heavy handed and the graver is caught between the leaves, there is the possibility of a leaf being broken out of the pinion, making another " rough " pinion necessary.

When shortening the leaves, turn a groove carefully at the correct length just to reach the arbor and then proceed to turn away the surplus. If a leaf is broken, it will break only up to the groove previously turned and the pinion will not be spoiled.

Next turn the leaves until the wheel fits snugly and lies flat, and then check that the wheel is true as well as flat. This is important, as a 'scape wheel which is not true can cause endless trouble. If it is true, rivet the wheel on carefully.

Fit the screw ferrule on to the arbor which adjoins the rivet, and cut the pinion head to length and leave it smooth.

A solid brass ferrule about 6 mm. in diameter is then selected and fitted to the pinion ; it should be tight enough to hold but not so tight that it cannot be pulled off easily.

Remove the brass ferrule and place the wheel and pinion in the turns and mark where the shoulder of the bottom pivot will be positioned. It is almost certain to be all but flush with the pinion face. Turn a deep undercut into the pinion face, but keep it very small as it spoils the appearance if spread half-way across the face of the pinion. At the same time, back-slope the arbor from the shoulder of the pivot into the pinion face.

The Bottom Pivot

The next operation is to turn the bottom pivot.

These small pinions usually have six leaves, with pivots as small as ·0025 in., or at most ·004 in. The general temptation is to try to file them, with disastrous results. The only satisfactory way is to turn the pivots into the holes, leaving them smooth and with the shoulder perfectly square.

Polishing the Pivots in Centres

Do not attempt to polish or burnish these pivots on a bed, but polish with the pivots in centres. If they are rested on a bed to polish they will become ridged and may possibly break off. The runner with a centre very near to the edge can have the edge stoned off, until the end of the pivot will rest in the remaining centre and stand slightly above or beyond the extreme edge of the runner. A polisher, having about the same width as the length of the pivot, is rested on the pivot and in a few seconds it can be polished almost without risk. Shorten and round up the pivot.

Polish the face of the pinion, being very careful not to let the polisher slip sideways, because if this should happen the pivot may break off. Use a light bow for this job.

Remove the screw ferrule from the arbor on the other end and replace with the solid brass ferrule which is fitted on to the pinion head. Mark the position of the top shoulder and shorten the arbor, allowing sufficient on which to turn a pivot. Allowance can be made for a long pivot but this is a matter of individual taste. As this top arbor is springy a sharp graver will be required. Turn the pivot down until it will fit closely into the top hole, and then polish. Next use the graver to turn the pivot to the correct length and round up as before.

The Lantern Runner

The operation of rounding up is carried out by putting the pivot through a hole in a lantern runner. This is a runner which is drilled to admit a brass extension. The reason for using brass is to prevent the shoulder from being scratched or marked. The lantern runner is made as follows.

A rod of hard brass, the same size as the runner, is turned down

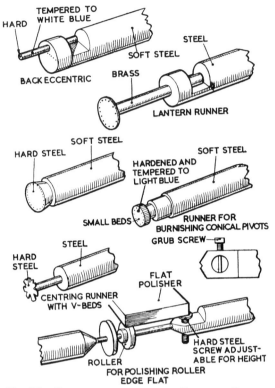

FIG. 95.—RUNNERS FOR USE IN THE LATHE OR TURNS.

to about half its diameter, like a pivot, about $\frac{5}{8}$ in. long. This pivot fits into a corresponding hole in the steel runner and is pushed in tightly so that it will not rock or move.

The runner is then put in the lathe and the rod is shortened to leave a very thin face which is the same diameter as the runner. The runner is then put in the turns and the back eccentric is pressed up against the brass face; at the same time the runner is given a full turn. The back eccentric will make a mark all the way round the face. On this line drill very small holes. The pivots are placed in these holes to round them up.

If, on the other hand, the pivots instead of being square-shouldered are conical, the length of the pinion is measured from the ends of the pivots and not the shoulders. (See Fig. 96.) Thus a different tool has to be used for taking the total length of the pinion.

Making Total Length Tool

It is very easy to make a suitable tool for taking the total

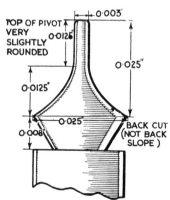

FIG. 96.—CORRECT PROPORTIONS OF TYPICAL BALANCE STAFF PIVOT.

length, which we will call, for convenience, a "two-screw" gauge.

A piece of square brass rod, about $\frac{3}{16}$ in. square, is bent under heat to form a U-shape, about $1\frac{1}{2}$ in. in overall depth, with the two sides measuring about an inch (see Fig. 97). The measurements need not be exact.

The two sides have two holes drilled in each. The first two should be in the centre of the rod and perfectly in line with one another. They should be near the ends of the two sides. The holes are tapped to 10 or 12 B.A. The other two holes are drilled about $\frac{3}{16}$ in. further down the arm.

A saw cut is made joining these holes together. Then a hole is drilled centrally but at right angles to the other two holes. This hole will be divided by the saw cut. One side of the hole is tapped to about 14 B.A. and the other is opened out for clearance. This provides a location for a locking screw, and by tightening the screw the saw cut is brought together and closes the top screw-hole.

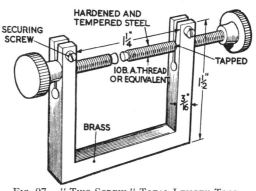

Fig. 97.—"Two-Screw" Total Length Tool.
For use with conical pivots only.

Next prepare two hardened and tempered steel rods, threaded to about 10 or 12 B.A., according to the size of the tapped holes. One end of each rod is squared and back-sloped, and on the other end of each is fitted a small thumb nut. These nuts must be secured tightly so that they do not come undone.

How to use the Total Length Tool

One rod is shorter than the other and this is screwed up tightly against the arm of the bent square rod. The other rod is longer and is moved up and down according to the size of the job. When using this tool, make certain that the short rod is screwed firmly in position. Unscrew the long rod and rest the short one against the lower jewel-hole and screw in the long rod until it just meets the top jewel-hole. Then adjust the locking screw which tightens the thread to prevent the long rod moving.

Finally, unscrew the short rod to disengage the tool from the watch and when removed screw the short rod back into position.

The distance between the ends of the two rods will be equivalent to the exact length of the pinion or balance staff.

HOLLOW CENTRE PINION

With a hollow centre pinion, which is the next item to be considered, the first operation is to open the hole to accommodate the centre arbor. Some of these pinions are very hard and cannot be opened by means of an ordinary broach, so it is necessary to make one specially for the purpose.

Making Half-round Broach

To make a suitable broach, choose a piece of silver-steel rod which is slightly larger than the size of the hole required. File the rod to the correct taper and corresponding to the centre arbor, and finish with a smooth file.

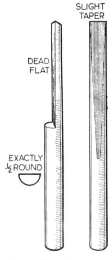

SLIGHT TAPER

DEAD FLAT

EXACTLY ½ ROUND

Fig. 98.—D-shape or Half-round Broach.

Next measure the rod with a micrometer and file it exactly to half its size, making it a D-shape, or half-round, with one side perfectly flat and the edges quite sharp.

Cover the broach with fine iron binding wire and harden in water. The iron wire prevents the broach from being burnt and also helps to keep it straight instead of warping. After the broach has been hardened, the flat side is stoned to make it smooth and free from burrs. This type of broach will cut very hard steel.

Here a note of warning must be added. The broach should be turned only one way and on no account should it be turned backwards and forwards, otherwise the hole will tend to become oval or even square and as such will be useless.

When the hole is to size, make a hardened and tempered steel arbor to fit the hole in the pinion from end to end. This arbor must have clean centres on it. Place the pinion on the arbor and then between centres in the lathe or turns and ascertain that the pinion runs perfectly true. If the pinion runs out of true it should be rejected and another obtained.

SWISS CENTRE PINION

With the Swiss the centre wheel is near the back of the watch and the pinion is " down ", or near the front or pillar plate. We will deal with a Swiss pinion first.

Fit a screw ferrule on the arbor, turn the wheel seat and mount the centre wheel and rivet it on.   Clean the riveted face and, without reducing the pinion arbor, cut a deep undercut into the pinion face.   Now the shoulder of the top pivot will be almost flush with the pinion face, so turn the top pivot until it fits the hole closely or even tightly, and turn the shoulder so that it is square and as close as ·002 in. from the face. Next, back-cut the shoulder and merge it

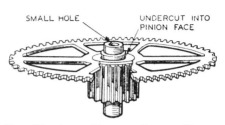

SMALL HOLE   UNDERCUT INTO PINION FACE

FIG. 99.—SWISS HOLLOW CENTRE PINION ("PINION DOWN").

with the undercut in the pinion face.   Do not reduce the diameter of the shoulder.

Checking for Length

Polish the pivot and face up the pinion face and polish.   Fit the screw ferrule on the end which has been worked on and just clear of the end of the pivot.   Mark off and cut the pinion head to length.   Mark off the bottom pivot shoulder and turn the pivot as before and polish.   Turn a deep undercut into the pinion face and back-slope the shoulder of the pivot to merge with the undercut in the pinion face.   Keep the pivot shoulder as large as possible. Face up and polish the pinion face.

Remove the screw ferrule from the pinion and place the pinion between the frame and check for freedom and endshake, etc.   Then shorten the bottom pivot to the correct length.   The pivot should be long enough to keep the cannon pinion from fouling the plate, but at the same time should be as short as possible, otherwise the motion work will take up too much room.

Shorten the top pivot until the distance or length between the ends of the pivots is equal to the pattern.   This length can be checked by putting the centre arbor in the pinion and then placing the cannon pinion in position.   If this is correct the pinion is finished.

Using Solid Brass Ferrule

If a screw ferrule is not available, a solid brass ferrule placed tightly on the pinion head will do as well, if not better.   The advantage with the solid brass ferrule is that it can be put on at the beginning of the job and left on until it is finished.

Another point of great importance is that under no circumstances should an attempt be made to turn the pinion without a true arbor through it.   It is simply asking for trouble to try to turn it on male centres, or by holding the pinion in a lathe collet or split chuck. The slightest lack of truth will cause great difficulty in getting the hands to run flat and clear of each other, apart from an uncertain barrel and centre pinion depth.

ENGLISH CENTRE PINION

An English centre pinion is turned in exactly the same way, except that in the majority of English watches the pinion is " up " and the wheel " down ", this being the reverse of the Swiss.

Solid Centre Pinion

The solid centre pinion, whether English or Swiss, follows the same rules as the hollow centre pinion, but, of course, the solid pinion has the centre arbor solid with it. Most watches, English or Swiss, use the solid pinion instead of the hollow type and it has great advantages.

Fitting the Cannon Pinion

The main difference between the two is that with the solid the cannon pinion snaps on, and is held in position by a small groove cut in the arbor and a pip or small bulge driven into the side of the cannon pinion. When putting in a new pinion, this pip or bulge must be broached away cleanly.

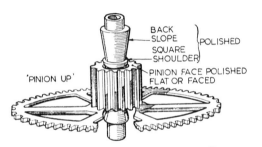

FIG. 100.—ENGLISH HOLLOW CENTRE PINION (" PINION UP ").

The cannon pinion is fitted on to the arbor so that it is tight enough to carry the motion work, yet still capable of being turned to set the hands from the keyless work. The pip or bulge is then punched into the cannon and the cannon is pushed on, without moving it round, until it rests on the shoulder. In this position the cannon is then moved round once or twice and pulled straight off. There will be a distinct ring marked round the pinion arbor. Turn a shallow groove precisely on this mark and

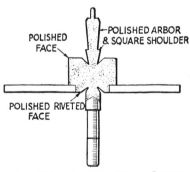

FIG. 101.—ENGLISH SOLID CENTRE PINION (" PINION UP ").

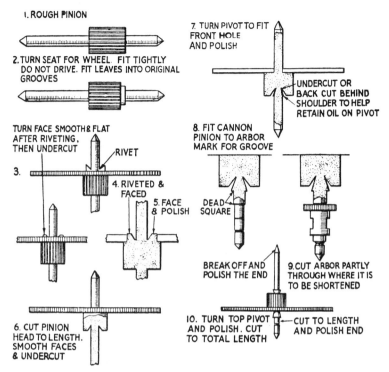

FIG. 102.—METHOD OF " WORKING IN " OR TURNING IN A SWISS SOLID CENTRE PINION, USING TURNS OR LATHE (" PINION DOWN").

push the cannon on again. It will give a slight snap when it reaches the shoulder and will not rise up when the cannon is moved round to set the hands, and will fit as tightly as before.

The only object of this snap action is to prevent the cannon from riding up. If, on the other hand; the cannon does ride up, then the groove has been turned in the wrong place and must be corrected. If the cannon rides up only a fraction and stays there, the groove is slightly too high and the easiest way to remedy it is to broach out the pip and put one a little nearer the top of the cannon. If the cannon will not snap on, the groove is too low and must be extended towards the end of the arbor until the cannon can be snapped on.

We have already dealt with a Swiss 'scape pinion where the wheel is riveted to the pinion : we will now deal with the English type of 'scape pinion where the wheel is mounted on a collet made either of brass or gold, and sometimes even of steel.

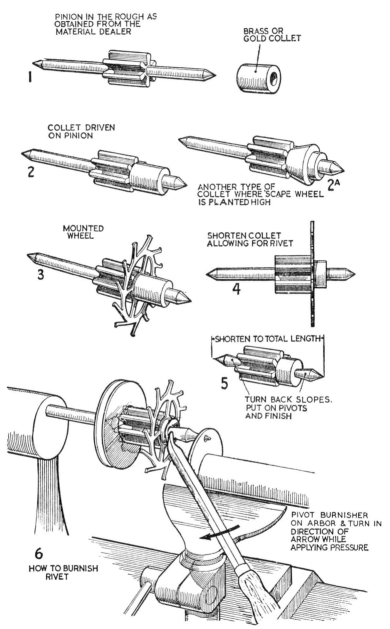

PINION IN THE ROUGH AS
OBTAINED FROM THE
MATERIAL DEALER

BRASS OR
GOLD COLLET

1

COLLET DRIVEN
ON PINION

2

ANOTHER TYPE OF
COLLET WHERE 'SCAPE WHEEL
IS PLANTED HIGH

2A

MOUNTED
WHEEL

3

SHORTEN COLLET
ALLOWING FOR RIVET

4

SHORTEN TO TOTAL LENGTH

5

TURN BACK SLOPES.
PUT ON PIVOTS
AND FINISH

6

HOW TO BURNISH
RIVET

PIVOT BURNISHER
ON ARBOR & TURN IN
DIRECTION OF
ARROW WHILE
APPLYING PRESSURE

FIG. 103.—TURNING IN AN ENGLISH 'SCAPE PINION AND MOUNTING THE
'SCAPE WHEEL BY BURNISHING THE COLLET OVER THE WHEEL.

ENGLISH 'SCAPE PINIONS

English 'scape pinions are sometimes square-shoulder pivots and sometimes conical. When one refers to conical pivots it is rather misleading, as the pivot is perfectly straight, but the shoulder is conical to give extra strength. When turning these pinions the procedure is slightly different. (See Fig. 103.)

The first job is to fit a solid brass ferrule to the pinion head, not forgetting that the pinion will be very slightly tapered. Next turn the arbor to a gradual taper and finish with oilstone dust. Always turn the arbor on the side nearest to the larger part of the pinion.

Making a Brass Collet

Choose a piece of brass rod, preferably best brass as this is much better for the purpose than easy cutting brass, and place the rod in the lathe. Drill it slightly smaller than the pinion arbor and fit it to the arbor by broaching as the hole should be tapered. Use a piece of brass rod slightly larger than the pinion. Cut the collet from the rod and tap it on to the pinion arbor tightly, but do not drive it on too hard as the pinion arbor may bend.

Turn this brass collet down until the 'scape wheel can be pushed tightly on to the collet. Sometimes the pinion itself acts as the seat for the wheel, and in this case turn the collet until the wheel rests on the pinion face. Turn the collet partly down so that it can be riveted over to hold the wheel. Do not turn the brass down to the arbor, but leave sufficient to hold firmly on the arbor.

Shorten the pinion head to the correct length and mark the place for the shoulder of the pivot on the arbor. Make the undercut into the pinion face with a back-slope behind the pivot.

Turn the pivot as before and polish, and then polish the face of the pinion. Mark off the shoulder of the other pivot and turn and polish the pivot. Next, bevel the corner of the pivot shoulder.

Rubbing or Burnishing the 'Scape Wheel in Place

Place the 'scape pinion with the wheel just pushed on into position in the movement with the lever and pallets. Try for endshake and freedoms in the holes, etc., and also make certain that the 'scape wheel will engage in the centre of the pallets or on the stones. If everything is in order proceed to mount the 'scape wheel.

Fit the brass ferrule on the pinion head and place the wheel and pinion in the turns with the pivot on the colleted end in the lantern runner, or safety runner as it is sometimes called. Then with a wheel rubber, which is a special burnisher for the job, burnish the rivet over the centre of the wheel until the wheel is perfectly flat and tight. If carried out correctly a polished ring will show. Undercut the rivet just a little, but do not remove the polished or burnished ring. Smooth the remaining brass on the arbor, but do not remove it, and then bevel the corner where it joins the arbor near the pivot shoulder. Shorten and round up the pivots and the job is completed.

Making a Wheel Burnisher

The burnisher or wheel rubber is easy to make and is useful for countless other jobs. A graver which is too soft for general use can be adapted for the purpose.

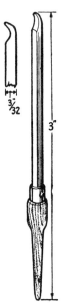

First soften the end and file it flat on two sides to a gradual taper until it is about ·02 or twenty-thousandths of an inch thick. File the end across the flat at an angle of 45° to a point on one side. Back-cut both the pointed side and the other side to make the edge stand out. Round this end with a smooth file and harden it. Reduce the hardness or draw the temper to a pale straw colour. Finally, polish the point and the rounded edge until there are no sharp corners. When polished the rubber is ready for use ; fit a handle to it, of course.

How to use the Burnisher

To use the rubber, hold it firmly on the T-rest with the rounded point resting on the arbor or brass collet arbor and as close to the centre of the rivet as possible. Keep the burnisher against the arbor and with a circular motion bring the burnisher against the brass rivet, forcing the metal from the centre to the outside and over the wheel. This requires a little practice.

F I G. 104.—
BURNISHER
FOR WHEEL
MOUNTING
OR RUBBING
OVER THE
COLLETS.

There is no need to fear that the pivot which is being pressed against will break, as it will withstand this pressure. The risk of breakage is with the other pivot, but this should be quite safe if it is held securely in the lantern or safety runner.

Train wheels are often found mounted on pinions with brass collets. The procedure is the same as with the 'scape pinion.

THIRD PINIONS

We have dealt with 'scape wheels and pinions, centre wheels and pinions and fourth wheels and pinions, both Swiss and English. This leaves the third wheel and pinion. There is nothing special about the third wheel and pinion, but there are one or two points worth mentioning.

Sometimes with a large train, the fourth wheel will foul the third pinion leaves. This can be remedied by putting the third wheel on a collet with a gap between the wheel and pinion head, or by using a long pinion and cutting away the leaves where the fourth wheel is fouling. (See Fig. 106.)

Another point about third pinions, especially in Swiss wristlet watches, is where the pinion head is very short and runs almost flush with the top pivot. The result is that the oil from the pivot

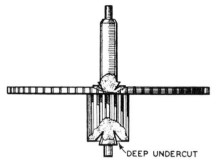

FIG. 105.—ENGLISH THIRD PINION ("PINION DOWN").

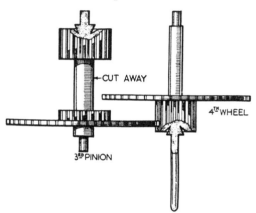

FIG. 106.—SWISS THIRD AND FOURTH WHEELS AND PINIONS.

Third pinion leaves turned away to free fourth wheel.

runs down into the pinion leaves and is carried by the centre wheel teeth over the balance.

A slight shake or jar while in wear causes the hairspring to jump up and just touch the centre wheel and collect some of the oil which the centre wheel has gathered from the third pinion. The consequence is that the hairspring becomes oily, the coils stick together, the watch gains about two hours or more and the third pivot fires in the hole through the oil being carried away.

So when fitting a new third pinion it is advisable to undercut the pinion face and leave the pivot and shoulder isolated and with a slight back-cut behind the shoulder. Do not weaken the pinion too

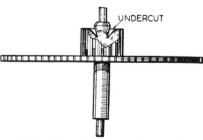

FIG. 107.—SWISS WRISTLET THIRD PINION ("PINION UP").

Showing undercut behind top pivot and shoulder.

much, of course, as it would be broken if the mainspring should break ; use discretion.

PALLET STAFFS

The greatest temptation with pallet staffs is to turn them in a split chuck, but do not do this. However short they may be, either turn them in between dead centres or use a wax chuck.

To turn them in the lathe a rod of silver steel is hardened and tempered. The rod should be just larger than the finished article. Place the steel in a split chuck and fit the lever and pallets, pushing them on tightly while the steel rod is still in the lathe. Then mark the pivot shoulder flush with the pallets.

Take off the pallets and turn the top pivot to size and straight. Polish the pivot holding the polisher underneath the pivot because with the polisher in this position it can be seen where one is touching. When the pivot has been polished, bevel the corner of the shoulder, shorten the pivot to length and round it up. Make certain that the pivot does not protrude above the pallet cock when it is through the hole. While it is still in the lathe, mark where the lower shoulder is to be positioned and cut it off by leaving a long cone behind or nearer to the collet. Leave enough for about the length of two pivots.

Wax Chuck for Turning Pallet Staff

Take out the split chuck and replace with a wax chuck. It is an advantage to have a chuck with a true cone cut in it as it is very useful. If one is not avaiiable, make a chuck and keep it for this sort of job.

Place the wax chuck in the lathe and with a long pointed lozenge-shaped graver turn a dead true cone, without a pip in the centre, about the depth of the length of the pallet staff. Check with a sharp pointed needle to see whether it wobbles, and if it does there is a pip which must be cleared.

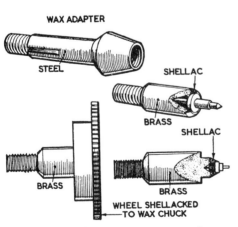

WAX ADAPTER
STEEL
SHELLAC
BRASS
SHELLAC
BRASS
BRASS
WHEEL SHELLACKED TO WAX CHUCK

Fill the cone with shellac and warm with the spirit lamp. Push the pallet staff into the cone, with the finished pivot resting on the bottom of the cone.

FIG. 108.—WAX CHUCKS FOR USE IN THE LATHE.

With a peg hold the pallet staff in place while the shellac is soft and revolve the lathe fairly quickly until the cone previously turned runs true. Allow the shellac to cool while still holding the cone true. As the finished pivot is running true and as the cone has not been disturbed the whole assembly must be dead true.

We can now go ahead and fit the other pivot, polish and finish up.

Boiling-out Pan

To remove the shellac, place the pallet staff in a boiling-out pan with some methylated spirit and warm over the spirit lamp. The shellac will be dissolved and a brushing is all that is required.

Put the pallet staff in the pallets, resting the pallets on a stake with a hole in it. Give a light blow on a punch which fits on the bevelled corner of the shoulder of the pivot and the pallet staff will be held tightly in place.

Screwed-on Pallet Staff

With the screwed-on type, the procedure is much the same, but it is necessary to make or obtain a " rough " staff or blank.

To make a blank, choose a rod of silver steel slightly larger than the hub of the pallet staff. Cut the rod to length or slightly longer than required and anneal it. Place the rod in a split chuck in the lathe and turn it down to the diameter of the threaded part of the pallet staff.

Put the thread on with a screw plate, harden it and temper it down to a dark blue colour. Replace it in the lathe and get the thread running perfectly true. Turn the shoulder or seat on which the pallets will lie absolutely square, and undercut the threaded part slightly even if one complete thread is turned away. While it is still in the lathe fit the pallets on the threaded arbor and notice if they lie flat on the shoulder or seat. If they do, the operation can be continued.

Mark the shoulder of the top pivot as close to the pallets as possible and then turn and polish the pivot. As before, bevel the corner of the shoulder, shorten the pivot and round it up. Where the lever and pallets are separate units, the pallet staff is screwed into the lever. Thus the shoulder must be close to the lever. With it still in the lathe mark off the position of the lower shoulder and cut with a long cone as previously, leaving it too long by about the length of a pivot.

Take it out of the lathe and put the finished end in a wax chuck and peg it true. Then turn the hub to its correct diameter, also the arbor and the bottom pivot. Finish and round up the pivot and the job is completed, except for checking.

When we turned the top shoulder we turned it almost flush with the pallets. Thus the pallets can be no higher without fouling the pallet cock. We may find that the pallets are too high and

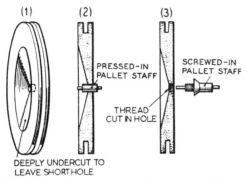

FIG. 109.—TURNING PALLET STAFF IN THE TURNS.

(1) Type of brass ferrule used. (2) Pressed-in type of staff in position for turning. (3) Procedure with screwed-in type.

we can easily lower them by turning the hub shoulder back a little, but if they were planted low we should be unable to raise them except by a new pallet staff. This is a point worth remembering, especially where a pallet staff is concerned; always aim to have the pallets high, only a matter of a few thousandths of an inch, of course. These jobs can be easily carried out in the turns and with practice can be done quickly.

Pallet Staff Turned in the turns

A piece of steel rod hardened and tempered is centred up to run true in the turns, and is then turned down to fit the pallets and polished.

Next it is shortened from the top, allowing sufficient for a pivot to be turned on the amount standing beyond the pallets. The pallets are then removed and the total length of the pallet staff is marked off and partly cut through, leaving it, as with a lathe, about a pivot's length too long.

A solid brass ferrule is then fitted on where the pallets fit. The end which has been cut is re-centred. The pallet staff rough is then put in the turns and the top pivot is turned and polished. The bow is changed round on the ferrule and the other pivot is turned and polished. The pivots are rounded off in the lantern runner.

The only difference with the screw pallet staff is the brass ferrule which is tapped and screws on instead of being pushed on. If a very short pallet staff is being turned in, the centre of the brass ferrule is turned thinly enough for the pallet staff to show through both sides of the ferrule.

BALANCE STAFF

The replacement of a broken balance staff is one of the most frequent repairs which has to be carried out by a watchmaker. The procedure is fairly simple, but nevertheless countless watches are spoilt by being fitted to unsuitable staffs, and also due to the fact that the job is unfortunately taken very lightly these days.

The author has often heard it said, " I can whip a staff in, in a quarter-of-an-hour " by workmen who have had about a year's experience in the trade. This time is not long enough for a workman to know what a balance staff is, let alone what it does.

In these days of interchangeable watches and materials, it is a great help if the correct counterpart of the broken staff can be obtained, but if it is one that is only " near enough " something will be ruined in the fitting. If a suitable replacement cannot be obtained, it is necessary to turn a new staff in to pattern, but before doing this check that the existing staff is correct. If there is any doubt, it is better to scrap it and start from the beginning.

Removing a Broken Staff

To remove the broken staff first extract the roller very carefully. Do not grasp a soft brass roller in steel pliers and twist as this will only cause damage and it will be necessary to make a new roller. The best method is to place the table roller in a split chuck in the lathe, making sure that it is held perfectly square, and then twist the balance and the roller will come loose. Sometimes the balance staff turns round in the balance. In this case, hold the hairspring collet seat in a pin vice with a good grip and twist the staff. If a lathe is not available, a collet in a screw-head tool will answer the purpose.

The Roller Extractor

Failing this, a roller extractor can be used, but care must be taken to avoid risk of damage. One type which can be made very easily is shown in Fig. 110.

A rod of brass is drilled and tapped. A piece of steel rod is threaded suitably and a thumb nut is fitted on the end. In the other end of the steel rod, a hole is drilled to take friction-tight small plugs having different-sized holes to suit small and large pivots.

Screwed on the outside of the brass rod is a shoe, having a flat plate at the end which is solid with it. This plate has a hole in the centre which is filed to the outside of the shoe in the form of a V. The shoe also has a section of the side filed away and joining up with the V. This is to admit the roller and the lower end of the balance staff. The plate at the end of the shoe is thin to allow it to pass between the roller and the balance arm.

The steel rod with a suitable plug is then screwed down on to the shoulder of the bottom pivot and sufficient force is exerted to push off the roller in this steel rod. The shoe is provided with extra plates to accommodate any size of roller.

Removing Balance-Spring Collet with Wedge

The hairspring is easily removed by means of the slot in the collet and a wedge. Do not remove a balance-spring collet by

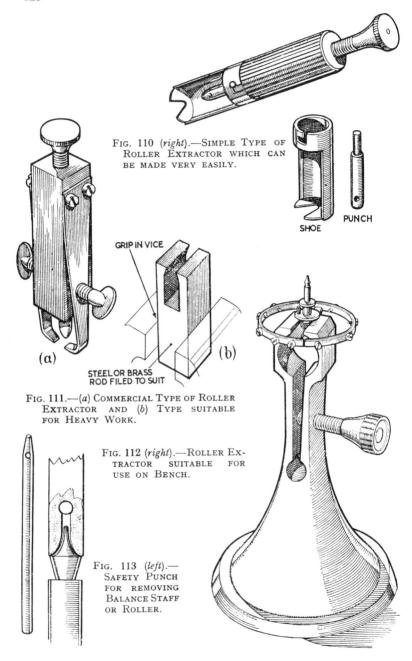

Fig. 110 (*right*).—SIMPLE TYPE OF ROLLER EXTRACTOR WHICH CAN BE MADE VERY EASILY.

SHOE   PUNCH

GRIP IN VICE

STEEL OR BRASS ROD FILED TO SUIT

(a)   (b)

Fig. 111.—(*a*) COMMERCIAL TYPE OF ROLLER EXTRACTOR AND (*b*) TYPE SUITABLE FOR HEAVY WORK.

Fig. 112 (*right*).—ROLLER EXTRACTOR SUITABLE FOR USE ON BENCH.

Fig. 113 (*left*).—SAFETY PUNCH FOR REMOVING BALANCE STAFF OR ROLLER.

placing a screwdriver blade, or a knife-blade, between the arm of the balance and underneath the collet. It only scores and marks the balance and makes it look shoddy and cheap. Wedges are easily made, and if several of different sizes are made, or separately as required, there will be no need to use the knife-blade as the wedge is quicker in use, more accurate and certainly safer as far as the hairspring is concerned.

A wedge is made from silver-steel rod which is filed to a very gradual taper to a thickness suitable to the slot in the collet. It is thinned at the end to pass between the first coil of the hairspring and the collet. The sides are draw-filed to prevent slipping and also back-tapered or wedge-shaped. Note that the large part of the wedge is placed towards the balance staff (see Fig. 114). This is also to prevent slipping. The wedge is placed in the slot and pressed in carefully until the collet turns easily, when it will lift off. Do not, of course, press the wedge in too far so that it splits the collet.

To remove the wedge place the hairspring collet on the bench, hold it down with tweezers and pull the wedge out. These wedges are also useful to twist or turn the collet to put the watch in beat.

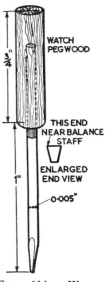

FIG. 114. — WEDGE TOOL FOR REMOVING SLOTTED BRASS BALANCE-SPRING COLLET.

Removing Staff from the Balance

Next remove the staff from the balance. Fit a ferrule on the roller arbor and place the balance and staff in the turns. With a lozenge graver undercut the rivet until only a small circle remains. Take out of the turns and remove the ferrule. Place the balance staff over a hole in the staking tool, or stake, which just admits the hub of the staff. Choose a small hole punch which fits on the cone of the top pivot and give a light blow on this punch and the staff will drop out.

When turning away the rivet do not remove any of the balance arm. It is bad workmanship to do so, and also makes it difficult to rivet a new staff satisfactorily.

Remove the endstones or endpieces and measure the total length of the staff with the " two-screw " gauge described earlier. As soon as the total length has been taken replace the bottom endstone.

Constructing a Height Tool

We now require the height of the balance. This can be determined by trial and error, but it is better to use a tool for this purpose (see Fig. 115). A watchmaker will find that this tool is almost a necessity and well worth making.

Select a brass tube about $\frac{3}{16}$ in. in diameter and another tube, or a brass rod, which fits the inside exactly. Smooth this tube or rod until it slides up and down inside the other without any side shake. Drill a large hole in this rod to about three-quarters of its length, and drill a small hole about thirty-thousandths of an inch in diameter through the remainder of the rod. The outer tube should be about $\frac{3}{4}$ in. long and the inner one about an inch long.

A piece of hardened and tempered steel rod ·03 in. thick is fitted to the small hole in the inner tube to act as a pump centre. One end of this rod is turned to a small conical pivot to pass through the average-sized jewel-hole for a balance staff, about four-thousandths of an inch.

Two steel jaws are made from plate steel, 20 gauge is a good thickness. They are identical in shape, but one jaw is shorter than the other and the holes are of different sizes, the one fitting on the outside tube being larger than the one fitting on the inside tube. Holes are drilled at the opposite end to the jaws. The hole

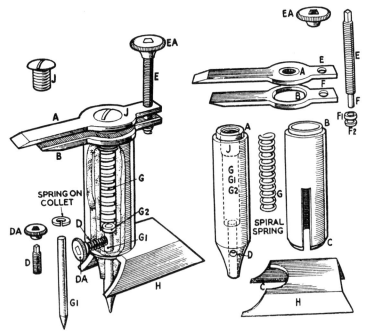

Fig. 115.—Constructional details of Height Tool for Balance Staff, Cylinders, etc.

drilled for the inside rod has a thread cut in it. The jaw fitted to the outside tube has a hole the same size as the core diameter of the screw-hole in the other.

The inside tube has a hole drilled through the side and into the small hole. This hole is tapped and a screw with a small thumb nut is fitted to the end. This screw holds the pump centre when it is set in place.

A piece of steel rod is threaded to the hole in the jaw fitted to the inside tube, and is turned down to its core diameter at one end closely to fit the hole in the other jaw. A hole is drilled through this pivot.

Coil up a piece of hairspring wire in the form of a spiral spring to fit freely over the pump centre, also fit a brass collet a little larger than a hairspring collet on the pump centre. This collet must fit like a hairspring collet, that is, tightly yet capable of being moved The larger hole in the smaller tube is tapped to take a screw.

Assembling the Height Tool

To put the pieces together, rivet the corresponding jaws on the inside and outside tubes tightly. Place the inside tube in position and make sure that it is free to move up and down inside the other.

Screw the threaded steel rod through the tapped hole in the inside jaw and through the hole in the other jaw, and place a pin in the hole which is drilled through this pivot. If the pivot has endshake between the pin and the shoulder of the pivot make a steel or brass collet to take up this endshake.

Make certain that the pump centre moves freely inside the small hole in the inner tube. Then fit the brass collet and push it about half-way down the pump centre, which should be about $\frac{3}{4}$ in. long.

Fit the spiral spring and place the pump centre in position in the inside tube. Tighten the screw which holds the spiral spring in place. Next fit a thumb nut on the threaded steel rod which passes through the jaws, and position the small screw with the thumb nut to hold the pump centre in place in the inside tube.

The base can be made as required. The only stipulation is that it must stand perfectly flat without wobbling and must be square with the outside tube so that the tool is upright.

A suitable base can be made from a piece of double-angle brass, or a square tube with one side open, about $\frac{3}{16}$ in. wide and an inch long. One end is filed to fit round the outside tube and is hard-soldered to it. It is then filed away to clear the thumb nut for the pump centre.

Taking Heights and Lengths

To use the tool, first unscrew the thumb nut controlling the jaws until the jaws meet. Ease the thumb nut controlling the pump centre and it will be pushed out as the spiral spring is released. Place the base of the tool in any convenient but flat part of the bottom plate and insert the pivot of the pump centre through the jewel hole of the balance staff and resting on the endstone. Then tighten the thumb nut to secure the pump centre.

Next, loosen the screw controlling the jaws until the pivot of the pump centre is just clear of the 'scape or pallet cock, and the space between the jaws will then be equivalent to the height of the balance seat of a staff. In other words, it will be the distance between the lower endstone and the 'scape or pallet cock.

We now have the total length of the balance staff and the height of the balance from the lower endstone. To find the correct height of the roller we can use the same tool. The pump centre has been set so we need not interfere with it. Put the tool base in the same place as before and unscrew the thumb nut controlling the jaws until the pump centre is just clear of the lever fork. The distance between the jaws will then be equivalent to the distance between the lower endstone and lever fork.

Turning in the Staff

We can now proceed to turn in the staff. Choose a piece of silver-steel rod slightly larger than the width of the balance arm at the centre. Fit it in a split chuck in the lathe and turn it roughly to size, but big overall, and leave cone centres at each end.

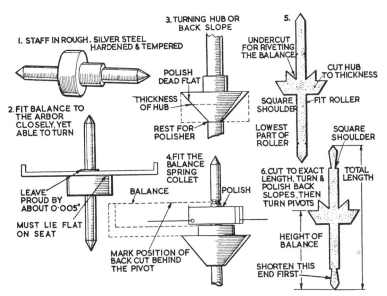

Fig. 116.—Correct Method of turning in a Balance Staff, showing Sequence of Operations.

Harden the rod and temper it to a dark blue colour. Commercial blue steel is only suitable for very cheap work. Place a screw ferrule on the end which will be used as the roller arbor and proceed to fit the balance. Turn it so that it is very smooth and leave a perfectly square shoulder for the balance seat. Do not polish the seat under any circumstances.

Turn the seat until its maximum diameter is only just smaller than the width of the balance arm ; it must be definitely smaller to enable the staff to be removed in the future without bending the balance.

Shorten the balance arbor until it stands about ·003 in.

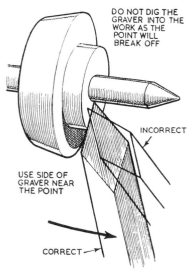

DO NOT DIG THE GRAVER INTO THE WORK AS THE POINT WILL BREAK OFF

INCORRECT

USE SIDE OF GRAVER NEAR THE POINT

CORRECT

FIG. 117.—TURNING AN UNDERCUT FOR RIVETING BALANCE.

above the balance when the balance is pushed flat on the seat. The balance must not fit this arbor too tightly, but so that when pushed on the seat it can just be moved with the fingers, that is, about as tight as a cannon pinion should be on the centre pinion.

Fitting the Hairspring Collet

The next stage is to fit the hairspring collet. This should be a good fit for about seven-eighths of its length and should push home tightly. The hairspring collet arbor should be very slightly tapered, about half-a-thousandth of an inch over its complete length.

Next the seat of the hairspring collet is undercut as deeply as possible as this is used to rivet the balance. Bring the top almost to a knife-edge as this makes riveting easier and safer.

Shorten the hairspring arbor until it stands just above the level of the hairspring collet, when the collet is pushed home. Do not shorten the remainder of the top of the staff at this stage, but just turn it down about half the existing size or about half the size of the hairspring collet arbor.

Thickness of the Hub

We now come to the hub of the staff, that is, the part of the staff behind the balance seat and the roller seat. The thickness of the hub is the difference between the height of the roller and the height of the balance. We set our height gauge for the height

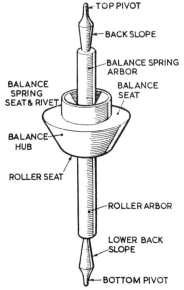

TOP PIVOT

BACK SLOPE

BALANCE SPRING ARBOR

BALANCE SPRING SEAT & RIVET

BALANCE SEAT

BALANCE HUB

ROLLER SEAT

ROLLER ARBOR

LOWER BACK SLOPE

BOTTOM PIVOT

FIG. 118.—DETAILS OF BEST-QUALITY BALANCE STAFF, ENGLISH OR SWISS.

of the balance from the 'scape cock in relation to the lower endstone and mark the lower part of the staff with the graver.

Reset the height gauge to get the height of the roller, or the height of the lever fork. Arrange to have the roller about half its thickness clear of the lever fork for freedom.

Using our first mark on the lower arbor of the balance staff as a starting-point, mark from there up the arbor the distance of the roller. Then add the thickness of the roller and its pipe if it has one, or, if a double roller, add the thickness of the table or impulse roller, that is, the roller in which the ruby pin is fitted. The remaining distance between the last mark and the balance seat is the thickness of the hub. Turn a deep groove into the hub here, keeping the side nearest to the balance seat perfectly square and being careful to coincide with the mark. A good plan is to keep clear of this mark until the end and then eliminate it.

Turning the Back Slope

The back slope can now be turned. This is not essential but looks much better with it than without. Turn the hub down to meet the bottom of the deep groove we have cut previously, without in any way reducing the diameter of the balance seat. The angle depends upon the thickness of the hub. If it is a cheap staff it can be left very smooth after using the graver, but if a quality staff this back slope must be polished flat.

Fitting the Roller

Next fit the roller. Turn the arbor down to taper slightly about half-a-thousandth of an inch over its length. If the arbor is to be polished, turn the arbor down, so that the roller can be pushed up the arbor with the fingers, until it is about double its thickness from its seat if a double roller, and about its own thickness if a single roller.

With a cheap staff let the roller up to about ten-thousandths of an inch from its seat, using the fingers as before. If the taper of the arbor is correct, the roller can be pushed up tightly either with tweezers or a pair of lead-lined pliers. On no account drive the roller on ; not only will it damage the roller, but it will be difficult to remove when required.

Measuring the Total Length

Reset the height gauge for the balance height and shorten the lower part of the staff to its exact length or to correspond to the distance between the jaws of the height tool. Next take the total length of the staff. Screw the balance cock firmly in place. Take off the endstones and with the " two-screw " gauge measure the total distance between the two jewel-holes.

A word of warning : do not measure with the gauge on the jewel-holes themselves, because the jewel-holes are sometimes sunk below the level of the brass and the staff would be short ; so measure across the solid part of the balance cock and pillar plate near the jewel-hole. Always measure accurately and do not allow little extras just in case ; it is a waste of time.

Shorten the balance staff from the top end, leaving the roller arbor severely alone as it is already correct, until it passes stiffly between the two centres of the " two-screw " gauge.

Turning the Pivots

It now only remains to fit the pivots. Do not make the mistake of grinding the pivots with oilstone slips, files or other contraptions, but turn the pivots down to size all the way. If the pivots are turned smoothly until they fit the jewel-holes, polishing or burnishing will give the necessary freedom. If a pivot is ground down with a pivoting file or an oilstone slip, especially when using a lathe, it is almost certain that an oval pivot will result ; this is extremely bad workmanship.

Before starting to turn the pivot, make sure that the centres of the staff are pointed and not flat at the ends. In addition, make certain that the back eccentric runner is in good condition and has a small centre on the extreme edge. If the pivot is ·004 in. the centre on the back eccentric runner must be ·002 in. or less from the edge, otherwise it will not be possible to reach the end of the pivot with the graver. Use a pointed graver which, although difficult to use at first, will with practice be far easier to manipulate than a shaped graver.

Length of Pivot

The length of the pivot should be twice the diameter, and the cone shoulder should be the same length as the pivot. Unfortunately, one cannot always observe this principle as jewelling varies considerably.

A good rule, which more often than not works out right in practice, is to make the length of the pivot twice the length of the jewel-hole, but no more, and the cone shoulder in proportion.

Pivot Burnisher

When the pivot fits the hole change the back eccentric with a hardened and tempered runner, but not one that is glass hard. On this runner small beds are made with a graver, or a small slitting file, and they should be very shallow as the pivot must stand well above the level of the runner. With a polisher or a burnisher give about half a dozen rubs on the pivot with a full length stroke of the bow each time ; this will polish the pivot and it will be true. The burnisher or polisher must be suitably shaped to match the pivot. It is always advisable to have at least three burnishers for different sizes or lengths of pivots.

Rounding up Pivots

The pivots can now be rounded up at the ends. This is carried out by putting the pivot through a lantern runner and stoning off the extreme centre of the pivot. A thin flat burnisher is then rubbed against the end of the pivot while the staff is revolved quickly (see Fig. 120). Do not shape the end to half a ball, but just off the flat, and be careful not to rub a burr on the side of the pivot itself.

Next put both endstones or endpieces in place, fit the balance on the staff, but do not rivet. Place the balance and staff in

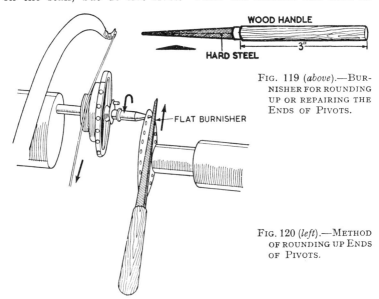

WOOD HANDLE

HARD STEEL

FIG. 119 (*above*).—BURNISHER FOR ROUNDING UP OR REPAIRING THE ENDS OF PIVOTS.

FLAT BURNISHER

FIG. 120 (*left*).—METHOD OF ROUNDING UP ENDS OF PIVOTS.

position and check up freedoms, endshake, etc., and if all is correct rivet the balance to the balance staff.

Riveting the Balance

This can be carried out with a polished punch or with a burnisher of the same type as is used for mounting a 'scape wheel to a brass collet. If a staking tool is available, select a punch which fits the hairspring collet arbor just freely. Place the stake in position, finding a hole which is only just free on the roller arbor. Place the balance and staff in the staking tool and fit the punch in position, resting over the hairspring collet arbor and on the collet seat or the rivet. Tap the punch with the hammer and then rotate the balance a little ; give another tap and again rotate the balance and continue until the balance has been given a full turn. The balance should then be firm and run perfectly flat and true.

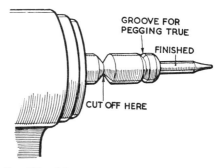

FIG. 121.—METHOD OF TURNING A BALANCE STAFF IN THE LATHE.

Staff is finished in wax chuck, see Fig. 108.

On no account tap the punch while rotating the balance, otherwise it will mark the roller seat.

Next replace the roller, being sure to place it in the correct position. With English work, the roller or impulse pin is generally in line with the arm of the balance ; in the Swiss it is often midway between the arms.

Finally, poise the balance and the job is completed.

All the measurements made with the tools mentioned can also be taken with a micrometer or a douzième gauge, but it is not so easy or so accurate.

Turning Balance Staff in the Lathe

When turning a balance staff in the lathe, do not attempt to turn one end and then reverse the staff and place it in another collet and turn the other end, otherwise it will almost certainly be badly out of true.

The best method is to turn the roller end first as the heights are all taken from this end. Fit the roller and turn and finish the pivot. The pivot can be polished while it is still in the lathe, but do not forget to turn the pivot all the way. Mark the position of the balance distinctly and turn a hollow towards the top end of the staff and well clear of the balance seat. (See Fig. 121.)

Next turn the steel off the full length of the staff. Take out the collet and replace with the wax chuck in which a deep cone has been turned.

Place the finished end of the staff into the cone, then warm the shellac and, when soft, peg the staff true by the hollow which has been previously turned. The staff will be true to the hollow.

Fit the balance and hairspring collet, etc., and undercut for the rivet. Take the total length with the " two-screw " gauge and shorten the staff to the correct length. This may mean taking the staff out of the wax chuck once or twice, but it should not take long.

When finished, boil out in methylated spirit to remove the shellac. Then proceed to rivet the balance. With a good-quality staff it is the general practice to turn a back slope behind the pivot as it helps to keep the oil on the pivot.

CHAPTER 7

GEARING AND MAKING WHEELS AND PINIONS

GEARING plays a most important part in watch and clock work. There is, and always will be, controversy of opinion with regard to proportions of wheels and pinions and, although theory is valuable, a sound knowledge can only be obtained from practical experience and by the use of common sense.

In watch and clock work we are governed by the fact of a watch or clock having hands which move at regular intervals, otherwise we could have odd numbers in the wheels and pinions. As it is, we are compelled to keep to regular proportions such as 10 : 1, 8 : 1, 6 : 1, and so on. The result is that the same teeth are engaged in the same pinion leaf at close regular intervals with consequent wear, also in equal proportion, and any irregularities are exaggerated. Engineers adopt the odd numbers in their gearing, with the result that any irregularities in the wheels are " ironed out ", as it is termed.

Maintaining Uniformity of Driving Force

The whole idea of gearing is transmission of power, and in watch and clock work uniformity of power. We have to imagine two rollers running together which, unless they are pressed together, will slip and will not be regular, also there will be a great loss of power. So with wheels we add teeth and with pinions we add leaves.

With high-numbered wheels and pinions, the problem is not difficult, and that is the reason why best-quality regulators and chronometers have high-numbered trains. Some regulators have pinions of 16 leaves. Generally speaking, a pinion is described as such if it has less than 20 teeth or leaves, but in actual fact a pinion is the follower and the wheel is the driver. With motion work, the minute pinion is a driver, and in some Swiss watches the centre pinion acts as driver and follower. The barrel in this instance drives the centre pinion, which does not carry a centre wheel but is geared into a steel wheel gearing into the third pinion—admittedly not a good arrangement.

Proportions of Wheel to Pinion

The most important considerations with wheels and pinions are the sizes and the profile of the teeth and leaves. We have to try to obtain the same action as that of the two rollers rolling together. So we will term the edges of the rollers the " pitch circles " and work from there.

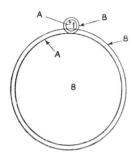

FIG. 122.—ILLUSTRATING THE IMPRACTICABILITY OF KEEPING TO THEORETICALLY CORRECT PROPORTIONS.

A, original rollers 8 : 1. B, plus 8 parts to larger and 1 part to smaller which is still 8 : 1, but an impracticable arrangement.

We will assume that the two rollers are 8 to 1 in proportion, the larger being 8 inches in diameter and the smaller 1 inch in diameter. If we add ·04 of an inch to each, to represent teeth and leaves, the proportion then becomes 8·04 : 1·04 which is 7·73 : 1. Likewise, if we reduce or cut teeth into these rollers at the same depth, that is ·04 of an inch, the proportion becomes 7·96 : ·96 which is 8·29 : 1. It is easy to see, therefore, why wheel-cutting must be correct. We must, by some means, restore the proportion with regard to the action which we have changed by putting teeth to these rollers. To maintain the correct proportions, we must add 8 parts to the larger and 1 part to the smaller. This is not practicable, as the intersection possible would be unsafe, and so we compromise. In working out the sizes we allow on the circumference three teeth and spaces for the wheel and one leaf and space for the pinion. These additions make the pinion proportionately smaller, and this means loss of power. We obtain uniformity, however, which is the most important point in watch and clock work, but the loss must be very small.

Calculation to find the Size of a Missing Wheel and Pinion

If a wheel and pinion are lost, we must have some means of obtaining the dimensions or measurements. Assume that it is the third wheel and pinion. We know the number of teeth in the wheel and the number of leaves in the pinion : wheel 75, pinion of 10. We know the centre wheel is 1 inch in diameter and has 80 teeth. To proceed, measure the distance between the centre and third holes. This will give the radii of the centre wheel and third pinion added together. We will assume that this measurement is ·542. As we work on the diameters we double this figure, which becomes 1·084 inches, that is the sum of the pitch diameter of wheel and pinion.

We know the full diameter of the centre wheel is 1 inch, but we want to know the pitch diameter, so we multiply 1 inch by $\pi(3\cdot1416)$. This is the full circumference. We divide this by 83 instead of 80, allowing for the three teeth and spaces ; then we multiply by 80 and again divide by 3·1416. Thus the calculation is

$$\frac{1\cdot000 \times 3\cdot1416 \times 80}{83 \times 3\cdot1416} = \cdot963 \text{ inch,}$$

which is the pitch diameter of the wheel.

Taking this away from 1·084 inches, we get 0·121, which is the pitch diameter of the third pinion. Therefore the calculation to find the full diameter of the pinion is $\dfrac{\cdot121 \times 3\cdot1416 \times 11}{10 \times 3\cdot1416} = \cdot133$ inch. Thus the third pinion will be ·133 inch in diameter.

We can now proceed to find the full diameter of the third wheel. The distance of centres between the third and fourth holes is ·425, and doubling this figure as before we get ·85 inch. The number of teeth in the missing third wheel is 75. The fourth pinion

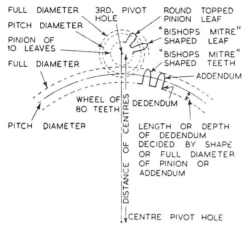

FULL DIAMETER — 3RD. PIVOT — ROUND TOPPED
HOLE — PINION LEAF
PITCH DIAMETER
"BISHOPS MITRE"
PINION OF — SHAPED LEAF
10 LEAVES
"BISHOPS MITRE"
FULL DIAMETER — SHAPED TEETH
— ADDENDUM
WHEEL OF — DEDENDUM
80 TEETH
PITCH DIAMETER — LENGTH OR DEPTH
OF DEDENDUM
DECIDED BY SHAPE
OR FULL DIAMETER
OF PINION OR
ADDENDUM
DISTANCE OF CENTRES
CENTRE PIVOT HOLE

Fig. 123.—Illustrating how Dimensions are Calculated.

Showing also different shapes of pinion leaf in which the working size is the same, yet the full diameter is larger.

measures ·11 inch over its full diameter and has 10 leaves. Therefore the pitch diameter of the pinion is $\dfrac{\cdot11 \times 3\cdot1416 \times 10}{11 \times 3\cdot1416} = \cdot1$ inch. This leaves us ·75 inch for the pitch diameter of the wheel. Therefore the calculation to find the full diameter of the wheel is $\dfrac{\cdot75 \times 3\cdot1416 \times 78}{75 \times 3\cdot1416} = \cdot78$ inch.

Thus the wheel will be ·78 inch and the pinion ·133 inch.

The shape of the pinion leaves in this instance would be, of course, semicircular at the top with straight sides, whereas the wheel teeth would be shaped like a bishop's mitre.

If we make the pinion leaves the same shape as the wheel teeth the full diameter must be larger, but the pitch diameter will remain unaltered. If we continue the curve of the pinion leaf, the full diameter of the pinion will also increase, but the pitch will still remain unchanged. The space at the base of the leaves becomes narrower, of course, but this part does not come into action.

This form of shaping is very useful. For example, the pinion

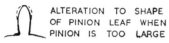

ALTERATION TO SHAPE OF PINION LEAF WHEN PINION IS TOO LARGE

FIG. 124.—RE-SHAPING PINION LEAF TO IMPROVE PROPORTION.

leaves can be reshaped in this form when either a watch or a clock has been supplied with a pinion which is too large and is run in such a position that the holes or bearings cannot easily be repitched, such as a hole which has been jewelled.

Epicycloidal and Hypocycloidal Gearing

The type of gearing generally used in watch and clock work is of epicycloidal construction, the principle involved being that of a circle rolling upon a circle. Gearing of this type is much more convenient than other forms, although it is not ideal. Hypocycloidal is another form of gearing also used by watchmakers on

FIG. 125.—
PRINCIPLE OF
EPICYCLOIDAL
AND HYPO-
CYCLOIDAL
GEARING.

  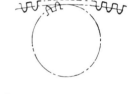

(a) EPICYCLOIDAL GEARING   (b) HYPOCYCLOIDAL GEARING

various occasions, the principle in this instance being that of a circle rolling within a circle. This type of gearing is used in minute repeaters and in some calendar watches.

The methods employed in each case are very similar, but wherever hypocycloidal gearing is used both wheel and pinion drive are driven alternately, and thus have to be carefully made.

Involute Gearing

The best gearing of all is, of course, involute, the whole action of which is rolling one tooth on the other. The teeth of both the driver and the follower are exactly the same shape and are made with the same cutter.

A hob or hobbing cutter is used to cut the teeth, and the wheels are cut in a hobbing machine. The hob resembles a worm gear, the thread of which is interrupted by grooves so as to form cutting faces. When machining the teeth, both wheel and hobbing cutter are revolving while the teeth are being cut.

The size of the cutter is worked out according to threads per inch, the threads per inch corresponding to the number of teeth and the circumference of the wheel. Any wheel made with this cutter will be the same pitch, whatever the circumference of the wheel, but the number will, of course, change. With epicycloidal and hypocycloidal gearing, however, each wheel and pinion requires a separate cutter.

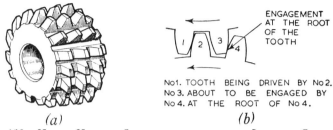

ENGAGEMENT AT THE ROOT OF THE TOOTH

No1. TOOTH BEING DRIVEN BY No2.
No 3. ABOUT TO BE ENGAGED BY
No 4. AT THE ROOT OF No 4.

(a) *(b)*

FIG. 126.—HOB OR HOBBING CUTTER USED FOR CUTTING INVOLUTE GEARS (*a*), AND ILLUSTRATING PRINCIPLE OF INVOLUTE GEARING (*b*).

It is difficult to cut an involute pinion below 20 leaves, as there is insufficient metal near the centre of the pinion to enable the proper shape to be obtained.

Finding the Number of Teeth in a Missing Wheel

Earlier in this chapter we worked out the size of a missing wheel and pinion ; we will now deal with the calculation for determining the number of teeth in a missing wheel.

With a watch we must first find out the number of vibrations the balance makes in an hour, or, if a seconds train and it is a missing third wheel, we can work from the centre wheel and fourth pinion. We will deal with this first.

The fourth wheel turns 60 times in an hour and has a pinion of 10 leaves. The centre wheel has 80 teeth and the third pinion has 10 leaves. The calculation is $\dfrac{80 \times x}{10 \times 10} = 60$, where x is the number of teeth in the missing wheel. Therefore $8x = 600$ or $x = 75$. Thus the number of teeth in the missing wheel is 75.

If the wheel and pinion are missing we can obtain the ratio of the two by similar means. The centre wheel is 80 as before, and the fourth pinion has 10 leaves. The calculation is $\dfrac{80 \quad x}{10 \times x} = 60$, that is $\dfrac{60}{8} = \dfrac{x'}{x}$ or $\dfrac{7 \cdot 5}{1} = \dfrac{x'}{x}$. Thus the ratio of the wheel and pinion is 7·5 : 1, or a wheel of 75 teeth and a pinion of 10 leaves.

In conjunction with our previous calculations for the size of the wheel and pinion we can obtain exactly what we require. If not a seconds train, we must work from the centre wheel at one end and the number of vibrations the balance makes in one hour. We will assume that we have counted the vibrations of the balance and it is 18,375. The fourth wheel and pinion are missing, but we have the rest of the train to work with. It is centre wheel 80, third wheel 70 with pinion of 10, 'scape wheel of 15 teeth and 'scape pinion of 8 leaves. We count the 'scape wheel as 30, as it is engaged twice. The calculation is $\dfrac{80 \times 70 \times x' \times 30}{10 \times x \times 8}$, which is equal to 18,375. Therefore $\dfrac{2100x'}{x} = 18{,}375$, which is 8·75 : 1, and this is the ratio of the missing wheel and pinion. Multiply each by 8 and we obtain 70 : 8. Thus a wheel of 70 teeth and a pinion of 8 leaves are required.

These calculations apply to a clock in the same way, except that we work from the number of vibrations a pendulum performs in the hour.

Stretching a Wheel

Sometimes a watch will stop and the slightest movement will start it again. This may be caused by a shallow fourth and 'scape depth. This can be corrected in two ways, either by fitting a new fourth wheel which is slightly larger, or by stretching the fourth wheel teeth and putting the wheel through the topping machine to reshape the teeth. This stretching operation has to be very carefully carried out, because only the teeth themselves must be

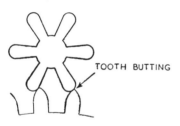

TOOTH BUTTING

Fig. 127.—Pinion of Correct Size pitched too Shallow, causing Teeth to Butt.

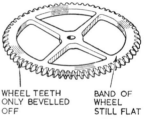

WHEEL TEETH ONLY BEVELLED OFF   BAND OF WHEEL STILL FLAT

Fig. 128.—Showing Method employed to stretch Wheel Teeth.

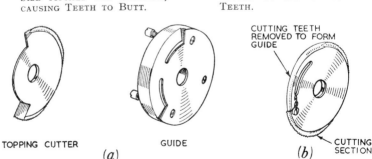

TOPPING CUTTER   GUIDE   CUTTING TEETH REMOVED TO FORM GUIDE   CUTTING SECTION

(a)   (b)

Fig. 129.—Types of Topping or Rounding-up Cutters.
(a) Cutter with separate guide. (b) Cutter and guide combined.

Fig. 130.—Wheel-
topping Machine
or Rounding-up
Tool.

A. Slide controlling
depth of cut.
B. Cutter.
C. Support for wheel.
D. Runner (only one
visible).
E. Slide to adjust
squareness.
F. Driving wheel.

stretched and not the band of the wheel. If the band is stretched,
the wheel will become five or six sided according to the number of
arms in the crossing out and be completely ruined.

First choose a topping cutter which suits the wheel teeth, because
once they are stretched this is almost impossible. Use a gauge
to see how much the wheel is enlarged, and also use a stake having
a hole which just fits the pinion head or the arbor of the pinion on

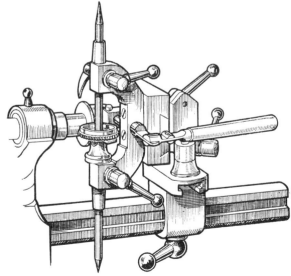

Fig. 131.—
Modern Type
of Topping
Machine
which is
fitted to a
Lathe.

The topping
machine is used
to reshape the
wheel teeth to the
required size after
stretching.

ENGAGEMENT FAR TOO EARLY. DRIVE TAKEN AWAY FROM TOOTH FIRST ENGAGED. PINION TOO LARGE

60 TEETH

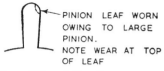

PINION LEAF WORN OWING TO LARGE PINION.
NOTE WEAR AT TOP OF LEAF

FIG. 132a (*left*).—PINION TOO LARGE, CREATING EXCESSIVE FRICTION AND LOSS OF POWER.

FIG. 132b (*above*).—WEAR CAUSED BY PINION TOO LARGE.

which the wheel is mounted. Then tap each tooth in turn with a light steel hammer, rotating the wheel until all the teeth have been slightly flattened. Place the wheel in the callipers to test for truth and, if true, continue until the wheel is stretched just a little more than required.

Finally, put the wheel through the topping machine until it is to the required size and stone up the wheel teeth to remove burrs.

The same treatment can be given to any wheel, but where a going barrel is involved a new barrel is the only remedy.

Sometimes a bad depth is caused by a large pinion. This means that the leaves of the pinion are too far apart in relation to the wheel teeth. As a rule this calls for a new pinion of the right size and often a new wheel as well, because a large pinion wears a notch in the teeth and even if the correct size of pinion is fitted, the worn notch will still cause trouble (Fig. 132b).

Reshaping Pinion Leaves

Another source of trouble with both watches and clocks is a small 'scape pinion. It is always preferable in a clock having a

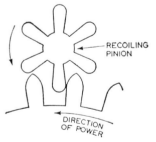

RECOILING PINION

DIRECTION OF POWER

FIG. 133a.—PINION TOO SMALL, CAUSING TROUBLE WITH A RECOIL ESCAPEMENT.

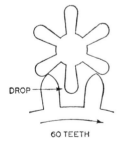

DROP

60 TEETH

FIG. 133b.—PINION TOO SMALL, CAUSING LOSS OF POWER DUE TO DROP.

FIG. 133c. — RESHAPING WHEEL TOOTH TO IMPROVE A SMALL PINION ERROR.

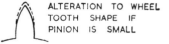

ALTERATION TO WHEEL TOOTH SHAPE IF PINION IS SMALL

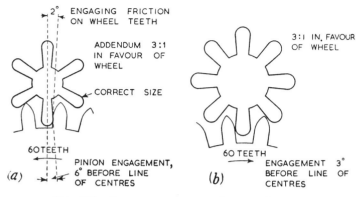

FIG. 134.—ENGAGEMENT BEFORE LINE OF CENTRES.

(a) Pinion of 6 leaves correct for size.　　(b) Pinion of 8 leaves correct for size.

verge or a recoil escapement to have the 'scape pinion full-size. In each of these types the 'scape wheel recoils or goes backwards and as such the 'scape pinion acts in a dual capacity, that is, as a driven pinion when the 'scape wheel is giving impulse and as a driver when the wheel is recoiling. With a watch having a lever escapement when the 'scape wheel is locked on the pallet, the wheel has to recoil owing to the draw to unlock.

Thus if the 'scape pinion is small the pinion leaf will butt on the top of the wheel tooth gearing into it, and will stop the clock or watch. It is always as well to examine for this fault.

These pinions are invariably low numbers of 6, 7 or 8 leaves and are difficult to mesh properly, owing to the engagement being before the line of centres. The practice has always been to have a thin leaf pinion for a pinion of 6 leaves, but it does not always work out satisfactorily. Sometimes trouble can be overcome if a pinion of 6 leaves has thick tapering leaves, and is shaped something like a star wheel but with convex sides (Fig. 135).

FIG. 135.—STAR-SHAPED PINION OF 6 LEAVES.

Shape is similar for a pinion of 5 leaves.

Although pinions of 5 leaves are not often met with, this particular shape is practicable. (Some small Swiss watches and some of the old clock watches were made with pinions of 5 leaves.) The author has overcome trouble by replacing a pinion of the recognized shape by one that may be termed a star-wheel pinion. The idea is to hold back the outgoing wheel tooth to allow the incoming tooth to engage in the pinion leaf by just the same amount later,

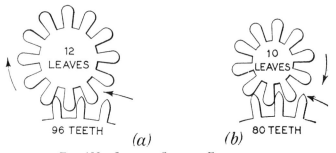

FIG. 136.—LINE OF CENTRES ENGAGEMENT.

(a) Pinion of 12 leaves. 2 : 2 addendum for wheel and pinion. Engagement on line of centres.

(b) Pinion of 10 leaves. 2·5 : 1·5 in favour of wheel. Engagement on line of centres.

and thus reduce the engaging friction. This particular trouble does not arise with a pinion of 12 leaves, because the engagement takes place on the line of centres as is the case with numbers higher than 12.

Making a Cutter

The cutting of wheels and pinions is a simple matter if we can keep to standard sizes, because ready-made cutters can be obtained. The problem arises when we are replacing a standard size because it is incorrect. A special machine is required to make the usual milling-cutters, but as it is far too expensive to buy machines to do all these jobs we are required to make cutters ourselves.

To make a cutter, choose a good piece of steel ; an old file well

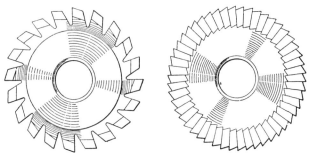

FIG. 137a.—MACHINE-MADE MILLING-CUTTERS USED FOR CUTTING WHEELS AND PINIONS.

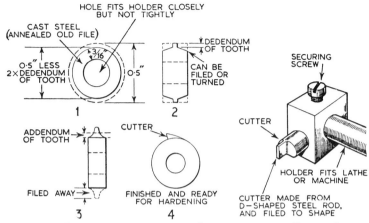

FIG. 137b.—PROCEDURE FOR MAKING A SINGLE-BLADED OR FLYING CUTTER
AND SHOWING TYPE OF CUTTER HOLDER USED.

annealed is the best. We will assume that a lathe or a wheel-cutting
engine is available. Drill a hole in the old file to fit the cutter
holder closely, and mark a circle about $\frac{3}{16}$ of an inch clear of the
hole. Then allow about $\frac{1}{8}$ of an inch of metal beyond this and cut
it off the file. File away most of the excess metal up to the $\frac{3}{16}$-inch
circle, leaving a block standing up about $\frac{1}{8}$ of an inch wide. The
cutter will be made on this block. File the top of the block perfectly flat and square with the hole. Next file the sides down,
leaving a smaller block standing up to act as the blade.

Thickness and Shape of the Blade

The thickness of the blade will be decided by the size of the
wheel or pinion we are cutting. First obtain the diameter at the
pitch circle, or the pitch diameter, say, of a pinion. Next measure
the circumference and divide this by double the number of teeth.
The reason for doubling the number is, of course, that our calculations give us tooth and space and we want only the space. This is
the thickness of the blade to start with, as this would make tooth
and space equal. Do not forget that we are cutting the space and

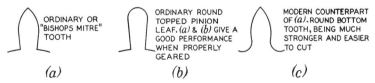

FIG. 138.—SHAPES OF WHEEL TEETH AND PINION LEAVES.

Showing (a) " Bishop's Mitre", (b) round topped pinion leaf, and (c) round
bottom shape used for both wheel teeth and pinion leaves.

leaving the tooth standing, so we shape the cutter to the side of the tooth and both sides must be identical. In this connection, the diagrams of teeth reproduced in Fig. 138 will be useful in determining the shape of the blade.

If a leaf or tooth with a round-shaped root is required, the top of the blade must be semicircular.

If we are cutting a convex-shaped tooth or leaf, the blade must be concave and the cutter must be thinner near the top, otherwise the leaf will be too thin at the base. Always remember that a parallel-bladed cutter leaves the tooth thinner at the base than at the top, because the circle is smaller or the circumference is less.

If not very experienced, it is suggested that a pinion of about the same size be obtained and used as a guide to judge the length of the blade, especially if a small pinion is to be cut. With larger pinions, the length of the blade should be double the addendum of the wheel or pinion.

When the cutter is to shape, harden and temper it to a pale straw colour. The cutter will then cut brass or steel. This type of cutter is known as a single-bladed or flying cutter. High speed is necessary when using the cutter, also a slow feed. To obtain smooth teeth or leaves the cutter must be polished on the cutting faces and the clearance must be about 25°.

Cutting a Pinion without an Engine or a Lathe

The cutting of a wheel and pinion can be performed even without a lathe or a wheel-cutting engine. It is rather a crude method, but may be useful in certain circumstances. A dividing plate can easily be made for a pinion, but with a wheel it is a lengthy operation.

Let us assume that we require a pinion of 7 leaves. Turn up a disc of brass ·279 inch in diameter. This will give seven divisions exactly $\frac{1}{8}$ of an inch apart. Set the dividers $\frac{1}{8}$ of an inch apart and mark the brass disc all the way round near the edge ; file slots if preferred, or drill holes. Fit the disc tightly on to the pinion blank and place between centres in the turns. Next, a piece of steel is attached at one end of a rod in the form of a T, and the rod is fitted into the T-rest socket, with the ends standing proud. In these ends are slots in perfect line with each other. The whole is hardened. A file holder fits exactly into these slots. A piece of flat steel, the same thickness as the space of the pinion leaves and shaped up as a file, is fitted into the file holder.

A piece of steel with the ends shaped accordingly is screwed to the body of the turns to act as the index and hold the dividing plate in position. A slot is filed in the pinion blank to the required depth, the dividing plate is then turned one slot or hole and another slot is cut, and so on all the way round. When this operation has been completed, the file is replaced by one of a different shape and the process is repeated. The pinion is finally touched up by hand, then hardened, tempered and polished.

The Dividing Head

The modern dividing head, however, is a very different proposition. The operation is often carried out by using degrees of a circle. A wheel is fitted on the mandrel of the lathe and geared into this, and fitting exactly is a worm which has been cut and ground perfectly true. Fitting on to this worm are various wheels which can be substituted according to the numbers required. The worm does one turn for each tooth of the wheel, which is mounted on the mandrel of the lathe. Thus if the wheel has 50 teeth and we mount a wheel on the worm having 20 teeth, one tooth of this wheel represents one-thousandth of a turn of the mandrel. With a wheel of 40, each tooth represents one two-thousandths of a turn, and so on.

Again, with a wheel of 60 on the mandrel, a wheel of 6 on the worm represents 1 degree for each tooth. This method has unlimited scope and is extremely accurate.

For example, if we wanted to cut a 'scape wheel of 15 teeth, all that is necessary is to have the 60 wheel on the mandrel and the 6 wheel on the worm (or any number on the worm with a multiple of 6). The division of the wheel is 24° for each tooth, the angle of the face of the tooth is 24° and the angle at the back of the tooth is 36°. Therefore, by using a wheel of 6 on the worm, each division is 1°.

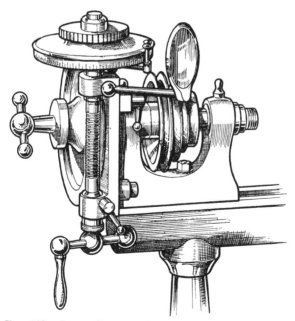

Fig. 139.—Lathe Dividing Head, using a Worm Gear.

A. Cutter.
B. Cutter holder.
C. Wax chuck.
D. Vertical slide.
E. Dividing plate.
F. Slide rest.
G. Index.
H. Revolving head-stock.
I. Driving pulley.
J. Drive from electric motor.
K. Adjustment for height of slide and cutter.
L. Nut to secure head.
M. Split chucks.
N. Spanner.
O. Lathe foot for bench.

Fig. 140.—Lorch Lathe set up as Wheel- or Pinion-cutting Machine.

It can be seen, therefore, that it is easy to set up the cutter accurately, and by using a wheel of 36 on the worm we can set up to one-sixth of a degree. We will, however, deal with a 'scape wheel in more detail later on.

Points to observe when Cutting Wheels and Pinions

In workshops, of course, these elaborate tools are not available unless we care to make the attachments for ourselves.

Wheels and pinions are either cut on a wheel-cutting engine furnished with a number of individual dividing plates (alternatively with various numbers on one plate), or on a lathe having a slide rest with a vertical slide attached (Fig. 140).

The lathe must have the pulleys on the extreme outside to enable a dividing plate or plates to be attached. The lathe or engine must be provided with an index which fits either into holes or slots in the dividing plates and holds the plate and the lathe mandrel firmly in position. If cutting a small wheel it can be shellacked to a wax chuck, but if a large wheel it must be mounted on a sleeve, or on a special attachment which clamps the wheel firmly. Everything in a wheel-cutting machine must be very firm, otherwise the cutting will be rough and chattery.

A pinion must be cut between dead centres to ensure truth and, if small, the body of the blank must be supported.

Procedure for Cutting a Wheel

To cut a wheel, first line up the cutter. In other words, make sure the cutter will run absolutely dead to the centre of the collet otherwise if it is the slightest bit high or low the teeth will be " drunk ", that is, leaning over. Make certain that the cutter is also parallel, otherwise the space made by the cutter will be too wide, or if much out of parallel will leave no tooth at all.

Next turn up the blank. Choose a piece of good-quality brass and hammer it hard, then file one side flat, leaving file marks on it. Fix the blank with shellac on to the wax chuck and turn it perfectly true and exactly to the required size. Then put on the necessary dividing plate.

Place the index in the first hole and always make a point of starting from there. Lead the cutter in until the curve of the addendum just shows on the blank, then cut the next two teeth. Take away the index and move the dividing plate until the three cut teeth are easily seen. If not quite up, fetch the plate back and

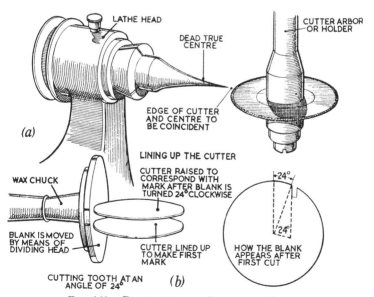

FIG. 141.—PROCEDURE FOR CUTTING A WHEEL.

(a) Setting up for wheel or pinion.
(b) Setting for cutting tooth off the radial.

then bring the cutter a little nearer and cut the three teeth again. As soon as these three teeth are just up, proceed to cut all the teeth.

If, on examination, the front of the wheel teeth are up and the back are not, the slide rest is out of square. If only a little, leave it alone, but if much out of square, line up on the blank ; it will mean spoiling the wheel but it is worth while, as the next one will be satisfactory.

It is always a lot of trouble to set up for an individual wheel, but once it has been carried out wheels can be cut to that particular size indefinitely.

Cutting a Pinion

When cutting a pinion the same setting up is required, but being smaller in diameter the setting up is more critical ; also the feed

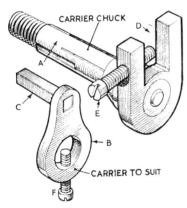

Fig.   142.—Carrier   Chuck   and Carrier for Pinion Cutting.

Carrier chuck A fits in lathe and holds carrier B, which grips pinion arbor pin C held in joint D by screw E. Screw E is loosened to examine pinion. The carrier screw F is adjustable.

must be slow as the cutter has much more metal to remove owing to the length of the pinion head.

The pinion blank has a carrier screwed to it firmly, and the chuck on the lathe head has a firmly fixed driving joint. On no account move the adjustable carrier screw, otherwise the division of the pinion will be most inaccurate. Cut two leaves first and see if they are in order, and then proceed to cut all the way round. With clock pinions, and some of the larger watch pinions, a slotting cutter is used first to save the heavy wear on the shaping cutter.

Making a Pinion from Pinion Wire

It is often possible to use pinion wire for making clock pinions. This is steel rod drawn to the section of a pinion. As purchased, the wire is not ready for use, but has to be shaped up and usually bottomed out. For these purposes bottoming files and rounding-

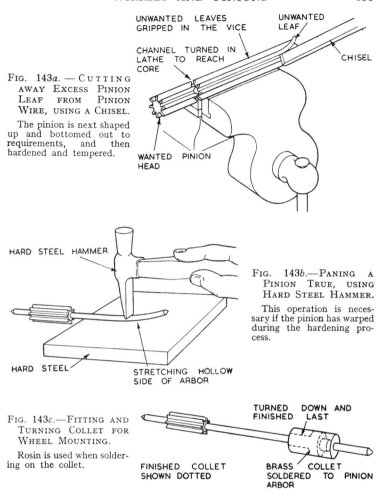

FIG. 143a. — CUTTING AWAY EXCESS PINION LEAF FROM PINION WIRE, USING A CHISEL.

The pinion is next shaped up and bottomed out to requirements, and then hardened and tempered.

UNWANTED LEAVES GRIPPED IN THE VICE

UNWANTED LEAF

CHANNEL TURNED IN LATHE TO REACH CORE

CHISEL

WANTED PINION HEAD

HARD STEEL HAMMER

FIG. 143b.—PANING A PINION TRUE, USING HARD STEEL HAMMER.

This operation is necessary if the pinion has warped during the hardening process.

HARD STEEL

STRETCHING HOLLOW SIDE OF ARBOR

FIG. 143c.—FITTING AND TURNING COLLET FOR WHEEL MOUNTING.

Rosin is used when soldering on the collet.

TURNED DOWN AND FINISHED LAST

FINISHED COLLET SHOWN DOTTED

BRASS COLLET SOLDERED TO PINION ARBOR

up files are available. Bottoming files are thin flat files which only cut on the edge, the sides being smooth. Rounding-up files cut on the flat side but the other side is rounded and smooth and joins the flat side in a knife-edge, so that the side of one leaf can be filed without marking the next leaf.

First cut a length of wire a little longer than required. Place the wire in the lathe, or throw, and mark the length of the pinion head on its correct place and turn a slot down to the solid arbor. The excess pinion is then cut away with a chisel. The last excess leaf is often removed with a file, or nippers. The pinion is then shaped up and bottomed out to requirements. Harden and temper

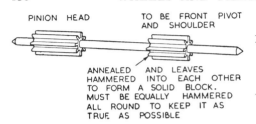

PINION HEAD

TO BE FRONT PIVOT
AND SHOULDER

ANNEALED AND LEAVES
HAMMERED INTO EACH OTHER
TO FORM A SOLID BLOCK.
MUST BE EQUALLY HAMMERED
ALL ROUND TO KEEP IT AS
TRUE AS POSSIBLE

FIG. 144. — PROCEDURE
FOR MAKING CENTRE
PINION OR FRENCH
LOCKING PINION.

In this case the pinion
wire is annealed.

it to a dark blue colour. Centres are filed on the arbor at each end
and drawn over until the arbor at each end runs true.

Stretching the Pinion True

The pinion head will probably be out of truth ; if so pane it true
with the ends of the arbor. This is carried out by stretching the
metal on the hollow side. On no account try to bend it true by
hitting with a hammer on the raised side ; it may break, and in
any case it will not come true this way. Use the pane of the hammer
for stretching, and do not hit all in one place but spread the blows
over the hollow side (Fig. 143*b*).

The pinion leaves are then smoothed up with emery powder and
oil, and when all marks have been removed should be polished with
diamantine. Next the arbor is turned true but not smooth. A
nick is then turned where the brass collet is to rest. The brass
collet is fitted on the arbor so that it is an easy fit, but not floppy.
All traces of grease or oil are removed and the arbor is tinned with
soft solder. The collet is soldered on and then cleaned in liquid
ammonia, or any alkaline fluid, to prevent rusting or corrosion.

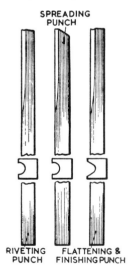

SPREADING
PUNCH

RIVETING
PUNCH

FLATTENING &
FINISHING PUNCH

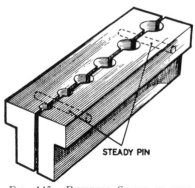

STEADY PIN

FIG. 145.—RIVETING STAKE IN TWO
SECTIONS.

Used for riveting wheel on to brass
collet where pinion is at other end of arbor.

FIG. 146 (*left*).—PUNCHES FOR RIVET-
ING CLOCK PINIONS.

The collet is then turned true and the wheel is mounted, but not riveted on. Face up the pinion and smooth or polish the arbors. Put on the pivots. The length of the pinion complete can be measured by pinning the plates together and laying the pinion against them. The distance between the plates is the distance between the shoulders of the pivots, providing of course the holes have not been sunk into the plates.

Riveting on the Wheel

With an English centre pinion, or a gathering or locking-wheel pinion in an English or French striking train, the pinion wire is annealed. Where the pivot and shoulder are larger than the arbor, the leaves of the pinion wire are hammered carefully round until they appear to be solid with the arbor. The pivot and shoulder can then be turned on this block, and, if carried out correctly, will appear to be solid all through (Fig. 144).

The wheel is riveted on with two punches, one having a slightly rounded end and the other a flat end. The stake is usually in two sections (Fig. 145), because the pinion head may be larger than the collet, and the pinion head would not pass through a hole small enough to support the collet while riveting.

The punches are half-round in shape and riveting is carried out in sections. Use the round-faced punch first to spread out the rivet, and then follow up with the flat one until the riveting is flat. Then clean the rivet with a graver.

CHAPTER 8

WATCH ESCAPEMENTS

THE escapement of a watch or clock is the mechanism which transmits the motive power from the train to maintain the vibration of the balance or pendulum. The term "escapement" is really self-explanatory, that is, allowing the 'scape wheel to escape or be released at uniform intervals.

LEVER ESCAPEMENTS

With a watch or carriage clock, the lever escapement is the most popular. Although both the ratchet-tooth and the club-tooth lever escapements were of English origin, the English continued to use the ratchet tooth long after the Continental makers had dropped it in favour of the club tooth. One often comes across old English keywind watches which were provided with club-tooth escapements. All modern lever watches have club-tooth escapements.

There is, however, little to choose between them as both escapements give extremely good performances.

The Club-Tooth Lever Escapement

We will deal first with the club-tooth lever escapement (see Fig. 147). In this form of escapement the impulse is divided between the 'scape wheel and the pallets.

Some craftsmen prefer the impulse equally divided and some favour more on the wheel teeth and less on the pallets, and vice versa. From a practical point of view the author prefers the impulse equally divided, especially if the stones are not visible. In other words, if the jewels are set flush with the steels and not as they are set to-day, standing beyond the steel.

One advantage of the modern method of fitting the stones or jewels is the ease of replacement; but with the old arrangement where the stones are not visible, replacement is a very different story. We will deal with this later.

With the club-tooth escapement, the wheel teeth are stronger than in the ratchet-tooth form, and its great advantage is that losses are much less. The undercut at the heel of the tooth reduces the amount of drop to a minimum, and thus greater impulse or impulses over a longer period is possible.

The impulse possible with a 15-tooth club wheel is 9°, although in theory 10° is possible. With a 15-tooth wheel there is 24° between two teeth and this 24° is divided between two pallets.

158

The Locking

The two pallets are termed the entrance and the exit pallet respectively. The entrance pallet is the first engaged and when this pallet releases the tooth, the tooth drops between the two pallets ; when the tooth is released from the exit pallet, it drops outside the pallets. The exit pallet is sometimes referred to as

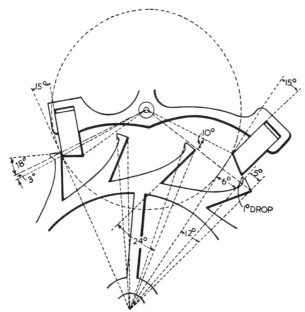

Fig. 147.—Club-tooth Escapement with 10° Pallets and Equidistant Lockings.

the hook pallet owing to its shape. Thus we have 12° for every completed action, that is, locking, impulse and drop.

Theoretically the locking is 2°, but in practice this is almost impossible, 3° being a safe and necessary locking.

" Draw "

With locking we have to consider draw or angle of draw. When the wheel tooth drops on to the locking face of the pallet there is always a chance that it may not hold there and, therefore, we have " draw ". That is, the locking face is angled back from the radial so that the wheel will pull the pallets towards itself or into itself. 12° draw on the entrance pallet is found to be sufficient but the exit pallet needs 15° draw, because there is always a tendency for the wheel to throw off the exit pallet, so often both pallets have 15° draw.

This draw action performs two functions : the wheel is held on to the locking face of the pallet and, also through the medium of the pallets and lever, the guard pin is held clear of the edge of the roller or the lever is held against its banking pin.

For the guard to be clear of the roller edge we must have " run " or, as it is often termed, run to the banking. Run is the amount the lever and pallets move after the wheel drops and this run is controlled by the banking pins ; so we have 3° locking and 1° run.

If we try these actions slowly, the lever, as it is moved across from one banking pin to the other, first unlocks and releases the wheel tooth ; the corner of the tooth then starts to push the lever and pallets across to the other side.

" Drop "

If the wheel tooth is watched carefully it will be noticed that the corner of the tooth runs the whole length of the pallet. Then as soon as the corner of the tooth reaches the back corner of the pallet, the plane or impulse face of the tooth comes into action and works on or pushes the outside corner of the pallets, continuing the push which the corner of the tooth started, until the lever is moved its maximum distance and then the tooth drops off. This " drop " is about 1° in a club-tooth escapement, which is all loss. In theory we still have 8° of impulse, but unfortunately we lose still more.

Recoil

When the wheel tooth is locked and the pallets are drawn to the banking pin, the 'scape wheel has gone forward a short distance. Thus when we wish to unlock the wheel tooth we move the lever away from the banking pin and as we do so the wheel recoils or goes backwards owing to the draw.

If a wheel is moving backwards it has to stop before it can change direction to go forwards ; also if a wheel or any other object is to be moved, the inertia or the resistance which is offered has to be overcome. Therefore, three factors, recoil, inertia and moving forwards, are involved before the wheel can give impulse to the pallets. All this time the pallet is moving away from the wheel.

The Impulse

In a very good escapement this loss will be 2°, but in a poor one the loss can be as much as 4°. Thus for 12° we lose 3° locking, at least 2° at the start of the impulse, and at least 1° drop at the end. Therefore the greatest impulse obtainable in a first-class escapement is 6°.

This does not take into consideration the freedom of the pivots in the jewel-holes, which is, of course, the side shake in the pallet staff and 'scape pinion pivot holes. A degree can be lost here as well. If the pallet stones of an older watch are examined, a small pit will be seen near the front of the impulse plane where the 'scape wheel tooth continually drops.

The Lever and Pallets

This impulse is given to the balance by means of the lever. The modern lever generally comprises lever and pallets in one piece. With modern English watches, however, the lever is a separate unit and is pinned to the pallets with two brass pins.

A lot of Swiss platform escapements have the lever as a separate piece. The lever is pinned in the same way as English levers, but where the English have a pushed-in pallet staff the Swiss and other Continentals have a screwed-in pallet staff.

The idea of having lever and pallets in two pieces is to enable them to be poised, which is, of course, lacking in the modern lever and pallets. They are, however, made extremely light in weight and adjustment can be made for the amount that they are out of poise. The poise does, nevertheless, affect the rate of a watch.

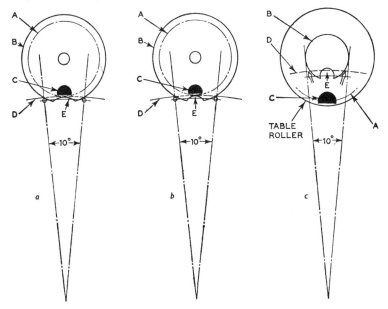

FIG. 148.—SHOWING GUARD OR SAFETY ACTION.

Comparison between 3 : 1 and 3½ : 1 single roller and illustrating the advantage of a double roller.

(a) Single roller, lever and roller proportions 3 : 1. A. Pin circle. B. Roller edge or guard circle. C. Impulse pin. D. Dotted line showing intersection. E. Roller crescent. Guard unsafe.

(b) Single roller, 3½ : 1, showing a greater and safe intersection.

(c) Double roller, 3 : 1. A. Pin circle. B. Guard circle. C. Impulse pin. D. Line showing intersection. E. Roller crescent.

Length of the Lever

The length of the lever varies with different manufacturers. With the single-roller escapement the least proportion can be $3\frac{1}{2}$: 1, that is $3\frac{1}{2}$ parts lever to 1 part roller, of the distance between the balance and pallet holes. With a double roller the proportion can be 3 : 1.

The point arising with the length of the lever is the balance arc. As we know, the lever escapement is a detached escapement, and the aim is always to have the maximum detachment. By detachment we mean when the balance is running completely free of everything, obstruction or impulse of the escapement. Thus the maximum detachment is obtained with a double roller which has a lever and roller proportion of 3 : 1 [Fig. 148 (c)].

As we have seen, the modern club-tooth escapement has 10° pallets. With a double roller we can have 8° pallets and with a 3 : 1 lever and roller we can reduce the balance arc to 24°. With a single roller, on the other hand, we are unable to get less than 30° balance arc, and then only if everything is perfectly constructed The reason for this is that anything less than 30° intersection of the guard pin into the roller would be unsafe and would allow the lever to get out of position or " overbanked ".

Single and Double Roller

The terms " single roller " and " double roller " need explaining. With the single roller, the guard or safety action and the impulse

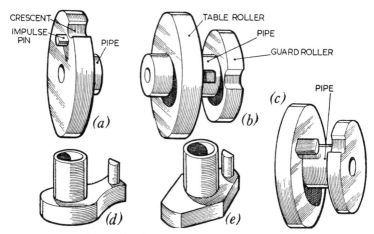

FIG. 149.—LEVER ESCAPEMENT ROLLERS.

(a) Ordinary single roller. (b) English double roller comprising separate table and guard rollers. (c) Swiss double roller all in one piece. (d) and (e) Types of table roller. Type (d) is used when guard roller is situated above table roller, to enable balance to be removed.

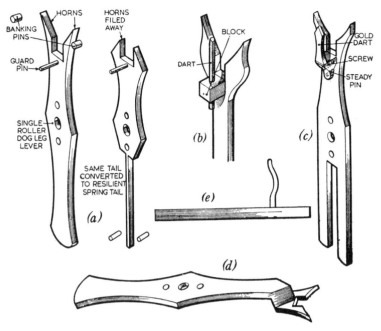

FIG. 150.—VARIOUS TYPES OF LEVER.

(a) English single-roller lever and showing conversion to resilient spring tail.
(b) Swiss double-roller lever, showing the dart.
(c) English double-roller lever, tuning-fork type.
(d) Single-roller with solid guard.
(e) Waltham type guard pin for single-roller.

pin are on one roller, actually two roller actions in one [Fig. 149 (a)]. The roller edge acts as the safety edge, or guard roller, and a small crescent is cut to permit the guard pin to pass when the impulse pin is in the lever notch.

The impulse pin is fitted inside the roller edge and just behind and perfectly central with the roller crescent [see Fig. 149 (a)]. So we have two circles, the roller edge and the pin circle, the pin circle obviously being the smaller to obtain a safe and sound hole to secure the pin.

" Dart" Guard and Guard Pin

The double roller has a table roller which holds the impulse pin and a separate roller for the guard or safety action [see Fig. 149 (b) and (d)]. The great advantage of the double roller is the fact of the guard roller being smaller ; a greater intersection can be obtained for the same amount of movement of the lever. The Swiss seldom use the single-roller escapement these days, because the double roller is easier to manufacture and will still function with a large margin of error, also the double-roller escapement is easier to alter after machining.

With the single-roller escapement, the guard pin is fitted into the lever just behind and central with the lever notch. It stands perpendicular to the lever [see Fig. 150 (a)].

With the double roller the guard is termed the " dart ". In all first-class watches the dart is screwed and steady-pinned to the lever, either above or below it. It is parallel to the lever and the extreme point is often just level with the mouth of the lever notch. In some cases it extends beyond to the level of the horns [see Fig. 150 (c)]. In English watches, the guard or dart is made in gold ; the Swiss generally use steel.

The Swiss often used a single-roller lever where the guard pin was solid with the lever. The lever was made solid, usually of steel, and was stepped down at the notch end, leaving the guard standing proud [see Fig. 150 (d)]. It had an advantage in that the guard pin could be closer to the notch, but this was outweighed by the great disadvantage that it tended to dig into the roller edge and stay there, thus stopping the watch, and once this happened a new lever was the only remedy.

The Lever Notch

The next item is, of course, the lever notch (see Fig. 151). There has been much controversy about this, but it has been proved in practice that the notch depth is very critical. It must be right whether it is a cheap or an expensive watch.

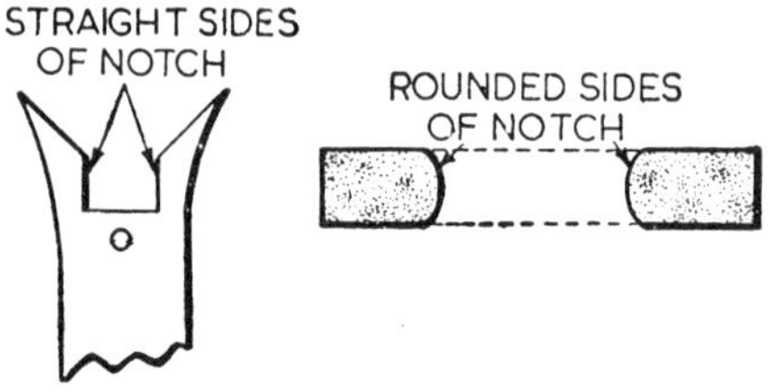

FIG. 151.—LEVER NOTCH.

Firstly, the impulse pin must fit the notch closely. The amount of freedom should be discernible only with a strong eyeglass. The notch should be smooth and the sides parallel to each other. The perpendicular sides should not be flat, however, but rounded so that only a small amount of metal is engaged by the impulse pin.

Tests for Notch Depth

The depth of the notch can be roughly tested by banking the lever to drop, that is, bending the banking pins (if not adjustable) and banking the lever so that the wheel tooth only just drops.

On turning the balance, the impulse pin should be felt scraping past the corner of the notch, but it must just scrape. If the impulse pin will not pass into the notch, the notch is too long and should be shortened. On the other hand, if the pin passes freely into the notch, the notch is too short or the depth is too shallow and must be corrected. Various opinions are held regarding this lever and roller depth and one is that if a watch loses in the short-arcs or in the hanging positions the notch should be shortened. The point is this, *never shorten a notch unless certain that it is too long.* A deep notch is bad practice, but a shallow notch is even worse and is the cause of many obscure troubles.

Another way to try a notch depth is to assemble the movement and put just a small amount of power on the train, then slowly lead the balance through the notch. As soon as the lever

FIG. 152.—CORRECT AND INCORRECT NOTCH ACTION.

reaches the centre, place a piece of thinly cut pegwood, or a fine pivot broach, against the side of the lever and, while still turning the balance, hold the lever back against the impulse pin. If the wheel tooth does not drop, the notch is shallow. If the wheel does drop, the notch is not shallow, but it may be deep.

When the wheel has dropped, notice if the impulse pin still continues to move the lever ; if it does, the notch is too long. A word of warning here ; do not be deceived by the guard pin or dart action.

Checking Dart Action

Sometimes the guard pin or dart is too deep and will carry the

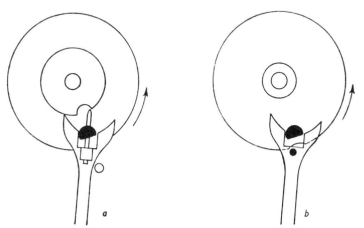

FIG. 153.—SHOWING POSITION OF IMPULSE PIN, DART AND GUARD PIN AS WHEEL TOOTH IS DROPPED WHEN ALL ACTIONS ARE CORRECT.
(a) Double roller 3 : 1. (b) Single roller, 3½ : 1.

lever over after the pin has left the notch. This can be checked by noticing the amount of shake between the roller edge and the banking pins. See how far the lever will move after the wheel has dropped. If the shake between the roller and the banking pins is

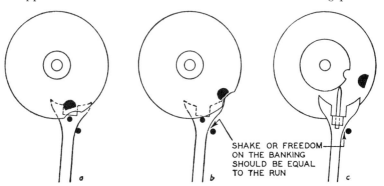

SHAKE OR FREEDOM
ON THE BANKING
SHOULD BE EQUAL
TO THE RUN

FIG. 154.—SHOWING POSITION OF GUARDS AND BANKING PINS, ALSO POSITION WHEN WHEEL TOOTH IS DROPPED.

(*a*) Single roller, showing the run to the banking. (*b*) Single roller, showing shake on the banking. *Note :* horns are unnecessary. (*c*) Double roller, showing lever horns as part of the guard action.

equal to the amount of run or the amount the lever moves after the wheel has dropped, everything will be in order. If, however, the run to the banking is greater than the shake between the roller edge and the banking pins, the guard or dart must be shortened.

Correcting a Deep Guard Action

In the case of a single roller, turning and repolishing the roller edge will correct the action, but the alteration must not be excessive as the guard may become unsafe. With a double roller, shorten the dart a little until this is corrected but be careful not to shorten it too much. Always remember to keep the run as little as possible ; it is all loss, also it interferes with the lever and impulse pin depth if excessive (see Fig. 152). The lever and roller action is the same for a ratchet-tooth as for a club-tooth escapement.

Another point which also applies to both escapements is always make certain that the wheel teeth are clear of the belly of the pallets, because this often causes a lot of trouble. If not visible, this can be traced by placing a small quantity of red dye on the 'scape-wheel teeth and setting the watch going. If there are traces of dye on the belly, it is obvious that the wheel will foul and must be cleared accordingly.

Angle of Impulse Planes on Wheel Teeth

A further consideration with the club-tooth escapement is the angle of the impulse planes on the wheel teeth. The impulse plane of the tooth must not be parallel to the impulse plane of the pallets at any time. At the beginning of the engagement only the locking corner of the wheel tooth must be in action.

As the wheel tooth gives its impulse to the pallets the corner runs along the plane to the end of the pallet, and then the corner of the pallet is engaged by the impulse plane of the tooth. The wheel is circular and as such has a circular path. Thus, as the wheel turns, the impulse plane on the teeth swings round and the heel of the tooth gets nearer to the pallet. If the impulse

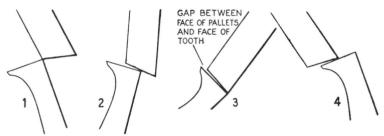

FIG. 155.—SHOWING HOW IMPULSE IS GIVEN.

1, 2 and 3. Corner of tooth pushing pallet stone. 4. Impulse plane of tooth continuing the push.

plane of the tooth were parallel to the impulse plane of the pallet, the impulse plane of the tooth would be completely lost and the action would be the same as a ratchet-tooth wheel with very thick teeth.

If a watch comes to hand with this fault, the vibration will be poor and sluggish and should be corrected. There are two ways in which it may be remedied and one depends on whether the locking is deep or shallow. If the locking is deep, the angle of the impulse planes of the pallets can be raised. If the locking is shallow, the only way is to replace the 'scape wheel and alter the angle of the impulse planes as well.

Correction by Stretching Pallet Arm

Sometimes the inside freedom of the wheel and pallet is close. In this case the pallets can be opened by stretching the inside of one arm of the pallets. If the wheel tooth runs parallel to the entrance impulse plane of the pallets, stretch the entrance pallet arm.

If the exit pallet angle is high, stretch the arm of the exit pallet. Great care is required to avoid breakage.

Replacing a Broken Dart

One of the troubles encountered with the modern wrist watch is in connection with the dart [Fig. 150 (b)]. The dart in these watches is in the form of a pin fitted through a hole in a block solid with the lever, and situated just behind the notch and on the underside of the lever. These darts or pins get broken off short and sometimes it is difficult to get them out for replacement. A good tool for removing the broken dart is a pair of old tweezers suitably modified as shown in Fig. 156.

File the points off until a strong part of the tweezers is reached. Tie the ends together and drill a small hole through one side near the front edge, but quite sound, and mark the other part of the tweezers with the drill to get the position right.

PIN OR
PUNCH

SLOT

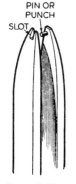

Next, where the tweezers have been marked, file a narrow slot to a short distance beyond that mark and through to the edge at the other end. Then fit a pin or punch through the drilled hole and taper the pin so that it is very thin, and shorten to about ·02 of an inch in length. The pin must be slightly smaller than the average dart and must pass through the slot in the tweezers. Finally, harden and temper the tweezers and smooth them. Shorten the ends to suit the average lever, and the tool is ready for use.

FIG. 156.—
TWEEZERS
FOR REMOV-
ING BROKEN
DART.

To use, place the slotted side of the tweezers on one side of the block of the lever and place the pin or punch on the other side against the remains of the dart. Then apply slight pressure and the broken dart will be pushed out.

Cutting a Club-Tooth Wheel

To cut a 'scape wheel for a club-tooth escapement, three cutters are required : one to cut the impulse planes, another to cut the locking face and a third for the heel of the teeth. It is necessary to have the dividing plate with a 360- or 90-division circle. (*Note*. If a 90-division plate is used, each division is 4°.)

The blank is turned from hard brass or steel and shellacked firmly on to the wax chuck. The blank must be exactly to size.

The impulse planes are cut first [Fig. 157 (*a*)]. The cutter is perfectly flat and square and must at first be set perfectly central. The cutter is led to the blank slowly until it makes a scratch. The dividing plate is then turned 18° which corresponds to the angle for the impulse planes of the teeth. The cutter is then moved out of central until it corresponds with the scratch previously made. We can now start cutting. The cutter is led in until the back of the cutter reaches the blank, then the whole 15 impulse planes are cut.

The Locking Face of the Tooth

Next remove the cutter and replace with the second [Fig. 157 (*b*)]. This cutter must be set at 24° corresponding to the angle of the locking face of the tooth.

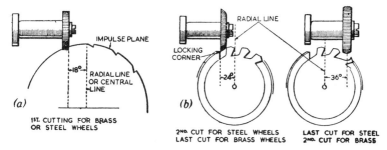

FIG. 157.—CUTTING A CLUB-TOOTH 'SCAPE WHEEL.

If we set the cutter to the same setting as the previous one and then move the cutter the extra 6° we shall be in order. We have to " pick up " the blank at the right place, so we lead the cutter in very lightly, make a mark and examine it. We then move the dividing plate a hole or 1° at a time, until the locking corner and the beginning of the impulse plane previously cut coincide, when we can proceed until all 15 locking faces have been cut. This second cutter also cuts part of the band of the wheel and, therefore, must be let in to the correct depth.

The Heel of the Tooth

The third cutter is used to cut the remaining band of the wheel, also the backs of the teeth and the heels. It must have a long blade as it has to cut to a greater depth to clear another tooth [see Fig. 157 (b)].

The cutter at present is set at 24° from the central position and we now have to take it 24° out of central the opposite way. Therefore we must move the dividing plate 48° in the opposite direction and set the cutter just to clear the head of the already partly cut tooth. This may mean another 12° or even 15° to be in position. The cutter has to be led in a long way to reach the back of the tooth, so lead it in until it starts to cut and then examine to see if the heel is " up " ; if not, lead in a little more until the heel is only just " up ". It is far better to leave a mere line than cut too much as this will make the wheel too small.

When the heel is right " up " carry on and cut the whole 15 teeth, and the wheel is finished as far as the teeth are concerned. Always remember that the heel controls the size or diameter of the wheel.

Making Swiss Lever and Pallets

To make a pair of pallets, or lever and pallets, is a very skilful job and one can give only an insight into the procedure, leaving the rest to the experience of the craftsman himself.

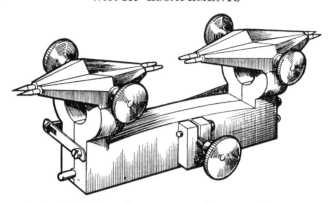

FIG. 158.—DEPTH TOOL USED FOR PLANTING WHEELS
AND PINIONS, ESCAPEMENTS, ETC.
The tool is also useful for examining separate actions.

First choose a piece of plate steel slightly thicker than the thickest
part of the pallets, and about three times as long as required and
about twice as wide.

Use a depth tool and set it carefully to the exact distance between
the 'scape and pallet holes (see Fig. 158). On the piece of steel
plate, draw a straight line through the centre and continue it the
whole length of the steel. Drill a very fine hole perfectly upright
in about the centre of this line (Fig. 159).

With the depth tool, mark off on this same line the distance
apart of the 'scape and pallet holes and, where it crosses the line,
drill another small hole, also perfectly upright. Next measure
the distance that the pallet and balance staff holes are apart and
mark it off on the piece of steel on the opposite end to the 'scape
and pallet distance. Again drill a hole. All three holes will now
be in a perfectly straight line, which they must be if everything
is to be correct at the start.

Next the hole representing the 'scape hole must be broached
open to allow the 'scape pinion or pinion arbor to go through
it without shake. Place the 'scape wheel in such a position that
the heel of the tooth rests precisely on the line A. We will naturally
take it for granted that the wheel turns clockwise.

The heel of the next tooth, in an anti-clockwise direction, will
give the position of the dropping-off corner of the entrance pallet, B.
Hold the wheel and steel plate firmly and indicate the position with
a small but distinct mark—a dot will do. Then mark where the
locking corner of the next tooth in a clockwise direction rests,
C, making sure that the 'scape wheel does not alter its position
in the process. This will give the position of the hook or exit
pallet locking face.

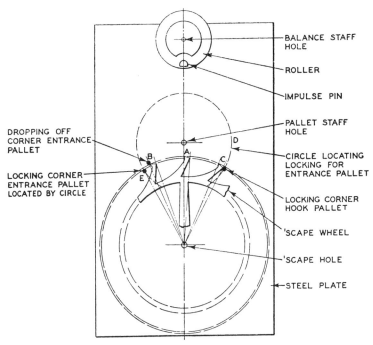

FIG. 159.—PROCEDURE FOR MAKING CLUB-TOOTH LEVER AND PALLETS TO
DEPTH (1).

Position of Pallet Stones

Next measure the distance between the pallet-staff hole and
the mark made for the exit pallet locking face, allowing a little less
for freedom, and then scribe a full circle, D. This circle will
pass through the locking corner of the entrance pallet. Thus
both locking corners will be on the same circle, E. Place the
'scape wheel so that the locking corner of the tooth rests on this
circle on the entrance pallet side, E (Fig. 160).

Mark with a small dot where the heel of the third tooth in a
clockwise direction rests, F (Fig. 160). This will indicate the position
of the dropping-off corner of the hook pallet, but does not allow
for freedom and we must make another small mark slightly anti-
clockwise to allow for this. These marks give the width of the
pallet ston s and their relative positions. We now obtain the
position of the lever notch before proceeding any further.

Lever Notch Position

It is easier if the roller is taken off the balance staff and the
impulse pin is removed (Fig. 159). The roller is mounted on a

172

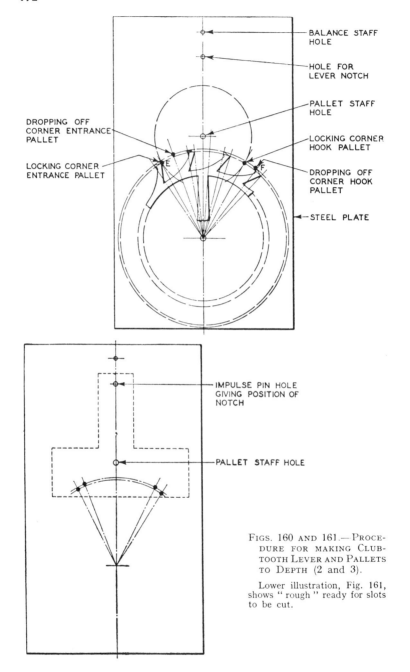

BALANCE STAFF HOLE

HOLE FOR LEVER NOTCH

PALLET STAFF HOLE

DROPPING OFF CORNER ENTRANCE PALLET

LOCKING CORNER ENTRANCE PALLET

LOCKING CORNER HOOK PALLET

DROPPING OFF CORNER HOOK PALLET

STEEL PLATE

IMPULSE PIN HOLE GIVING POSITION OF NOTCH

PALLET STAFF HOLE

FIGS. 160 AND 161.— PROCE-
DURE FOR MAKING CLUB-
TOOTH LEVER AND PALLETS
TO DEPTH (2 and 3).

Lower illustration, Fig. 161,
shows " rough " ready for slots
to be cut.

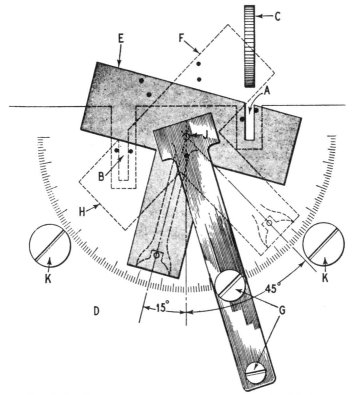

FIG. 162.—PROCEDURE FOR MAKING CLUB-TOOTH LEVER AND
PALLETS TO DEPTH (4).

Cutting the slots for the pallet stones.
A. Entrance pallet slot. B. Exit or hook pallet slot. C. Saw in lathe for
cutting entrance pallet slot. D. Brass plate with degree lines. E. Pallets in
1st position. F. Pallets in 2nd position. G. Clamp fixing screws. H. Dotted
lines showing how lever can be formed. J. Stud on which to rest pallet-staff hole.
K. Screws for holding plate on to slide rest of lathe.

small arbor and this arbor is let through the hole drilled in the
plate, marking the balance-staff hole. The impulse-pin hole is
placed on the line facing the pallet hole (Fig. 159). The position
is then marked and a small hole, a little smaller than the impulse
pin, is drilled through the plate. It now remains to cut the slots
for the stones.

Cutting Slots for the Stones

Remove the 'scape wheel and file away the excess metal, leaving
our various marks clear (Fig. 161). Choose a piece of brass plate and
drill a small hole, *J* (Fig. 162), about the size of a pallet staff, near
the centre of the metal and about ¼ inch from the edge. Scribe a

1

74 WATCH ESCAPEMENTS

line at right angles to the edge of the brass plate and passing through the drilled hole, *J*. Then with a protractor, mark off from the line 15° on the left-hand side looking from the back of the plate towards the hole, and mark off 45° on the other side. These marks must be made accurately. Scribe a line joining up the 15° and the 45° marks to the drilled hole.

Next fix an arbor through the hole in the brass plate and fit the steel plate or rough pallets tightly on this arbor. Place the hole drilled for the lever notch on the 15° line, and hold the plate firmly by means of the clamp and the two shouldered screws, *G*.

Use of Slitting Saw

Set a slitting saw in the lathe and fix the brass plate on to the slide rest. The gauge of the slitting saw should be equivalent to the thickness of the pallet stones, and we obtain this measurement from the markings on the steel plate.

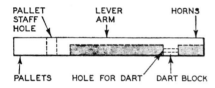

Fig. 163.—Procedure for making Club-tooth Lever and Pallets to Depth (5). Filing up lever and pallets after stones have been fitted.

Adjust the slide rest to bring the marks on the steel plate into position and cut a slot ; do not cut this slot too deeply at first.

Unclamp the steel plate. Place the hole drilled for the lever notch on the 45° line and clamp the plate firmly as before. Again adjust the slide rest until the marks coincide with the saw and then cut another slot.

Finishing the Lever and Pallets

Unclamp the steel plate once more and place the pallet stones in position. Set the depth tool to the distance between the 'scape and pallet holes and test the rough lever to see if it is in order. The slots may have to be cut deeper, and one or two other alterations may have to be made, although it should be necessary only to file up to shape, cut or file the lever notch and the horns.

Cut away the lever arm, as shown in Fig. 163, so that a block is left to take the guard pin, and thin the fork to the correct thickness. Then drill a small hole in the block for the dart. Finally, finish the pallets according to quality.

The Ratchet-Tooth Lever Escapement

As the ratchet-tooth escapement is similar in principle to the club-tooth type, it is only necessary to describe the differences.

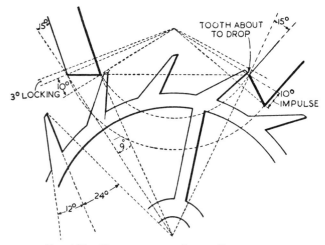

FIG. 164.—RATCHET-TOOTH LEVER ESCAPEMENT.
Showing necessary inside shake or freedom.

Most ratchet-tooth escapements have invisible stones. In other words, the steels are the pallets before they are jewelled. The steels are slotted, the stones being fitted in and then ground flush with the steelwork.

The ratchet-tooth escapement has all the impulse on the pallets and none at all on the wheel teeth. The teeth are different in shape, being almost pointed (see Fig. 164). The locking faces of the wheel teeth are cut back 24°, the same as the club-tooth wheel, but in some of the older escapements the wheel teeth are cut back

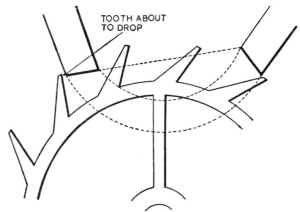

FIG. 165.—RATCHET-TOOTH LEVER ESCAPEMENT.
Showing necessary outside shake or freedom.

only 20°, the idea being to reduce losses by decreasing the amount necessary for drop. The objection to this arrangement, however, is the difficulty of obtaining proper draw on the exit pallet.

Freedoms

The disadvantage of the ratchet-tooth escapement is that the wheel must have drop for freedom, but it has to have excessive drop. In theory with 2° locking there is 2° drop, but it works out differently in practice. We have 3° locking in practice and we must have 3° drop. When the 'scape wheel is locked it has to recoil to unlock and the pallet has to move away from the wheel. At the same time, the other pallet moves into or towards the wheel. Therefore we have two actions : the wheel, by its recoil, moving nearer to the pallet and the pallet, in unlocking, also moving nearer to the wheel.

The ratchet-tooth owing to its shape, however, has no space into which the pallet can move and, therefore, if the drop is insufficient the corner of the pallet fouls the back of the tooth. It is this fact which gives the club-tooth escapement its superiority. If the drawings of these two escapements are studied these points will be obvious. When the entrance pallet is unlocking, the exit pallet fouls the wheel tooth, and vice versa.

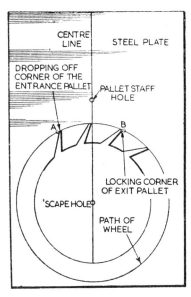

FIG. 166.—MAKING RATCHET-TOOTH PALLETS TO DEPTH (1).

Making Ratchet-Tooth Pallets

The procedure for making pallets for the ratchet-tooth escapement is very different from that just described. The pallets are made to work as they are, unlike the Swiss style of lever and pallets in one piece where the stones are adjustable for depth and are a separate unit.

The first operation is the same, except that we need not, of course, consider the position of the balance staff. The steel plate is drilled with holes for the 'scape wheel and pallet staff (see Fig. 166). Draw a line joining 'scape and pallet holes, passing through the dead centre of both and continuing beyond the pallet hole.

Marking the Steel Plate

Pallets for the ratchet-tooth escapement embrace three teeth and four teeth span the pallets. If we place the 'scape wheel so that one tooth rests on the line joining the pallet and 'scape holes, the next tooth, in an anti-clockwise direction, will denote the line of the dropping-off corner of the entrance pallet, *A*. The tooth on the opposite side will denote the locking point of the exit pallet, *B*. Then mark where these teeth lie on the path of the 'scape wheel by means of two dots.

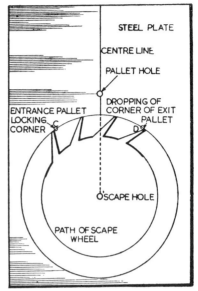

FIG. 167.—MAKING RATCHET-TOOTH PALLETS TO DEPTH (2).

Next move the wheel a distance corresponding to half of the space between two teeth. This distance can be measured with the dividers on another part of the circle of the 'scape wheel. Make certain that the wheel is moved exactly half the space. Between the two marks made previously are two teeth. Make a dot on the path of the 'scape wheel where the next tooth in an anti-clockwise direction lies (see Fig. 167), also make a dot where the next tooth in the opposite direction rests, *D*.

There should be four teeth outside these last two dots and these marks denote the locking corner of the entrance pallet and the dropping-off corner of the exit pallet. Draw a line carefully from each of these four dots joining up with the 'scape hole on the steel plate and continue the lines beyond the marks in the path of the 'scape wheel (see Fig. 168). We now have two pairs of lines joining up with the 'scape hole.

Filing Steel Plate to Shape

Next remove the 'scape wheel. Then file away the metal between the two inside dots retaining the lines and dots, but just clearing the circle marking the path of the 'scape wheel inside the pallet nibs, and leave the pallet hole sound. A rectangular shape can be filed out providing the lines and dots are visible. File away the metal on which the 'scape wheel was resting, but leave sufficient metal where the dots are marked, because the nibs protrude into the path of the 'scape-wheel teeth. Cut away all the excess metal, leaving a tail at the back to enable the correct angles to be obtained.

Angle Plates

To obtain the correct angles, an angle plate can be devised. This takes only a few minutes to make and can be made either in a wheel-cutting machine or by hand using a protractor, provided that the angles are correct.

If we place the rough pallets on the plate, as shown in Fig. 169, with the pallet staff hole on the stud, with the tail of the lever resting along the 15° line and the line on the pallets coinciding with the line on the plate, we can obtain the angle of the locking face of the entrance pallet.

Next we consider point A, which is the locking corner of the entrance pallet. If a line is drawn passing exactly through

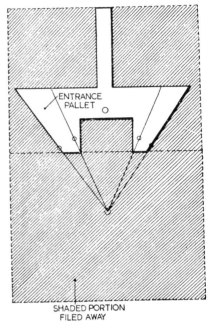

FIG. 168.—MAKING RATCHET-TOOTH PALLETS TO DEPTH (3).

Roughly shaping the pallets.

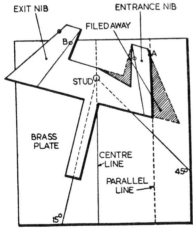

FIG. 169.—MAKING RATCHET-TOOTH PALLETS TO DEPTH (4).

Shaping the locking face of the entrance pallet or nib.

this point and parallel with the centre line of the angle, it will give the correct angle including draw. The pallets can then be filed to shape, removing the shaded portion as shown in Fig. 169. If we move the tail of the pallets to the 45° line, this will give the correct angle of the exit pallet locking face.

By the same procedure, if a line is drawn through point B (Fig. 170), and again parallel to the centre line on the angle plate, it will give the correct locking angle including draw. The excess metal can be filed away, as indicated by the shading in Fig. 170, leaving the nibs long, as before, and, of course, retaining the tail.

Impulse Angles

We can now deal with the impulse planes and great care must be taken with this last operation. Another angle plate is required, but this can be made quite simply (see Fig. 171).

The stud in the centre of the plate must fit the pallet hole closely. Place the rough pallets on the stud, making sure that they are the right way up, with the centre line on the pallets coinciding with the centre line on the angle plate. Make a mark on the

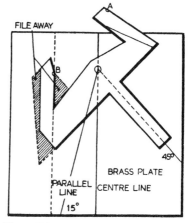

FIG. 170.—MAKING RATCHET-TOOTH PALLETS TO DEPTH (5).

Shaping the locking face of the exit pallet or nib.

plate where point *A* rests and make another mark where point *C* rests.

Move the tail of the pallets until the centre line coincides exactly with the line showing 10° on the angle plate. *A* will now be *A2* and *C* will be *C2*. It is *A2* and *C* which we now have to consider, so make a mark where *A2* lies on the plate and, of course, there is already a mark at *C*. Take the pallets off the plate and draw a straight line on the angle plate joining *A2* and *C*. Draw this line carefully. Then file away the nib until the end coincides with the line *A2C*, with the centre line of the pallets coinciding with the 10° line on the angle plate. When this operation has been completed, put the pallets back on the plate, with the tail centre line coinciding with the centre line on the angle plate.

Make a mark where points *B* and *D* lie on the angle

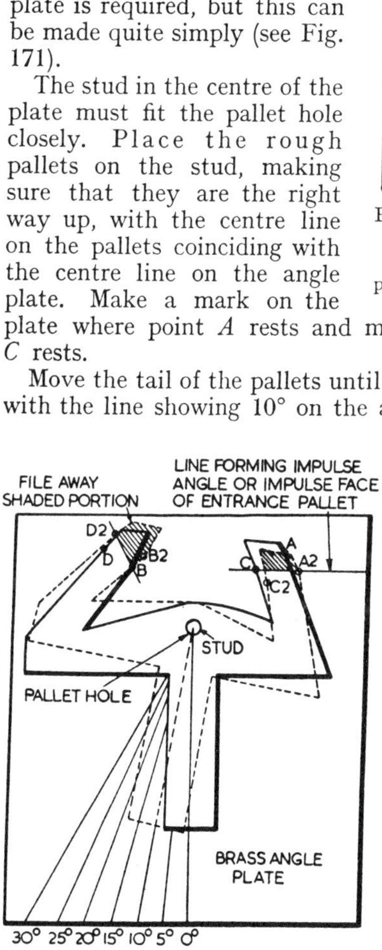

FIG. 171.—MAKING RATCHET-TOOTH PALLETS TO DEPTH (6).

Filing the impulse planes.

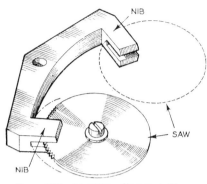

FIG. 172.—MAKING RATCHET-TOOTH
PALLETS TO DEPTH (7).

Slotting the pallet steels to take jewel slips. Each nib is slotted separately with saw in a different position relatively.

plate. Again move the pallets until the centre line coincides with the 10° line on the angle plate.

Next make a mark on the angle plate where D lies at $D2$. Remove the pallets and draw a straight line joining B and $D2$. File the exit nib at the end until it coincides with the line $BD2$, with the line on the tail coinciding with the 10° line on the angle plate. This is the correct impulse angle of the exit pallet.

Jewelling the Pallets

File up to shape at the back, remove the tail and generally make symmetrical, and the pallets are ready for jewelling.

There is, of course, no freedom anywhere and also no locking. The pallets are, however, 12° in length, so we can file the locking faces of both entrance and exit pallets until they are free. This will give 3° locking. Great care must be taken to keep the angles exactly as they are, otherwise the pallets will be useless. The pallets should now be mounted on a true arbor and put up in the depth tool with the 'scape wheel. The depth tool must be set at the correct distance of centres of the 'scape and pallet holes.

The pallets are jewelled by cutting slots horizontally in the nibs and then fitting slips of ruby or sapphire firmly in place with shellac. The stones are then ground flush with the steels.

Club-tooth pallets of this type can be made in exactly the same way. All these operations are, of course, for an individual job and the procedure is very different for mass production.

Making a Roller to Depth

A word about making a lever and roller may not be out of place, as these parts do get lost and sometimes they are spoiled by indifferent workmen. A roller is easy to make if the dimensions are known, but if not it is difficult. (With any escapements which the author made, he found it advisable always to keep a note of the length of the lever and the radius of the pin circle of the roller.)

The roller is roughed out from silver-steel rod, a piece being chosen slightly larger than required. If the lever is placed in position and the distance between the balance-staff hole and the lever is noted, this will give an idea of the size.

Place the rod in the lathe and drill a hole in the rod to fit the balance sta,ff. Then turn the pipe of the roller, if it has one, and with a parting tool cut it off to the approximate length to suit the roller. Make an arbor on which to turn the roller and be sure it is true. Open the banking pins to give the lever plenty of play. Fit the rough roller on to the balance staff and see if it is in the correct position. Make any necessary adjustments and also turn the roller to the correct diameter to give the required freedom of the guard pin with the banking pins wide.

Drill a small hole about half the size of the lever notch and fit a steel or brass pin tightly in the hole. Fit the roller on the staff and place them in the frame with the lever. Bring the balance round and notice where the pin engages the notch ; if this cannot be seen, apply red dye on the pin to make a mark on the notch where it engages. If only a little too deep, the hole can be filed back slightly to correct it ; but if a lot too deep, another rough roller must be made. If the depth of the pin and notch is shallow but only slightly so, the hole can be filed outwards, but if a lot too shallow, again another roller will be required.

Shaping the Pin Hole

When the pin engages correctly, broach the hole in the roller to take the correct size of impulse or ruby pin. As it is now the hole is round, but it requires to be D-shaped. To alter the shape of the hole, a template can be made from a piece of hardened and tempered steel rod shaped to suit the pin ; an old pallet staff filed flat on one side will answer the purpose.

Push the template into the pin hole with the flat side to the front of the roller and make sure it is tight. Tap the front of the roller with the pane of the hammer and force the front of the roller against the template until the hole is the right shape. Remove the template and try the pin in the hole to see that it fits properly. The author uses a pin-hole tool for carrying out this job (see Fig. 173).

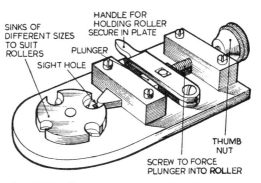

SINKS OF DIFFERENT SIZES TO SUIT ROLLERS

SIGHT HOLE

PLUNGER

HANDLE FOR HOLDING ROLLER SECURE IN PLATE

THUMB NUT

SCREW TO FORCE PLUNGER INTO ROLLER

Fig. 173.—Tool for shaping Pin Hole and partly making the Crescent.

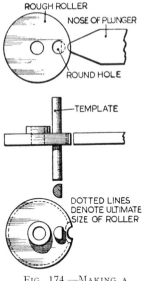

FIG. 174.—MAKING A
ROLLER.

Shaping the pin hole for
single or double rollers.

Making the Roller Crescent

Next file the crescent to remove the hammer marks, if a hammer has been used for shaping the hole. Then harden the roller and temper to a dark blue colour. Place the roller on a true arbor and clean the back with oilstone dust until clean and smooth.

Bank the lever to drop by bending the banking pins back, so that the 'scape-wheel teeth will just drop as the lever reaches the banking pins.

Fit the roller on to the balance staff and then place into the frame to see if the roller is correct for size. The roller should be just tight against the guard pin, with the lever in its present position ; if not correct, turn the edge of the roller on a true arbor until the roller is the right size.

Polishing Roller Edge and the Crescent

Polish the edge so that it is flat and square. The best way of polishing is in the turns, using a runner with a guide screw, and a zinc polisher and diamantine (see Fig. 175).

Next polish the crescent. This can be carried out by hand, holding the roller in the thumb and finger and taking care not to slip, otherwise the already polished edge will be spoilt. A better method is to use a roller crescent tool, as the crescent can be kept flat and there is no risk of slipping (see Fig. 176). After the crescent has been polished, the flat of the roller is polished on a zinc block with diamantine.

Finally, when polishing has been completed satisfactorily, carry out the usual tests to see that all is in order.

Fixing the Impulse Pin

Fixing the impulse pin in the roller is a simple job if carried out in the right way. A suitable tool, which can be made quite simply for this purpose, is shown in Fig. 177.

A piece of copper wire about 16 gauge and $2\frac{1}{2}$

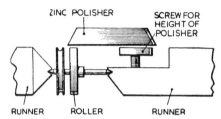

FIG. 175.—RUNNER FOR POLISHING ROLLER
EDGE FLAT.

inches in length is filed to a long gradual taper. A large brass block or ferrule is fitted tightly on to the tapered wire about $\frac{3}{4}$ inch from the thinner end.

On the other end a square is filed on which to fit a handle, this being necessary as the tool will be made hot. The roller is placed on the end of the tapered wire and the block is heated

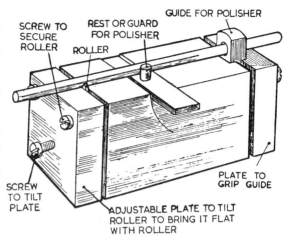

FIG. 176.—TOOL FOR POLISHING ROLLER CRESCENT OF SINGLE OR DOUBLE ROLLERS.

until shellac will melt at that end. The impulse pin is placed in position in the roller. A very small quantity of shellac is applied to the pin, and while still liquid the impulse pin is pushed back and forth in the pin hole to work the shellac through. The pin is then fixed in its correct position and the block is allowed to cool. The pin should then be firm and if the correct amount of shellac has been used it will be a clean job.

Securing Loose Impulse Pin without Removing Roller

Sometimes a roller is extremely firm on the balance staff and the impulse pin is loose. A tool made in a similar way can be used with safety. Instead of tapering the wire, it is hammered flat and thin. A slot is cut in the flattened part just wide enough to pass across the average roller arbor of a balance staff. The tool is placed between the balance and the roller from the opposite side to the impulse pin. The block is warmed and the heat passing to the roller melts the shellac.

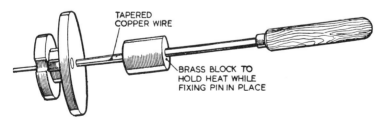

FIG. 177.—TOOL FOR FIXING IMPULSE OR RUBY PINS.

The pin can be fixed in position without any trouble and there should be no risk of blueing the balance or staff in the process.

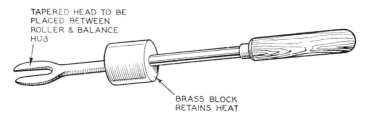

FIG. 178.—TOOL FOR SECURING IMPULSE PIN WHEN ROLLER IS TOO TIGHT TO BE REMOVED WITH SAFETY.

The tool must be removed from the flame as soon as it is hot enough to melt the shellac : a little applied near the end will soon show when melted and can be cleaned off before the tool is used.

Making a Lever to Depth

Making the lever, also without measurements, is quite an undertaking. First take the distance of centres, of the balance and pallet holes in a depth tool. Choose a piece of lever steel or a piece of flat steel suitable for the job. File a V at one end and then in the centre of it, cut or file a notch to fit the existing impulse pin (see Fig. 179). Then drill a small hole central with the notch to take the guard pin. Do not make too large a hole, about ·006 inch will be large enough.

Next make a dot on the lever to indicate the approximate position of the pallet-staff hole. Take the roller off the balance staff, mount the roller on an arbor and then place it in one side of the depth tool. Reverse one of the runners on the other side of the depth tool. Place the rough lever between the two runners, with the pointed runner sticking into the dot on the lever. Press the two runners together fairly hard to hold the lever in place. Try the depth and, if too deep, make another dot nearer the front ; if too shallow, make a dot nearer the back and so on until it is correct. Then drill the pallet-staff hole.

Fit the rough lever on to the pallets and pallet staff, fix the roller on to the balance staff and place them all in the frame to check that the lever is correct. Open the banking pins wide to do this. Then put the lever in angle, hold the lever and pallets in a pair of suitable tongs and carefully drill the pin holes.

File the front of the lever to the correct width to suit the banking pins when they are perfectly straight. Then file the rest of the lever to shape and near poise. Harden the lever, clean it and temper to a dark blue colour.

Polishing the Lever

Next polish the horns. The horns of the lever in a single-roller escapement serve no useful purpose and are merely ornamental, but they are always retained.

After the horns have been polished, polish the lever notch and do not forget that the acting sides are rounded. The edges of the lever are polished in a swing tool. If the edges are rounded, the swing tool is moved backwards and forwards when polishing. A bell metal polisher shaped to the lever is used with diamantine. The tail is polished by hand. It is smoothed with a fine emery buff, then rubbed with wet diamantine on a piece of pegwood.

The top and bottom flat surfaces of the lever are polished by hand, using a flat zinc polisher and diamantine. The lever is held on a piece of flat willow wood held firmly in the vice.

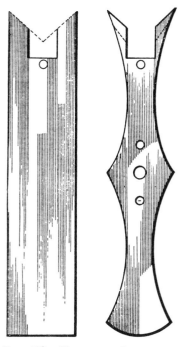

FIG. 179.—MAKING A LEVER TO DEPTH WHEN A SEPARATE UNIT.

A great deal of pressure is needed to obtain a good polish.

The brass pins are made to fit the lever and pallets tightly. The ends of the pins are rounded and burnished. The guard pin is treated in the same way. All three pins must be tight.

Tool for Putting Lever in Angle

Make sure the lever is in angle when it is pinned up. If out of angle it can be corrected in a special tool which can be made in a few minutes (see Fig. 180). A light tap on a piece of brass rested on the tail of the lever will ease the lever into its correct position.

To test a lever in angle, lead the balance round until the tooth of the 'scape wheel drops. Then with a sharpened piece of pegwood hold the lever against the impulse pin while still moving the balance. If the lever moves, notice the amount of movement carefully.

Reverse the direction of the balance, holding the lever against the impulse pin and see how far the lever moves after the wheel tooth has dropped. If there is equal movement on each side

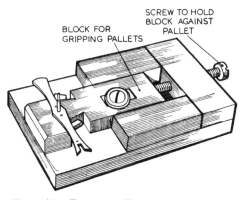

FIG. 180.—TOOL FOR PUTTING A LEVER IN ANGLE WHEN A SEPARATE UNIT.

the lever is in angle. On the other hand, if the lever moves *after* the wheel has dropped, and on the other side the lever drops back on to the roller the lever is out of angle.

Bending the Lever

If the lever and pallets are all in one piece the lever must be bent towards the direction in which it moves after the wheel tooth has dropped, or in the direction in which it falls also after the wheel has dropped. The lever can be bent by means of pliers shaped as shown in Fig. 181.

In the case of a separate lever, the pallets are held firmly in the tool described previously, a brass or ivory punch is placed against the tail of the lever and tapped lightly with a hammer. This will bend the pins very slightly and give the lever the required movement. The same rule applies as regards the direction in which the lever is moved.

FIG. 181.—NOSE OF BENDING PLIERS.

Resilient Levers and Escapements

The resilient type is generally a standard form of escapement with certain modifications, usually consisting of a special type of 'scape wheel or a lever with horns which are parts of a spring.

The most successful was undoubtedly the spring tail type made by Messrs. E. Dent & Co., Ltd. This was an ordinary lever escapement without any additions whatever. The lever itself was the whole secret.

The horns of the lever were polished away to form inclined planes from the outside of the lever leading up to the mouth of the notch [see Fig. 150 (*a*)]. The banking pins were at the tail of the lever and the tail of the lever was thinned almost to the thickness of a chronometer detent spring. The belly of the pallets was provided with slightly more clearance to allow the pallets to move towards the 'scape wheel more than usual. Thus, if the watch were over-banked, the impulse pin would run up the inclined plane, the spring tail would give and the impulse pin would drop into the notch.

Another type, made by Nicole Neilson's, had an ordinary ratchet-tooth escapement, but the wheel teeth had little steps acting as the bankings or substituting the banking pins (Fig. 182).

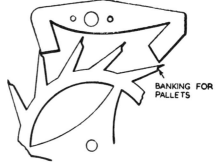

FIG. 182.—RESILIENT LEVER WHEEL AND PALLETS BY NICOLE NEILSON'S.

There are no banking pins on the lever.

When the watch was over-banked the pin running up the inclined plane would force the lever backwards. The corner of the pallet would over-run the step and allow the lever to move far enough for the impulse pin to drop into the notch.

Cole's resilient was not so popular because the wheel, which was something like a club-tooth wheel, had always to be specially cut ; also it had a great tendency to set.

Savage's Two-Pin Escapement

Another type of lever escapement which we must mention is Savage's two-pin escapement. By this we do not mean two pins in place of an impulse pin. The two pins in a two-pin escapement are not impulse pins at all, but are the unlocking pins. The impulse pin is the guard pin which performs two functions : firstly as the guard pin and secondly to give impulse to a small square notch in the roller (see Fig. 183). This square notch replaces the passing crescent in an ordinary single-roller escapement.

The whole idea was to get the first engagement of impulse on the line of centres so as to eliminate engaging friction. The pallets were 15° instead of the usual 10°.

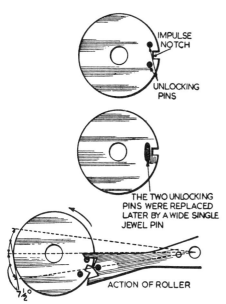

FIG. 183.—SAVAGE'S TWO-PIN ESCAPEMENT.

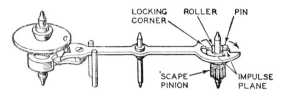

FIG. 184.—SINGLE-
PIN LEVER ES-
CAPEMENT.

Impulse is de-
livered by a roller
and pin to the tail of
the lever.

It was a good escapement and gave a good vibration to the balance, but unless very well made it could cause trouble.

Roller instead of 'Scape Wheel

A further interesting type of lever escapement had a roller with a ruby pin substituted for the 'scape wheel (see Fig. 184).

The pallets were in the tail of the lever, and it was almost impossible to keep the pin and the pallets lubricated, with the result that they required attention about every three months.

Pin-Pallet Lever Escapement

The pin pallet is another form of lever escapement used for cheap watches and alarm clocks ; but it has little to recommend it except cheapness of production.

In this escapement the impulse is all on the wheel and very little, if any at all, on the pins (see Fig. 185). Everything depends upon the wheel teeth. If the angle of draw is wrong the watch will continually fail to lock, although the escapement may be deep.

If the wheel teeth get worn, which they often do, a new wheel, if obtainable, is the only remedy. If a wheel is unobtainable it is better to scrap the article rather than waste time and money on it. If the pins in the pallets are worn they can be replaced, but always replace with the right size of pins or trouble will ensue.

Another trouble is oil, more so when the bankings are the band of the wheel and not pins. The oil runs away from the pallet pins and wheel teeth, spreads, and leaves the pins and wheel quite dry.

The Rack Lever

A form of lever es-capement sometimes encountered is the rack

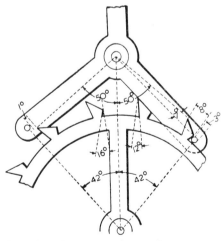

FIG. 185.—PIN-PALLET LEVER ESCAPEMENT.

lever. The watches are usually very old and have fusee keywind full-plate movements. The balance staff is an ordinary train pinion usually of 6 or 7 leaves. The rack lever is pinned to the pallets

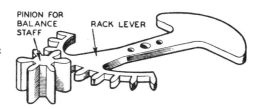

FIG. 186.—RACK LEVER ESCAPEMENT.

PINION FOR BALANCE STAFF RACK LEVER

in the ordinary way. The objection to this type is the fact that it is never detached and, of course, the amount of wear is more than with any other form of escapement.

Some had 'scape wheels of 30 teeth, about twice the size of the ordinary 'scape wheel, and all had ratchet-shaped teeth. This

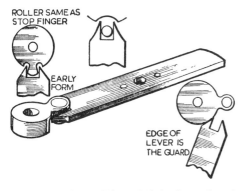

ROLLER SAME AS STOP FINGER

EARLY FORM

EDGE OF LEVER IS THE GUARD

FIG. 187.—CLUB ROLLER— AN EARLY FORM OF LEVER ESCAPEMENT.

particular form (Fig. 186) had no fourth wheel, only the centre, third and 'scape wheels.

A number of watches were made, but the escapement had only a short life. The repairer should find no difficulty with a rack lever, providing the principle of the lever escapement is understood.

THE DUPLEX ESCAPEMENT

The duplex was a very popular escapement at one time, but owing to its expense lost popularity with the trade. If a watch with a duplex escapement were accidentally dropped it often meant that a new balance staff and a new ruby roller were required, and possibly a 'scape wheel and pinion as well. Nevertheless, the duplex escapement is capable of a very good performance, and although now obsolete is quite often encountered by repairers.

The 'scape wheel was provided with two sets of teeth, one horizontal and the other perpendicular (see Fig. 188). The horizontal teeth were pointed with one side radial, and these acted as the locking teeth. The vertical or perpendicular teeth were triangular in shape and gave the impulse to the impulse roller on the balance staff. The only objection was oil on the locking teeth and ruby roller. The ruby roller or locking roller was fitted on the balance staff and kept in position with shellac. It had a slot cut to permit the passing of the wheel to give impulse.

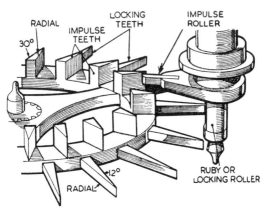

Fig. 188.—DUPLEX ESCAPEMENT.

Most duplex 'scape wheels had 15 teeth, which was the best arrangement, but some had 12 teeth and were not a success. The impulse teeth, *which must never be oiled*, get badly worn at times so that they miss the impulse pallet altogether and thus fail to give any impulse and the watch stops. Sometimes this can be remedied by altering the position of the wheel on the pallet or by turning the pallet in the same direction as it receives impulse or, in other words, by giving a little more drop to the wheel teeth.

The duplex, like the chronometer, is a single-beat escapement, that is it receives impulse only on one side or in one direction. The reverse vibration merely unlocks the wheel and thus it is able to set very readily. It has to be perfectly in beat, otherwise it will be constantly stopping.

Putting Duplex Escapement in Beat

To put a duplex in beat the same rules apply as in a chronometer. From the position of rest lead the balance round until the locking tooth drops into the slot in the ruby roller, release the balance and the watch should start off. Then bring the balance to rest and lead it round once more in the opposite direction until the impulse tooth drops off the impulse pallet. Again release the balance and the watch should start off.

Under no circumstances must the balance be removed while there is any power on the 'scape wheel. The train must be either firmly wedged or the mainspring let down. With a fusee watch do not forget that there is power in the maintaining spring and this must always be let down. If there is power and the balance is removed, damage will result to the 'scape wheel, making a new one necessary ; if a jewelled impulse roller, a new jewel will be required as well because the 'scape wheel is released and rushes down.

Repairs to Duplex Escapement

The duplex is a difficult escapement to repair. The jewel-holes must always be a close fit on the pivots, and the endshakes of the balance staff and 'scape pinion must also be close.

The intersection of the impulse teeth and impulse pallet is very small and the smallest amount of wear on the teeth will let the teeth miss the pallet. A new wheel is the best remedy, although a duplex wheel is expensive as it has to be cut specially for the job. It can be avoided, however, by fitting two wheels in the following manner.

If the locking teeth are in order the impulse teeth can be turned away and, in their place, a ratchet-tooth 'scape wheel can be substituted and mounted on top of the locking wheel. It has to be correctly positioned, however, and must be the same size as the circle of the old teeth. The ratchet-tooth wheel can be lightened by sinking out the middle. The author has carried out this repair successfully on many occasions.

Sometimes, especially with an English watch, the jewelling can be brought nearer to avoid the wear in the 'scape-wheel teeth. This is done by scraping the 'scape hole in the plate, a little on the side nearest to the balance hole, and then burnishing the pipe of the 'scape jewel-hole to enlarge it until it fits the enlarged hole in the plate. This will place the 'scape wheel slightly nearer to the balance staff and will often overcome the trouble.

Sometimes when this is carried out the impulse pallet will foul the tooth of the wheel on its return vibration. A slight polishing of the impulse pallet will clear it. This fouling is occasionally caused by having a ruby roller too large, and if a smaller one can be fitted without the wheel mislocking it is a distinct advantage.

Cutting a Duplex 'Scape Wheel

The duplex 'scape wheel is a difficult wheel to cut. The blank is made from hard plate brass and is turned first to the full diameter of the locking teeth. It is then placed in a true step chuck and turned out with the slide rest, leaving the band on which the upright or impulse teeth are cut. This band must be the same height and diameter as the old one before it was worn.

Four cutters are required for the wheel : two for cutting the locking teeth and two for the impulse teeth. A dividing plate with 30 or a multiple of 30 is required.

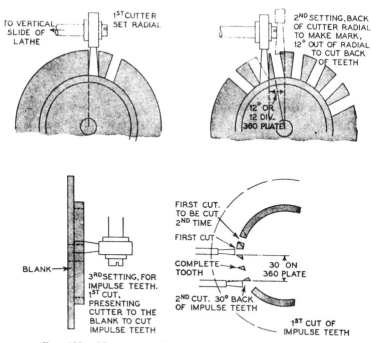

FIG. 189.—METHOD OF CUTTING A DUPLEX 'SCAPE WHEEL.

Setting up the Cutters

The locking teeth are cut first. The first cutter is radial and cuts the locking face and half the space (see Fig. 189).

The second cutter is 12° off the radial as the backs of the locking teeth are at an angle of 12° to the locking face. This cutter cuts the back of the tooth and half the space. It is not advisable to cut all the metal away at once ; it is far better to take two or three cuts, even if it does take a little longer.

The impulse teeth are radial at the front, and the back is 30° to the front of the tooth or the radial. These teeth can be cut with one cutter by two separate settings, but it is quicker with two unless a cutter has to be made specially for the job.

The wheel is crossed out to leave it as light as possible. Great care must be taken in crossing the wheel out, otherwise a broken tooth may result. A duplex 'scape wheel must always be mounted to run perfectly flat and true.

Turning in Duplex Balance Staff

The balance staff of a duplex is turned in, almost in the same way as an ordinary balance staff. The only difference is the roller arbor. The ruby roller arbor is turned so that it is extremely thin to fit the hole in the ruby roller. The roller must fit easily but without play, as it is shellacked in place, and a small brass or gold collet is fitted between the end of the ruby roller and the pivot. The author always places both pivots on the balance staff and then turns the ruby roller arbor last. It requires care, but it is the quickest way. The adjustment is carried out by moving the impulse roller, the ruby roller being left alone once it has been fixed.

Some duplex watches had a banking pin and a movable banking roller on the balance staff. It allowed the balance to vibrate only a little more than a turn and a half.

One type of duplex had a banking pin in the arm of the balance standing perpendicular. The balance-spring had a raised bulge from the last coil, and, when the spring expanded a certain amount, the pin banked on the bulge on the spring ; this was the banking.

The Crab-Tooth Duplex

Another type of duplex is called the crab-tooth duplex. It has been referred to as a Chinese duplex, but it is difficult to understand the reason.

With this escapement impulse was given every fourth vibration and, with a 14,400 train, would beat seconds, although if the seconds hand were watched closely the three movements of the dumb vibrations were visible. Most, if not all, had centre-seconds or sweep-seconds hands.

The crab-tooth escapement had one of the most difficult 'scape wheels to cut, but only a few watches of this type were made.

They had only a short life.

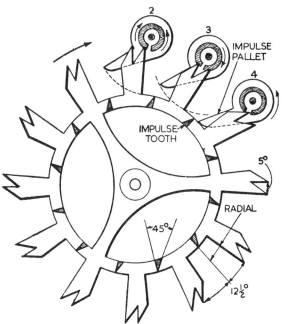

Fig. 190.— Crab-tooth Duplex Escapement.
Beats seconds with a 14,400 train.

THE CYLINDER ESCAPEMENT

The cylinder escapement followed the old verge escapement which was fitted vertically in the movement, and as the cylinder was the first to be arranged horizontally it was originally referred to as the horizontal escapement. It is now generally known as the cylinder escapement, which is a much more appropriate name and is self-explanatory.

The balance is mounted directly on a cylinder which runs on pivots in exactly the same way as a balance staff. This cylinder can be likened to the pallets in an ordinary movement, as it takes the impulse from the 'scape wheel. The cylinder is cut away leaving a little more than half ; and the 'scape wheel, which has all the impulse on its planes, engages each lip alternately. As the wheel tooth finishes its impulse the tooth drops. Then the succeeding tooth drops on to the solid part of the cylinder, resting there until the cylinder returns and unlocks that tooth and it gives impulse. Each tooth is engaged firstly on the outside of the cylinder and then on the inside (see Fig. 192).

The escapement is a frictional-rest type and is never detached.

In some of the older watches the cylinders were made of ruby and were extremely delicate ; also many old watches, particularly the early English, had brass 'scape wheels, but all the more modern cylinders have steel wheels. Some of the brass wheels were made in three tiers, that is five teeth on different planes. The object was to distribute the wear on the cylinder. Some were even made with five tiers. The cylinders for these older watches were made by hand and never mass-produced. The cylinder escapement is now used only for cheap watches and the Swiss produce the 'scape wheels and cylinders very cheaply.

Most cylinder escapements have a 'scape wheel of 15 teeth, but many were made with wheels of 10, 12 and 13 teeth. A certain type of chronograph, used at one time for timing projectiles, had a cylinder escapement with a 'scape wheel of 10 teeth and gave 1/100 of a second reading. These chronographs have been superseded by the lever type.

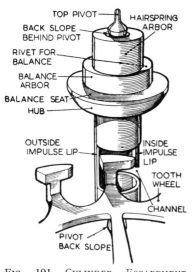

FIG. 191.—CYLINDER ESCAPEMENT, SHOWING DETAILS OF THE CYLINDER.

Turning in a Cylinder

To turn in a cylinder, first obtain a suitable " rough " from the material dealers, but, if obtainable, a finished one is better. Make sure the cylinder is the right size. The safest way to check the size is to place the 'scape wheel in the depth tool and reverse one of the runners in the other side so that the pointed end is inwards. Set the depth tool so that the point of the 'scape wheel tooth is central, using the pointed runner as a guide. Then fit the runner in the right way again and insert the cylinder. Then test to see if the shake or freedom of the teeth is the same inside as it is outside the cylinder. If there is too much outside shake and too little inside, the cylinder is too small, and vice versa.

It is always safest to fill the aperture of the cylinder with shellac to strengthen it while working on it, because the cylinder is very delicate.

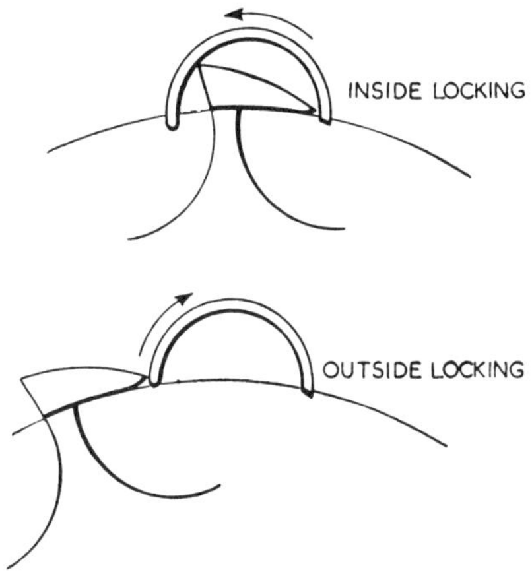

INSIDE LOCKING

OUTSIDE LOCKING

FIG. 192.—CYLINDER ESCAPEMENT, SHOW-
ING HOW IMPULSE IS GIVEN.

With the height tool, described previously, take the height or distance of the bottom rim or band of the 'scape wheel, as this has to pass freely through the channel of the cylinder.

Next, shorten the bottom of the cylinder to agree with the gauge. Then set the gauge for the height of the balance without interfering with the cylinder, because it is correct as it is now, but turn the brass collet to leave the balance seat the right height. Fit the hairspring collet and then turn the backslope behind the balance seat or hub. Undercut the balance arbor for the rivet. Next take the total length of the cylinder, shorten from the top or balance spring collet end to the exact length and fit the pivots. Then boil the cylinder in methylated spirits to remove the shellac and it only remains to mount the balance.

Mounting the Balance

On the balance is a guard pin and the balance must be mounted in the correct place in relation to the cylinder. Fit the balance on its seat and put the balance in place with the 'scape wheel.

Apply light pressure to the 'scape wheel and lead the balance round until the pin in the balance rests on the banking pin, either at the back of the balance cock or some other convenient place which will be obvious.

The 'scape wheel tooth should not pass over the lip of the cylinder; if it does, rotate the balance on the cylinder until the banking pin prevents this. Then reverse the direction of the balance and try it on that side. Sometimes the 'scape tooth will pass both ways, and if this happens fit an extra banking pin or a larger one, as this must be prevented. If the tooth passes over the lip on either side it will stop the watch. A balance on a cylinder can vibrate only a little, less than half a turn each way. The best vibration is about a third of a turn each way.

The lips of the cylinder must be oiled whether it is a jewelled cylinder, or a brass or steel wheel. The endshakes of the cylinder and 'scape pinion must be close and under no circumstances excessive. One of the troubles with the cylinder escapement is that the band of the 'scape wheel fouls either the top or bottom of the channel in the cylinder. The only remedy is to alter the height of either the cylinder or the 'scape wheel, whichever is the easier.

Some cylinder watches were fitted with compensation balances, but the other natural errors in the escapement made them superfluous. In these instances, the banking pin was fitted into the solid part of the cylinder instead of in the balance.

Angle Locking

A fault which is often obscure is that known as angle locking. This is often caused by an inexperienced workman stoning the points of the 'scape wheel teeth when a cylinder has been of the wrong size. With an old watch it can be caused by wear. The only way to correct it is to bring the teeth up to a point again by stoning the inside of the teeth, not the impulse plane. If any alteration is required to a cylinder 'scape wheel, it should be made to the backs or the dropping-off corner.

When the cylinder itself wears, the height can be altered to bring a different part of the cylinder into action, but movement of this nature is rarely possible. It can be carried out only if the channel in the cylinder is wide and the wheel runs nearer to one side than the other. Usually it means a new cylinder.

Making a Cylinder

Sometimes an old cylinder watch is received for repair in which the wheel is reversed. The cylinder is also reversed and, if a replacement is required, the only way is to make it by hand. It is not a difficult job.

A rod of steel is drilled to the same size as the length of the 'scape-wheel tooth. It is then mounted on an arbor and turned until it is free between two teeth of the 'scape wheel. Next it is fitted on to a piece of brass wire which fits the inside of the tube tightly. The lips and the channel are cut almost to the correct size and shape. The cylinder with the brass still in it is hardened and tempered to a dark blue colour. It is then removed from the brass wire, mounted on an arbor and then highly polished.

Polishing the Inside of the Cylinder

When the outside has been polished a piece of soft iron or soft steel wire is inserted in the cylinder, so that it is an easy fit, and is then placed between centres. A ferrule is fixed on the cylinder itself. The wire is charged with diamantine and, by means of the ferrule and a bow, the cylinder is rapidly revolved around the wire, which will polish the inside of the cylinder. The lips are then polished to their correct shape. It only remains to drive on the brass collet to which the balance and hairspring collet is fixed, and then fit the two cylinder plugs.

Cylinder Plugs and their Removal

In Swiss cylinders the plugs are in one piece and the pivots are turned on them (see Fig. 193). In the English type a brass plug is used, in which a smaller steel plug is inserted. This is a good idea as it is easier to remove and replace the plugs when required.

A specially shaped punch and stake are required to remove a cylinder plug. The punches are easy to make. A piece of flat steel rod about 2 inches long has a tapering recess filed out first, leaving a solid piece at the end (see Fig. 194). The solid piece is then filed away, leaving a projecting pivot, which is used for removing the plug. It must be slightly smaller than the plug but not too small. The solid end of the punch should be filed at an angle so that the main force of a hammer ,blow will be directed to the pivot on the punch.

Sometimes the plugs are so tight that there is great risk of breakage. The best way to ease the plug is to lay the cylinder carefully on a hard steel stake and tap it gently all the way round with a steel hammer. This will stretch the shell of the cylinder very slightly, enabling the plug to be removed easily.

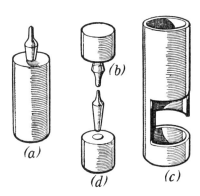

FIG. 193.—CYLINDER PLUGS.

(a) Swiss top cylinder plug.
(b) Swiss bottom plug.
(c) Cylinder " shell ".
(d) English type plugs.

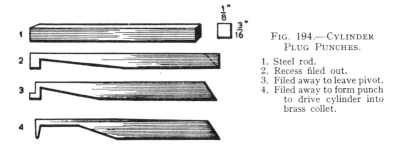

FIG. 194.—CYLINDER
PLUG PUNCHES.

1. Steel rod.
2. Recess filed out.
3. Filed away to leave pivot.
4. Filed away to form punch
   to drive cylinder into
   brass collet.

Ruby Cylinders

To repair a broken ruby cylinder is a formidable job and the author cannot, in all fairness, advise anyone to attempt to make one. If the customer is willing, but first obtain permission, replace with a steel cylinder ; its action will be the same.

There are various types of ruby cylinder ; some are simpler than others. In some the entire cylinder is made of ruby, while others the lips only are of ruby let into a steel cage or skeleton.

One form of ruby cylinder which can be replaced, however, is that used by Bréguet, the eminent French horologist. The procedure is as follows.

Choose a rough ruby or sapphire and fix it in a wax chuck. First drill a hole to the required depth with a chip of diamond brazed into a piece of brass wire. Then cut the stone through until the hole is exposed. Wax it up again with the hole running true. Polish the hole with a piece of iron wire charged with diamond powder, using high speed, but do not drive it in. Remove the stone from the wax chuck as soon as the wheel tooth is free inside the hole.

Turn a piece of brass wire in the lathe so that it is only just free in the hole, then place the hole over the brass wire and fix the jewel on to the wire with shellac. At high speed again, turn the outside of the jewel to the required diameter, using a piece of bort brazed to a piece of brass as a graver. Then polish with an ivory polisher and diamond powder. When the stone has been polished, take it out of the lathe and polish the unwanted jewel away while still on the brass wire. If one has worked to size it will fit the groove in the balance hub and will only need fixing with shellac. The plugs do not fit the cylinder but are a separate unit.

The Chariot

At one time some cylinder watches and platform escapements had the balance cock screwed into a chariot, which was screwed and steady-pinned into a shaped sink cut into the pillar plate.

The object, of course, was to make the 'scape wheel and cylinder depth adjustable.

It certainly has its advantages and saves cylinders being mutilated. The author had a good-quality cylinder watch recently where someone had filed off the fronts of the lips of the cylinder to shallow the locking, and thus spoiled the cylinder.

The endpiece screw into the chariot is very short, so always make sure that it does not protrude through the chariot and interfere with the endshake of the cylinder.

THE VIRGULE ESCAPEMENT

The virgule escapement, sometimes called the hook escapement, is an old escapement which is now obsolete, although some are still in existence. It is actually a cylinder escapement with all the impulse on the cylinder and none on the wheel. It has the failing of friction and losses, and is also difficult to keep lubricated.

The wheel teeth resemble a cylinder 'scape wheel with the teeth themselves removed, leaving only the stalks.

The action is shown in Fig. 195. The wheel tooth is about to drop on the locking point at B inside the cylinder. The hook, or impulse pallet, is swinging towards the wheel to complete its vibration. On its return the tooth is released at B and runs along the impulse pallet giving impulse. The pallet can travel all the way round until the back of the hook hits the tooth at C, or vice versa. Thus, the balance has to be banked like a cylinder.

After giving impulse the tooth drops and the next tooth drops on to the outside of the cylinder at point A. The next vibration is a "dummy" vibration and no impulse is given. All that happens is that the tooth is unlocked from the outside of the cylinder at A and drops inside the cylinder, being locked at point B, thus it is similar to the duplex and is a single-beat escapement, besides being a frictional-rest type and never detached.

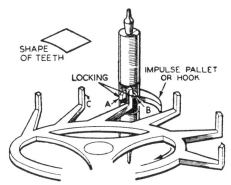

Fig. 195.—Virgule or Hook Escapement.

Although now obsolete, a number of these escapements are still in existence. It is actually a cylinder escapement with all of the impulse on the cylinder and none on the wheel.

When the pallet locking corners get worn they can be touched up, but if the wheel becomes worn a replacement is necessary. The wheel must definitely lock on both pallets. It is put in beat in the same way as a duplex.

The cylinder is made solid, but has plugs exactly the same as an ordinary cylinder. In replacing the virgule, the hook must have about 20° impulse and it is solid with the cylinder.

CHAPTER 9

CLOCK ESCAPEMENTS

THE earliest type of escapement was that fitted to the old verge clocks. In addition, the earliest watches had verge escapements, which were subsequently superseded by the horizontal or cylinder escapement as mentioned in the preceding chapter. The verge or crown-wheel escapement is, of course, now obsolete, although many verge watches in fairly good condition are still in existence. As the verge escapement may also be encountered by repairers in many types of antique clocks, we will include a description of its action after first dealing with the more modern forms of clock escapement which are of greater practical interest.

THE RECOIL ESCAPEMENT

The anchor and recoil escapement, although first introduced in the latter part of the seventeenth century, is still one of the most popular escapements for domestic clocks, with, of course, modern improvements in design added. In comparison with other escapements it is fairly easy to make, and seems to perform well even with rough usage and despite the fact that some are badly made. The 'scape wheels vary between 30 and 35 teeth, according to the train and the preference of various makers. The pallets embrace six, seven or eight teeth, but the most popular is seven.

The recoil escapement performs well with a good vibration, as against the " dead-beat " which performs very well on a small vibration. The reason a recoil escapement gives a good vibration is because the pallets are planted close to the 'scape wheel. In fact, the distance between the 'scape and pallet-staff holes is only the radius of the 'scape wheel plus half the radius, or, to be more correct, the radius multiplied by 1·4. With the anchor type, the distance is more usually the diameter of the wheel.

This rule has not been adhered to in most of the clocks handled to-day. Consequently when a clock requires a new pair of pallets, it is cheaper to make them to depth, instead of repitching and blocking up holes, which, unless well done, always looks a botched job.

Making Recoil Pallets to Depth

The best procedure is to make a drawing of the pallets on a piece of stiff paper, fix it on to a suitable piece of steel and file up to shape. First make a hole in the paper in which the 'scape pinion arbor can be fitted tightly. Then take the measurement between the pallet arbor and the 'scape hole in a depth tool, or a vernier, and mark the distance near the centre of the paper, joining the hole and the mark just made by a straight line (see Fig. 196).

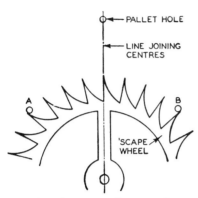

FIG. 196.—MAKING A PAIR OF RECOIL PALLETS TO DEPTH (1).
'Scape wheel 30 teeth.

Place the 'scape wheel on the paper with one tooth resting on the line joining the 'scape and pallet holes. Count four teeth in an anti-clockwise direction, and make a pencil mark where the point of this fourth tooth rests, *A*. This will indicate where the entrance pallet is first engaged.

Next make a mark where the fourth tooth in a clockwise direction rests, *B*. This point will be the dropping-off line of the exit pallet.

Move the wheel in an anti-clockwise direction to exactly half the distance of the space between two teeth (see Fig. 197). Then make a mark where the fourth tooth in a clockwise direction from the centre line lies, *D*. This will give the position of the first engagement of the wheel tooth with the exit pallet.

Make a further mark where the fourth tooth in an anti-clockwise direction rests, *C*. This mark will denote the position of the dropping-off line of the entrance pallet.

The Impulse Angles

These marks do not allow for freedoms or the impulse planes. To obtain these, draw a straight line joining the mark for the first

FIG. 197.—MAKING RECOIL PALLETS TO DEPTH (2).

Obtaining the impulse planes.

A. First engagement, entrance pallet.
B. Dropping-off line, exit pallet.
C. Dropping-off line, entrance pallet.
D. First engagement, exit pallet.
E. Circle scribed to line joining point *A* to point midway between *D* and *B*.
F. Line joining point *A* to point between *D* and *B*.
G1, G2. Radial lines passing through *C* and *B* respectively.

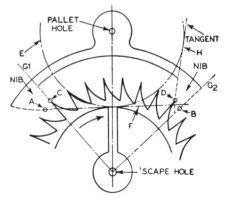

engagement on the entrance pallet, A, and to pass midway between the two marks denoting the first engagement and the dropping-off line of the exit pallet (points D and B). This will give the angle of impulse on the entrance pallet, F. Next by scribing a circle from the pallet hole, just to meet this line at one point, will enable the impulse angle of the exit pallet to be obtained. A tangent of this circle passing through point D, that is, the first engagement on the exit pallet, will give the impulse angle of the exit pallet.

We now have the impulse angles. If we draw radial lines to the 'scape hole from points C and B, they will cross the lines denoting the impulse angles, and will give a guide to the dropping-off corners of both pallets (see $G1$ and $G2$).

Next cut the drawing to shape with a pair of scissors and, of course, leave a margin all round. Fix it with glue on to a piece of steel suitable for making the pallets, and drill a hole to take the pallet staff or arbor tightly at the point on the drawing for the pallet hole. Then cut out, or file up the steel to correspond exactly with the drawing.

Amount of Impulse

At this stage the pallets will be tight everywhere. The impulse is too great, as each pallet has double the amount of impulse that is required. This has to be halved, and yet the pallets kept central, so we remove half of the amount from each side. We do not want to alter the impulse angles, so we file away the metal on the dropping-off line, that is, the line $G2B$ on the exit pallet and $G1C$ on the entrance pallet. Do this very carefully, and try the pallets in the frame after each alteration, and make certain that an equal amount is removed from each side. If too much metal is filed away, there will be too much drop, and this will result in loss of impulse.

As soon as the pallets are just free, harden the nibs. First harden one nib, then hold it in a heavy pair of tongs and harden the other. The tongs will prevent the heat softening the first nib which has been hardened. It only remains to clean up the pallets themselves, and polish the impulse planes with a zinc polisher and diamantine. This will give the necessary freedom.

Leave the impulse planes slightly curved where the action takes place, but quite flat across so that the action will not be affected by the endshakes. Elsewhere the pallets look nice if straight-grained with emery paper wound round a file.

THE GRAHAM DEAD-BEAT ESCAPEMENT

Under ideal conditions the Graham dead-beat escapement is undoubtedly the best of all clock escapements, other than turret clock escapements. It is used mostly for regulators, with a long

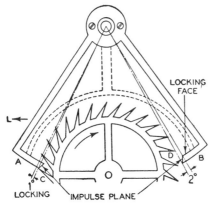

FIG. 198.—OLD PATTERN GRAHAM DEAD-
BEAT ESCAPEMENT.

Pallets span 14 teeth. 'Scape wheel 30
teeth, giving dead seconds.
Dotted lines show how pallets are sometimes shaped.
        A. Entrance pallet.
        B. Exit pallet.

heavy pendulum and con-
stant motive power, that
is, of course, weight-
driven. It is affected by
changes of motive power,
the friction increasing appreciably as the power
increases.

It was made originally
with the pallets spanning
14 teeth, but this has been
superseded by an escape-
ment having the same principle in which the pallets
span eight teeth. The
former requires less power
to keep it going, and thus
the slightest thickening of
the oil affects the rate.
The arrangement whereby
the pallets span eight teeth
requires more power to
keep it going, and, as such,
the thickening or thinning of the oil is less troublesome, although still
a factor to be reckoned with. The vibration must be kept as small
as possible, and, as a regulator requires the slightest amount of
supplementary arc, this type of escapement is ideal.

Action of the Dead-Beat Escapement

The action is simple to understand if the two drawings in Figs. 198
and 199 are studied. In
Fig. 198, the tooth *C* is
resting on the locking of
the entrance pallet *A*.
As the pallets move
towards the left, the
tooth *C* reaches the im-
pulse plane and pushes
the pallet towards *L*.
At the same time, the
pallet *B* is moving into
the path of the wheel.
As the tooth *C* reaches
the end of the impulse
plane, the tooth *D* drops
on to the locking face of
pallet *B*.

When examining this

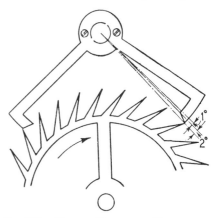

FIG. 199.—MODERN DEAD-BEAT ESCAPEMENT.
'Scape wheel 30 teeth.   Pallets span 8 teeth.

escapement make absolutely certain that the tooth drops cleanly on to the locking face and not on to the impulse plane. In the drawing, the locking, or rest as it is often called, is 1°, but it can be less ; if a regulator is well made, $\frac{1}{2}$° is ample. As the pallets move in the opposite direction, this same action takes place, and the same rules apply with regard to the locking.

The pivot holes must be a good fit on the pivots. Any play in the holes will destroy the qualities of the escapement. The locking faces and the impulse planes must be smooth and polished. They are jewelled in the majority of regulators, usually with agate or garnet, and only a few are jewelled with harder stones. The wheel teeth, as a rule, wear as well as the pallet faces, but the wear is much less. The pallet faces must be repolished if badly worn. If the wheel teeth are slightly worn they can be touched up, but if badly worn a new wheel is necessary.

Shape of Pallets

Fig. 198 gives an outline of the shape of the pallet arms as sometimes used. There is no advantage or disadvantage in the shape ; it is purely a matter of choice.

There is 2° of impulse and, as stated before, 1° locking or rest. The locking faces are arcs struck from the pallet arbor. The wheel teeth are cut back from the radial, so that only the points of the teeth are in action. They can be cut back from 10° to 24°. The advantage with 10° teeth, is that the drop can be less, but as there is no recoil to the wheel in unlocking, it can, in any case, be kept small.

HALF DEAD-BEAT ESCAPEMENT

For clocks with half seconds or shorter pendulums an escapement termed "half dead-beat" is used. In this form, the action is very similar, but the locking faces are curved to introduce recoil. In other words, the locking faces are struck with a larger radius instead of from the pallet arbor, as in the case of the perfectly dead-beat. The half dead-beat possesses the advantages of the dead-beat and recoil escapements. The escapement was originally used with seconds pendulums, but was discarded.

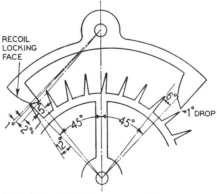

FIG. 200.—HALF DEAD-BEAT ESCAPEMENT.
The locking faces are recoil.

BROCOT'S PIN-PALLET ESCAPEMENT

The Brocot pin-pallet is another dead-beat escapement which performs best with a long heavy pendulum. The escapement is easy to produce, but unfortunately, it is rarely in good order when brought in for repair. Whether it is put out of order by incompetent workmen, it is difficult to say. The fault seems to be that the pallet pins are too large and will not clear, unless the escapement is left very shallow and mislocking. The action under these circumstances is like a recoil without enough impulse, and, of course, the clock stops. The escapement is seldom found in any but French house clocks.

The pallets are semicircular steel pins, or sometimes jewel of a cheap kind (see Fig. 201).

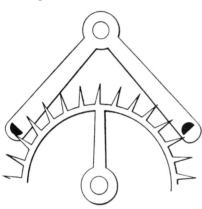

Fig. 201.—Brocot Pin-pallet Escapement.

A " dead-beat " with half-round pallet pads in hard steel or common jewel.

Steel pallet pins are better as they can be easily replaced and, if left quite hard, the wear is very little. The pallets usually embrace 10 teeth, and with a 'scape wheel of 30 teeth have about 4° of impulse, but the impulse varies in accordance with the number of teeth in the 'scape wheel and the number of teeth embraced by the pallets. The thickness of the pins should be half the distance between two teeth, less the necessary freedom. The 'scape-wheel teeth should be radial on the acting face ; any other shape is a nuisance, and also detracts from the performance of the clock. The backs of the teeth vary, but a straight angular back is all that is required. The pallets are planted a little more than one and a half times the radius of the 'scape wheel from the 'scape pivot hole. They do not work well if any closer.

Making the Pallet Pins

When making the pallet pins or pads, choose a piece of steel rod which will pass between two teeth when the rod intersects the wheel by its own diameter (Fig. 202).

Always take great care with this measurement, erring, if at all, on the small side. The clock will function with the pads on the small side, but it certainly will not if they are too large. They must be cut exactly in half, and should be checked carefully with a micrometer. If less than half there will be serious loss of impulse, and if more than half the pads will not be free in the 'scape-wheel teeth. When putting the pads into the pallets, the flat side must not be brought into action at all, but they should be parallel with the acting face of the 'scape-wheel teeth to obtain the maximum impulse and the maximum freedom. Sometimes the holes or sockets for the pallet pins are too large ; if so, a piece of steel rod which fits the hole can be used if turned down on the acting part to the correct size.

Adjustable Turntable

There is usually an adjustable turntable in which is the pallet arbor pivot hole. The object of this table is to correct the inside and outside freedoms of the pallet and wheel teeth. It does not adjust the depth.

If the wheel mislocks, the arms of the pallets must be closed, and if the locking is too deep they must be opened. Great care is required as a little adjustment makes a lot of difference. The wheel teeth should drop just on the centre line of the pallet pin, and the wheel should not recoil or move when the pallet pin runs to the band of the wheel. If attention is given to these various points no trouble should be experienced with this escapement. Naturally, the pivots and pivot holes must be in good condition, the pivots must be smooth, and the holes perfectly round and a good fit.

Self-setting Crutch

The crutch, with this type of escapement, is generally self-setting, that is, the crutch screws on to the pallet arbor and is just friction tight. When the pendulum is given a good swing, the pallet pins bank on the band of the wheel and the clock is put in beat. The crutch gives way each time the pins meet the band of the wheel, and eventually settles in the central position in relation to the pallets.

Sometimes bad workmen solder the crutch to the pallet arbor, presumably because they cannot find the fault. This is very bad

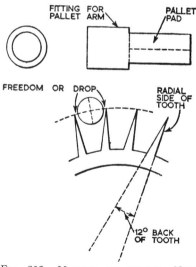

FIG. 202.—METHOD OF MAKING NEW PALLET PADS FOR BROCOT PIN-PALLET ESCAPEMENT.

practice and should not be tolerated. If the crutch is a little too easy, it can be tightened up without difficulty.

The collet on which the crutch is mounted is generally slotted, and to tighten the crutch it is only necessary to close the slot a trifle. A smear of oil on the thread of the pallet arbor will prevent the crutch from seizing up.

THE PIN-WHEEL ESCAPEMENT

The pin-wheel escapement is another useful clock escapement, and has been fitted to turret clocks with favourable results. It is a " dead-beat " and, as such, performs best with a long heavy pendulum. Instead of teeth on the 'scape wheel, semicircular pins projecting from the rim of the 'scape wheel give impulse to the pallets (see Fig. 203).

The length of the pallet arms seems to vary with different makers ; some arms are very long, while the length of others is about the diameter of the 'scape wheel.

French Pin Wheels

The number of pins in the 'scape wheel also varies. Some have all the pins arranged on one side of the rim, although French clocks generally have pins on both sides, the object being to have the pallet arms of the same length. Another difference is that the pins are small and circular (see Fig. 204). When the pins are on one side of the rim, one pallet arm is shorter than the other.

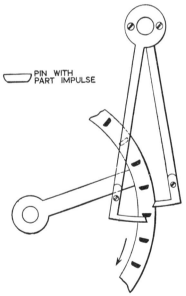

PIN WITH PART IMPULSE

Again, some have the pins shaped in such a way that the impulse is divided between the pins and the pallets. If the pins are very small, however, as is the case with some French clocks, better results are obtained with the arrangement whereby all the impulse is on the pallets.

Fig. 203.—English Type Pin-wheel Escapement.

Pins on 'scape wheel are shaped to give impulse.

Oil-bath Lubrication

The main difficulty with this escapement is keeping the pins and pallets lubricated. One or two French clocks handled by the author have had a little oil bath on the pallets themselves, and after a considerable period the oil has been retained and has kept well (see Fig. 204).

One advantage of the pin-wheel escapement is that it does not lose impulse when the pallet arbor holes get worn. The action is similar to the Graham escapement, inasmuch as it has a locking face and an impulse plane, and the impulse is given in a similar way.

The arms are screwed to the collet mounted on the pallet arbor, and the arbor is tangential with the 'scape wheel instead of central as is usual, so the impulse is in one direction, that is, downwards.

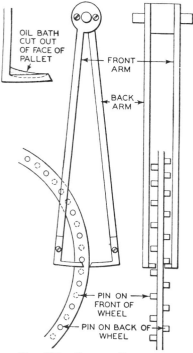

FIG. 204.—FRENCH PIN-WHEEL ESCAPEMENT.

Round pins are situated on both sides of 'scape wheel; thus arms are the same length. Note the little oil bath.

Replacing the Pins

The pins sometimes get worn and have to be replaced, but they seem to function for a very long time before this is necessary. It is a long job to replace the pins, but it presents no great difficulty. The best way is to replace with round pins, and halve them in a wheel-cutting machine with a suitable cutter.

The pallet faces often need repolishing, and again there is no difficulty, but care is required to preserve the angles.

THE GRAVITY ESCAPEMENT

The double three-legged gravity type, as used in the clock of Big Ben, is by far the best escapement for large turret clocks (see Fig. 205). The impulse is given indirectly or, to be more accurate, not by the clock mechanism itself, and as such is referred to as a remontoire. The clock train sets up the impulse, and has no influence on the pendulum, or at most very little if in order. The impulse

210

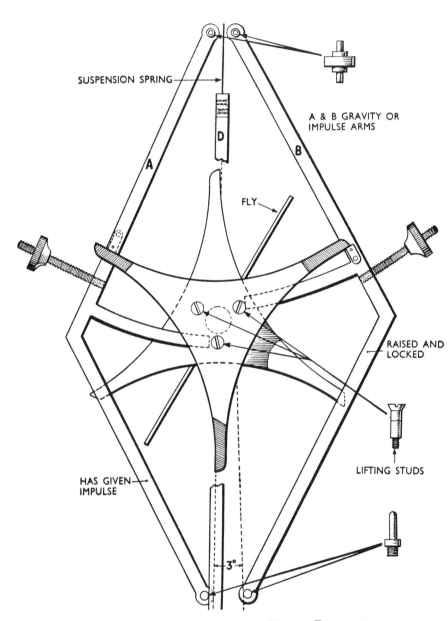

SUSPENSION SPRING

A & B GRAVITY OR
IMPULSE ARMS

D

A

B

FLY

RAISED AND
LOCKED

LIFTING STUDS

HAS GIVEN
IMPULSE

3°

FIG. 205.—DOUBLE THREE-LEGGED GRAVITY ESCAPEMENT.

is given through the action of gravity, as the name of the escapement implies. The clock train lifts two gravity arms, one on each side of the pendulum rod, and it is the weight of these arms falling alternately which gives the impulse to the pendulum.

Action of Double Three-legged Gravity Escapement

Fitted on the 'scape pinion is a pair of what may be described as wheels of three teeth. These two wheels are joined together by a pinion of three leaves, which is probably the best term to describe it, although it actually consists of three studs set equidistant to each other. The wheels are positioned like a wheel of six teeth, also equidistant to each other. One wheel acts underneath the gravity arms and the other works above them with the three studs between. These are actually the locking teeth. The pinion of three leaves acts as lifting studs for the gravity arms.

In Fig. 205 the locking-wheel tooth is locked at block B, the pendulum rod is moving towards the bottom of the arm, and will lift the arm to unlock the locking wheel. As the locking wheel turns, the pin or stud engages the lifting arm A, raising this arm and the gravity arm A, and places the block underneath in the path of the locking wheel A.

The gravity arm B is released and rests on the pendulum rod, and its weight provides the impulse given to the pendulum. A fly on the pinion arbor prevents the escapement from tripping. Without the fly, the gravity arm would be thrown up beyond the path of the locking wheel and the locking wheel would run through. The fly slows the locking wheel sufficiently to prevent this.

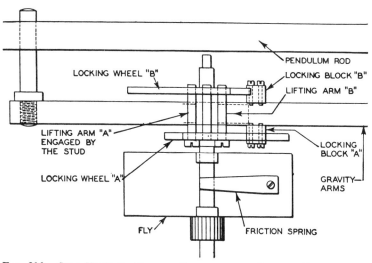

FIG. 206.—SIDE VIEW OF DOUBLE THREE-LEGGED GRAVITY ESCAPEMENT.

If this locking is too deep, it interferes with the pendulum as extra work is created for the pendulum to unlock. This unlocking is the only connection between the pendulum and the clock train itself. This section of the clock must always be in good order. If the locking blocks or the locking arm become worn, they must be repaired or renewed.

The studs which engage the pendulum rod at the end of the gravity arm are often in the form of small rollers to ease the friction. The gravity arms are supported either on studs, or on short pivoted arbors spanned by cocks screwed to the frame of the clock.

Other Forms of Gravity Escapement

Some forms of gravity escapement have arms which are sprung, or the arms themselves are long springs. The whole action is the same, but the springs provide the impulse instead of gravity.

Sometimes a supplementary weight is added to the gravity arms. This takes the form of a screw and adjustable nut fixed in the gravity arm itself. The total weight of the arm is increased or decreased by simply screwing the nut towards the arm to decrease the weight and drawing the nut outwards to increase it. This means of adjustment is usually found in regulators having a gravity escapement.

There are other types of gravity escapement, but the principles are very similar. The double three-legged gravity type is undoubtedly the best.

THE VERGE ESCAPEMENT

As mentioned at the beginning of this chapter, the verge or crown wheel is the oldest form of escapement and, although obsolete, is still of interest, as verge clocks needing repair are often met with by repairers. Although this chapter deals solely with clock escapements it will not be out of place to deal with the watch verge as well, because the principle of both is very similar, except, of course, that the watch has a balance instead of a pendulum.

The verge is really a kind of recoil escapement and is never detached. Fig. 207 will assist in enabling the action of the escapement to be understood.

Pallet A is receiving impulse and pallet B is falling into position to receive the next tooth. There is no locking in this escapement. The teeth are set at right angles like a contrate wheel, and the verge is set centrally across the wheel. Unless the verge is central, the drop is unequal and the escapement seems out of beat. If the escapement is close and the drop is unequal, the wheel will not pass.

In a watch there are dovetailed slides in the pottance to enable the drops to be made equal ; also the back pivot of the 'scape pinion is carried in a follower. In some followers the pivot hole is eccentric, but it is best placed centrally. The idea is for adjusting the contrate and 'scape depth, but, in actual fact, it is merely a nuisance. The follower is useful for setting the 'scape or crown wheel deeper or shallower into the verge by closing up or increasing the endshake.

The 'scape wheel, of course, is referred to as the balance wheel in a watch and as a crown wheel in a clock.

If the top pivot of the verge is broken it can be pivoted. By using a hollow sinking tool, the brass in the collet can be cut away round the steel and the steel broken away. A plug can then be fitted in tightly and a pivot turned on it. If the bottom pivot is broken, however, a new verge is the only remedy.

Turning in a Verge

It is not a difficult operation to turn in a verge. First find a brass ferrule which will fit tightly on to a piece of pegwood. Cut a V-slot lengthwise in the pegwood, and place the verge in the slot. Then replace the piece of pegwood which has been cut out, using it as a wedge (or use another suitable piece), and push the brass ferrule on tightly. Turn the balance seat first, as high as possible, and do not forget that the hairspring collet fits underneath the balance and not above as is usual. Care must be taken to see that the hairspring collet is free of the 'scape or balance wheel. It is pivoted in the usual way. The bottom pivot is awkward to polish, but with care it is fairly easy. Sometimes the pallets have to be shortened, and this can be done with an oilstone slip.

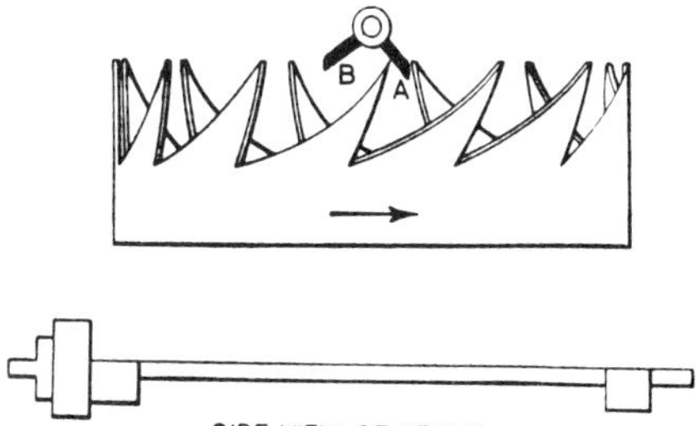

SIDE VIEW OF VERGE

FIG. 207.—VERGE ESCAPEMENT FOR WATCHES.

The pallets can be opened or closed, by twisting the verge in the centre, to about 95°–100° of each other. This is carried out by splitting a full-length piece of pegwood and placing it on the bottom pallet. The brass collet on the verge is placed in a pin vice, and the pin vice is held in a bench vice. Place the verge in the right position according to whether the pallets require to be opened or closed. If to be closed, arrange the pegwood to lean towards the top pallet, and vice versa. With a fine blowpipe flame directed into the centre of the verge, midway between the two pallets, the weight of the pegwood will twist the verge as soon as the verge is hot enough. It will twist well before the verge is softened.

The Verge Clock

Usually the pendulum of the verge clock is fitted directly on to the verge itself, and the back pivot of the verge is a block filed to a thin knife-edge and resting on a V-bed. The end of the pivot is banked by a cap nicely pierced and shaped, and also has a block fitted on the cap to prevent the verge from rising up out of the bed and allowing the 'scape or crown wheel to run through.

The later type of verge clock had a crutch, and the pendulum had a separate suspension very similar to present-day models.

Repairs to a Verge Clock

The knife-edge of the verge sometimes gets badly worn. This can be replaced by cutting a slot in the block at the back end of the verge, and fitting and pinning in tightly a new piece of steel which has been filed to shape. Make sure the knife-edge itself is true with the arbor of the verge ; if not, the clock is sure to stop, or, if the clock does manage to keep going, it will keep bad time. It is always a mistake to convert a verge clock to a recoil escapement. If the verge escapement is put in order, it will give quite a good performance. The pallet pads can always be repolished if worn. If the wheel is badly worn, however, it must be recut and set in deeper. There is an endpiece screw, at the bottom end of the crown-wheel pinion, to adjust the escapement depth.

The verge itself is not difficult to replace. It is made from a piece of strip steel, which is filed to shape, hardened and tempered. It is twisted in the same way as a watch verge, by making the centre hot and twisting with pliers. The brass collet is driven on, or soldered in place. The block or collet is drilled to take the pendulum rod, and is fitted and riveted tightly.

CHAPTER 10

KEYLESS WORK, SELF-WINDING MECHANISMS AND MOTION WORK

BEFORE the advent of keyless mechanisms it was necessary, of course, to use a key for the purpose of winding a watch. Nowadays watches are all keyless, and some of the better-quality keywind movements have been converted to keyless. A few key-wind watches, however, are still in existence and need repair from time to time.

ENGLISH KEYLESS WORK

English keyless work has always been more robust than the Continental, although for a period the English adopted a similar style. The form of keyless mechanism now provided with most English movements is known as the rocking bar. (See Fig. 36, page 41.)

English Rocking Bar

The English rocking-bar mechanism is simple in construction. The winding button is fitted to a winding pinion, which passes through the pendant, in fact the hole in the pendant is the bearing for the winding-pinion arbor. The button is usually fitted on to a square on the pinion arbor, and fixed firmly in place by a gold nut sunk into the button. The arbor and pinion are made from a solid steel rod, and the teeth on the pinion are cut at right angles, or are bevelled according to the particular watch.

The movement is removed from the case without interfering with the winding pinion. The winding pinion and winding button completely seal the pendant, as far as dust and dirt are concerned, but will not exclude water. English watertight watches are provided with a helmet which screws over the button and pendant.

Push-Pieces

With the English watch, where a push-piece is used for setting the hands, little trouble should be experienced, providing it is well fitted and of the proper length. The disadvantage, of course, is that the watch has to be taken off the wrist to set the hands, whereas with the modern Swiss wrist watch the button can be pulled out and the hands set without removal from the wrist.

The argument at one time was that the English wrist watch performed so well that the hands rarely needed resetting ; thus the push-piece was all that was required, and the extra expense was unnecessary. Nowadays, the Swiss wrist watch gives such a good performance that this argument no longer holds good.

The Winding Pinion

The winding pinion of the English watch is geared into a large bevelled wheel, which is the central wheel of the rocking bar. It is held in place either by a steel collar screwed to the front plate of the watch, or by the rocking bar itself as well as the collar.

Sometimes the rocking bar is underneath the bevelled wheel, and sometimes it is above. The former arrangement is much better because the rocking bar prevents the plate from being scored by the bevelled wheel, and the keyless mechanism is smoother in action.

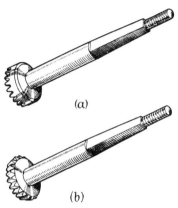

(a)

(b)

FIG. 208.—ENGLISH WINDING PINIONS.

Showing (a) ordinary type and (b) winding pinion with bevel leaves.

Transmission Wheels

When the rocking bar is below, the two transmission wheels, which gear into the bevelled wheel, are held in place by shouldered screws with the heads sunk into the wheels.

When the rocking bar is above, the two transmission wheels run on studs which are fixed permanently into the rocking bar. Again the objection is the two transmission wheels running on the pillar plate and scoring the plate. The two transmission wheels are positioned one on each side of the central bevelled wheel, and one is geared directly into the winding ratchet situated on the barrel arbor. The other is for setting the hands.

When the push-piece is pressed, it moves the rocking bar, takes the transmission wheel out of gear with the winding ratchet and places the other transmission wheel into gear, either with the minute wheel itself, or into a steel idle wheel, which is fixed to the front plate by a shouldered screw with the head sunk into the wheel.

A spring also screwed to the front plate, either from the inside or on top with the rocking bar, acts on the rocking bar and keeps the keyless mechanism in gear with the winding ratchet all the time.

This latter feature is most necessary because if the winding mechanism were continuously in gear with the motion work, it would stop the watch or, at the very least, would hold up the motion work and make the watch unreliable.

Some Constructional Requirements

If the push-piece, for some reason or the other, becomes tight or not properly free, there is always the possibility that the keyless mechanism may remain in set hands and stop the watch. Never put oil on a push-piece, otherwise it will soon fail and stick.

The weak points in this rocking-bar keyless mechanism are, of course, the winding pinion and the bevelled wheel. The cause is usually bad construction, or bad fitting of the movement into the case.

If the movement rises up when winding, the depth of the winding pinion becomes shallow, and although it may not slip at first, once it does the teeth of both pinion and wheel will be stripped of their teeth. The movement, therefore, must be held firmly near the pendant. If necessary, a strong pin on each side of the pendant can be fitted into the movement and let underneath the rim of the case. For the same reason, the movement must not be allowed to turn or twist out of position.

Bolt and Joint

Some English watches were made on the bolt and joint principle to reduce the cost of manufacture. There was no dome to the case and the back was solid with the band. The movement was held in place, usually, by a joint at the figure 10 and a spring bolt on the opposite side of the movement.

These movements always had the tendency to rise up, and as a result the winding pinions had to be constantly replaced.

Tongued-type of Winding Mechanism

A distinct improvement on the arrangement where the winding pinion is in the pendant was made in another type of English watch. In this model the winding pinion was in the watch frame itself, and was constructed with a protruding tongue piece and a female tongue or slot as a winding stem. The winding button was fitted on to the stem in the same way as the winding pinion. The movement was removed from the case, as before, without interfering with the button and stem.

These watches never failed in the keyless work, but the winding stem had to be lined up properly with the winding pinion, otherwise the winding action was very heavy and uneven.

The small winding ratchet was another disadvantage of these English wrist watches, especially the small ladies' size, because the winding always tended to be hard, just as though the watches had too strong a mainspring. Nevertheless they were fine watches generally.

Shifting-Sleeve Mechanisms

Another type had a similar winding mechanism to the Swiss watches and it is probable that the rough movements were sent to

CASTLE WHEEL CROWN WHEEL

FIG. 209.—CROWN AND CASTLE WHEELS.

Sometimes referred to as winding pinion and clutch wheel.

LARGE CROWN WHEEL

FIG. 210.—LARGE CROWN WHEEL, SIMILAR TO SWISS KEYLESS WORK.

Switzerland for the keyless work to be added. These were fitted with a shifting-sleeve mechanism, having a crown and castle wheel with the large crown wheel fitted to the underside of the top plate. The winding ratchet was solid with the barrel arbor. Usually the teeth on the wheels were of the buttress type and were, therefore, very strong and smooth in action.

The winding stem was similar to the Swiss, and had the usual square section for the castle wheel to work on. Some models, however, had a half-round section on the winding stem, and, of course, a correspondingly shaped hole in the castle wheel. The castle wheel was held in place by a return spring, which had a drop post on to which the push-piece operated to set the hands.

A very similar type, also with a shifting sleeve mechanism, had the tongued type of winding, but in this model the usual type of winding stem was not used. It was divided into two parts. One part was in the pendant, and the other part was between the frame held in by a steel bridge.

The stem in the movement ended in a tongue, and the other half was a female tongue or slot, which was fitted into the pendant. Thus, the movement could be easily removed from the case, without removing the winding stem. The only drawback was the winding button.

Removing the Winding Button

The button screwed directly on to the pendant half of the stem, and to unscrew this button often presented difficulty. The best way to unscrew it with safety was to make a tool of hardened and tempered steel which would fit the female tongue exactly, and then with this in the slot it was safe to use force to remove the button. If gripped with pliers, the slotted head was likely to break. An alternative way was to file up a piece of brass to wedge the slot, and it was then safe to grip the slotted head.

There was no rocking bar, and the central wheel was screwed by a steel collar to the front plate. The collar was held by three screws. The winding wheel was also screwed to the front plate with a shouldered screw.

A push-piece was used for set hands, and this pressed on a post on the return spring which placed the castle wheel into gear with the idle transmission wheel, which in turn was always in gear with the minute wheel.

Old Pattern English Keyless Work

There are two other types of English keyless work worth mentioning. One is rather an old type, but some are still in use. It had the usual type of winding pinion in the pendant, but the rest of the mechanism was different.

The movement was held in the case by a steel bridge screwed and steady pinned on the top plate. On this bridge a bevel wheel was mounted on a hollow stud and was held in place by a screw with a large head. This wheel was mounted at an angle of 45° and connected the winding pinion and the main winding wheel.

The main winding wheel was sunk out on the underside, and a click and spring were fitted in the sink. On the barrel arbor square was fitted a fine-toothed ratchet wheel, having a pipe solid with it. A pin went through the pipe and the barrel arbor square to hold the ratchet on firmly. The main winding wheel fitted this pipe, and the click and spring lay round the ratchet when the winding wheel was in place. A steel cap held the main winding wheel in place, and this cap was fixed to the ratchet by two screws.

The main winding wheel also geared into a transmission wheel, which was fitted on a movable lever. The centre arbor was a large pinion, and, when the push-piece was pressed, the movable lever with the wheel attached moved into gear with the centre arbor wheel.

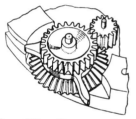

FIG. 211.—ROCKING BAR, BEVEL WHEEL AND TRANSMISSION WHEEL PIVOTED BETWEEN THE PLATES.

The big disadvantage with this type was that when the watch was fully wound, it was impossible to set the hands forwards, only backwards, and in the ordinary way when the hands were being set forwards the watch was being wound at the same time.

English Pattern Unsafe to Let Down by Button

The second type, Fig. 211, made by the same firm, had the winding pinion and push-piece as usual, but the bevel wheel was screwed to another wheel with a rocking bar between, and these were either pivoted between the frame, or ran on a stud. On this rocking bar was a steel post on which ran a transmission wheel, and this wheel was the connection between the bevel wheel and the winding mechanism in one position, and the set hands mechanism in the other. The winding ratchet was fitted to a square on the bottom of the barrel arbor, and had a pipe which acted as the lower barrel arbor pivot. The winding ratchet teeth were of the buttress type.

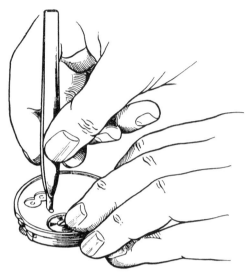

FIG. 212.—PLACING A PIECE OF PEGWOOD AS A
WEDGE TO PREVENT WHEELS COMING OUT
OF GEAR WHEN LETTING DOWN MAIN-
SPRING.

The mechanism was fairly straightforward, but care had to be taken when the watch was let down. In the ordinary way, if a watch is fully wound and will not run down, the first thing to do is to replace the movement in the case, without putting the dial on, then ease the click on the winding ratchet and let down the mainspring by allowing the button to slide slowly through the fingers until the spring is completely down.

With this particular type, if this were carried out, as soon as the click was taken out of the winding ratchet, the mainspring would go down with a rush, resulting in broken stopwork, broken barrel teeth and a damaged centre pinion—a very costly accident.

The best way to let down these watches was by wedging the rocking bar transmission wheel into gear with the winding ratchet. A piece of sharpened pegwood placed in the hole in the pillar plate and against the tail of the rocking bar was the only safe way, and it had to be wedged tightly at that. The keyless work was extremely good and wound very smoothly, but this point had to be watched very carefully.

Fusee-Keyless Mechanisms

With a fusee watch, the fusee is turning while the watch is running down, unlike the going barrel where the barrel arbor remains stationary until the watch is rewound. Thus a system of winding had to be introduced which would automatically disconnect the winding from the fusee.

Various types of mechanism were devised, and some were better than others. We will not consider the badly constructed types, as they had only a short life. On the other hand, the better ones are still in use and still give good service. The best types of pocket chronometer were provided with fusees, and thus had fusee-keyless work. The majority of tourbillons and quite a lot of karrusels were also fusee-keyless watches.

Kullberg Fusee-Keyless Mechanism

One type, used mostly by Messrs. V. Kullberg, has an ordinary train pinion as the winding pinion. The central wheel is provided with two sets of teeth, one being set at right angles to the other on the plane of the wheel, in a similar way to the Swiss idle or larger crown wheel. These right-angled teeth are geared into the winding pinion. The rocking bar is not a fixture in the ordinary sense, as it is held down by a steel cap which is screwed to the pillar plate, but is permitted to move from side to side. Also on this rocking bar is a transmission wheel, which rests either on a steel screw-head, or on a steel bar shaped like a triangle. (See Tourbillon movement, Fig. 297, page 357.)

A spring acting on the rocking bar keeps the transmission wheel against the steel bar or screw-head, whichever is used. The screw-head is fixed in such a position that the teeth will engage with each other correctly. When the winding button is turned, the transmission wheel rides up the steel triangle, and this forces the rocking bar over, and, at the same time, the central wheel moves with it and into gear with a wheel which is screwed on to the fusee steel. This fusee steel is the steel centre of the fusee on which the complete fusee is mounted.

As soon as the winding button is released, the rocking bar drops back carrying the central wheel with it, and everything is clear of the steel wheel on the fusee.

The set-hands mechanism is the same as usual. The rocking-bar transmission wheel is pushed into gear with either the minute wheel itself, or an idle wheel. The idea of the idle wheel in any keyless watch is to prevent the hands from being moved when putting the keyless mechanism back from set hands to winding.

Sliding-Spring Fusee-Keyless

The sliding-spring type of fusee-keyless work is, of course, a most efficient form of mechanism. It may appear complicated, but the principle is quite simple. It was invented by Sutton of Clerkenwell.

Around the lower fusee hole or bearing the pillar plate is turned out, leaving a raised block. Sometimes a fusee piece, as it is called, is let into the plate and screwed firmly in position. The fusee piece is a rod of brass turned down, leaving a step which fits into a sink in the pillar plate. The fusee piece carries the lower fusee hole.

Running freely on this raised block is a steel ratchet wheel, which is sunk or turned out almost to the teeth. Into this sink is fitted a flat steel spring, which has a raised steel post shaped almost like a triangular hairspring stud. This post is solid with the spring.

Fitted on the same raised block, on the plate, and on top of the

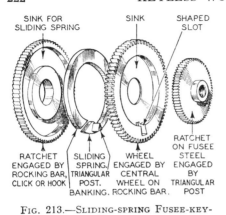

SINK FOR SLIDING SPRING

SINK

SHAPED SLOT

RATCHET ON FUSEE STEEL

RATCHET ENGAGED BY ROCKING BAR, CLICK OR HOOK

SLIDING SPRING. TRIANGULAR POST.

WHEEL ENGAGED BY CENTRAL WHEEL ON BANKING. ROCKING BAR.

STEEL ENGAGED BY TRIANGULAR POST

FIG. 213.—SLIDING-SPRING FUSEE-KEY-LESS MECHANISM.

steel ratchet wheel, is a steel wheel provided with ordinary teeth. This wheel is also sunk out to accommodate a smaller steel ratchet wheel, which is screwed on to the fusee steel. Also in this same wheel, a triangular space is filed out corresponding to the raised post on the flat steel spring, mentioned previously. The raised post is long enough to reach the top of the steel gear wheel, and it fits closely, but not tightly, the triangular space filed out in this wheel.

The central wheel is above the rocking bar, and gears directly into the gear wheel running on the fusee piece. On one side of the rocking bar is a transmission wheel for set hands, but the other end of the rocking bar terminates in a click, or hook. This engages in the steel ratchet running around the fusee piece or block.

Action of the Sliding-Spring Mechanism

The action is as follows. As the button is wound, it moves the central wheel which, in turn, rotates the gear wheel, which is running around the fusee piece. At the same time, the click holds the ratchet wheel, which is underneath the gear wheel.

As the gear wheel turns, the triangular post, by reason of its shape and the shape of the hole filed in the gear wheel, is pressed inwards, because the ratchet, in which the spring and post are fitted, is held by the rocking bar click. Thus, the triangular post being pressed inwards, engages the ratchet wheel screwed on to the fusee steel itself. The steel post is arranged so that as soon as it reaches the bottom of the teeth in the ratchet wheel screwed to the fusee, the post itself banks on the solid part of the spring of which it is a part. Thus the post is engaged with the fusee ratchet, is banked on the spring, the spring slides around in its sink, and the watch is wound.

As soon as the button is released, the steel post jumps back into the gear wheel and is disengaged from the fusee winding ratchet, and the fusee is free to run clear of the keyless work.

When the push-piece is pressed in, the click is disengaged from its ratchet wheel, and the hands can be set without any interference with the winding. The spring with the steel post is the weak point. However, if properly made, there is no reason why it should ever fail.

Making the Sliding Spring

Making a steel spring should not present difficulty to a craftsman. The spring can be made from rod silver steel, or steel plate. If using rod steel, cut a piece about the thickness of the gear wheel and the ratchet wheel combined, that is, the two wheels which run on the fusee block.

File one side perfectly flat and fix it on a wax chuck. Turn it until it fits tightly into the sink of the ratchet wheel. Turn the middle out first, of course, otherwise it will not be possible to fit it into the sink. Also turn it slightly tapered, so that it goes into the ratchet with a slight snap. The sink itself is slightly undercut to prevent the spring rising, or working out when being pushed around.

Make a dot anywhere on the steel ring, but midway between the inside and outside circles. Then soften the shellac on the wax chuck and peg the steel ring true and flat with this dot. Then proceed to turn away all the metal, leaving the metal around the dot as soon as it is turned true. This will leave a circular block, the same size or diameter as the width of the steel ring.

Turn the remainder down until it becomes flush with the top of the turned-out ratchet. To find this dimension, first measure the total thickness of the ratchet wheel, then the remaining metal where the wheel has been sunk, take one from the other, and the result will be the depth of the sink and the thickness of the spring.

To obtain the correct thickness of the spring, first measure the thickness of the wax chuck. Once this measurement is known, when the spring and chuck are measured together the difference must be the thickness of the spring. When the spring has been made to the correct thickness, remove it from the chuck and finish the rest by filing.

Shaping the Spring

First file the post to shape and keep it flush with the extreme outside of the ring. If it has to be narrowed, file it from the inside. The side, which is engaged by the shaped hole in the gear wheel above, must be carefully filed to correspond with it. The inside corner must be just free of the fusee winding ratchet. When this stage is reached, harden the spring and temper it down just lower than dark blue. Temper the spring in brass filings, but keep the filings away from the post so that the post remains slightly harder, because it is subject to a lot of wear.

The next operation is to cut the spring. Care must be taken to do this the right way. The slot must be cut from a point about ·025 inch away from the post on the outside to a point almost coinciding with the post on the inside of the ring. Thus, as the post is pushed towards the centre, it will bank on the opposite side of the slot. If cut in any other way, all the strain is taken by the spring itself and, of course, it will break. The ring is thinned from about two-thirds the way round, in other words, about one-third is thinned. The spring must be strong enough to return smartly to its position and yet not too strong that it cannot be pushed in by the shaped hole in the gear wheel above.

Hunter or Half-hunter Fusee-Keyless

Another type of fusee-keyless work can be used if the watch is a hunter or a half-hunter. The keyless work is the same as usual with one exception. The transmission wheel on the rocking bar, which usually gears into the winding ratchet in a going barrel movement, instead of being on the rocking bar itself, is on a separate bar, which runs on a stud in circle with the central wheel. This bar is movable and can swing in and out of gear with a gear wheel, which is screwed on the fusee steel. Thus, when this wheel is in gear with the fusee winding wheel it will wind.

A steel piece passes through the plate and the band of the case, and projects just above the seat of the front cover of the case. As the front cover is closed, it presses on this projection, pushing it in and puts the transmission wheel out of gear with the fusee winding wheel, and thus the fusee can run freely.

The foregoing description has covered most of the points of interest in English keyless work, so we will now deal with the Swiss and American mechanisms.

SWISS AND AMERICAN KEYLESS MECHANISMS

Some of the older Swiss and American models were provided with rocking bars, and even in some modern wrist chronographs the rocking bar is employed, usually because of the minute recording, or for some other reason depending on the layout. It is not necessary to go into detail, as the principle is very similar to the English.

Many cheap Swiss watches have rocking bars, but of a very poor quality. The most popular is the shifting-sleeve type, which is a good keyless mechanism and trouble free, if correctly made. The amount of wear is very small, except, of course, in the cheaper models.

Swiss watches now use pull-out-piece hand-setting, the push-piece being completely out-of-date. Some older models, however, with push-piece hand-setting are still met with by repairers.

There are two methods of pull-out-piece hand-setting used in keyless work, the ordinary system and that which is termed " negative-set ".

Negative-set System

With the negative-set system, the keyless mechanism is always in set hands and is put into winding by a stem in the pendant, having a screwed-in sleeve, which is sprung to allow the stem to be held in two positions. This is carried out by means of a barrel-shaped bulge on the winding stem and the claw-like end of the screwed-in sleeve in the pendant.

Sleeves

A weakness of this form of keyless work is the sleeve. These sleeves, owing to the constant strain in pulling out the stem, break or lose their elasticity and have to be replaced.

Sometimes, the ordinary pull-out hand-setting mechanism

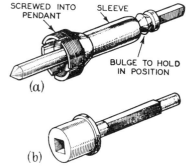

FIG. 214.—WINDING STEMS FOR NEGATIVE-SET KEYLESS WORK.

Showing (a) external stem, and (b) internal or female stem.

has been adapted in some way to suit this particular type, but the author considers that this is a change for the worse, unless it is a question of replacing an old worn-out movement, or one that is hopelessly damaged.

The modification is often carried out by removing the snap action of the trigger or pull-out piece and adding a spring, which keeps it in the out position. The stem is shortened, or replaced by a shorter one having a female or hollow square. The usual arrangement is a male square on the outer stem and a female square on the inner one. The shifting-sleeve principle is used, that is a crown and castle wheel between the plates.

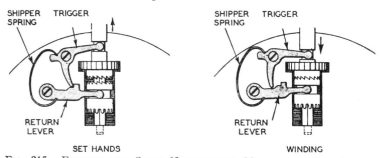

FIG. 215.—ENGLISH AND SWISS NEGATIVE-SET MECHANISM WITH CROWN AND CASTLE WHEEL CLUTCH ACTION.

The English used this same idea ; one type was very similar to the American Elgin and another favoured the Swiss.

Waltham Negative-set Mechanism

The American Waltham is a most ingenious type of negative-

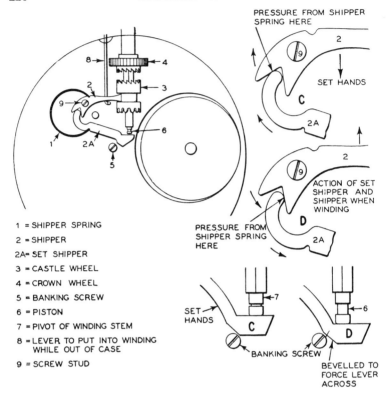

1 = SHIPPER SPRING
2 = SHIPPER
2A= SET SHIPPER
3 = CASTLE WHEEL
4 = CROWN WHEEL
5 = BANKING SCREW
6 = PISTON
7 = PIVOT OF WINDING STEM
8 = LEVER TO PUT INTO WINDING
     WHILE OUT OF CASE
9 = SCREW STUD

Fig. 216.—Waltham Negative-set Mechanism.

set mechanism. The crown and castle wheels have well-cut ratchet teeth. They have the appearance of having been made with two cutters. The bottom corner of each tooth is slotted, so there is no possibility of a root which can prevent a firm engagement. There are two levers; one runs on a stud in the form of a small cheese-headed screw, having a V-slot to engage into another lever, the end of which is engaged by a piston. This piston passes right through the inner female winding stem, and is engaged by the male square on the stem in the pendant.

The two levers are held together by a " shipper " spring, as shown in Fig. 216. The lever with the V-slot is tapered off at the other end, and this end lies in the turned groove of the castle wheel. Thus, this is the return lever or " shipper ". The action is as follows.

When the button is pulled out, the piston in the inner winding stem is pushed out and carries the lever engaged by its end. This lever at the other end engages with one side of the V-shaped end of the return lever, and by the pressure of the shipper spring forces the return lever to carry the castle wheel into gear with an idle wheel, which gears into the minute wheel. Thus the hands can be set.

When the button is pushed in, the piston in the inner female winding stem is also pushed in, engages the foot of the lever and pushes it downwards, or towards the centre of the movement. Just underneath, and towards the back of the foot of this lever, is a screw acting as a stud. As the foot is pushed down, it engages the stud and is forced across as well as downwards, and this changes its action into the return lever. Instead of pushing the return lever (or shipper) downwards, it acts on the other side of the V, pushing it upwards, and pushes the castle wheel into gear with the crown wheel. Thus the watch is ready to be wound.

Elgin Negative-set Mechanism

The Elgin has a slightly different principle. The lever which engages the piston is held in place by a shouldered screw and is extended across the plate, and at its end is a post which passes through the pillar plate by way of a slot and engages with the return lever. The return lever has a spring which tends to keep the castle wheel permanently in position for winding. The lever engaged by the piston is also acted upon by a spring, which is strong enough to overcome the strength of the return spring.

When the button is pressed, the piston is pushed in and this moves the lever downwards and also forces the post out of action with the return lever. The return spring then draws the return lever upwards, and places the castle wheel in mesh with the crown wheel and the winding. It is a very simple and effective form of keyless work.

Keeping Mechanism in Winding when out of the Case

These negative-set watches invariably have some means of keeping the mechanism in winding, if it is required to run the movement out of the case.

The Waltham has a slide near the inner winding stem, which can be pulled out by the thumb nail, or by means of a pair of tweezers. The slide engages with the return lever, which is drawn up with the castle wheel, and thus out of set hands.

The Elgin has a small pawl which acts as a banking. A part of the pawl protrudes just over the edge of the movement. When this is pulled over, it renders the spring inoperative, the return spring takes control and the watch is in winding.

Swiss Keyless Work

The general run of Swiss keyless work functions in the opposite or obvious way, inasmuch as the watches are permanently in winding.

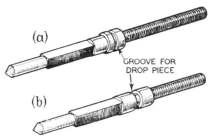

GROOVE FOR DROP PIECE

Fig. 217.—Swiss Winding Stems.

(*a*) Winding stem with crown wheel running against a shoulder. This saves wear on the plate.
(*b*) Ordinary type of stem.

The winding stem has a turned groove and the drop piece of the trigger works in it. Thus the trigger prevents the stem from falling out, or acts as an old type bridge spring. This trigger, or pull-out piece, is fitted to a screw which is pivoted between the plates and can move freely. However, it must be arranged to have very little endshake or sideshake. If it has much of either, the winding stem is liable to pull right out when the hands are being set.

Another fault with the screw is that the slot is often cut too deeply. Consequently, when trying to tighten or loosen the screw, half of the head may break off and the watch may have to be partly dismantled to remove the stem. When replacing these screws, never leave them too hard ; they should be hardened and then tempered to a light blue colour.

Making a Trigger

Another weak point is the trigger itself. Some, of course, are stronger than others and give no trouble. If an up-to-date model, the correct replacement can often be obtained, but if a year or two old, it is unlikely and a new trigger will have to be made. Then, again, some are easy to make and others are difficult.

The best way is to choose a piece of plate steel, a little fuller than the required thickness of the finished trigger. File it roughly to shape to fill the whole space between the return lever or spring, when it is pushed right down into set hands. Mark the screw-hole, and drill and tap it suitably. The hole should provide a close fit for the screw, but on no account must it be loose in the thread. Then file the metal away carefully, so that the rough trigger only just clears the crown and castle wheels.

Next file away sufficient metal to enable the return lever to be locked in the set-hands position. Then move the rough piece so that it just releases the return lever, place the winding stem in the correct position for winding, and mark the steel to outline the position of the drop piece. Then file the metal to shape, leaving the block standing so that it is just broad enough to fit the groove in the winding stem and is as long as the diameter of the stem.

Setting the Trigger in Place

The next operation is to put the trigger in place and mark where the pin or stud is to be fitted. Drill a hole smaller than required and check it for position before proceeding to broach the hole to size. If not quite right, the hole can be adjusted by filing it to the correct position—hence the reason for first drilling a small hole. When these actions are correct, harden and temper the piece to a dark blue colour. Then clean it and remove any surplus metal.

Thin the trigger, so that it can be lifted high enough to remove the stem, especially if the watch has an enamelled dial ; if too thick the dial may get cracked. Also leave the drop piece as long as possible.

Altering a Return Lever

Sometimes with these types of keyless work, as the winding stem is put in place, the castle wheel slips underneath the return lever. This often occurs where the dial has to be fitted before the move-ment is placed in the case, as is necessary where side screws are used. If the watch is put into set hands with the trigger unscrewed, this trouble will not arise.

If, however, it still happens despite these precautions, it is probably due to the nose or tongue of the return lever being shallow in the castle-wheel groove. This can be corrected by softening the return lever, and using a pair of bending pliers to raise a slight projection where the return lever engages the castle wheel. Then, of course, the return lever must be re-hardened and tempered.

Making a New Return Lever

Sometimes a return lever has to be replaced, usually when the lever and spring are in one piece. In this instance, choose a piece of good-quality steel plate, which is almost correct for thickness. File away sufficient metal to enable the rough just to drop in the space available, or as large as possible, providing it will lie in the space.

Drill the screw- and steady-pin holes, and then fit the steady pin. Next, file the tongue which lies in the groove of the castle wheel. File the tongue so that it is slightly high in relation to the groove. Make sure the trigger is in the correct position for winding, then file away the surplus metal, leaving ample metal where the trigger engages. Thin the spring part almost to the correct thickness and length, but leaving it as long as possible. At this stage, if the screw securing the spring to the plate is sunk into the spring, sink it with a pivoted sinker. Then harden and temper the rough spring, and let it down to a light blue. Then thin the rough, if necessary, and if it has warped during hardening, the thinning operation should bring it up perfectly flat.

Next file the acting face for the trigger carefully to shape. The acting face is usually an inclined plane, so make the slope as gradual as possible. If too acute, a lot of force will be required to pull the stem into set hands.

After this operation, thin the spring to the correct strength and do not leave it too strong. Providing it returns the castle wheel smartly to the crown wheel, the weaker the spring the better. It will look nice if the edges are burnished and the rest straight-grained with an emery block. Do not use an emery buff, as a buff will make it look out of flat.

Drifting a Square Hole

While on the subject of keyless mechanisms, a word or two about new pieces will not be out of place. Square holes are often required with many keyless mechanisms. With a flat wheel, the square hole can easily be filed out. The wheel is placed in the lathe and a small circle is marked with a graver point where the corners will reach. If this circle is not broken into, the wheel must be true and the hole will be perfectly square.

With a castle wheel, or a winding pinion for an English hunter, or a winding stem with a female square, it is a different matter. It is difficult to file a long hollow square and be sure of it being square all the way through, and so we " drift " the hole, as it is termed. That is, we make a square punch which is exactly the same size as the square hole we wish to make.

Making Drifts

It is better to use two drifts : a tapered drift and a straight one. The steel used for making the drifts must be of good quality and must be filed very carefully to ensure absolute accuracy. Use a micrometer and measure the sides every few moments.

The piece to be drifted must be well annealed, and drilled to the core diameter of the square, or the length of one side of the square. The drift must be hardened in water, and the temper drawn to a very pale straw. Also do not make the drift any longer than necessary.

Place the tapered drift in the hole with oil, and place the piece to be drifted on a solid stake, or in a vice. Hit the drift hard and truly with a hammer of a weight suitable to the size of the piece being drifted. When it sounds solid, rest the piece on its side and hammer the flat sides of the piece until the drift becomes loose, being very careful not to mishit and strike the drift.

Repeat the process until the drift will pass through completely, and then follow with the straight drift. When the straight drift passes through, the hole must be to size, provided that the drift has been made correctly.

Brass is drifted in the same way for clock keys, etc.

Removing Broken Screws

It often happens that a screw is broken in its hole. If the screw is hardened and tempered, a sharp blow on a punch, made just slightly smaller than the screw, will drive it out. If the screw is soft, drill a hole through the centre. Then push a square piece of hardened and tempered steel into the drilled hole and use it to remove the screw, or the remains.

A screw broken in a Swiss barrel arbor can present great difficulty. It can often be removed by using two sharp-pointed gravers to grip the remains of the screw. If it seems impossible to remove it by this means, soften the arbor and the screw, and drill out the screw. Then re-harden and temper the arbor, and re-polish. This is often the easiest way, unless a new arbor can be purchased ready-made.

A steel screw in a brass plate can be removed by leaving the plate, stripped of all other steelwork, in a strong solution of alum for about 48 hours. The screw will be partly dissolved and can then be pegged out.

MOTION WORK

In some watches the link between the keyless work and the motion work is carried out by pivoted idle wheels. Sometimes two wheels are used and sometimes only one. Again the minute wheel may also be pivoted, but this is not usual. The minute wheel usually runs on a stud. Sometimes the stud is merely pushed tightly into the plate, but with the better-quality movements, the minute wheel-stud is screwed in and a small screw may be added to prevent the stud from unscrewing.

Cutting the Teeth

It may happen that these wheels are stripped of their teeth due to the motion work being too tight.

Usually it means that they have to be specially cut and it is a tricky operation to turn them in. They must first be turned to their correct thickness, and faced up on both sides. The undercuts are polished with a hollow polisher of a corresponding shape.

The pivot is turned so that it will fit and be of the correct height, and is left long with a safety cut in case of accident. The ferrule is then placed on the pivot, the other pivot is turned to size and polished, and a safety cut is turned. The ferrule is then reversed and the other pivot is polished. The pivots are then shortened and rounded up.

The wheels are cut in the same way as a pinion. It is better if the roots of the teeth are rounded, as this form is stronger ; also the teeth must be as thick as possible.

Sometimes the smaller wheel is a bevel wheel, but it presents no difficulty. The headstock of the lathe is adjusted to the correct angle, and the teeth are cut like a contrate wheel. The angle of the headstock controls the bevel.

Motion Work Centre Arbors

The motion work consists of the minute wheel and pinion, the

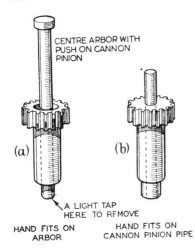

CENTRE ARBOR WITH
PUSH ON CANNON
PINION

(a)   (b)

A LIGHT TAP
HERE TO REMOVE

HAND FITS ON
ARBOR

HAND FITS ON
CANNON PINION PIPE

Fig. 218.—Motion Work Centre
Arbor and Cannon Pinion.

(a) Hand fits on to the centre arbor.
(b) A neater arrangement where the
hand is fitted on the cannon pinion pipe.

cannon pinion in a watch and the cannon wheel in a clock, and the hour wheel.

In a watch, the cannon pinion is either a " snap-on " as it is termed, or fits tightly on a centre arbor. The centre arbor passes through a hollow centre pinion. The majority of Swiss watches now use the snap-on cannon pinion, and only in the older models is a centre arbor used. With key-wind movements the centre arbor, or centre square as it was called, was essential to enable the hands to be reset. This centre arbor must not fit too tightly, but just tight enough to carry the hands.

After a time the arbor tends to work loose and the hands fail to carry. If the arbor is placed on a filing block and rolled with a round file a burr can be raised, which is sufficient to tighten the arbor in the centre pinion hole. Always place a little oil on the centre arbor when assembling the watch.

Removing a Centre Arbor

To remove a centre arbor, hold the cannon pinion in a lathe collet or screw-head tool, and with a pair of brass-nosed pliers, grip the centre arbor and twist it, when it should come out easily. On the other hand, if it is not possible to get a grip on the centre arbor, the best way is to knock it through with a punch.

If the centre arbor protrudes above the cannon pinion, as it does sometimes, a sharp tap with a brass hammer will dislodge it. However, do not use a punch, or hammer, if the centre holes are jewelled, as the holes will be smashed. The only way is to take off the centre bar or bridge, and then remove the arbor. If both centre holes are jewelled, rest the centre pinion on a stake, and drive the arbor against the face of the pinion.

With the snap-on cannon, a pin vice can be screwed tightly on the cannon pinion and then, by twisting carefully and pulling perfectly straight, it is possible to remove the cannon. Care must be taken not to pull sideways, as a broken centre pinion may result.

Tightening a Snap-on Cannon Pinion

At times the cannon pinions work loose and have to be tightened.

This is carried out by putting a broach through the cannon with a flat side towards the pip. (See Fig. 102, page 119.)

If, as in English watches, a thin groove is cut in the centre pinion arbor, the pip can be deepened by using a small centre punch. In most Swiss watches, however, the groove is long and gradual. In this case, the correct tool is a chisel-shaped punch, which should be used at an angle. A brass stake having a V-shaped groove is also required.

The stake is held firmly in a vice, and the cannon pinion with the broach through it is rested in the V-shaped groove. A suitable punch is placed against the pip, the punch is given a sharp but not a hard blow with a hammer, and the cannon should then be tight. If the cannon is too tight, it is often better to remove the pip completely and make a new one. If the pip is only partly removed the cannon will ride up, as it will also if the pip is in the wrong place. It is an operation which has to be carried out intelligently.

English Clock Motion Work

In clocks the action is altogether different. The cannon has a friction spring between the cannon wheel and the shoulder of the centre pinion, and the hand and cannon wheel are kept in place and at the correct tightness by a hand collet and a pin. There must be a trace of oil between the collet and boss of the minute hand. Likewise where the cannon is friction tight there must be a little oil, otherwise it will fire or seize up.

With the friction spring, the hands can be tightened by slightly bending the spring to increase the pressure against the collet.

French Clock Motion Work

The French carriage timepiece, in which the hands are set from the back, often has the motion work between the frames, and the hour-wheel pipe is the bearing for the centre pinion. The centre pinion is hollow, and the pivots of the centre pinion are on the centre arbor.

The pinion is held on the centre arbor by a small spring, which fits a slot or groove in the centre arbor. This spring does not give tension, but prevents the pinion from riding up and down. The arbor itself must fit the centre pinion and, if loose, can be rolled with a round file until it fits correctly.

Spring-held Motion Work

Some other types have a spiral spring held in place by a brass collet which is driven on tightly. To tighten the hands, the collet is driven on a little more to increase the tension of the spring. In these types, the minute hand fits directly on to the centre arbor.

With watches and better-quality clocks, the minute hand fits on to the cannon pinion itself, although some of the cheaper watches had a centre arbor which protrudes and the hand was fitted to it.

The advantage with the cannon pinion fitting is that the hour wheel can be easily banked and thus the endshake kept very close. Where there is but little room in a watch this is a distinct advantage. Machine-made watches often have a spring washer placed between the dial and the hour wheel to take up the shake.

Motion Work of Centre-Seconds Watches

With centre-seconds watches of the older pattern, where the centre pinion is placed off centre, the motion work is different.

The cannon pinion is really a cannon wheel. Instead of the cannon pinion, a wheel is pushed tightly on the centre arbor and this wheel gears into the minute wheel, and the minute wheel drives the cannon wheel.

It is a bad arrangement, as there is a lot of backlash in the teeth, also any inaccuracies are exaggerated. It is very difficult to get the seconds hand and the minute hand to correspond. Various arrangements have been tried, but without success. A spring washer on the hour wheel was the only thing that could be fitted with any hope of success ; but if there were any inaccuracy in the wheels, or the dial, it was just as bad.

The modern counterpart is provided with ordinary motion work. The centre pinion is hollow, of course, but the cannon pinion snaps on to the hollow centre pinion.

Some eight-day watches have indirect drive for the cannon wheel, but the teeth are triangular in shape and kept together with a spring, generally working on the minute pinion pivot which takes up all the backlash.

Another type has the minute wheel mounted directly on to the centre arbor. This also has a lot of backlash to the minute hand and it is difficult to tell the time within a minute.

Calculations for Motion Work

Calculations for motion work are quite simple. As the minute hand turns twelve times to one revolution of the hour hand, all calculations are based on 12, except, of course, in the case of true 24-hour dials. The equation is :

$$\frac{\text{minute wheel} \times \text{hour wheel}}{\text{minute pinion} \times \text{cannon pinion}} = 12.$$

Thus with a cannon pinion of 12 gearing into a minute wheel of 36, and an hour wheel of 48 gearing into a minute pinion of 12 the equation will be :

$$\frac{36 \times 48}{12 \times 12} = 12 \text{ or } \frac{3}{1} \times \frac{4}{1} = 12.$$

If a minute wheel and pinion are lost, the numbers can easily be found. If the remaining hour wheel is 48 and the cannon pinion is 14, we may express the equation as

$$\frac{48}{14} \times \frac{x}{x_1} = 12$$

therefore,

$$12 \div \frac{48}{14} = \frac{x}{x_1} \text{ or } \frac{7}{2} = \frac{x}{x_1}$$

The equation then becomes $\frac{48}{14} \times \frac{7}{2} = 12$

or

$$\frac{48}{14} \times \frac{28}{8} = 12$$

This is a much-favoured motion work. The numbers are finally decided by the distance between the minute stud and the centre pinion, or the distance of centres. In the case of a minute wheel of 28 teeth the distance of centres will be $1\frac{1}{2}$ times the pitch diameter of the cannon pinion. The same applies to the minute pinion.

With most centre-seconds watches of the old type, the minute wheel and cannon were of the same number, so the ratio between the minute pinion and hour wheel was 12 : 1.

Where the minute wheel is mounted directly on to the centre arbor and acts as the driver instead of the cannon pinion, as is usual, the ratios vary according to the model. The minute wheels sometimes take four hours to complete one revolution and thus the cannon is at a ratio of 4 : 1 to the minute wheel, the reason being that the cannon revolves once per hour and the hour wheel and minute pinion must be 3 : 1 ratio.

In clocks the ratios are just the same. With a number of clocks the cannon wheel and minute wheel have the same number of teeth and thus the proportion of the hour wheel to the minute pinion must be 12 : 1. A minute pinion of 6 leaves and an hour wheel of 72 teeth is the usual arrangement.

The motion work of clocks will be explained further in Chapter 13 dealing with striking mechanisms.

" UP-AND-DOWN " INDICATOR MECHANISM

It is appropriate to include in this chapter a description of the " up-and-down " mechanism, as it is called. This is a mechanism for showing whether a watch is wound up or run down. Usually a hand, or some form of indicator, is fitted on the dial itself.

Fusee " Up-and-down " Mechanism

The mechanism is quite simple in respect of a fusee watch, because the fusee when being wound up runs one way, and in running down runs the reverse way. A pinion on the fusee steel gearing into a larger wheel is all that is required.

If the fusee makes four turns from top to bottom and we want

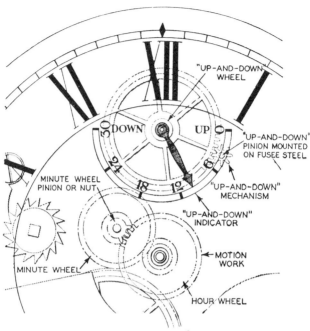

Fig. 219.—Motion Work and " Up-and-down " Mechanism as fitted to a Fusee Watch or Chronometer.
The indicator hand shows the extent to which the piece is wound.

to show the hours it is run down, we can fit a pinion of 8 leaves on the fusee steel and a wheel of 40 teeth gearing into it. The wheel of 40 teeth will either be pivoted in the frame at the end, or run on a stud. The hand will travel on the dial four-fifths of a turn and if this four-fifths is divided into four, each will represent eight hours and can be marked on the dial.

Some fusees make 4½ turns, while some, as in the case of marine chronometers, make 8½ turns with a 2-day and 16 turns with an 8-day. The proportion between the pinion and the up-and-down wheel can be made accordingly. With an 8-day, it is generally marked off on the dial in days.

Going-Barrel " Up-and-down " Mechanism

With a going-barrel watch, however, the " up-and-down " mechanism is very different. When the watch is being wound the keyless work is turning, but while the watch is running down, the barrel turns and the keyless work remains stationary. Thus a very different arrangement from the fusee is required. It has been carried out in many ways.

One method uses a threaded pipe fitted on the barrel arbor

square, and on to this threaded pipe a threaded steel collar is fitted. Several holes are drilled through the collar to enable a pin, which is fitted tightly into the bottom of the barrel, to be inserted in the most convenient hole. The collar also has a groove turned in the side which is engaged by a pin on a pivoted arm, which also engages a rack. This rack is geared into a pinion on which the up-and-down hand is fitted.

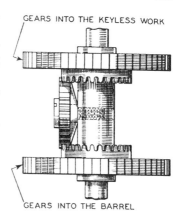

GEARS INTO THE KEYLESS WORK

GEARS INTO THE BARREL

FIG. 220.—DIFFERENTIAL MECHANISM USED IN GOING-BARREL " UP-AND-DOWN " INDICATORS.

As it is being wound, the square on the barrel arbor turns and carries the threaded pipe. As it does so, it draws the collar downwards by reason of the thread. Likewise as the barrel turns, the pin in the barrel, which also fits a hole in the steel collar, turns the steel collar, while the pipe on the barrel arbor remains stationary, so the collar runs up the thread and carries the hand back again.

Differential used in Going-Barrel Indicator Mechanism

The differential is, of course, the best arrangement, although slightly complicated (see Fig. 220). The mechanism takes up very little space and can be placed between the plates. It is now used in the automatic or self-winding wrist watch, which is a good idea as the owner needs a guide as to whether the watch is wound or not.

Pivoted between the plates is an arbor and on this arbor are two wheels each provided with two sets of teeth. One set of teeth on one wheel is geared into the barrel, and a set on the second wheel is geared into the keyless wheel.

The other set of teeth on each wheel is set at right angles, and both are geared into a pinion, which is held by a shouldered screw and runs freely on the side of the arbor pivoted between the plates. Thus whichever wheel is revolving, the pivoted arbor also turns. The mechanism is trouble-free, and wear is not worth considering.

AUTOMATIC OR SELF-WINDING MECHANISMS

In addition to the keyless watch, which was an advance on the keywind, the "automatic" or self-winding watch is now extensively made, and thus another advance is registered. The earlier automatics were not provided with ordinary keyless work as well, and thus, if the self-winding mechanism failed, or the owner did not wear it, the watch stopped. The later models, however, are

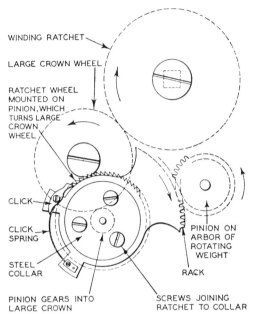

WINDING RATCHET

LARGE CROWN WHEEL

RATCHET WHEEL
MOUNTED ON
PINION, WHICH
TURNS LARGE
CROWN
WHEEL

CLICK

CLICK
SPRING

STEEL
COLLAR

PINION ON
ARBOR OF
ROTATING
WEIGHT

RACK

PINION GEARS INTO
LARGE CROWN

SCREWS JOINING
RATCHET TO COLLAR

FIG. 221.—PRINCIPLE OF SELF-WINDING AS
APPLIED TO JAEGER-LECOULTRE AND OTHER
MOVEMENTS.

provided with ordinary winding in addition to the self-winding mechanism.

The Self-winding Principle

The movement is as usual, but of a smaller caliper than the case suggests. This is to make room for the rotor or rotating weight, sometimes referred to as the "pendulum" or oscillating weight, which is mostly fitted or pivoted in the centre of the plate (Fig. 221).

The arbor on which the weight is fitted is a pinion which runs in a jewel-hole in the barrel bar, and is spanned by a bridge which also has a jewel-hole for the top pivot of the pinion. This pinion is geared into a rack that is part of a unit, having a click and a very fine click spring, which keeps the click engaged with a ratchet wheel. This ratchet wheel lies on the rack and is held in place by a steel collar, which is fixed by three screws to this same ratchet and is shouldered through the rack.

Fitted to the ratchet is a pinion, which is pivoted into the barrel bar and is geared to the large ratchet wheel of the keyless work. The same bridge, which supports the top pivot of the weight, also carries, in a jewel-hole, the top pivot of the wheel and pinion on the rack.

Buffer Springs

When the weight moves in one direction, the click slides over the ratchet wheel and does not engage; but when the weight moves in the opposite direction, the click engages with the ratchet and turns it a number of teeth according to the length of the swing. As the ratchet turns, the pinion fitted to it also turns, and, as it is geared into the large ratchet wheel attached to the barrel, which in some cases carries another click spring, the watch is wound.

On one end of the weight is a buffer spring, and there is also a similar spring on a buffer spring bridge on the opposite side of the weight. The object of these buffers is to absorb the shock should the watch receive a violent swing. This model, which is made by Jaeger-LeCoultre, is provided with an up-and-down indicator.

Rotor Full Circle Wind

The latest automatics have a rotor or fully rotating weight which can run the full circle either way, but not all models wind both ways. One well-known model by Rolex is very good.

The rotor is secured by a screw with a large head. The screw head is drilled and tapped to take a locking screw, which protrudes into the rotor itself to prevent the screw from coming undone while in use. The movement is completely covered by the extra plate or cap, into which the top pivots of the self-winding train are supported.

An arrow indicates the trigger screw—a very sensible idea. It saves trying other screws, if not familiar with the type of watch, when the winding stem has to be removed.

The rotor arm fits on a square attached to an arbor passing through the cap or plate, and pivoted between the back plate and the cap. On the other end of the arbor is another square, and fitted on to this square is a three-bladed spring, acting as triple clicks and springs combined.

The triple clicks, as they are termed, engage in a wheel very similar to the small crown wheel in an ordinary keyless mechanism, that is, it has ordinary gear teeth, and ratchet teeth set at right angles which run on a pivot on the same arbor. Thus, as the rotor moves, it carries the arbor with it and also the triple clicks.

As the rotor moves in one direction, the clicks pass over the ratchet teeth and do not engage. As the rotor moves in the opposite direction, the clicks gather the ratchet teeth and turn the wheel with it. This wheel gears into the wheel of a wheel and pinion, and the pinion gears into the wheel of a second pair and on to a third pair in the same way. The last pair has a large pinion, which gears directly into the winding mechanism by means of a wheel connected to the winding ratchet through the medium of a click and ratchet. The object of this connection is to enable the watch to be wound in the ordinary way, without the self-winding mechanism rushing round.

There is also a supplementary click on the first pair of wheels of the self-winding mechanism. This prevents the train from running back, should the rotor fail to move far enough to wind the watch a full tooth of the winding ratchet. There is, of course, the usual click on the winding ratchet, so it is perfectly safe to lift the cap or plate to remove the self-winding train.

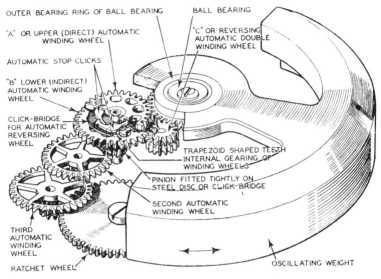

OUTER BEARING RING OF BALL BEARING   BALL BEARING

"A" OR UPPER (DIRECT) AUTOMATIC
WINDING WHEEL

"C" OR REVERSING
AUTOMATIC DOUBLE
WINDING WHEEL

AUTOMATIC STOP CLICKS

"B" LOWER (INDIRECT)
AUTOMATIC WINDING
WHEEL

CLICK-BRIDGE
FOR AUTOMATIC
REVERSING
WHEEL

TRAPEZOID SHAPED TEETH
INTERNAL GEARING OF
WINDING WHEELS

PINION FITTED TIGHTLY ON
STEEL DISC OR CLICK-BRIDGE

SECOND AUTOMATIC
WINDING WHEEL

THIRD
AUTOMATIC
WINDING
WHEEL

OSCILLATING WEIGHT

RATCHET WHEEL

FIG. 222.—PRINCIPLE OF FULL CIRCLE BOTH WAYS WINDING AS USED BY
" ETERNA-MATIC ".

Full Circle Wind Both Ways

A later model is the " Eterna-matic ". This model is a little thicker than usual to make room for the oscillating weight and the self-winding train. The advantage it possesses is that the weight not only runs a full turn both ways, but also winds both ways. This is carried out very simply (see Fig. 222).

The oscillating weight, which acts like a rotor, revolves on ball bearings that rest on a steel cap top and bottom, and these caps are again held by a screw on to a brass stud. Fitted on the underside of the rotor is a steel wheel, which is geared directly into two further wheels.

One is the top brass wheel of a type of differential gear which we will call A. The other is the top half of a small double wheel of two small wheels fitted together which we will call C. This differential consists of the brass wheel A and a larger brass wheel below, which we will call B. The small double wheel C gears into the lower wheel B. The small double wheel C revolves in the same direction as wheel A, because they both gear into the steel wheel fitted on to the weight.

Double wheel C, acting as an intermediate, gears into the lower brass wheel B and turns it in the opposite direction to wheel A. Thus wheels A and B are always revolving in opposite directions. These wheels A and B run freely on the arbor of a hollow pinion, and the lower wheel B is held in place by the pinion head on which it rests. The top wheel *A* is held in place by a pressed-on steel collar which fits the pinion arbor.

The Clicks

Mounted tightly on the pinion arbor and turning with it is a steel disc. This disc is between the two brass wheels *A* and *B*, and has four clicks, two above and two below. Two engage the top brass wheel *A* and the other two the brass wheel *B*. These clicks are so arranged that click springs are unnecessary. The head of the latter engages the tail of the former and pushes the nose into the path of the protuberances on the inside of each wheel *A* and *B*.

The pinion and the disc can only turn anti-clockwise. Thus as wheel *A* is turning clockwise by the movement of the weight, the back of the clicks are engaged and the wheel merely pushes by. At the same time wheel *B* is turning anti-clockwise, and through its direction the noses of the clicks engage the protuberances and grip them, and the disc with its pinion is turned in the correct direction, that is, anti-clockwise.

The weight on a reverse swing turns wheel *A* in an anti-clockwise direction. The click on *B*, which is turning clockwise, slides over, but the clicks engage wheel *A* and the disc and its pinion are turned in the correct direction, that is, anti-clockwise. Thus whichever way the weight moves, one of the wheels, either *A* or *B*, is turning anti-clockwise and thus winding the watch.

The rest of the mechanism is quite straightforward. There are two wheels and pinions between the differential and the winding ratchet. This is a reduction gear, as the pinions are the drivers. The pinion of the last wheel and pinion is geared into the winding ratchet on the barrel arbor. The click to hold the mainspring acts on the large crown wheel, instead of, as usual, on the barrel arbor or winding ratchet.

Removing and Replacing the Mechanism

The self-winding mechanism is mounted on the supplementary plate, and on taking out three screws the whole mechanism lifts off. Care must be taken when replacing the mechanism, because the last pinion is pivoted in the top plate of the movement as well as in the supplementary plate. Make certain, therefore, that the pivot enters the hole, and the pinion does not jamb on the tops of the winding-ratchet teeth.

Another model which winds both ways is the Felsa. The connection wheel between the pinion and the weight rocks left and right as the weight reverses on a pivotless lever. It first gears into one wheel and then into another geared to it. It is very simple in operation.

CHAPTER 11

BALANCES AND BALANCE-SPRINGS

THE time-controlling element of a watch is formed by the balance and balance-spring, or hairspring as it is often called. The same, of course, applies equally to a clock fitted with a platform escapement.

It is the number of vibrations of the balance over a given time which necessitates a correct train of wheels with the correct number of teeth on the wheels and leaves in the pinions.

Matching Balance and Balance-Spring

If a balance could be made in such a way that there were no interference from any source whatsoever and no friction at the pivots, a balance-spring could be fitted to it which would completely control the number of vibrations over a given period of time. Unfortunately this is not possible in practice, and each watch has to be considered separately when it is a question of fine timekeeping.

There is, of course, such a thing as selective assembly, where the balances and balance-springs are made to a standard pattern and the best balance and the best, or most suitable, balance-spring are paired together. Very good results are often obtained by this method.

Compensation Curb Pins

One big problem with balances is the question of compensation for temperature variations, involving losses in heat and gains in cold temperatures.

In some of the older watches compensation curb pins were used and some very good results were obtained. One index pin was a fixture and the other pin was fitted to a bimetallic arm, usually consisting of brass and steel fused together. Thus, in the higher temperatures the movable pin moved closer to its partner and made the watch gain to compensate for losses due to the expansion of the balance and spring and, of course, the pin moved away in the colder temperatures. The reason for the movement of the pin is because brass expands more in heat than steel and as the brass is fused on the outside of the arm, the arm is bent inwards in heat, and vice versa.

Then came the gold balance and the nickel-steel or " Invar " balance-spring. With nickel-steel the coefficient of thermal expansion is very small and it was, therefore, an improvement on the plain balance with a steel balance-spring.

Compensation Balances

The compensation balance, invented by Arnold, was a great advance. Fig. 223 shows a compensation balance in which a bimetallic rim is used, consisting of brass and steel fused together. The rim itself is cut through to allow the arm to close in and open outwards in heat and cold respectively. It was found that this was insufficient to compensate fully for the changes in rate, so movable weights or screws were added to the rim to enable the balance to be adjusted according to the error. Therefore, if a watch is losing in heat more weight is moved to the cut end of the arm, and thus more weight moves inwards and lightens the balance accordingly.

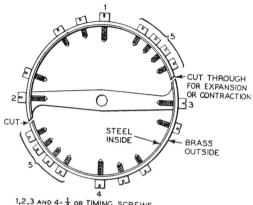

1,2,3 AND 4 = ¼ OR TIMING SCREWS
5 = COMPENSATING SCREWS

FIG. 223.—BIMETALLIC COMPENSATION BALANCE.

The proportion of the two metals used extensively is 3 : 2. For example, if the rim were ·02 inch thick, there would be ·012 inch of brass and ·008 inch of steel. This, however, is not a standard and various makers adopt different proportions.

The types of balance are innumerable, however, and we cannot hope to mention them all. The principle is all that is required.

Non-Magnetic Balances

The fact of watches becoming magnetized created a further problem and much research was carried out on this subject.

Some balances were so soft that there was every chance of bending them, however carefully they were handled. However, balances made of nickel-steel and brass were very successful and easy to handle, as they were almost as hard as those made of brass and steel. Palladium balance-springs were used in conjunction with these balances, with extremely good results. Added to this, of course, the 'scape wheel, pallets, lever and roller were made of gold of low quality. A gold 'scape wheel was not necessary, but it gave a good appearance. Sometimes just phosphor-bronze was used for the lever, pallets and roller. Thus, the whole escapement was non-magnetic, except, of course, the 'scape pinion, pallet staff and balance staff, but their influence was negligible.

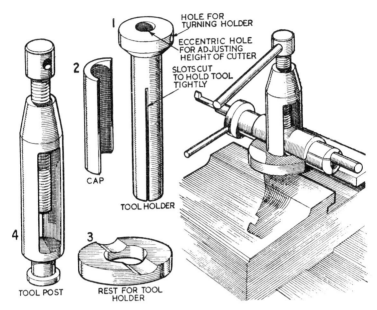

FIG. 224.—TOOL HOLDER FOR SLIDE REST AND METHOD OF ADJUSTING THE HEIGHT OF CUTTER.

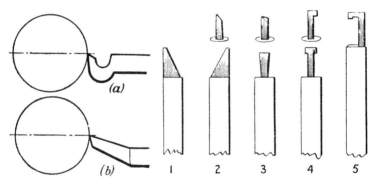

FIG. 225a.—SLIDE REST CUTTER FOR TURNING STEEL.

(a) For making heavy or deep cuts.

(b) For finishing or smooth cuts.

Note angle for cutting edges and position when presented to the work.

FIG. 225b.—SLIDE REST CUTTERS FOR TURNING BRASS.

1 and 2. Tools for general turning, left- and right-hand cutting.

3. Tool for turning square-sided sinks.

4. Boring tool for turning out holes.

5. Tool for turning bottom of a barrel with clearance for a barrel hook.

Making a Balance

Balances are usually made by specialists, but occasionally a balance is required that cannot be bought and consequently has to be made by the repairer himself. A few hints on the subject may, therefore, be useful.

In the first place, it should be emphasized that it is advisable to use a slide rest for the entire job, as this will ensure accuracy. (See Figs. 224 and 225.)

A rod of good-quality steel is essential, the diameter of which must be larger than the full diameter of the balance by about ·045 inch. A true hole of the required size is drilled into the rod to a good depth, or deeper than the thickness or height of the balance. A sink is turned in the rod so that the inside diameter corresponds to the diameter of the steel in the finished balance and reaches to within about ·005 inch of the outside diameter of the steel rod. The depth is equivalent to the full height of the balance and should be made a little deeper to allow for cleaning later on.

Next, part off the steel rod so that it is slightly thicker than the depth of the sink and still solid and sound. Then turn a ring of brass which will fit the sink and stand above the steel.

Fusing the Bimetallic Rim

Mix some jeweller's borax with perfectly clean water and make into a thin paste. Make certain that there is no oil or grease, or any foreign matter, in the steel sink ; in other words, be sure the surfaces are quite clean. Then coat the sink completely with the borax paste and also the brass ring. Place the brass ring in the sink. Fill the drilled hole with black lead, or charcoal, to prevent the brass running into it when melted. Do not use oil or grease in the hole as it may spread over the metal and prevent the brass from joining properly with the steel.

Heat until the brass ring melts and then allow the whole to cool slowly. The turned sink will be completely full and will overflow, probably over the steel, but this does not matter providing that brass does not enter the hole in the steel.

Turning the Balance to Size

Fix the rough balance on a wax chuck and peg it perfectly true and flat. Place the solid part of the balance against the face of the chuck, because the other side will probably be covered with brass. Turn the face of the rough balance making it flat and then turn the steel off the outside edge. Remove it from the wax chuck, clean off the wax in methylated spirits and proceed to hammer the brass on the edge evenly all the way round.

Wax the rough balance back on to the chuck with the front, that is the side just turned flat, against the face of the chuck and

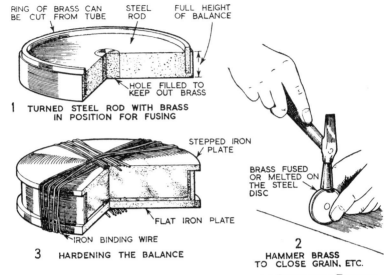

FIG. 226.—PROCEDURE FOR MAKING AND HARDENING A BIMETALLIC BALANCE.

make certain it is dead flat and perfectly true. Then turn the face until the balance is of the correct thickness. Now proceed to sink the balance to the correct depth, leaving the right amount of steel in the rim. Turn the sink very smoothly as it saves a lot of work when finishing the balance later.

Next turn the outside edge of the balance to the correct size If all the measurements of the pattern balance have been followed the brass and steel will be of the same proportion as the pattern, File out the bottom of the balance leaving the arms, and file the rest true with the steel in the rim and leave smooth.

Drilling and Tapping the Rim

The next operation is to drill and tap the rim for the screws. This is best carried out in the lathe using a dividing-plate and the vertical slide to hold the drill. This will ensure that all the holes are opposite each other and are also at the correct angle.

Hardening and Tempering the Balance

If a good-quality balance is required, this is the stage at which to harden and temper the steel in the balance. Two pieces of iron are necessary. A disc must be turned from one piece to fit the sink and to stand slightly above the top of the balance. The other piece is used to make a disc slightly larger than the total diameter of the balance. One is fitted inside the balance and the other is placed flush with the bottom of the balance and then the whole is wired firmly together or, better still, clamped together with a mild-steel clamp.

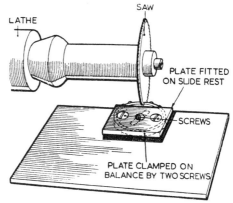

FIG. 227.—How Balance is cut by Saw in the Lathe.

The whole assembly is then heated until it becomes a cherry-red colour, when it is plunged into water which has oil floating on the top. The idea of the oil is to stop the steel cracking and help to prevent warping.

After hardening, the balance is cleaned until it is bright. It is next covered with brass filings, leaving the steel arm just visible, and then tempered until the steel turns a pale blue colour.

Next proceed to polish the balance rim and smooth the sink inside the balance. The top rim is polished by laying the balance on a piece of cork and using a tin block, about twice the size of the balance, held in the hand. When all has been cleaned and the necessary parts polished, the balance is cut.

Cutting the Balance

This is carried out by clamping the balance to a plate fitted on to the slide rest. A saw is held in the lathe and the balance is led to it slowly. If carried out slowly, the balance will not distort and will be easier to bring flat and true afterwards. The balance can be cut with or without the balance staff fitted.

To make the balance true, use either the figure-of-8 callipers, or the pair with cross-over centres mentioned earlier. The staff, of course, must be riveted to the balance to bring the balance true and flat.

Tools for Bending the Arm

Two tools are necessary for bending or twisting the arm of the balance, if it is not to be marked or bruised. These tools are quite simple to make.

Choose a piece of brass rod of about $\frac{3}{16}$ inch diameter. Drill two holes near the centre to leave a gap of ·025 inch between the holes. Drill the holes about ·04 inch in diameter. Fit an ivory pin firmly into each hole and standing up about ·075 inch above the brass.

The tool is used by placing a pin on each side of the rim, and twisting wherever required.

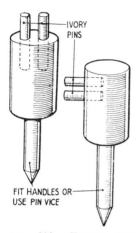

IVORY PINS

FIT HANDLES OR USE PIN VICE

FIG. 228.—TOOLS FOR BENDING BALANCE ARM TO TRUE BALANCE AFTER IT HAS BEEN CUT.

The other tool is similar, except that the brass is filed flat on one side and the pins are put in on the side or at right angles to the rod. These dimensions, of course, apply only to a balance of the size used in a gentleman's pocket watch. For wristlet and bracelet watch balances, proportionately smaller pins and a narrower gap between them are necessary.

In factories, of course, a different method of making balances is employed. The arm and rim is stamped out in a press and the screw-holes are drilled in automatic machines. The balance is produced complete for a very small figure, although this cannot be carried out for an individual balance as the cost would be prohibitive. Consequently a balance often has to be made the hard way.

Uncut Balances

The latest balances are not cut, but are made in such a way that under heat the balance becomes egg-shaped. Whether these balances will maintain their compensation qualities, like the brass and steel balance, remains to be seen. They have the added advantage, however, of being used in conjunction with an " Elinvar " balance-spring which does not require much compensation.

All that is necessary is to compensate for other errors, such as thickening or thinning of the oil and unequal changes in the escapement and the train. This is accomplished by an " Affix " added or screwed on to the solid rim. The " Affix " is bimetallic and is similar to part of the rim of a brass-and-steel balance, and the adjustment is the same.

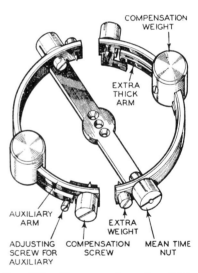

COMPENSATION WEIGHT

EXTRA THICK ARM

AUXILIARY ARM

EXTRA WEIGHT

ADJUSTING SCREW FOR AUXILIARY

COMPENSATION SCREW

MEAN TIME NUT

FIG. 229.—KULLBERG AUXILIARY COMPENSATION BALANCE FOR MARINE CHRONOMETERS.

Used to restrict expansion of balance in low temperatures.

Middle-Temperature Error

The greatest difficulty with the brass-and-steel balance is the middle-temperature error. Correct adjustment can be made for high temperatures, but when the piece is put into a low temperature it is almost certain to lose or go slower. The use of palladium balance-springs helped a lot in this direction, but did not solve the problem.

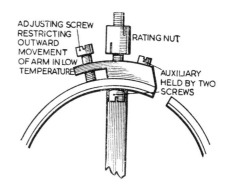

FIG. 230.—AUXILIARY COMPENSATION BY JOHN POOLE.

Helped to correct in the lower temperatures.

Auxiliaries

The best device for overcoming this difficulty is probably the auxiliary invented and applied by Victor Kullberg, the celebrated chronometer maker. The advantage of this type is that there are no pieces riveted or screwed on, but everything is made from the solid.

The balance is made in the usual way and only the rim itself varies. About half-way round the rim it is divided into two sections. The upper section is as usual, except at the extreme end, but the lower half is left appreciably thicker on the inside. The extreme end is drilled and tapped and a screw is fitted, which engages on a protuberance at the extreme end of the top section of the rim.

The weights are fitted on the solid part of the rim, and at the extreme end of the top section is a compensating screw supplementary to the weight. The auxiliary acts in the low temperatures and prevents the compensation arm moving too far out. The adjusting screw is moved to quicken the rate in the cold temperatures. This balance is extremely efficient, and properly adjusted the middle-temperature error is negligible.

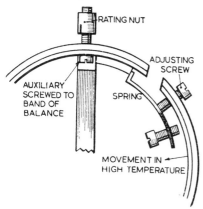

FIG. 231.—AUXILIARY COMPENSATION BY MOLYNEUX.

Helped to correct in the higher temperatures.

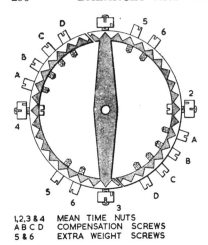

1,2,3 & 4 MEAN TIME NUTS
A B C D COMPENSATION SCREWS
5 & 6 EXTRA WEIGHT SCREWS

FIG. 232.—UNUSUAL TYPE OF COMPENSATION BALANCE MADE IN A WHEEL-CUTTING ENGINE.

John Poole, Mercer, Molyneux and Professor Airy all invented types of auxiliaries, but these are met with only occasionally.

In one interesting type of balance encountered by the author, the rim must have been made in a wheel-cutting engine. The steel blank had small star wheel teeth all the way round and thus when the brass was fused on the rim there was an equal amount of brass and steel. This watch gained a Kew certificate and, although unorthodox, obtained good marks for compensation. It is difficult to explain the reason, but as a matter of interest a sketch of the balance is reproduced in Fig. 232.

Balance-Springs

Balance-springs have been made in nearly every kind of metal and have even been made in glass. At one time, the material used most frequently was hardened and tempered steel. To-day, it is generally the practice to use an uncut balance, as mentioned previously, in conjunction with a self-compensating spring made in one of the alloys of the nickel-steel group, such as " Elinvar ". The advantage of this alloy, invented by Professor Guillaume, is that its coefficient of thermal change of elasticity is very small, which makes it a particularly suitable material for balance-springs.

Making " Elinvar " Balance-Springs

To make an " Elinvar " balance-spring, first choose the correct size of wire required. The best way is to measure the old spring, if available, and copy it with regard to thickness and height, or if not of the correct dimensions it can be used as a guide. If a pattern is not available and it is not wished to resort to lengthy calculations, various hairsprings can be tried until an idea is obtained of the required dimensions. Experience counts a lot in this matter.

Construction of Winder and Barrel

Having chosen the wire, make a barrel a little larger than the diameter of the balance-spring when finished, or a sink can be turned in a plate of German silver. The depth should be about three times the height of the wire. A cover is made to fit into the

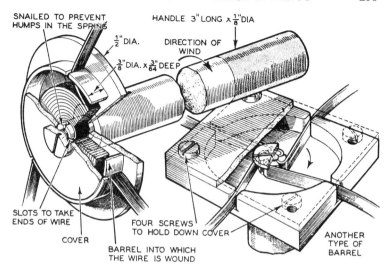

SNAILED TO PREVENT
HUMPS IN THE SPRING

HANDLE 3" LONG x ⅛"DIA

½" DIA.

DIRECTION OF
WIND

⅜"DIA. x ¾"DEEP

SLOTS TO TAKE
ENDS OF WIRE

COVER

FOUR SCREWS
TO HOLD DOWN COVER

BARREL INTO WHICH
THE WIRE IS WOUND

ANOTHER
TYPE OF
BARREL

FIG. 233.—METHOD OF MAKING BALANCE-SPRINGS, SHOWING TWO DIFFERENT
TYPES OF BARREL FOR WINDING THE SPRINGS.

barrel or sink, but not too tightly. Then file three slots in the edge of the barrel, as shown in Fig. 233, wide enough to allow the wire to pass through.

Next make an arbor on a piece of brass rod about 3 inches long. First turn the brass rod down to the same size as the centre of the finished but unmounted balance-spring. Then drill or open the hole in the barrel and cover, making it the same size as the brass rod. Drill a true hole in the brass rod and tap it. Then fit a screw having a long head. One of about 12 B.A. will do, but if a small balance-spring is being made a smaller screw must be used.

Cut three radial slots in the end of the brass rod slightly shallower than the height of the wire and the same width as the wire. Snail the slots so that the beginning of the wire will not be bumpy or, in other words, lower one side of the slot by the thickness of the wire and gradually slope upwards to the front of the following slot, as shown in the diagram.

Winding the Wire into the Barrel

If a flat balance-spring is being used, wind three pieces of wire together into the barrel or sink. If, on the other hand, an overcoil is to be used on the balance-spring, wind only two pieces of wire in together. The number of pieces of wire wound into the barrel together controls the distance apart of the coils. To wind the wire into the barrel, cut off three lengths of wire about 12 inches long. Place the arbor from the underside of the barrel through the barrel. Fit one end of each piece of wire in the slots in the arbor, and tighten the screw to hold the wire firmly on the winder.

Replace the cover and hold it firmly on to the wire. Turn the arbor carefully and wind the wire round it. When the arbor becomes very stiff to move, lift the cover carefully and see if the wire has wound evenly and tightly round the arbor. Do not turn the arbor when it becomes stiff as the centre of the wire may be broken. When the barrel or sink is full and tight, clamp the cover firmly on the coiled-up wire. Then remove the winder.

The Hydrogen Oven

The springs have next to be set. This is carried out by placing them in a hydrogen oven at a temperature of about 1500° F. and keeping them at that temperature for about five minutes. The reason for using the hydrogen oven is to prevent the spring going black and to avoid difficulty in cleaning.

To remove the springs from the barrel, place the barrel in a box and hit it several times with the palm of the hand ; the springs will come out and separate at the same time. They are then ready for use.

Steel Balance-Springs

The same procedure applies to steel balance-springs as regards winding them into the barrel. Steel, however, has to be hardened and tempered if it is to be used on a good-quality watch.

If a cheap watch, the wire can be wound in to the barrel in the ordinary way and heated until the springs turn to a dark blue colour or midway between light and dark blue. They can then be removed from the barrel and dipped in a weak solution of hydrochloric acid to clean them. Then the springs are blued on a brass plate which is quite flat.

Hardening and Tempering the Steel Spring

To harden and temper better-quality springs fill the barrel with soft soap, including the hole in the barrel and cover, so that it is completely sealed. This will exclude the air and prevent the springs becoming heavily fire-skinned or blackened.

The barrel and cover are bound tightly with iron binding wire. The whole is then made red hot and plunged into a jar containing water with about an eighth of an inch of oil floating on the top. The purpose of the oil is to lessen the shock and prevent the springs cracking.

After hardening, place the barrel complete into a pan with brass filings. Clean a piece of steel ; an old roller or lever, or a steel endpiece will do. Cover the barrel with the brass filings, and then place the piece of steel on top so that it is visible. Heat the pan until the piece of steel turns to a light blue colour. Remove the

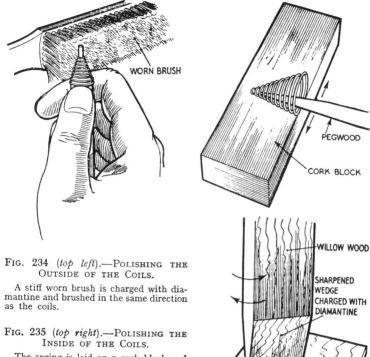

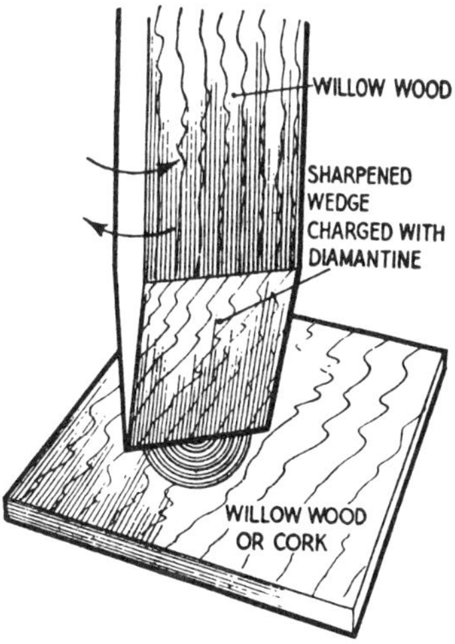

FIG. 234 (*top left*).—POLISHING THE
OUTSIDE OF THE COILS.

A stiff worn brush is charged with diamantine and brushed in the same direction
as the coils.

FIG. 235 (*top right*).—POLISHING THE
INSIDE OF THE COILS.

The spring is laid on a cork block and
stroked from side to side.

FIG. 236 (*bottom right*).—POLISHING
THE TOP AND BOTTOM OF THE COILS.

The spring must be turned periodically
so that each coil receives the same treatment.

barrel at once and cool it, otherwise the springs may become
too soft.

Polishing the Balance-Spring

Remove the springs from the barrel. Then polish the coils
inside and outside, and also top and bottom. It is a simple matter
to polish the outside of the coils. A large piece of tapered pegwood
is used, the spring being placed over the point and stretched downwards so that the coils rest on the wood. The outside coils are then
polished, by means of a short-haired watch brush charged with
very wet diamantine and oil, until they become quite bright.

It is not so easy to polish the inside coils. The spring is placed
on a piece of flat cork. A piece of pegwood is sharpened to a gradual

taper and covered with wet diamantine. The spring is held edge-wise to the cork and the centre coils are pushed away until the coils will all lie on the cork. The pegwood is then moved from side to side, sliding over the inside of the coils. By working on a different section in turn, eventually every coil will become polished. It only requires practice, so do not despair if not successful at first. Be careful not to treat one section of the spring more than any other, and do not put too much pressure on the spring. These springs are fairly strong, but can be damaged.

Usually the brush treatment at least cleans the top and bottom of the spring. If the spring needs polishing, however, a piece of willow wood, sharpened to a knife-edge and charged with wet diamantine, can be used. This is placed on the spring as it rests on a flat piece of cork and is turned backwards and forwards to polish the top and bottom of the coils. If a little nervous of these jobs, practise on an old balance-spring at first until the knack has been acquired.

Cleaning the Spring

When all of the spring has been well polished, clean it in benzine and dry in sawdust. If the spring does not blue very well, clean it again and wash in methylated ether. Then dry quickly on a previously warmed brass plate. Ether is very highly inflammable, so do not have the spirit lamp alight while using it.

Blueing the Spring

Blue the spring on a perfectly flat brass plate, in air. Watch the spring carefully, as it changes colour very quickly. It is far better to leave a slight trace of purple rather than a pale colour. Some prefer a purple blue as it looks richer.

Pinning Balance-Spring to Collet

The next operation is to pin the spring on to the collet. If a steel balance-spring collet, put the collet tightly on a hardened and tempered, tapered steel rod. If a brass slotted collet, use a tool filed to a round and having a pointed bulge on one side. This bulge enters the slot in the collet and prevents it from moving.

Break off a piece of surplus spring from the end and keep it handy. Break out sufficient of the centre coils to make room for the collet ; always allow a full coil freedom from the collet to the first turn of the spring. On the other hand, if it is proposed to have an internal terminal curve, leave about two turns clearance from the collet to allow for manipulation.

Straighten the extreme end of the inner coil to correspond to the length of the hole in the collet. Put this straight piece through the hole and obtain an idea of the shape required to enable the balance-spring to run true when pinned up. After making certain that the inner coil is correctly shaped, remove it and replace by the

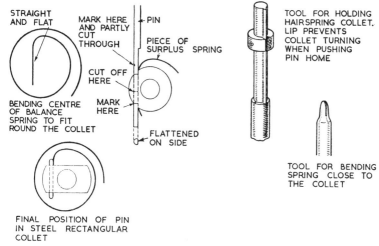

FIG. 237.—PROCEDURE FOR PINNING BALANCE-SPRING TO THE COLLET FOR BOTH ROUND AND RECTANGULAR TYPES OF COLLET.

surplus piece of spring broken off earlier. See that the spring will lie flat and true and, if necessary, broach the hole in the collet until it does ; it will save a lot of trouble later.

Making the Pin

Remove the piece of spring and proceed to make the pin. First file a slightly tapered brass pin (not carrot shaped) until it passes through the hole in the collet. Then file one side flat ; about a third of its diameter will be about right. Place the surplus piece of spring in the hole in the collet. Push the pin in with a twisting movement and notice if the spring is carried round with the flat of the pin ; if necessary, smooth the hole in the collet until it is. When all is in order, push the pin in tightly.

Shortening and Fitting the Pin

With a sharp penknife-blade make a small cut on the thinner end of the pin where it leaves the collet, and as near to the collet as possible. Then make another cut about the diameter of the pin, away from the collet on the thicker end of the pin. Remove the pin from the collet and shorten the pin from the thinner end, cutting it shorter by an amount equivalent to the diameter of the thicker end of the pin. Round up the end of the pin and see that it is smooth and not pointed.

Next, the cut made previously at the thicker end of the pin is made deeper and continued all the way round until it is partly through. Then with the sharp edge of a burnisher rested in the cut, the wire is given one or two turns to burnish the edges.

Place the proper balance-spring in position and insert the pin partly in the hole. Turn the pin, with the flat side resting on the spring, until the spring is quite flat. Notice whether the spring is true with the collet ; if not, alter it and put it back on the collet again and continue until in order.

When the spring is flat and as true as possible, push the pin in carefully as far as it will go, then break it off at the place partly cut through. Then with a pair of strong, flat-ended tweezers, one leg each side of the collet, push the pin right home. If the pin has been marked correctly it will be flush with the collet each side and should be well finished, having one end rounded and the other with burnished edges.

Rectangular Steel Collet

If a steel collet of the rectangular type, the pin protrudes about twice the thickness of the balance-spring on each side of the collet, both sides being equal in length. Mount the collet with the spring on a true arbor and put it between dead centres in the lathe, or turns, or in a pair of callipers fitted with a marker. Test the spring for flatness and truth and carefully carry out any necessary alterations. On no account bend the spring backwards if it has been bent forwards too much, as the elasticity of the spring will be spoilt. It is far better to bend the spring forwards half a dozen times until correct, rather than bend once and too much.

Tool for Bending Close to the Eye

When the spring runs close to the collet it is awkward to bend, but a little tool can be made to simplify this operation. A piece of round steel rod about $\frac{1}{16}$ inch diameter is filed down to a taper. The end is then slotted with a slitting file about twice as far as the average balance-spring is high. The edges are rounded and smoothed.. If the slot is tapered, straighten it by closing with a hammer while still soft. Then harden and temper, leaving it a dark blue colour.

To bend the spring near the centre, the tool is placed over the part of the spring to be bent and is twisted accordingly. Sharp or gradual bends can be carried out with ease.

When the spring is flat and perfectly true, mount it on the balance and count the number of vibrations, using either a watch as a standard, or a vibrator.

Counting the Spring for Timing

A good method is to hold the balance-spring by the outside coil in a pair of tweezers and allow the balance to drop by its own weight, letting the lower staff pivot rest on the glass of the watch being used as a standard. Then turn or twist the tweezers sharply and the balance will start vibrating. As the spring winds up, when the balance turns in one direction, the balance rises clear of the glass, and on the return journey or vibration the spring unwinds and the balance falls and taps on the glass. If the tweezers are held at a constant height, the taps can be counted while at the same time looking at the seconds hand of the watch. This is a very accurate way of counting the vibrations.

When counting, the double vibration only is counted as it is almost impossible to count both, especially if an 18,000 train or faster.

Therefore, if an 18,000 train, 150 double vibrations per minute are counted ; a 16,200 train, 135 per minute ; and a 14,400 train, 120 per minute. Always start counting on the dead second and finish just before the dead second, otherwise the watch will be slow. When close to time, count for a longer period than one minute.

Another important point, if the watch has an index, the balance-spring is held in the tweezers at the point where the index pins will embrace the spring ; therefore always allow extra for the distance between the pins and the stud. If a freesprung watch, allow only the thickness of the stud or length of the stud hole.

If a flat balance-spring, it can be pinned up straight away. Make the pin as before, but leave it as for a steel rectangular collet, that is, about twice the thickness of the pin standing out on each side of the stud.

The Overcoil

If an overcoil is required, place the balance-spring with its collet on the balance cock with the collet dead central with the cock jewel-hole. Notice where the index pins are placed in relation to the spring. Also notice where the outside of the drop piece of the stud lies. If there is plenty of room between the outside of the drop piece of the stud and the second coil of the balance spring, it is possible to have a longer overcoil, or " terminal curve ", as it is termed.

Fit the balance-spring collet in place with the spring on the balance, put the balance in the frame with the balance cock in place and notice where the hole in the stud is in relation to the top of the collet. This will give the correct height of the overcoil. An overcoil which is too high is difficult to lower, apart from the risk of spoiling the spring.

Bending the Spring

The next operation is to bend the balance spring. A pair of strong tweezers, with a pin fitted tightly in one leg and passing freely through a hole in the other, is all that is essential for the job. Various tools are available, but for a craftsman who does not specialize in springing this is by far the best.

The average balance-spring has room for an overcoil which has length equivalent to three-quarters of a turn of the body of the

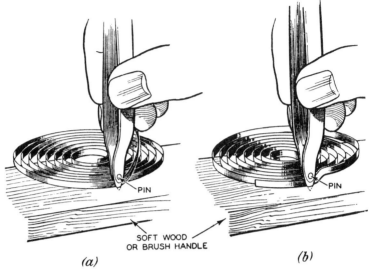

PIN

PIN

SOFT WOOD
OR BRUSH HANDLE

(a)   *(b)*

Fig. 238.—Making the Double Bend to form the Elbow for the
Overcoil.

(a) The first bend is made by pressing the spring into soft wood. The pin prevents
the spring from sliding and being marked, and also decides the point of bending.
The bend can be sharp or gradual.
(b) The second bend is made to bring the overcoil parallel to the body of the spring.
Note that the spring is not drawn in proportion, the size having been greatly
exaggerated for the purpose of illustration.

spring.   Therefore we will turn up an overcoil from a point three-
quarters of a turn from the end of the spring.

Place the spring the correct way up on a piece of flat willow, or
use the handle of a watch brush.   Hold the spring at the three-
quarter turn with the tweezers and press the spring into the wood.
Do not press too hard at first ; it is far better to repeat the operation once or twice rather than bend too much.   Hold the spring
in the tweezers all the time, however, as it may be difficult to find
the exact place where bending has been started should it be laid
down.   When the spring is bent sufficiently, turn it over and grip
it in the tweezers a little nearer the end of the spring.   Examine
the spring to see if the elbow will be the right height.   Adjust if
necessary by moving the tweezers nearer to the previous bend to
lower the elbow, or further towards the end of the spring to raise it.

Bending up the Overcoil

When satisfied that all is in order, press the spring into the wood
again, and the bend will bring the overcoil parallel to the body of
the spring.   Again be careful not to bend too much.   When the
overcoil is parallel to the body of the spring it remains to be shaped,

and the section embraced by the index pins brought concentric and in the right place.

The spring can be bent by using an ivory roller fitted to revolve freely on a steel rod. The spring is laid edgewise on a strip of wood. The roller is moved along the length of the spring with a fair amount of pressure. As the roller moves along, it bends the spring evenly and in a perfect curve.

The same effect can be obtained, however, by the use of suitably shaped bending tweezers. It is always as well to have several pairs of bending tweezers, each having a different curve. It is not easy to bend a hardened and tempered steel balance-spring and avoid marking or scratching the spring. Often it is well worth while to heat the tweezers. The main thing to remember when bending is that the last quarter turn of the overcoil must be concentric or true with the balance-staff hole. Another is to keep the rest of the overcoil as near as possible to the outside coil of the body of the balance-spring. The reason will be given later.

Pinning to the Stud

When the spring is to shape, or as near as can be judged, mount the spring on the balance and place both into the frame with the balance cock and the stud in its permanent place. Turn the balance and watch the overcoil, making sure that the concentric part of the overcoil passes through the index pins without assistance and then through the hole in the stud. If necessary, alter the overcoil until it does.

Dismantle the balance and spring and make the pin for the stud in the same way as for the collet previously described. Place the end of the balance-spring through the stud, insert the pin and move it until the overcoil is in place to hold the body of the spring parallel to the balance cock. Then push the pin home, break it off to length, and give a final push with a pair of tweezers.

Turn the balance-cock over with the balance-spring in place, and make certain that the hole in the collet is perfectly in line with the jewel-hole in the balance cock. If it is not, there is likely to be strain where it is pinned into the stud. Correct this and the job is completed.

One other point worth considering is to see that the spring is set properly after bending. A good plan is to place the balance-spring, collet and stud in a boiling-out pan and cover well with good-quality clock oil. Heat it over a spirit lamp until the oil starts to smoke. Then place the pan on a steel block to cool it quickly. Wash the spring in benzine, dry in box dust and it is ready for use.

Isochronism

The original idea of an overcoil was to distribute the weight of the balance-spring evenly over the balance, even while the balance was vibrating, and the Bréguet spring, as it was called after the inventor, was a big move in the right direction. It opened up the possibility of correct isochronism.

Isochronism means equal time. For a watch isochronism implies that the time of vibration of the balance should be the same whatever the arc of vibration, that is, in both the long and short arcs.

Long and Short Arcs

We say that a watch is in the long arcs when it is in a horizontal or lying position, either " dial-up ", or " dial-down " ; and in the short arcs when hanging up or vertical, that is, in the " pendant-up ", " pendant-down ", " pendant-right " or " pendant-left " positions.

When a watch is in the " dial-up " position the balance is running on the end of one pivot and is supported only by the other pivot. Therefore, as the friction is less, the vibration is greater or longer. When a watch is hanging up, the balance is supported by, or runs on, the sides of two pivots. Thus, with at least twice the friction, the vibration of the balance is less or shorter. Theoretically, the time of vibration should be the same in each case, but in practice this is not so. With a chronometer, or a deck watch, although always supported in the " dial-up " position, they still must be isochronous. Any variation in this case is caused by changes in the motive power.

Terminal Curves

If a balance could be supported in some way without any interference, that is impulse or friction, and kept going, the time of vibration would no doubt be the same. As this is impossible we must obtain what we want by practical means. This is carried out by the manipulation of terminal curves, in such a way that we create points of resistance to bending into the overcoil or the inside of the spring where it joins the collet. We can have even in a flat balance-spring a terminal curve to the collet which will alter the time of vibration.

The marine chronometer and some pocket chronometers have helical balance-springs, which are really all overcoils and no actual body, and these also have terminal curves to allow for alterations for isochronism. Again, there is the " duo in uno " balance-spring which is a flat and helical balance-spring combined made from a continuous length of wire. (See Fig. 31, page 37.)

Manipulation of the Balance-Spring

The general tendency is for all watches to lose in the short arcs. By this we mean that they lose when hanging or being worn in the pocket, or on the wrist. The only way to correct this error is by adjusting the balance-spring, provided, of course, that the rest of the movement is in good order. It is impossible to time a watch accurately if there are errors in the train, mainspring or the escapement.

If a watch is more than about half a minute slow in the short arcs there are certain to be mechanical faults requiring correction before manipulating the balance-spring. The author has known a bad barrel and centre pinion depth give a loss to the short arcs by about 4½ minutes. However, we will assume that everything is in order so that we may proceed with our description.

We know that if we bend a poker or a rod made of steel, or any other metal, it is impossible by ordinary means to straighten it without leaving any trace of the bending. The reason for this is that the metal is stretched on the outside of the bend and compressed on the inside, and in each case is harder than the rest of the metal. Therefore this is why resistance is offered and also why it bends in an adjacent place when straightening. This is the basis of balance-spring manipulation.

If a watch is losing in the short arcs, it is the same as gaining in the long arcs. Therefore by altering the rate of the long arcs we can adjust the difference between the two. If we put a bend or a curve in the overcoil, we immediately create a resistance to the bending point. The result is that when the balance vibrates a certain distance, the spring always bends where there is the least resistance. When the vibration is great enough it not only bends the spring at the least resistance, but also at the greatest resistance. Thus, when the vibration is shorter the bend acts as a supplementary movable stud and shortens, or apparently shortens, the acting length of the spring. The bend is overcome when the balance is vibrating further, or the vibration is longer.

How to Isochronize the Spring

The procedure is often difficult, especially when the watch has an index, because it reduces the length of the overcoil available for manipulation.

The main difficulty is the fact that if an overcoil is bent in one place it is necessary also to bend it in another place to bring the balance-spring central ; otherwise the balance would be forced against the pivots on one side and eased off the pivots on the other, with distinct disadvantages. Another great problem is that one rule does not apply in every case, and, as a result, each watch, or chronometer, has to be considered separately. We can, however, have a basis on which to work.

It was mentioned earlier when bending up the overcoil that the overcoil should be kept as near as possible, and as far round as possible, concentric with the outside coil in the body of the spring. The reason for this is to enable us to start from the body circle of the spring.

If we bend the spring at the elbow, at the top of course, and bend the overcoil towards the centre of the spring, the overcoil moves

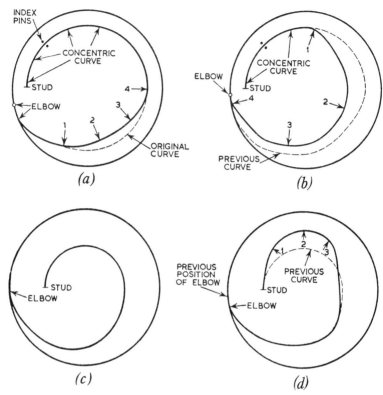

FIG. 239.—METHOD OF TERMINAL CURVE MANIPULATION.

All changes are made to quicken the short arcs. The lack of smoothness is intentional, to enable the alterations to be more easily seen.

(a) Alteration will quicken short arcs by about 5 seconds per day.

(b) Alteration will quicken short arcs by about 10 seconds per day. (In both examples, (a) and (b), the springs have index pins.)

(c) and (d) Alteration to overcoil on free-sprung watch to quicken the short arcs.

bodily over ; so we must bend it somewhere else to bring the spring true. The only place we can bend it is near the concentric curve for the index pins. Therefore, push the index hard over to fast, as far as it goes in fact, and, just clear of the pins, bend the spring to bring the curve in the correct position for the spring to be true again.

As the spring is wound by the balance, the spring will bend the overcoil at the index pins and later at the bend we have made. Therefore the balance-spring acts as a longer spring on a long vibration and acts shorter on the short vibrations, with the result that the short vibrations are faster and the long vibrations are slower relatively.

The amount of improvement is limited, of course, because it is a short overcoil. A long overcoil, such as in a free-sprung watch, is a much easier proposition.

We will take the following examples as a practical illustration.

Adjustment for Watch Losing in the Short Arcs

In Fig. 239 (a) the watch is losing in the short arcs. The concentric curve for the index pins is marked by arrows. The overcoil or terminal curve is bent from the dotted line to take up the new position denoted by the full line. The best way to do this is to bend at point No. 1 first. Take no notice of the body of the spring at this stage. No. 2 bend slightly flattens the coil. No. 3 bend does the same thing to the coil at that place. Use flat-nosed tweezers for this operation.

The last bend at No. 4 is the important one. This bend must be carried out with the tweezers as hot as they can possibly be held. Curved tweezers must be used and the spring held square in them, otherwise a twist will be introduced which will spoil the spring. Squeeze the spring gently and watch the action carefully. As this bend should make the spring concentric with the balance-staff hole, it is necessary to put the spring in place on the balance cock to check first before bending, in case the spring is bent too much. As soon as the spring is central, the maximum bend possible is finished. Make sure the spring lies quite flat with the balance cock and that the elbow will clear the side of the stud. When all is in order, set the balance-spring by heating in oil and allowing it to cool quickly, as described earlier.

Sometimes the first change is insufficient and we have to make a more drastic alteration. For this second adjustment we go as near to the index as we possibly can. We make a fairly sharp bend at point No. 1. From No. 1 to No. 2 the spring is very slightly flattened and a bend is made at No. 2, then another at No. 3. These last two are only very slight bends. It will be noticed that in each case the elbow moves nearer to the stud, so be careful it does not foul in action. Do not forget to see that the spring runs flat and true.

In each case, the balance-spring bends first at the index pins as the balance winds up the spring, and, as this is so in every instance, we can ignore it. As the balance carries on, it bends next at point No. 4 in the first spring. Then as the balance continues to wind up the spring, the next bend is at point No. 1.

Therefore, we have a greater bend for each period of the vibration of the balance. Thus the spring is acting as though the spring is shorter until the various bends give way to the greater strain as the spring is wound up. In other words, the greater the vibration the longer the spring acts, and thus the watch tends to go slower. On the return vibration the same applies in reverse. The first bend is at point No. 1, then at point No. 4 and lastly at the index pins, with the same results.

Position of Index Pins

In Fig. 239 (*b*) the same action is increased. The spring first bends at point No. 1 and next at the index pins. Then it bends at point No. 2 and lastly at point No. 3. Point No. 4 will come into the picture at an ineffective stage, and it is there only to centralize the body of the spring.

In both these drawings (*a*) and (*b*), the springs have index pins, and if any alteration were made to their position the isochronism would be spoilt. In actual fact, therefore, the index is a nuisance to a fine watch. A practice of some old craftsmen was to cut off the index pins and make the watch free-sprung. Some may rather approve of the idea and, although the author has not been guilty of the practice himself, he would not consider it advisable to replace the pins in a watch from which they had previously been removed.

Many years ago an argument was in progress amongst some craftsmen that a watch could be isochronized by the index. What was actually happening was that a watch had been isochronized with the index in a certain position, and when the index was put in that particular place the watch was again isochronous. It was rather misleading.

Adjustment for Free-sprung Watch

With free-sprung watches we have a greater scope for adjustment. Fig. 239 (*c*) shows an ordinary overcoil on a free-sprung watch. This particular watch was slow in the short arcs or short vibrations.

By bending the overcoil from the stud, three resistance points were created, as shown in the next diagram (*d*). During the short vibrations the spring was easily bent at point No. 3 ; as the vibration increased point No. 1 was bent and at its greatest vibration point No. 2 was therefore bent. After this alteration the watch was made isochronous. The amount of bending was severe, and had to be carried out very carefully.

If a spring has been bent too much, do not bend it back to correct it as the spring will be spoilt. A bend must be made somewhere else to counteract the error. It will probably spoil the final isochronism, however, and, if it is a very particular job, a new spring may be the easiest remedy.

The watch can have a terminal curve at the collet or inner coils of the balance-spring.

Position for Pinning-in at the Collet

In Fig. 240 (*a*) the spring is pinned to the collet in the ordinary way.

In (*b*) the spring leaves the collet perfectly straight, and thus has a certain resilience. In other words, under strain of a long vibration it will bend in the direction of the arrow.

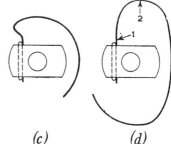

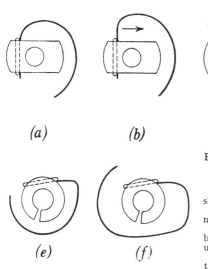

(a)   (b)   (c)   (d)

(e)   (f)

FIG. 240.—POINTS OF ATTACHMENT
TO THE COLLET.

(a) The ordinary attachment.
(b) A straight section to quicken the short arcs.
(c) A more severe bend when (b) is not sufficient.
(d) Maximum adjustment that can be carried out with any advantage using an inner terminal curve.
(e) and (f) Same principle as applied to round type of collet.

In (c) the spring bends backwards, thus giving the spring greater scope to bend under strain ; while (d) gives the maximum degree as a coil is removed from the eye of the spring and a terminal curve in the truest sense of the word is introduced. It must be pointed out that these curves give only a margin of a very few seconds per day.

The maximum movement of the spring in the case of (b) and (c) is to occupy the position of (a). In the case of (d), it has points 1 and 2 where it can bend as the strain increases.

The drawings (e) and (f) are of the same springs, but using round brass collets instead of the steel rectangular type shown in the other diagrams.

These curves tend only to quicken the short vibrations relatively ; actually they slow down the long vibrations. The rule with all balance-spring adjustments is to quicken the short arcs and introduce resistance in the terminal curves, and to slow the short arcs and smooth out any resistance in the spring. By " smooth out " we mean to have long gradual curves instead of a series of short curves.

Positional Errors

Isochronism must not be confused with positional errors. A watch may have positional errors and still be isochronous. A watch is isochronous when the mean of the rates of the four vertical positions is equal to the rate when the watch lies flat in the " dial-down ", or " dial-up ", position.

Rates of Watches

Some rates of watches taken from the rate book are reproduced in the following charts.   These watches have been timed in the usual six positions in room temperature, but heat and cold trials have not been made.

If these rates are examined and analysed it will be seen that No. 1 watch is isochronous.   First bring them all to their pairs. We can ignore the dial-down position as it is the same as dial-up.

CHARTS SHOWING RATES OF WATCHES

No. 1   Watch No. 05040

Date	Collective Variation from Day to Day (Secs. per day)	Daily Error (Secs. per day)	Regulator Error	Daily Rate (Secs. per day)	Position of Watch
April					
16th	+ 4·0	+ 4·0	—	+ 4·0	Dial-up
17th	+ 10·0	+ 6·0	—	+ 6·0	Pendant-up
18th	+ 12·0	+ 2·0	—	+ 2·0	Pendant-down
19th	+ 20·0	+ 8·0	—	+ 8·0	Pendant-left
20th	+ 20·0	0·0	—	0·0	Pendant-right
21st	+ 24·0	+ 4·0	—	+ 4·0	Dial-down

Dial-up   + 4·0
Pendant-up   + 6·0⎫
Pendant-down + 2·0⎭ = 8·0 ÷ 2 = 4·0 seconds per day.
Pendant-left + 8·0⎫
Pendant-right   0·0⎭ = 8·0 ÷ 2 = 4·0 seconds per day.

No. 2   Watch No. 05043

Date	Collective Variation from Day to Day (Secs. per day)	Daily Error (Secs. per day)	Regulator Error	Daily Rate (Secs. per day)	Position of Watch
June					
11th	+ 3·0	+ 3·0	—	+ 3·0	Dial-up
12th	0·0	— 3·0	—	— 3·0	Pendant-up
13th	+ 3·0	+ 3·0	—	+ 3·0	Pendant-down
14th	0·0	— 3·0	—	— 3·0	Pendant-left
15th	+ 3·0	+ 3·0	—	+ 3·0	Pendant-right
16th	+ 6·0	+ 3·0	—	+ 3·0	Dial-down

Dial-up   + 6·0
Pendant-up   0·0⎫
Pendant-down + 6·0⎭ = 6·0 ÷ 2 = 3·0 seconds per day.
Pendant-left   0·0⎫
Pendant-right + 6·0⎭ = 6·0 ÷ 2 = 3·0 seconds per day.

Note.—All these trials are of 24 hours' duration.   Thus, when adding the rates of two side positions, the result must be divided by two to obtain the mean of the two positions.   The same applies when taking the mean of four positions : the total of the four positions must be divided by four.

The pairs added together equal 48 hours, and, therefore, we divide by 2. This gives us $+ 4\cdot0$ seconds per day for each pair, and as the dial-up position is also $+ 4\cdot0$ seconds per day the watch is isochronous, although the watch has positional errors.

Next analyse the second chart. Here we have slow and fast rates, and so we must bring them to a common sign. Therefore, we add 3 to all and the results will be unaltered as regards errors. When the calculation is worked out the watch is $+ 6\cdot0$ seconds per day in the dial-up position and the mean of the positions is $+ 3\cdot0$ seconds per day. Thus the watch is slow in the short arcs by 3 seconds per day and is not isochronous.

If examined carefully, the pendant-up position is 6 seconds slower than the pendant-down position, and the pendant-left position is 6 seconds slower than the pendant-right position. At first glance, it may appear that by correcting the positional errors the watch can be made isochronous, but this is not so. If we poise the balance it may bring the positional errors to nil, but the watch will still be 3 seconds faster dial-up, and the only way to correct this is by altering the terminal curve of the balance-spring.

Poising Callipers

A convenient way to poise a balance is in a pair of poising callipers. The callipers can be either figure-of-eight, or the cross-over type described earlier, and it is better if they are jewelled.

The callipers can be easily jewelled by the craftsman himself. Choose a jewel-hole and an endstone from an old watch; it is preferable to use a full-size jewel-hole. Set the hole in a small rectangular brass plate and screw and steady-pin the plate to the jaws of the callipers, so that it is square and upright. Set the endstones in plate brass, or if already set they can be screwed in place. They can then be taken off to clean the jewel-hole when necessary. The other part of the callipers can be serrated, or knurled, as shown in Figs. 24 and 25, page 21.

Poising the Balance

Place the balance in the callipers so that it can revolve freely. Hold the callipers in a convenient position with the part not in use resting on the bench, and stroke the serrations with a pair of tweezers, or a screwdriver blade.

If the balance is in perfect poise, it will revolve and keep on revolving at increasing speed. If out of poise, however slight, the balance will come to rest with the heaviest part at the bottom.

The author finds this a convenient method of poising the balance, although, of course, a special poising tool can be used if required.

Always bear in mind, however, that the poise of the balance itself is not the only item that has to be considered. There is the weight of the balance-spring, the amount supported by the stud and the amount supported by the balance itself. All these have

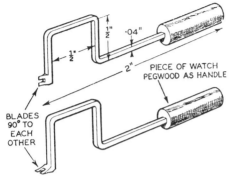

FIG. 241.—SCREWDRIVERS
FOR ADJUSTING QUARTER
SCREWS WHILE MOVE-
MENT IS IN THE CASE.

Great care is necessary to
avoid bending or damaging a
staff pivot ; thus the shaft
must be thin.

an effect on the poise of the balance. Thus, it does not follow if
the balance itself is perfectly in poise without the balance-spring
and out of the frame that it is in poise with the spring in place and
the balance in the frame.

When poising a balance, especially if it is a cut balance, do
not handle with warm hands, but always use tweezers. Hold it
by the inside and outside of the rim and not across the top and
bottom, otherwise the balance will be badly marked and will look
shoddy and cheap. The reason for not handling the balance with
warm hands is because the arm may bend inwards under the heat
and mislead with regard to poise.

Reducing Balance Screws

Another point, always file screw-heads carefully using a very
smooth file and, when almost in poise, finish off in a screw-head
tool. Do not use drills or three-cornered chamfering tools to cut
the screw-heads, but treat the balance with care, leaving it in
as good a condition as when received, or better if possible. A
mutilated balance is not only a nuisance but an eyesore to any
craftsman.

Quarter Screws

Most good-quality watches have quarter screws or nuts, or, as
they are sometimes termed, mean time screws. When the positional
errors are small, they can be corrected by adjusting the quarter
screws. (See Fig. 241.)

The rule is to draw the quarter screw in the fastest position ;
that is, if a watch is gaining in the pendant-up position the pendant
screw, or the quarter screw nearest to the pendant when the balance
is at rest, must be unscrewed or drawn out by the appropriate
amount. Under no circumstances unscrew any other than a quarter
screw.

If the watch is keeping correct time lying flat or dial-up, the
pendant-up position being fast, the pendant screw is drawn out

and its opposite number is screwed in by exactly the same amount. However, make certain that there is no mechanical fault causing these positional errors, otherwise screw adjustment will only make things worse.

Small Watches and Index Pins

Errors will result if the index pins are not in their correct position. The spring must be close in the pins, and if an oiler, or a pricker, is carefully wedged in between to ease the pins open, the spring should play evenly between them and not hard on one or the other.

In small watches where the balance-spring is thin and weak a very small amount of play must be visible, otherwise the spring will be bent or buckled when the index is moved towards slow or retard.

Compensation for Temperature Variations

When adjusting a fine watch it has to be compensated in order to obtain a constant rate in all temperatures.

First, however, after a balance has been cut and made true it must be set and tested again for truth under extremes of temperature. One way to set it, is to revolve the balance and staff in a pair of callipers held just near enough to the flame of a spirit lamp to close up the cuts completely without distorting the balance.

Another way is to place the balance in oil and heat it. Treat the balance two or three times in this way and then test the balance for truth after it has cooled. If still true, everything is in order. If not correct, true it up again and repeat the process until it will withstand the high temperature and return to truth when cooled.

To test in a cold temperature, place the balance in a small quantity of ether on a glass and then blow vigorously on it, using a blower, or watchmaker's bellows. When the ether evaporates, the temperature drops well below freezing point. Then test for truth when the balance warms up.

After these tests and settings have been carried out we can proceed to adjust the watch for temperature variations.

Temperature Tests

First test the watch in room temperature to get it somewhere near a mean-time rate. Then place the watch in an oven at a temperature of about 92° F. for two trials each of 24 hours' duration. Take the mean of the two trials and compare it with the trial in the room.

If the difference is faster in heat, the screws must be moved away from the free or cut end of the arm towards the back or the fixed end. Conversely, if the difference is slow in heat, the screws must be moved from the fixed end towards the free end of the arm. As the watch gets nearer to final adjustment it may mean just exchanging heavy screws for light ones, or vice versa.

After the tests in heat have been completed and the error between 92° F. and 67° F., or room temperature, does not exceed 1 second per day slow in heat, carry out the tests in cold at a temperature of 40–42° F. The test is easier to carry out in a refrigerator, if one is available, but failing this an ice-box can be used.

The watch must be placed in a box lined with waterproof packing material before it is put into the refrigerator. When removed, the box must not be opened until the condensation has been dried, otherwise the piece will be rusted.

When the rate is taken it will probably be found that the watch is slow by two or more seconds per day. This means that the arm has moved outwards a little more than is required. If the screws are moved to compensate for this error, the watch will be slower in heat. This is where an auxiliary is particularly useful. The outward movement of the arm is restricted by the auxiliary in the cold temperature and thus the difference between the temperature in heat, 92° F., and the middle temperature, 67° F., can be decreased and the cold adjusted accordingly by the auxiliary. With palladium balance-springs the middle-temperature error is not so apparent, but with an auxiliary the error is almost eliminated. The same applies to " Elinvar " springs where the errors to be adjusted are less.

Over-Compensated Watches

Sometimes a watch is over-compensated, that is, all the weight is at the fixed end and the balance is still fast in heat. If a serious error, the balance must be changed. If the error is only small, additional holes can be drilled in the fixed end of the arm to move the screws a little farther back, or four screws can be replaced by two of the same weight as the four.

If the screws are all grouped at the free end and the watch is still slow in heat, platinum screws can be substituted to give the extra weight. A platinum screw will generally replace two made of gold.

Final Tests

When the compensation is correct, poise the balance and again test in heat and cold, and room temperature to see if any alteration has taken place while poising the balance. Now that the balance is in perfect poise and the compensation is correct, test the watch in the vertical positions and then in the dial-up position to see if it is isochronous. If necessary, the watch must be made isochronous at this stage. The diagrams given previously will give a guide as to the procedure, whether the watch is slow or fast in the short arcs. Take all the final rates for full 24 hours. Short trials of less than 24 hours are unsatisfactory.

Isochronous Errors

Isochronous errors are not all in the balance-spring. The modern watch, with the lever and pallets in one piece, has to be adjusted for the lack of poise in the lever and pallets. Endshakes in the escapement being excessive, or unequal, are another cause. Other errors can be caused by the staff, pallet staff, or 'scape pinion pivots not being truly round or not fitting the holes properly, or the pivots being of the wrong shape.

Balance-Staff Pivots

The balance-staff pivots should always be very carefully made. The actual pivot must be perfectly straight and only the shoulder should be conical for strength. The pivot should be long enough to pass through the jewel-hole by its own diameter.

In some of the cheaper watches where the endstone stands some distance from the jewel-hole, a longer pivot is necessary unless the jewelling can be pushed nearer to the endstone, which is the correct way. Make absolutely certain that the pivot does reach the endstone. A balance-staff pivot must always be turned until it fits the jewel-hole, and the polishing or burnishing should give ample freedom. There should be just visible freedom or sideshake of the pivot in the hole. The endshake should not exceed ·001 inch in any part running on conical pivots.

Depths

Another point is gearing. The fourth wheel and 'scape pinion depth must be correct, or if low numbered pinions must have a minimum of engaging friction. It is unwise to have a pinion too small, but it is better to err slightly in favour of a small pinion rather than a large one ; of course, it must be only very little on the small side. The lever notch and impulse pin depth is also very critical, as explained previously in Chapter 8.

The rest of the train has also to be considered. A bad barrel and centre pinion depth, or a bad centre wheel and third pinion depth will completely spoil the rate of a watch.

The mainspring obviously is of major importance and too strong a mainspring is not advisable except, of course, in the case of a fusee. A fusee watch invariably needs a slightly stronger mainspring owing to the losses due to the fusee equalizing the pull or power of the mainspring.

Jewelling Requirements

Another important point is the jewelling. The hole must be perfectly round and must be set quite flat. The endstone must also be set flat and not in any way askew. There must be a small gap between the endstone and the back of the jewel-hole ; about ·002 inch is sufficient. The main idea is to create capillary attraction in the oil. If this is in order the pivot is running in a small oil-bath.

The hole itself should be olive-shaped, that is, the sides, instead of being parallel to each other, should be rounded so that only a small surface is engaging the pivots when the watch is vertical. The idea of this is to ease the adhesive friction on the pivots.

The rubbing friction remains the same whether the hole is straight or olive-shaped. Another advantage of the olive-shaped hole is that there is less risk of binding should there be any lack of uprightness in the staff.

CHAPTER 12

PENDULUMS

THE most important consideration with a pendulum is the rigidity of suspension. A pendulum supported on a flimsy bracket or back cock cannot keep time. Also it must traverse a straight path, that is, it must not " roll " or wobble. Rolling may be caused by bad alignment at the suspension, or may be due to a bent or distorted suspension spring. The crutch out of alignment will also cause the pendulum to roll. A suspension spring which is too weak will also cause this trouble. The suspension

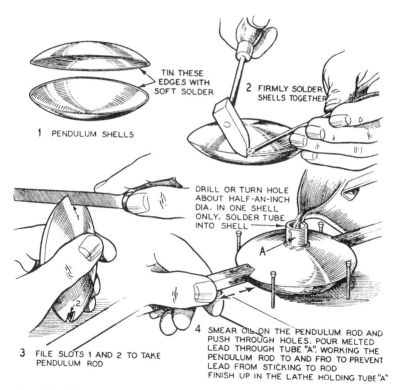

TIN THESE
EDGES WITH
SOFT SOLDER

1 PENDULUM SHELLS

2 FIRMLY SOLDER
SHELLS TOGETHER

DRILL OR TURN HOLE
ABOUT HALF-AN-INCH
DIA. IN ONE SHELL
ONLY. SOLDER TUBE
INTO SHELL

A

3 FILE SLOTS 1 AND 2 TO TAKE
PENDULUM ROD

4 SMEAR OIL ON THE PENDULUM ROD AND
PUSH THROUGH HOLES. POUR MELTED
LEAD THROUGH TUBE "A". WORKING THE
PENDULUM ROD TO AND FRO TO PREVENT
LEAD FROM STICKING TO ROD
FINISH UP IN THE LATHE HOLDING TUBE "A"

Fig. 242.—Making a simple Pendulum using Brass Shells and Brass Rod.

Shells are soldered together and filled with lead to form the bob. No means is provided for temperature compensation

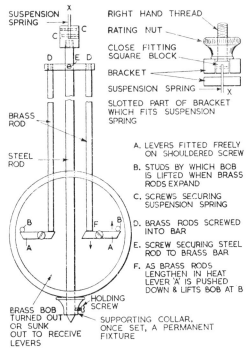

A. LEVERS FITTED FREELY
   ON SHOULDERED SCREW

B. STUDS BY WHICH BOB
   IS LIFTED WHEN BRASS
   RODS EXPAND

C. SCREWS SECURING
   SUSPENSION SPRING

D. BRASS RODS SCREWED
   INTO BAR

E. SCREW SECURING STEEL
   ROD TO BRASS BAR

F. AS BRASS RODS
   LENGTHEN IN HEAT
   LEVER 'A' IS PUSHED
   DOWN & LIFTS BOB AT B

FIG. 243.—ELLICOTT PENDULUM.

Compensation is effected by the expansion of the
two brass rods which lift the bob through pivoted
levers.

must never be too strong, but should be consistent with the weight of the pendulum.

The pendulums described earlier are affected by changes of temperature and various methods of compensation have been introduced at different times.

Ellicott Pendulum

The pendulum originated by Ellicott was devised on a cantilever principle. The greatest disadvantage was the considerable amount of friction, and consequently the pendulum was only partially compensating and was discarded.

The bob was supported by two pins which rested on the long ends of two levers pivoted in the pendulum bob. The opposite or short ends of the lever were acted upon by two strong brass rods. The bob was also supported by a central rod which was anchored permanently. Thus as the central rod lengthened, the brass rods expanded and pushed the bob upwards.

Harrison's " Gridiron " Pendulum

A more effective pendulum was invented by John Harrison known as the " Gridiron ". This consists of pairs of brass and steel rods arranged alternately, with each pair anchored to a cross-bar. There is a central steel rod on which is fitted a rating nut and the first pair of brass rods rests on this nut. Thus as the control rod lengthens in heat, the bob is pushed upwards according to the expansion of the pairs of rods (Fig. 244).

This method of compensation was not entirely satisfactory in practice as so much depended on the quality of the metal and the method used in its working. The " Gridiron " pendulum is still in use in some Continental regulators.

Regulators and other fine clocks are fitted either with mercurial compensated pendulums, or the zinc and steel type. The Westminster clock " Big Ben " is fitted with a zinc and steel pendulum (Fig. 246) and it gives an extremely good performance.

For the cheaper grades of regulator, pendulum rods of straight-grained deal are used with a cylindrical composition bob made of lead, having a small amount of antimony added for hardening purposes and also to prevent tarnishing.

Fig. 245 illustrates the construction of this type of pendulum.

Zinc and Steel Compensated Pendulum

When constructing a pendulum of the zinc and steel type, owing to the difficulty of obtaining suitable materials, iron can be used in place of

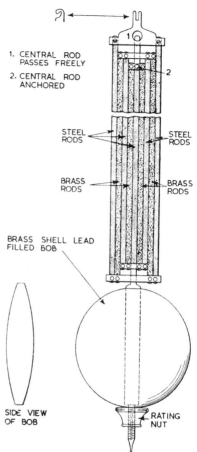

1. CENTRAL ROD PASSES FREELY

2. CENTRAL ROD ANCHORED

STEEL RODS

STEEL RODS

BRASS RODS

BRASS RODS

BRASS SHELL LEAD FILLED BOB

SIDE VIEW OF BOB

RATING NUT

FIG. 244.—HARRISON'S "GRIDIRON" PENDULUM.

Compensation is effected by pairs of brass and steel rods arranged alternately, usually four of brass and five of steel. The principle is good, but not sufficiently accurate for modern requirements.

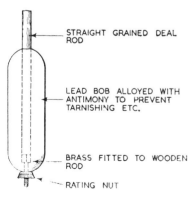

STRAIGHT GRAINED DEAL ROD

LEAD BOB ALLOYED WITH ANTIMONY TO PREVENT TARNISHING ETC.

BRASS FITTED TO WOODEN ROD

RATING NUT

FIG. 245 (left).—WOOD ROD PENDULUM.

The rod must be straight grained. Pendulum gives a good performance on cheaper types of regulator.

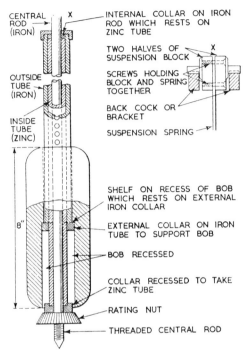

CENTRAL ROD (IRON)

OUTSIDE TUBE (IRON)

INSIDE TUBE (ZINC)

INTERNAL COLLAR ON IRON ROD WHICH RESTS ON ZINC TUBE

TWO HALVES OF SUSPENSION BLOCK

SCREWS HOLDING BLOCK AND SPRING TOGETHER

BACK COCK OR BRACKET

SUSPENSION SPRING

SHELF ON RECESS OF BOB WHICH RESTS ON EXTERNAL IRON COLLAR

EXTERNAL COLLAR ON IRON TUBE TO SUPPORT BOB

BOB RECESSED

COLLAR RECESSED TO TAKE ZINC TUBE

RATING NUT

THREADED CENTRAL ROD

FIG. 246.—ZINC AND STEEL COMPENSATED PENDULUM.

This is one of the best temperature compensating pendulums for commercial use. It is used in the Westminster clock "Big Ben", the most accurate public clock which is kept within two seconds of mean time.

steel. In this form of construction, the internal rod is of iron, and over this and fitting easily is a tube of zinc and again over this is a tube of iron. This outer iron tube has a series of holes drilled through the side to enable the air to act upon the zinc tube.

The internal iron rod is threaded and to it is fitted a rating nut, and just above this nut the zinc tube rests on a collar. The outer iron tube has a collar fitted to the top end which has a hole large enough to pass freely over the internal iron rod and rest on the top of the zinc tube. The other end of the outer iron tube has an outer collar which forms the seat for the bob.

Thus the bob is supported by the outer iron tube, which in turn rests on the zinc tube which is supported by the collar resting on the rating nut. The collar should not turn when the rating nut is adjusted. Therefore, the inner iron rod should have a flat side and the hole in the collar should be shaped accordingly. Some zinc rods have the inner or upper collar screwed on, to enable adjustment to be made to the acting length of the zinc tube.

Dimensions of Zinc and Steel Pendulums

When constructing a zinc and steel pendulum, the zinc rod should be left longer than required and shortened to requirements. Zinc has a greater coefficient of expansion than iron. The proportion of expansion between 32° F. and 212° F. is 28 : 12, that is, 28 for zinc and 12 for iron.

The best type of bob is one made of lead which is cylindrical in shape and is sloped at the top to minimize the collection of dust.

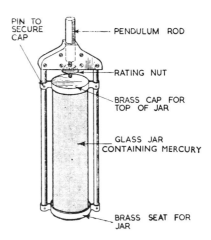

The length of the zinc tube for a seconds pendulum should be 28 inches if using an iron bob 8 inches long ; and if using a lead bob of the same size supported at the bottom, the zinc tube should be 24 inches in length. These tubes are slightly longer than required, but if a screwed top collar is used the error is taken up when adjusting the pendulum if it is over-compensated, that is when the time of vibration is fast in heat.

A suggested size for rod and tubes is : internal rod ·25 inch diameter, zinc tube free of ·25 inch or ·28 inch inside and ·65 inch outside diameter.

FIG. 247.—MERCURIAL COMPENSATED PENDULUM.

A glass jar is more common, although better results are obtained with an iron jar. It is used in best-quality regulators and gives an accurate performance.

However, these dimensions may be influenced by the materials available, as one has to depend on standard productions and specially made rods or tubes are expensive.

Mercurial Compensated Pendulums

Most mercurial pendulums consist of a glass jar containing mercury supported in a cradle or stirrup. The pendulum rod passes through a rectangular slot in the upper part of the cradle and the rating nut is situated between the jar and the upper part of the cradle, as shown in Fig. 247.

Although the arrangement using a glass jar provides a better appearance, a metal jar, usually of iron, is more efficient and is generally used with astronomical regulators and ordinary regulators where the pendulum is hidden. The reason for this is that glass is not a good conductor of heat, and thus the rod changes temperature quicker than the mercury, whereas with the metal jar this does not apply.

Some mercurial pendulums have a rod passing right through the glass jar with the rating nut at the bottom. The glass jar in this case takes the form of a cylinder open at each end. This cylinder rests in a brass cup and in the centre of it is a steel, or iron, tube through which the rod passes. The jar is put in place and cemented to the brass cup filled with mercury. The top cup is then put in place and cemented after the compensation has

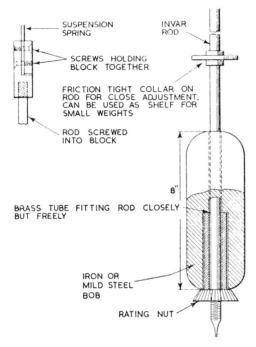

FIG. 248.—" INVAR " COMPENSATED PENDULUM.

The bob is of iron or mild steel, supported in the centre by a brass rod which rests on the rating nut. This principle gives the best results and is used with the Shortt free pendulum.

been completed. This form of mercurial pendulum certainly possesses an advantage where a pendulum has to be transported, but it is difficult to decide whether it has other advantages.

Dimensions of Mercurial Pendulums

The dimensions of a mercurial pendulum are glass jar 8 inches high and $2\frac{1}{2}$ inches in diameter externally ; and $7\frac{3}{4}$ inches high and 2 inches diameter internally. The height of mercury inside should be $7\frac{1}{2}$ inches. The mercury is added or withdrawn according to requirements. The usual weight of mercury to start with is 12 lb.

If over-compensated, mercury is withdrawn and conversely, if the time of vibration is slow in heat, mercury is added.

The pendulum rod should be about 34 inches long measured from the suspension spring to the upper part of the stirrup. If the rod passes right through the jar or is supported at the bottom, the rod must be longer by the length of the jar. These same rules apply to a metal jar.

" Invar " Compensation

The use of the nickel-steel alloy, " Invar ", is a comparatively new development in connection with the construction of compensated pendulums. In this type of pendulum, a cylindrical iron or mild-steel bob is used, and this is drilled to take a rod made of " Invar " as shown in Fig. 248.

As stated previously, the alloy is little affected by changes of temperature and consequently errors in the rod are negligible, but it is still necessary to provide some means of adjustment for errors in the bob and the clock mechanism itself, which all affect the time of vibration. For this purpose, a brass tube, which can be shortened as required, is fitted over the rod and is supported on the rating nut. The bob is recessed halfway so that the bob is supported in the centre. The top half is a close but not a tight fit on the pendulum rod. The idea of supporting the bob centrally is that in this position the expansion of the bob itself is ineffective.

This method of " Invar " compensation is very useful, but, where extreme accuracy is required, is not so effective as the zinc and steel, or mercurial pendulums.

A Method of Altering Rate to Close Limits

Where it is required to keep a regulator or a fine clock close to mean time, a friction-tight brass collar is fitted on the pendulum rod and this is moved up or down to adjust for very small errors.

Another use of this collar is to provide a platform on which small weights can be placed to alter the rate of the regulator. A small weight added to the platform will quicken the time of vibration, and a weight removed from the platform will make it slower. These weights can be placed in position, or removed, using a pair of tweezers and without stopping or interfering with the " going " mechanism.

This principle is used to keep the Westminster clock " Big Ben " within the required two seconds of mean time. In this case, pennies and halfpennies are used as weights. This raises the centre of oscillation by adding weight above the bob and lowers the centre when weight is removed.

The Centre of Oscillation

The centre of oscillation of a pendulum is the point where if all the metal in the pendulum were concentrated the time of vibration would remain unaltered. In a simple pendulum the position would be a little below the centre of the bob.

From a practical point of view this will cause little trouble when calculating the length of a pendulum.

Circular Error

Circular error is a fault to which all pendulums are prone. To vibrate in the same time, the pendulum must travel in a cycloidal path, whereas in the ordinary way it travels in a circular path, thus the long vibrations tend to be slow.

In these days only the cheaper clocks have a large vibration as close timekeeping is not required. Regulators, however, have a very small arc of vibration, and the circular error is negligible and can be ignored. It has been suggested that the circular error tends to cancel out the barometric error in the case of a larger vibration.

Barometric Error

Barometric error is very small and need be taken into account only where extremely close rates are required, such as, with astronomical regulators. The error has been eliminated in these regulators by means of magnets controlled by a mercurial barometer.

Determining the Length of a Pendulum

The formula for finding the time of vibration of a pendulum is :

$$\text{Time} = \pi \sqrt{\frac{\text{length}}{\text{gravity}}} \text{ in feet or } t = \pi\sqrt{\frac{l}{g}}$$

$$\pi = 3\text{·}14159, \text{ gravity} = 32\text{·}19$$

Thus if it is required to find the time taken for one vibration of a 12-inch pendulum the calculation is $3\text{·}14159 \times \sqrt{\dfrac{1}{32\text{·}19}}$. As the square root of 32·19 is 5·67434, the calculation taken a step further becomes $3\text{·}14159 \times \dfrac{1}{5\text{·}67434}$ or $\dfrac{3\text{·}14159}{5\text{·}67434} = \text{·}553$. The pendulum therefore performs one vibration in ·553 seconds.

Likewise, if the number of vibrations is known the length of the pendulum can be found. The revised formulae for this are :

$$t = \pi \sqrt{\frac{l}{g}}, \quad t^2 = \pi^2\frac{l}{g}, \quad \frac{t^2}{\pi^2} = \frac{l}{g} \text{ and lastly } g \times \frac{t^2}{\pi^2} = l.$$

CLOCK TRAINS IN COMMON USE

Vibrations per Hour	Centre Wheel (No. of teeth)	3rd Pinion (No. of leaves)	3rd Wheel (No. of teeth)	'Scape Pinion (No. of leaves)	'Scape Wheel (No. of teeth)	Length of Pendulum (inches)
3,600	96	12	90	12	30	39·14
3,600	80	10	75	10	30	39·14
3,600	64	8	60	8	30	39·14
4,500	75	8	60	8	32	25·53
5,400	80	8	72	8	30	17·39
6,000	80	8	80	8	30	14·09
6,480	96	8	72	8	30	12·14
7,200	96	8	80	8	30	9·72
7,218	84	7	78	7	27	9·73
7,320	90	8	84	8	31	9·46
7,500	100	8	80	8	30	9·01
7,800	100	8	78	8	32	8·34
8,022	84	7	78	7	30	7·9
8,400	84	8	80	8	40	7·18
8,556	84	7	78	7	32	6·9
8,826	84	7	78	7	33	6·5
9,600	84	7	78	7	36	5·5
9,894	84	7	78	7	37	5·15
10,560	84	7	77	7	40	4·5

Thus if it is required to find the length of a pendulum to give one hundred and twenty vibrations a minute, or a half-seconds pendulum, the calculation is $32 \cdot 19 \times \dfrac{\cdot 5^2}{3 \cdot 1416^2} = l$, that is $\dfrac{32 \cdot 19 \times \cdot 25}{9 \cdot 8697} = l$.

Therefore $\dfrac{8 \cdot 0475}{9 \cdot 8697} = l$ and the result in feet is $\cdot 81$, which is $9 \cdot 72$ inches.

This formula is all that is needed for determining both the length of the pendulum and the time of its vibration. A seconds pendulum is $39 \cdot 14$ inches long in London, but its length varies according to height from sea-level. The reason is that gravity varies at different heights and also in different latitudes. At the equator a seconds pendulum is only 39 inches long, whereas at the poles it is $39 \cdot 206$ inches. A pendulum for sidereal seconds is $38 \cdot 93$ inches long in London.

A list of clock trains in common use giving the length of pendulum required with each train is reproduced in the accompanying table.

Timing Machines

It is impossible to check a pendulum clock or any other frictional rest escapement on a timing-machine with an acoustic pickup as there is too much extraneous noise resulting in a very scattered undecipherable trace. However a device can be obtained where either a visible light – or infra red – beam shining on a photo-cell is interrupted by the swinging clock pendulum and "clean" electrical impulses are sent to the timing-machine enabling a good trace to be obtained. As when testing watches the rate shown is the performance of the timepiece at that moment which is not necessarily its rate for the whole 24 hours. Timing-machines usually have comprehensive instruction manuals which explain their use far better than a few paragraphs in a book.

CHAPTER 13

STRIKING MECHANISMS, REPEATERS, CLOCK-WATCHES, MUSICAL AND ALARM WATCHES

THE general run of clock striking mechanisms, whether English or French, is fairly simple to understand. The most important point to bear in mind, however, is that faults, when they do exist, are generally caused by worn pieces needing replacement. Therefore, do not file away pieces of metal indiscriminately, or bend pieces without careful thought as to the reason or the result. Such treatment will only lead to a ruined clock. Instead, use a process of elimination to find the fault : try each action separately and then two or three pieces together to make certain that the actions are correct.

Clock Striking Mechanisms

Two systems are involved with clock striking mechanisms, the " locking plate " and the " rack ". With the rack system, two alternative forms of striking mechanism are employed. In one type there is a warning and in the other the mechanism is released instantly by means of a flirt, as is the case with the French carriage-clock repeater described previously.

The English arrangement in respect of the warning action differs slightly from the French. In the system of rack striking used in English clocks the lifting piece releases the rack and the warning together, the striking train being released as the lifting piece is dropped. With the French system, the lifting piece raises the rack hook just sufficiently to push the locking piece clear of the locking wheel and pin, warns, and then drops the rack, after which the striking train is released.

Where a flirt is used, the action is simultaneous, that is, the rack hook, locking piece, rack and the train are all released at the same time.

A full description of these mechanisms will be found in Chapter 4, and if the illustrations are studied it will assist in understanding the description of the watch repeater which follows.

WATCH REPEATING MECHANISMS

A watch repeating mechanism has a separate mainspring and a train of wheels, but the mainspring is only wound up when the watch is required to strike the time. The action to repeat is carried out either by a slide let into the outside of the band of the case, or by a large push-piece let through from the movement to the

282

outside of the case. The slide is pulled either from the pendant of the case towards the joint, or from the joint towards the pendant.

Hour Rack and Slide and the Circular Rack

The slide is usually connected to a steel rack which turns on a stud screwed to the pillar plate. The teeth of this rack are geared into a pinion which is fitted and screwed firmly to a circular rack carrying twelve teeth corresponding to the twelve hours to be struck. These rack teeth engage a pallet, termed the hammer pallet, which is fitted on the arbor of the hour hammer. The rack, which is engaged by the slide, is known as the hour rack and has an extended arm which engages into the snail. Thus when the slide is moved, the circular rack is turned correspondingly and the appropriate number of hours is struck.

The slide is often fitted with a spring on the section inside the

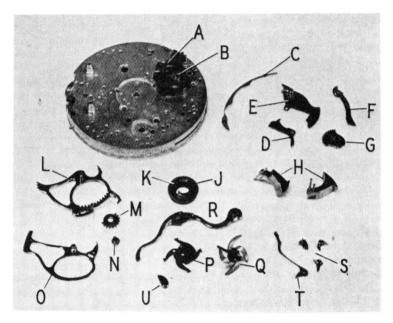

Fig. 249.—Pillar Plate of Minute Repeater from the Inside, with Parts of Repeating Mechanism.

A. Repeating train. B. Repeating barrel arbor. C. " All-or-nothing " piece. D. Supplementary rack with rack tail. E. Hour rack. F. Slide lever. G. Circular hour rack. H. Hammers. J. Ratchet teeth. K. Repeating barrel and mainspring. L. Quarter rack. M. Lifting wheel. N. Gathering pallet for lifting wheel of quarter rack. O. Minute rack. P. Quarter snail and surprise-piece screwed together. Q. Minute snail. R. Quarter jumper with disconnection lever joined together. S. Hammer pallets. T. Hammer return spring. U. Disconnecting pawl.

band of the case, so that as soon as the slide has been pulled, it can return immediately to its starting point and thus leave the repeating train to run without any obstruction. Where the slide is without a spring, the hour-rack lever, as it may be termed, that is, a lever fitted on the same stud as the rack and acting on it, is fitted with a spring which has the same effect, and through the medium of the lever pushes the slide back to its starting point.

The earlier types of repeater were not provided with a rack lever, but the rack itself was solid with the lever. Some of these models, however, had a spring on the slide itself.

Setting the Hour Rack

The hour rack and the pinion on the circular rack have to be meshed correctly, that is, the correct teeth of one rack must engage with certain teeth on the circular rack. This applies even to the very early repeaters as well as to the most modern. Also, with modern clock-watches the same principle is involved.

Usually the hour rack is provided with fourteen teeth, and the pinion on the circular rack has thirteen leaves terminating in a block or an uncut tooth. This block is used to take the screw which holds the pinion and the circular rack together.

When setting up this section, the first tooth of the rack must be against the block on one side, and when the rack is moved the full extent the last tooth of the rack must be against the block on the other side. The hour rack must be correctly set in this manner for the right number of hours to be struck.

Another point is that the modern rack is different from that used with earlier designs of repeater. The modern rack is not solid with the rack tail, or the part which engages the snail. In earlier repeaters, the rack was, in effect, solid, as the tail was screwed and steady-pinned to the rack, and the whole acted as one piece. With the modern rack, however, the tail is fitted on the same stud as the rack, but the tail end fits under the rack and slides backwards and forwards. The opposite end of this supplementary tail engages with a pawl screwed to the top of the rack, as shown in Fig. 250 (a). The action is as follows.

Operation of the Repeating Mechanism

As the rack is pushed towards the snail, the tail is moved against the solid rack, the opposite end of the tail engages with the pawl on the rack and this pawl pushes against the all-or-nothing spring and releases the quarter and minute racks. The purpose of this mechanism is to prevent the incorrect number of hours being struck should the slide be pushed or pulled insufficiently. With earlier repeaters, if the rack were not pushed in to the fullest extent, an hour or so less might be struck.

With the " all-or-nothing " mechanism, as it is termed, the slide

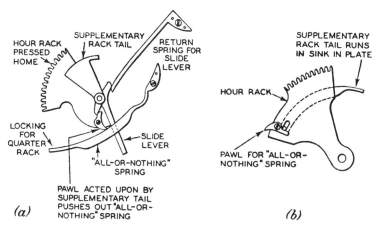

FIG. 250.—OPERATION OF SLIDE AND HOUR RACK WITH " ALL-OR-NOTHING "
ACTION.

Showing the most modern type (a), and a less popular but still very efficient type
of mechanism (b).

must be fully pushed in, otherwise striking is prevented. The
train of wheels runs down and that is all.

In another similar type of all-or-nothing mechanism the supplementary tail runs in a curved sink in the pillar plate under the
rack itself [see Fig. 250 (b)]. The tail has stout steel pins standing
up and passing through the rack. One pin, at the opposite end
to the engagement with the snail, stands beyond or above the hour
rack and engages with the pawl, which in turn engages with the
all-or-nothing spring.

The all-or-nothing action varies again with some of the older
modern-type repeaters. The snail itself is mounted on a movable
arm, and when the rack engages with it the snail moves away
carrying the movable arm. On the end of the arm is a thin, flat-
ended section on which rests an arm of the quarter rack.

As the snail is moved it carries the arm, or locking piece, away
from the quarter-rack arm and the quarter rack falls. The movable
arm runs on a stud screwed to the pillar plate and is kept down by
a shouldered screw filed to leave a triangular-shaped head to cover
the end of the arm. There is also a steel spring, screwed to the
arm, which rests in a slot cut in another stud near the locking end
of the movable arm. This spring also keeps the snail in the correct
position for locking the quarter rack and for engagement with the
cannon pinion at each hour for the change from one hour to another.

The Repeating Mainspring

The circular rack, with its pinion, has a square hole which fits
the barrel arbor of the repeating train. Thus, as the slide is pulled

or pushed, the repeating mainspring is wound up and the repeating mechanism comes into action on the running down. Therefore the amount the mainspring is wound up depends on the number of hours to be struck.

When assembling a repeater, always ascertain the number of running turns in the barrel. This varies quite a lot. There is no definite rule as to how much the mainspring should be set up ; it depends on the strength of the mainspring in relation to the amount of work to be done. Some repeaters will run on low power, while some require more.

A good plan is to wind the mainspring fully and place the circular rack about a quarter of a turn away from the hammer pallet. Then allow the train to run carrying the rack and notice the speed with which it strikes on running down each time the rack passes the hammer pallet. If it strikes fast on the first occasion and about right on the second, that is the section of the mainspring to use.

Sometimes the circular rack will fit any square on the barrel arbor, but usually the particular square is marked in some way and, of course, it is always advisable to use it.

The Barrel

A resting barrel is used. This type of barrel is a fixture or is pre-set and the great wheel is fitted to the barrel arbor. The great wheel is provided with a click and spring, and the arbor on which it is fitted has a ratchet wheel into which the clicks engage.

The arbor boss, that is, the block with the hook for the inner eye of the mainspring, is usually screwed on to the arbor and holds the great wheel in place. Sometimes this boss is pinned on. Check this point, therefore, before using force to dismantle the unit. It is usually fairly obvious.

If the boss is screwed on, use a pair of brass-nosed pliers. A right-hand thread is customary, but always be prepared for a left-hand one, as some are constructed the opposite way round for a particular reason, which again is usually obvious.

Sometimes, particularly with Swiss repeaters, the barrel is a separate unit and is fitted into the bar or bridge which spans the repeating train. Again the barrel has ratchet teeth on the edge, and a combined click and spring is screwed to the bar and engages with the barrel teeth. This is a very convenient method, as it gives greater scope in setting up the mainspring. In the ordinary way only quarter turns can be used, but this method subdivides the quarter turns and enables a better set-up to be obtained.

Speed-Regulating Devices

The train varies with regard to numbers, also as regards principle. Some have a governor to control the speed of striking. Others have a pinion with a heavy brass boss and an eccentric bush to adjust the depth of the pinion and the previous wheel. If the depth is reduced the train runs faster. Conversely, if the depth is increased the train runs slower. The amount of adjustment, of course, is very limited.

Another type has a small 'scape wheel and pallets to control the speed. Usually there is a steel post which fits closely into the plate and has a hole drilled through the side to take a very thin and springy brass pin. The brass pin is bent at a right angle to engage with a small metal weight which is mounted tightly on the pallet staff. If the pin is placed nearer to the weight the swing is reduced and the train runs faster, and if the pin is moved away the swing is increased and the train runs slower.

The pallets sometimes get worn, but if they have to be repolished do this extremely carefully, because once their setting is altered it will be very difficult to readjust and a new pair may be necessary. Some of these pallets are jewelled, but most are made just of plain steel and are flint hard.

Renewing Worn Holes of the Repeating Train

The best-quality repeaters have jewel-holes throughout, but some merely run in brass holes and thus get worn. When the holes become worn it is better if jewels are fitted, as it costs no more this way and saves a lot of trouble.

The greatest wear occurs at the pinion end of the first wheel and pinion. Where this pivot hole is on a separate cock it is easy to renew it, but where it is pivoted in the plate the hole is so very near to the edge of the sink, which is turned to clear the circular rack, that even a bush is almost impossible. The best way to renew this particular hole is to dovetail a piece of metal in and re-drill it.

Quarter Repeaters

Before we proceed with a description of the different varieties of repeater, it should be mentioned that the hour snail resembles the snail of a striking clock and is made in the same way, but, of course, on a much smaller scale.

With a quarter repeater there is a further snail fitted directly on to the cannon pinion. This quarter snail is exactly the same in shape as a quarter snail on a clock, but has underneath what is known as a " surprise-piece ".

The Surprise-Piece

The surprise-piece is fitted on the cannon pinion arbor and is kept in place by a tightly fitting steel collar which allows the surprise-piece to move freely without any appreciable play.

The surprise-piece carries a block which engages the star wheel on which the hour snail is mounted, and advances the star-wheel tooth at each hour. The hour snail is mounted on a star wheel

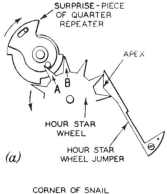

SURPRISE - PIECE
OF QUARTER
REPEATER

APEX

B
A
O

HOUR STAR
WHEEL

HOUR STAR
WHEEL JUMPER

(a)

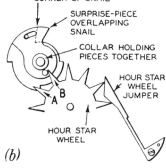

CORNER OF SNAIL

SURPRISE-PIECE
OVERLAPPING
SNAIL

COLLAR HOLDING
PIECES TOGETHER

HOUR STAR
WHEEL
JUMPER

B
A
O

HOUR STAR
WHEEL

(b)

FIG. 251.—ACTION OF SURPRISE-
PIECE.

(a) A. Tooth being engaged first.
B. Tooth pushing over surprise piece by action of hour star
wheel jumper.
(b) Showing completed action;
surprise piece covers low part of snail.

with twelve teeth, and is held in position by the usual jumper (see Fig. 251).

As the star wheel is turned by the block on the surprise-piece, the tooth runs up the inclined plane of the jumper until it reaches the apex. As soon as the apex is passed, the star wheel jumps forward, and as it does so the next tooth on the star wheel engages the back of the block on the surprise-piece and pushes it forward. The surprise-piece then covers the low section of the quarter-snail and stands in the path of the quarter rack, thus preventing quarters being struck at the hour. This surprise-piece is provided with all repeaters (see page 77), and is very necessary.

The Quarter Rack

The quarter rack runs on a stud screwed to the plate and is kept in place either by means of a shouldered screw with a shaped head, or by a spring which acts on it. Where the spring is underneath the rack, a screw is necessary to hold the rack down.

When the slide is pulled to the fullest extent, the quarter rack is released and the spring carries it back until the tail rests on the quarter snail; then, according to the depth of the snail, the number of quarters is struck. As soon as the slide is released, the hours are struck, and, at the last stroke, a pallet on the barrel arbor square engages with a step on the quarter rack and carries it forward.

The outside edge of the quarter rack is provided with two groups of three teeth, as shown in Fig. 252 (a), and each group engages with a separate hammer pallet. As the rack moves forward, a tooth of each group is engaged alternately and lifts and drops a hammer. Thus the two hammers, acting one after the other on gongs having different tones, produce the double-tone strike or " ting-tang " which indicates the quarters. As two teeth of each group are engaged, two double-tone strikes are given, and so on.

Some repeaters have three hammers which are brought into use

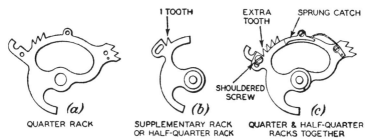

FIG. 252.—QUARTER AND HALF-QUARTER RACKS.

(a) Quarter rack. (b) Supplementary or half-quarter rack. (c) Assembled unit.

at the quarters, and in this case the rack is provided with three separate groups of three teeth.

As soon as the quarters have been struck, the hammer pallets are held away from the gongs and the racks, and the all-or-nothing piece drops into place and locks the rack.

Half-Quarter Repeaters

With the half-quarter repeater the mechanism is very similar, except that there is a supplementary or half-quarter rack, which is provided with one tooth only, as shown in Fig. 252 (b), and a double snail is used.

The quarter-rack spring acts on a pin fitted into the half-quarter rack, which is mounted above the quarter rack proper and is fitted free to move on the same collet as the quarter rack. Shouldered screws hold the racks together, but the half-quarter rack has elongated holes allowing the rack to move forwards or backwards by the distance of one tooth of the quarter rack.

The single tooth provided on the half-quarter rack either coincides with the last tooth of the group of three on the quarter rack, or stands beyond the last tooth of this group, thus making four acting teeth, as shown in Fig. 252 (c), the extra tooth allowing a single blow to be struck for the half-quarter.

Two arrangements are used, in one case the half-quarter rack is locked in the position to strike the half-quarter, and in the other is the reverse, or is in a position with the tooth coinciding with the last tooth of the quarter rack.

In the first case where no half-quarters are to be struck, the supplementary rack is pushed back off its locking piece and becomes coincident with the quarter rack, and in the second case the supplementary rack is pushed forwards off its locking piece.

The quarter snail on the cannon pinion is similar to two snails fitted one above the other and firmly screwed together (see Fig. 253). The upper snail controls the half-quarter rack, and the lower is the quarter snail proper and controls the full quarters and the quarter rack.

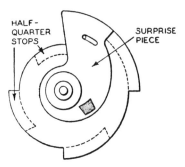

HALF-QUARTER SNAIL

FIG. 253.—DOUBLE SNAIL FOR HALF-QUARTER REPEATER.

Comprises one snail mounted below the other. The action is the same as an ordinary quarter snail.

This type is sometimes referred to as a seven-and-a-half-minute repeater.

Five-Minute Repeaters

With the five-minute repeater there are two snails which look alike and can be identical. Sometimes the snail is geared to the cannon pinion or is mounted on a twelve-pointed star in a similar manner to the hour snail or, again, may be mounted on the cannon pinion arbor in the same way as the quarter snail. The difference in the two snails is that on the highest step no blows are struck, on No. 2 step only one is struck, and so on. Therefore, at the lowest step only eleven blows are struck.

Usually the hour is struck on one gong and each five minutes is indicated by one blow on a different gong. This type is not so common as the quarter or minute repeaters.

Minute Repeaters

The minute repeater is the most useful of all. It strikes on pulling or pushing a slide as usual and reproduces first the hours, then the quarters and finally the minutes. Thus, at one minute

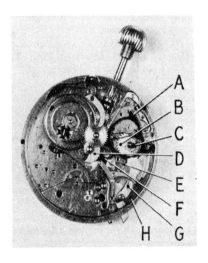

FIG. 254.—FIVE-MINUTE REPEATER

A. Five-minute rack.
B. Circular rack.
C. Gathering pallet.
D. Five-minute snail.
E. Supplementary rack tail.
F. Hour snail.
G. Hour rack.
H. " All-or-nothing " spring.

to one o'clock the repeater will strike twelve hours, three quarters and fourteen minutes.

As the principle of the mainspring and repeating train is the same as in the quarter repeater, also as the slide, rack lever, hour rack, circular striking rack and all-or-nothing spring are the same, it is unnecessary to describe these features in detail again.

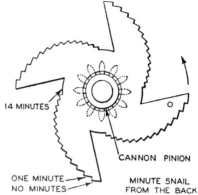

FIG. 255.—MINUTE SNAIL MOUNTED ON CANNON PINION.

Comprises four curved sections each of 14 steps.

The Minute Snail

In the minute repeater there is a minute snail which is fitted and riveted on to the cannon pinion and does not move except in conjunction with the cannon pinion. The minute snail comprises four curved sections, as shown in Fig. 255, each having fourteen steps corresponding with the fourteen minutes between each quarter. The quarter snail and a four-bladed surprise-piece are screwed together and are fitted to move freely on the cannon pinion arbor. As in the quarter repeater, a steel collar holds the surprise-piece in place (see Fig. 256).

The Quarter Jumper

The surprise-piece is not wholly dependent on the hour-snail jumper, but only at the hour. It has its own jumper, which comes into action every fifteen minutes or quarter of an hour. The object is to prevent the minute rack falling at the full quarters or at the hour. In most modern repeaters this jumper only comes into action when the repeating work is set in motion. The idea is to save wear and tear on the surprise-piece, which is particularly troublesome to remedy when it does occur.

The jumper is taken out of action usually by the slide as it returns to rest, or by a pawl

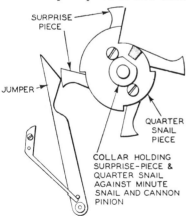

FIG. 256.—ACTION OF SURPRISE-PIECE WITH MINUTE REPEATER.

which is fitted on the repeating barrel arbor square and engages a lever joined to the jumper itself. As the repeating train runs down, the pawl on the barrel arbor lifts the lever and carries the jumper clear of the surprise-piece.

Gathering Click on Quarter Rack

The quarter rack differs by the addition of a piece which moves freely on it and is held in position by means of a shouldered screw. A spring which acts on this piece is also fitted and screwed to the quarter rack. Sometimes it is shaped like a double-ended click, but in the majority of good-class repeaters it is U-shaped with elongated sides. One side acts as the gathering click for the minute rack. The other side is so shaped that when it engages an extension of the hour hammer arbor, it releases and allows the rack to fall; it also arranges the position of the quarter rack in such a way that only when the quarters have finished striking can the minutes be struck.

The elongated click works in a similar way, but instead of engaging on the hammer arbor it engages either on the corner of the barrel bar or on a steel stud placed in position for the purpose. The action is the same ; as the racks fall together the tail of the click engages the stud and this lifts the click end out of the minute rack which carries on to its full fall. As the quarter rack returns, the click returns to the minute rack at the right time and carries the minute rack with it.

Gathering Wheel for Quarter Rack

The minute rack has ratchet-shaped teeth with which the click engages. The quarter rack has ten hypocycloidal teeth cut on the inside circle with eleven spaces. This is engaged by a flat steel wheel having eleven teeth only, the rest being cut away. Projecting from this wheel is a steel pin. This steel pin is engaged by a steel cam with a square hole and fits the barrel arbor square. The steel cam is turned half-way into a pivot and the steel wheel fits this pivot closely.

When assembling the repeater, the teeth in the steel wheel must be correctly meshed with the teeth in the quarter rack. Make sure that the two outside teeth of the steel wheel are engaged in the two outside spaces of the quarter-rack teeth, otherwise the quarters will not be struck correctly, apart from other troubles.

After this adjustment has been made correctly, pull the slide and allow the hours to be struck and, just before the last hour is reproduced, put the cam in place with the pin in the steel wheel. Make certain that the pivot on the cam is properly in the hole in the steel wheel and push it home. Do not forget to place a little oil on this pivot.

The cam engages the pin, turns the steel wheel and carries the quarter rack to strike the quarters. The click picks up the minute

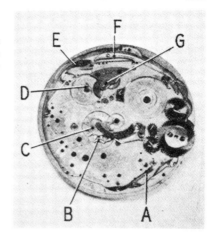

Fig. 257.—Pillar Plate of Minute Repeater from the Front with most of the Mechanism removed.

A. Quarter jumper spring.
B. Hour jumper spring.
C. Hour snail.
D. Repeating barrel arbor square.
E and F. Adjustable hammer stops.
G. Repeating train.

rack and the minutes follow immediately after the quarters have been struck.

The Minute Rack

The minute rack fits on the pipe of the quarter rack. It is provided with six ratchet teeth on one part of the periphery and fourteen similar teeth on another part. The fourteen teeth correspond with the fourteen minutes between each quarter. The minute-rack spring is screwed to the side of the pillar plate and engages a pin near the centre of the rack. Sometimes it is stepped to hold the minute and quarter racks down, or just rests on the minute rack itself and holds them down.

Adjusting the Hammers

There is nothing intricate about the hammers themselves. Sometimes they are pivoted between the plates, or they may have separate cocks. The hour-hammer arbor is often extended and acts as a stud, as mentioned earlier. As well as the arbor on which the hammers are pivoted, a stud is screwed into the hammer. This usually takes the form of a screw with the visible part of the thread turned away, and is situated near the arbor and passes through the plate. The plate is cut out in a curved slot to allow freedom of movement.

Near each hammer is a stop piece which is screwed to the plate. This stop piece is adjusted by means of screws which are put in from the top of the pillar plate and pass through the plate and engage with the hammer stops. The threads of the screws are turned to a long cone and as the screws are tightened against the stops, the cone moves the stops across the plate and adjusts the position of the hammers in relation to the gongs. When the hammers have been adjusted the screws which secure the stops must be screwed home tightly.

Securing the Gongs

The gongs must always be screwed firmly in place. Usually the gongs are in one piece and as they are very hard, if it is tried to bend them, more often than not they will break. Two screws are usually fitted through the block of the gongs to secure them, and as one screw is generally shorter than the other, be careful when replacing them.

The Hammer Pallets

The hammer pallets fit on to the hammer arbors. There are four pallets in a minute repeater ; two on the hour hammer and two on the minute hammer. They should be handled very carefully because they can be easily lost, and it is difficult to make replacements. Another warning, do not remove bits by filing as this can lead to all sorts of trouble.

The hour pallet presents least difficulty. It consists of a flat piece of steel filed to shape. A pin stands upright from the pallet, and is engaged by a spring which passes from the centre of the movement across the circular rack. The spring permits the pallet to give way when the rack is being pushed back as the repeating mainspring is being wound, and brings the pallet back into position to lift the hammer on the return of the circular rack.

The pallet for the first blow of the quarters is placed on the same hammer arbor and is above and resting on the hour pallet. The spring acting on the hour pallet has a flat section which fits in a slot in the quarter pallet. This allows the quarter rack to pass when falling and lifts the hour pallet in place on the return of the quarter rack. Each of these pallets engages in the stud screwed into the hammer near the pallet arbor and by this means the hammer is lifted.

The minute hammer also has two hammer pallets. The lower one lifts the hammer for the last stroke of the quarters, and the top pallet lifts the hammer for the minutes to be struck. The minute pallet is stepped downwards to engage in the hammer stud, which is usually shortened to enable the minute rack to pass. If this stud were long, it would engage in the teeth of the minute rack and would stop the repeating mechanism.

The pallets on the minute hammer are also provided with an additional spring, which acts in a hole drilled in the side of each pallet. The springs are screwed to the plate and are tapered off at the ends to enter the hole. As with the other pallets, the springs allow the pallets to give way when the racks are falling and bring the pallets back into position on the return journey and also prevent them from riding up.

Sometimes these pallets are slotted instead of being drilled, and

Fig. 258.—A Modern
Minute Repeater.

A. Minute rack.
B. Minute snails.
C. Slide rack.
D. "All - or - nothing"
    spring.
E. Jumper for surprise-
    piece.
E_1. Disconnecting tail.
F. Section of quarter rack
    which locks hammer
    pallets.
G. Gathering pinion for
    quarter rack.
H. Gathering pallet.
J. Hour snail and star
    wheel.
K. Hour snail jumper.
L, L_1, and L_2. Figure-of-
    eight end pieces.
M. Minute rack spring.
N. Trigger.
O. Return spring.
P. Minute rack tail.

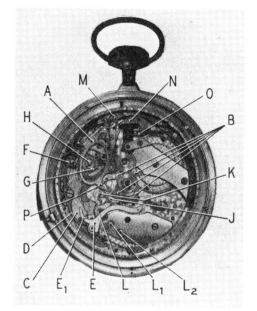

(*Reproduced by courtesy of Mr.*
R. John Low.)

flat-ended springs act as return springs. A modern minute repeater
is shown in Fig. 258.

Slide and Push Repeaters

The older repeaters, whether English or Continental, used the
pendant instead of a slide. The pendant fitted into a pipe and at
the end of the pendant inside the case was a round rod of steel
which was flattened, leaving a head at the extreme end. A bridge
screwed to the band of the case prevented the pendant from coming
right out, but allowed it to be pushed in. The pendant steel
engaged directly with the hour rack and some were extremely stiff
to operate.

Another type had a button and a steel stem which passed through
the pendant. To operate the repeating work it was necessary to
pull out the button a certain distance, give a quarter of a turn and
then push the button in again. This steel stem engaged directly
with the hour rack.

Some of these old repeaters had one hammer only, and the same
hammer was used for both hours and quarters. Very often the
hammers simply tapped the side of the case as there were no gongs.

The hammer pallets were also different. Instead of moving
sideways, as is the modern practice, they were lifted up to allow
the rack teeth to pass and were dropped into the path of the racks
as soon as the slide or hour rack reached the snail. Unless the rack

were pushed to the fullest extent, the repeating work could fail and was likely to stop the watch. The all-or-nothing piece prevents this.

Full Plate Repeaters

In the days of full plate watches, the repeating train, hammers, hammer pallets, circular rack, etc., were all between the plates, and some were very difficult to assemble. The type having a chain connection between the hour rack and the barrel arbor of the repeating train was particularly troublesome, especially when the chain became worn or was broken. Unless the length of the chain was exactly right it would not function. If the chain were short, the quarters would not be struck, and if it were long, the hours struck would be less than the correct number.

The greatest difficulty was when the repeater failed to strike the first hour, or failed to drop the last hammer for the third quarter. The only remedy was to replace the last two links of the chain by a brace. If the chain were still slightly short, the hole in the brace could be elongated by means of a steel polisher and oilstone dust. The length was critical to ·001 inch.

CLOCK-WATCHES

A clock-watch strikes the hours and quarters on passing in exactly the same way as a clock, but is usually a repeater as well. The clock-watch is generally provided with a small button in the side of the case which it is only necessary to push, about the same amount as a push-piece for set hands, to make the watch repeat.

It differs from the ordinary repeater inasmuch as it has a mainspring and a continuous train. The winding button when turned in the ordinary way winds the watch, and when turned backwards it winds the striking mainspring, but the fact of working the repeating button does not wind a mainspring.

The barrel arbor of the repeating train is superseded in a clock-watch by a wheel and pinion with a square arbor, otherwise most of the mechanism is the same as a repeater, except for the circular rack. In both the repeater and the clock-watch the hour rack turns the circular rack, the amount corresponding to the number of hours to be struck. On the repeater the mainspring is wound, whereas with the clock-watch their only function is the control of the hours to be struck. The mechanism is all mounted on what is, in effect, a movable platform which can be released at will, or is released by the going train of the watch. The mechanism varies from one type to another, but the main principle is the same, except in very old clock-watches.

Early Design

In this type either four cams are fitted on the cannon pinion, or cams are fitted on to the minute wheel. These cams engage a

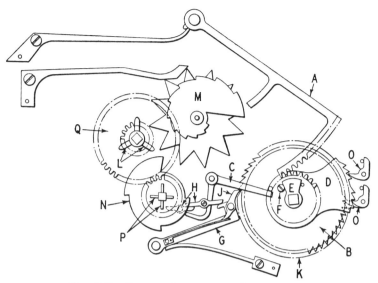

FIG. 259.—TYPICAL CLOCK-WATCH MECHANISM.

A. Hour control rack.
B. Circular hour rack.
C. Quarter rack tail.
D. Quarter rack.
E. Gathering pawl for quarter and minute racks.
F. Gathering post for pawl E.
G. Lifting and release arm.
H. Lifting pieces.
J. Releasing click.
K. Releasing and carrying ratchet.
L. Pawls for changing hour star wheel.
M. Hour star wheel and snail.
N. Quarter snail.
O. Hammer pallets.
P. Lifting cams.
Q. Minute wheel.

lever, which is held in place by a shouldered screw and is screwed to the plate. A spring acts on the lever and lies flat beside it, so that whichever way the cannon is turned the lever can move and still be returned to a resting position. This is to allow the hands to be set backwards.

When the hands are set forwards, the cams or pins on the cannon pinion engage the lever and lift it slightly and then release or drop it. On the rebound of the lever it lifts a click or hook-shaped lever which engages a ratchet-toothed wheel on the underside of the carriage, that is, the mechanism containing the circular rack, etc. As this ratchet is suddenly engaged, it knocks a pin on a wheel mounted directly above. This pin pushes a click out of engagement with another ratchet on which is mounted the circular rack, etc. This carriage immediately flies back until the hour rack is banked against the hour snail. The striking train is then released and starts running. The click, previously knocked out of engagement, gathers up the carriage and turns it. As it does so the circular rack strikes the hours, the quarter rack is gathered up as soon as the hours are struck and the quarters are struck if appropriate.

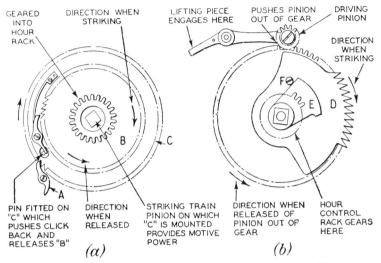

FIG. 260.—TWO DIFFERENT TYPES OF CLOCK-WATCH RELEASING MECHANISM.

(a) The most usual type of mechanism:
  A. Releasing click mounted on lifting arm.
  B. Body of striking carriage.
  C. Releasing ratchet, also carries striking carriage.
(b) Type used when striking and going trains are driven by only one barrel:
  D. Circular rack.
  E. Carrier pawl for quarter rack.
  F. Post on D which gathers up quarter rack carrier pawl.

As the watch strikes only on passing the quarters no minutes can be struck, but the minute rack has fallen just the same and has to be gathered up. A pin is usually fitted to the end of the minute rack either at the toothed end or at the tail end, and as the minute rack reaches the end of its journey this pin passes into a wheel in the striking train and stops it running.

When the release push-piece or button is pressed, the only thing it does is to push the gathering click out of action and release the carriage. If there are minutes to be struck it will strike hours, quarters and minutes in the same way as a minute repeater.

Clock-watches are often provided with some arrangement for acting as a strike-silent piece, or for striking the hours or quarters only. In the case of hours only, the quarter rack is prevented from falling, and with quarters only, the hour-hammer pallet is held back. Whichever striking arrangement is adopted, however, the train still runs the same amount.

Other Forms of Clock-Watch Mechanism

Some of the older models had a rack with a rack-hook and a gathering pallet, very similar to the striking mechanism of a grand-father clock. A type of warning was even provided to allow the

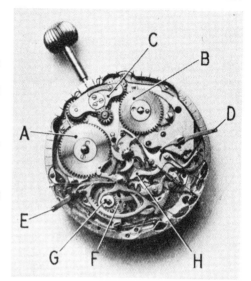

FIG. 261.—CLOCK-WATCH
MINUTE REPEATER.

With hour wheel and
minute wheel removed.

A. Striking train ratchet.
B. Going train ratchet.
C. Rocking bar.
D. Hours or quarter lever.
E. Strike-silent lever.
F. Hour rack.
G. Striking carriage.
H. Quarter jumper.

(*Reproduced by courtesy of Lord Harris.*)

rack to fall clear. Some were " flirted ", but the margin of safety was very small and any delay in the action meant failure.

Again, some old clock-watches had two separate trains, one for the striking mechanism and the other for the repeating. Both were completely independent of each other and each consisted of a complete set of snails, racks, etc.

Replacing and Re-adjusting Worn Parts

Most troubles experienced with a clock-watch are associated with worn parts, so always be extremely careful.

The lifting levers get worn, with the result that the actions are advanced and the striking train is released before the exact hour, or quarters. This can be remedied by stretching and repolishing, or replacing them if necessary. A further trouble is that the springs get worn into little hollows and are then sluggish in their action.

Another action which often gets worn is where the jumper spring works on the teeth of the hour star wheel. This spring or jumper must be repolished and the action carefully readjusted, otherwise the watch is very likely to strike an extra three quarters and four-teen minutes at the hour, or three quarters and fourteen minutes fast. If the jumper acts too early it will not strike the fourteen minutes. In a minute repeater, the hour and minute snails must be in step.

Oiling a Clock-Watch

It is most important, and cannot be emphasized too strongly, that a clock-watch must be oiled correctly, otherwise troubles will follow. Do not apply oil to the surprise-pieces, except at the extreme ends where they engage the jumper. If any oil gets between the surprise-piece and the minute snail it will prevent the surprise-piece from working owing to the suction. For the same reason, do not put any oil on the carrying ratchet wheel, because it is sure to spread and get in between the carrying ratchet and the ratchet on the carriage, and will prevent the carriage from being released.

Some surprise-pieces are fitted with a fine spring. The object of this spring is to keep the surprise-piece back flush with the edge of the minute snail, otherwise the minute rack might be obstructed. The spring must be set so that it is just strong enough to keep the surprise-piece back, but not so strong that it prevents the surprise-piece from being pushed forward by the jumper. This is used only when the jumper is put out of continuous action.

MUSICAL AND ALARM WATCHES

A musical watch plays a tune at regular intervals, and is usually combined with a repeater or a clock-watch. Some are released every hour, and some every three or four hours. The musical train and mainspring are always completely separate from the going train.

The train usually consists of a " comb ", as it is termed, or, failing this, a series of springs of certain thickness planted in a semicircle on the pillar plate between the dial and the plate. The barrel usually carries the lifting pins.

The Musical Work

The musical work is generally set off by a flirt and is stopped, after the barrel has moved a full turn, by a lever which carries a pin or is shaped at one end in the form of a click. On the barrel is a raised ring of brass with a small section cut away, the object of which is to allow the locking lever to fall and the click or pin to obstruct the train. There is another slide or push-button on the outside of the case to prevent the musical train being released. Sometimes it takes the form of a two-position slide. In one position the musical train is stopped, while in the other the tune is played and, if left in that position, the train will continue to run unhindered each time it is released by the motion work.

Alarm Watches

The alarm watch is not a formidable piece of mechanism. The whole principle amounts to a lever placed in a position to obstruct a train and escapement and release it at a predetermined time.

Some alarm watches have two separate barrels and mainsprings, while others take their power from the same mainspring as the going train.

In the type where one barrel does the work for the two, the first wheel and pinion of the alarm train act as the click. In other words, there is the usual winding ratchet on the barrel, but the winding ratchet gears into the first wheel of the alarm train. Thus, the barrel teeth drive the going train and the barrel arbor drives the alarm train.

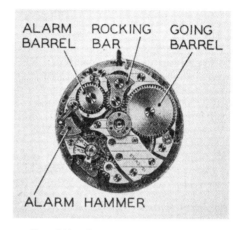

FIG. 262.—ALARM WATCH MOVEMENT.

The going is wound in one way and the alarm in the reverse direction.

To prevent the mainspring from being run down completely by the alarm train, a wheel is added having all the teeth cut in the usual way, except the last one. Thus, there is a block at one end. At the opposite end a tooth is cut away, leaving a space. When the watch is wound up, the wheel turns on the barrel arbor until it reaches the space.

On the same wheel is a pin which is acted upon by a spring. This spring keeps the wheel in such a position that it cannot get out of gear with the alarm train when it comes to the space, but clicks over on the last tooth before the space. When the winding is finished, the first tooth of the wheel is in gear and carries the power of the mainspring.

When the alarm train is released, it can run only for just under one turn owing to the block of uncut teeth which cannot pass the alarm pinion in which it gears. It can only run again if the mainspring is re-wound. There is no interference with the going train.

The Release Mechanism

The release mechanism is complicated in a few new models, but very simple in most cases. There is a steel spring screwed to the plate which passes under the hour wheel and across the frame of the watch. The free end of the spring is bent down at a right angle and passes into the frame in the path of either the 'scape wheel, or the hammer of the alarm train.

The hour wheel has a raised block, or a shaped pin, standing up from the body. The dial, or a plate on which the dial is mounted, is fitted with a wheel which turns stiffly. This wheel has a pipe which carries the alarm hand. A slot is cut in the side of the wheel which is near to the hour wheel. One side of the slot is straight and the other is sloped. This is in a corresponding position to the raised block, or shaped pin, on the hour wheel.

Sometimes there is a button to set the alarm hand, or it may be carried out from the pendant. In some cases the bezel is so fitted that it can be turned round without coming off, and a slot is cut on the flange into which the end of the alarm hand fits. Thus, to set the alarm, it is only necessary to turn the bezel until the hand points to the required hour of release.

When the alarm has been set, the raised block rests on a solid part of the wheel fitted to the dial plate. As the watch goes, the hour wheel turns and, as soon as the block reaches the cut-out, the alarm lever is released and rises out of the path of the alarm train. This lever or spring rests underneath the hour wheel.

Repairing Alarm Mechanism

Some alarm watches are made with an extra wheel which has exactly the same number of teeth as the hour wheel. This fulfils the same function, but has an advantage as it avoids a trouble sometimes experienced with the hour wheel. Where the hour wheel is pushed up by the spring or lever, it is possible for the minute hand to be knocked off unless the hand is fitted very tightly, which again is a nuisance as it may be difficult to remove.

When removing a tight minute hand another trouble may arise due to the raised block on the hour wheel becoming damaged in the process. When levering off the minute hand, if the hour hand is pressed or pulled up, it is more than likely that the block will be flattened, with the result that the release of the alarm will be uncertain. If it is tried to raise the flattened block, more often than not it will break off. The best remedy is to remove the damaged block and replace it by a steel one which can be screwed in and shaped suitably. Remember when shaping the block that the side in the direction in which the hour wheel turns must be sloped, and the opposite side must be vertical or even slightly under-cut, so that it will drop sharply and not in steps. If this action is sharp, the alarm release can be arranged within a minute or two ; but if not, within five or ten minutes is more likely.

Alarms with One Barrel for Both Trains

One type of alarm, which is fairly common nowadays, has one barrel only for both going and alarm trains. There are two winding wheels geared together. One wheel is squared on to the barrel arbor and is held in place by a small nut which is screwed on to the barrel arbor. The winding key is also screwed to this same arbor. There is no click on this wheel which in the ordinary way has a click and spring.

The other wheel is different from the usual type, as underneath it is provided with very fine ratchet teeth cut into the flat of the wheel. The arbor on which it is mounted has a square section on which is fitted a domed four-bladed steel spring, which acts as a click in conjunction with the ratchet teeth. The arbor is the first power of the alarm train.

There is no means of letting down the mainspring, also neither of the screws holding the two wheels in place can be moved until the mainspring is right down. If either is unscrewed, the mainspring will go down with a rush, with disastrous results. The best way is to run the alarm train out until the mainspring is down. As it is an eight-day watch or clock movement and the last pivots are small, it is unsafe to run down the mainspring by letting the going train run.

CHAPTER 14

CHRONOGRAPHS AND STOP WATCHES, CALENDAR WATCHES AND CLOCKS

A CHRONOGRAPH is a watch in which a chronograph mechanism has been added to an ordinary movement, to allow intervals of time to be measured without interfering with the normal timekeeping. In addition to the customary minute and hour hands, as well as the seconds hand in the usual place, the watch is provided with a sweep-seconds hand and usually a minute-recording hand positioned either at the pendant, or at the figure IX. The minute-recording hand records each complete revolution of the sweep-seconds hand, which is not always one minute as will be seen later.

The mechanism can be started, stopped and the chronograph hands returned to zero by pressing a push-piece on the side of the case, or, as is more common to-day, by pressing a push-piece which passes through the winding button.

The layout of chronographs varies considerably, but once the general principle has been mastered it should not be difficult to deal with the various types.

Six-Post Crown

Most chronographs record fifths of a second. This action is controlled by a six-post crown (or column wheel), that is, a ratchet wheel of eighteen teeth carrying six perpendicular posts (see *M*, Fig. 263).

A lever pivoted on a shouldered screw, or on a capped stud, passes from the button to the six-post crown, which is again pivoted, or runs on a shouldered screw fixed to the plate. The end of the lever near the push-piece has a post which is screwed in, or is solid with the lever and acts as a drop piece. This drop piece is engaged either by the push-piece itself, or by means of a sleeve or tube fitted on the winding stem of the watch. Thus when the push-piece is pressed in, it presses the end of the lever and, as the lever is pivoted in the centre, the opposite end of the lever moves outwards.

Fitted on this end of the lever is a click (or sometimes a hook) which is acted upon by a spring, the object of which is to keep the click in action with the eighteen ratchet teeth of the six-post crown. As there are eighteen teeth on the ratchet, each post engages with three teeth, thus providing the three separate actions of start, stop and return to zero.

When the push-piece is pressed, the lever moves and the click

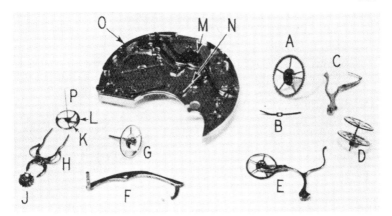

FIG. 263.—SPLIT-SECONDS CHRONOGRAPH TOP PLATE WITH PARTS REMOVED.

A. 60-minute-recording wheel (note heart piece).
B. Friction and lifting spring for minute-recording wheel.
C. Threefold piece ; double flyback jumpers and sliding piece to put minute-recording wheel out of action.
D. Fourth wheel and pinion with extra driving wheel for chronograph.
E. Arm carrying chronograph transmission wheel.
F. Starting arm for split seconds.
G. Central chronograph wheel on hollow arbor (note heart piece).
H. Split-second stop clams.
J. Eight-post crown (usually four-post type).
K. Pawl.
L. Pawl spring.
M. Six-post crown.
N. Brake for chronograph central wheel.
O. Lever to operate chronograph.
P. Split-seconds wheel. Arbor passes through G.

engages with one of the ratchet teeth and pulls or pushes the crown one tooth. This happens each time the push-piece is pressed. The lever has a spring acting on it which presses the lever back to its starting point. The click is so shaped that as the lever returns, it slides over the tooth it is about to pull and drops into it ready to pull the crown round another tooth, and so on.

Heart-shaped Cam

These six posts are all engaged by various levers and each lever has at least two different positions which it can occupy. We will deal with these in turn.

In the majority of cases, the centre pinion of the watch is hollow and the cannon pinion snaps on in the usual way.

Through the centre pinion a thin arbor passes and stands above the cannon pinion. On the other end is a fine-toothed wheel with as many as three hundred teeth. Mounted on the same arbor and usually above the wheel is a heart-shaped cam or heart piece. This heart piece fits the arbor closely and is screwed firmly to the wheel.

The arbor at this end has a pivot and runs in a jewel-hole fitted into a cock screwed to the plate.

The Minute-recording Wheel

This same cock spans another wheel provided with either thirty or sixty pointed teeth, depending on whether it is a thirty- or a sixty-minute-recording chronograph. This is known as the minute-recording wheel. It is mounted on an arbor which passes through the movement and projects just beyond the dial. This wheel has a heart piece mounted on the arbor and screwed to the wheel and is again pivoted and runs in a jewel-hole in the same cock. The purpose of the heart pieces is to enable each wheel to be returned to its starting point. They are acted upon either by separate levers, or by two joined together and running on a single stud. Either way is efficient.

Strong springs act on the levers to force them against the heart pieces. These same levers are held away from them by one of the six posts in the crown. When the crown is turned, as a space appears opposite the levers, the levers drop and apply the pressure of the spring on to the heart pieces. The heart piece is so shaped that any pressure exerted against its side will force the heart to the lowest point.

The Finger Piece

Underneath the central wheel is a cam or finger piece which varies according to the type of chronograph. This finger piece engages with a wheel, which is geared into the minute-recording

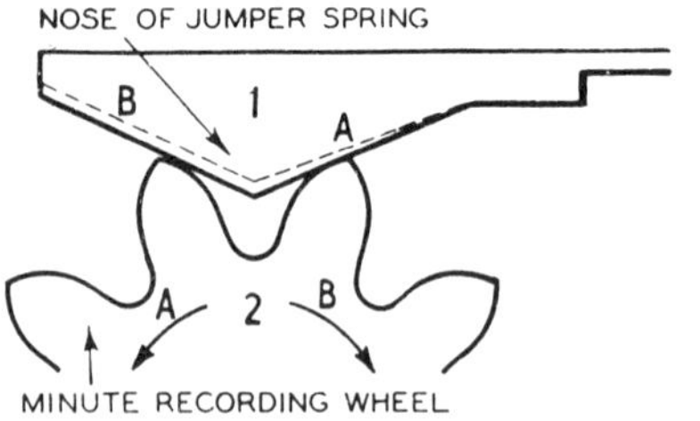

FIG. 264.—SHOWING ACTION OF JUMPER SPRING ON MINUTE-RECORDING WHEEL.

1. Jumper spring. 2. Minute-recording wheel. When the side A1 is reduced, wheel is moved in direction of A2. When the side B1 is reduced, the wheel moves in the direction of B2.

wheel and is mounted on a movable arm running on a stud screwed to the plate. When the chronograph mechanism is running, the finger piece engages with the wheel after it has completed one full turn, and advances it one tooth each time and also moves the recording wheel one tooth.

The minute-recording wheel is held in place by a very thin jumper spring. The object of this spring is firstly to keep the hand on the minute-recording arbor pointing exactly to a particular minute, and secondly to hold the intermediate wheel in the correct position for engagement with the finger piece. Otherwise the finger might easily engage on the top of a tooth and stop the watch. This action is often very critical.

Adjusting the Finger Piece

Sometimes the jumper is slightly out of position in relation to the finger piece and has to be adjusted. This adjustment is made either by moving the spring where it is movable, or, if a fixture, by altering the position of the point by polishing one side or the other of the nose. This will advance or retard the minute-recording wheel, according to which side of the nose is polished.

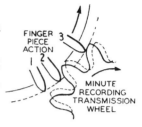

FIG. 265.—MINUTE-RECORDING ACTION FOR CHEAPER CHRONOGRAPHS.

The shake in the gearing makes action uncertain. Drawing shows incorrect action : finger engages too early and does not pass out clearly. Dotted teeth show correct position. Three positions of finger are shown.

This transmission wheel is also adjustable for the depth or inter-section between the finger piece and the wheel. This is carried out by means of an eccentric banking stud against which the arm is pressed. The finger piece must run in clear of the previous tooth, engage the correct tooth and then run out clear on the other side.

Driving the Chronograph Mechanism

The fourth or seconds pinion has a long pivot at each end. The front carries the ordinary seconds hand and on the back pivot is mounted a high numbered toothed wheel. This wheel provides the power to drive the chronograph mechanism, and is exactly the same in size and number as the central wheel which passes through the centre pinion and carries the sweep-seconds hand.

The Transmission Wheel

Another wheel of the same pitch, but not necessarily of the same number of teeth, is mounted on a movable arm or lever which is on either a stud, or a shouldered screw. Sometimes an eccentric stud is fitted on the plate and the lever pivots on it, or the stud may be mounted on a kind of turntable which can be moved by means of a twin-pointed key. The object of this is to adjust the depth of the intermediate or transmission wheel into the wheel mounted on the top or back fourth pivot. This wheel on its arm is always in gear and is continually running with the fourth wheel.

The opposite end of the lever is engaged or banked on one of the posts on the crown and is pressed against the post by a spring screwed to the plate.

When the crown is turned, the lever drops into a space and

moves over, carrying the intermediate wheel, which is running with the fourth wheel, into gear with the central wheel and this runs with it and in step with the fourth wheel. As the fourth wheel turns once a minute the central wheel does the same and, as the hand is fitted to the arbor, the hand also turns once a minute.

The depth or intersection of this transmission wheel is also adjustable, usually by means of an eccentric screw on which it is banked.

Action of the Chronograph Mechanism

The action, therefore, when the push-piece is pressed is that the crown is turned one tooth, the lever places the transmission in gear with the central wheel and at the same time the intermediate minute-recording wheel drops into the path of the finger piece. The two fly-back jumpers are lifted clear of the heart pieces and the chronograph is set in motion.

The second push turns the crown another tooth, the lever carries the transmission lever over and takes the wheel out of gear with the central wheel. The intermediate minute-recording wheel is moved out of the path of the finger piece, but the fly-back jumpers just rest on the edge of one of the posts and the chronograph is stopped.

The third push advances the crown another tooth and all the levers remain resting on the edge of a post on the crown, but the fly-back jumpers are opposite a space between two posts and are free to fall, which they do, on to the edge of the heart pieces wherever they may be. The heart pieces are then forced back to their starting point, that is zero, by the hands.

The foregoing is the sequence of operations which is always repeated when the push-piece is pressed three times in succession.

This type of chronograph is probably the simplest, and, although efficient for most purposes, lacks complete accuracy. There is no piece designed solely for holding the central wheel firmly when the chronograph mechanism is stopped. Thus as it is dependent on a skid spring under the central wheel, it can, and does, move a little either way, which is unsatisfactory for close timing.

The minute recording is also uncertain. When a chronograph has been running for 59 and four-fifths seconds the minute-recording hand should not record one minute, but at 60 seconds it must record the minute. As it may be kept running for 15 or 20 minutes, one cannot be certain of knowing the right minute with this type of chronograph. Therefore other methods have to be adopted where extreme accuracy is required.

Minute-recording Chronograph

The type of minute recording generally favoured for high-quality chronographs is arranged on an entirely different principle.

Mounted on the central chronograph wheel is a snail-shaped piece or cam. There is a lever pivoting on a stud, having an arm at one end which engages on the edge of the snail. Sometimes this arm terminates in a ruby roller, but actually it is no advantage. The arm should end in an almost sharp corner. The lever also has an arm at the opposite end carrying a hook actuated by a small weak spring, which presses the hook into engagement with the teeth of the minute-recording wheel.

The snail gradually lifts the lever as the chronograph is running and as it does so the hook passes over a tooth in the minute-recording wheel and drops into the next space. The arm by this time has reached its maximum height, which should be a little more than necessary, and as the snail ends with a straight drop to the centre, the arm falls and in doing so the opposite end, with its hook, pulls the minute-recording wheel one tooth.

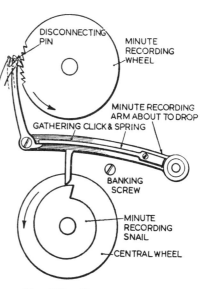

When the fly-back to zero action is carried out another lever with a V-shaped end engages with a pin in the head of the hook and lifts the hook out of engagement with the minute-recording wheel, and thus the wheel is free to run back to zero. This action is extremely rapid and can be adjusted to move the minute-recording wheel in less than a fifth of a second.

FIG. 266.—MINUTE-RECORDING MECHANISM, INSTANTANEOUS TYPE.

Used on high-quality chronographs when extreme accuracy is required.

Another Type of Minute-recording Chronograph

There is another type of chronograph having a large minute-recording wheel, which is moved directly by the finger piece without any intermediate wheel (see Fig. 263).

The central wheel is sometimes carried by a fine-toothed pinion, or wheel mounted on a pinion, geared into the third wheel. The actions of starting and stopping are carried out by moving the pinion in and out of gear respectively with the central wheel.

When the fly-back to zero action is carried out, a steel lever passes across the protruding top pivot of the minute-recording arbor and pushes the wheel down and out of the path of the finger piece on the central wheel. On this same lever is a jumper lever which, as usual, engages in a heart piece mounted on the wheel and pushes the wheel back to zero. The central wheel is pushed back in exactly the same way.

There is a thin, twin-armed spring under the minute-recording wheel, which acts as a skid or friction spring and also raises the wheel into the path of the finger piece when the chronograph work is set in motion.

Wrist-Watch Chronograph

A further type, usually used in wrist watches, has the centre pinion planted off centre. The fourth, which is a hollow pinion, occupies the centre of the watch. Where the watch has a seconds hand in the usual place, this hollow pinion in the centre is supplementary and is only carried by the third wheel.

Mounted on the hollow pinion is a brass collet, shaped like a small round table, and projecting from it are two sharp-pointed pins made either of brass, or steel. Passing through this hollow pinion is an arbor, which is a little thicker than the average seconds pivot. This arbor passes through the plate and the centre post, and projects above the minute hand. On this end is fitted the sweep-seconds hand. On the top end of this arbor is another brass table, to which is fitted a fibre or leather washer. This faces the two pins in the table mounted on the pinion. When the chronograph is running, these two tables, by reason of being pressed together by springs, act in exactly the same way as a small clutch.

The hollow pinion is carried by the third wheel and by means of the clutch carries the arbor passing through it and the chronograph hand runs. This same arbor carries a heart piece and also a finger piece to actuate the minute-recording wheel. The whole action is controlled by a crown in the usual way.

Adjusting the Springs

The springs are different from usual as they are hump-shaped, but fortunately are capable of adjustment. They are actuated by a pivoted lever which is pushed across them and also across another spring which rests on the top pivot of the central arbor. There are three tightly fitting screws in the lever which can, however, be turned to increase or decrease the depth of engagement.

The aim is to get all these actions collectively correct; if they have been disturbed it requires patience to put them right. Three of these springs have to be removed when the watch is cleaned and it may take time to replace them in the correct positions, but do not file or bend them. As the springs are provided with long holes where they are screwed to the plate, there is plenty of scope for adjustment; also they can be moved from side to side.

Wrist Chronographs with Additional Push-Piece

Another type of wrist chronograph, instead of having all three actions controlled by the one push-piece as usual, has a separate push-piece for returning the hand to zero.

The second push-piece cannot be pressed until the chronograph is in the stopped position. However, the first push-piece can be pressed to start and stop, and then when started again the hand will carry straight on from where it was previously stopped.

In a more recent type of wrist chronograph the six-post crown is eliminated. There are two push-pieces, as before. The first push-piece is pressed to start the mechanism. The second push-piece stops the mechanism when first pressed, and, when pressed again, returns the hands to zero.

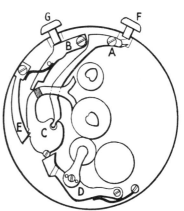

Fig. 267.—Wrist-type Chrono-graph having Two Push-But-tons and without the usual Six-post Crown (or Column Wheel).

A. Starting lever.
B. Stopping lever.
C. Combination lever for stopping and
    fly back.
D. Transmission lever.
E. Snap holding detent.
F. Starting button.
G. Stop and fly-back button.

A lever with a ball joint operates into a second lever provided with a socket, as shown in Fig. 267. This second lever occupies two positions, and acts as the stopping and fly-back lever. It is held in either position by means of a jumper spring acting on two pointed teeth.

The action of the first lever is to push the second lever back to its starting point, and that is its sole function.

The first push of the second push-piece places the lever into No. 1 position, and the second push places this same lever into No. 2 position.

Another lever carrying the transmission is held in place by a shouldered screw, and has a spring which keeps this transmission lever banked against a screw-head on the second lever. Thus the second lever either releases the transmission to gear into the central wheel, or pushes it out of gear.

The minute recording is as usual, but there is no provision for instantaneous minute recording, and a brake is not provided.

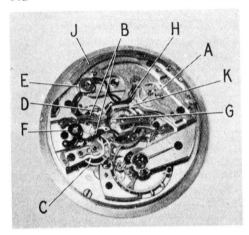

FIG. 268.—SPLIT-SECONDS CHRONOGRAPH MOVEMENT, SWISS.

A. Minute - recording wheel.
B. Split-seconds clams.
C. Extra fourth wheel.
D. Transmission chronograph wheel.
E. Six-post crown under steel cap.
F. Four-post crown under steel cap.
G. Central chronograph wheel under split-seconds wheel.
H. Tongued lever to disconnect minute recording.
J. Lever to operate chronograph.
K. Minute-recording arm.

Another type of a slightly different construction, but with the same principle, is also available.

Split-Seconds Chronograph

A more complicated design is the split-seconds chronograph, the uses and a brief description of which have already been given in Chapter 3.

The chronograph work itself is as usual. The centre pinion is hollow, as is also the arbor of the central wheel. The split-seconds arbor passes through the central arbor and stands above the ordinary chronograph hand. Fitted on to the top pivot of the central chronograph arbor is another small heart piece. Usually it is simply pressed on tightly so that it can be easily removed when required.

Mounted on the split-seconds arbor is a thin light wheel, which is usually made of steel. On this wheel is a pawl pivoted on a shouldered screw. Acting on this pawl is a fine spring, which is also screwed to the steel wheel (see Fig. 263).

The pawl acts in the same way as a fly-back jumper, as it brings the wheel always to the lowest part of the heart piece. This heart piece, as mentioned before, is fitted on the central arbor of the chronograph. Thus, the split-seconds wheel is carried by the central chronograph wheel, and the hands are fitted while the pawl or jumper is at the lowest part of the heart piece. The hands are placed so that they are coincident with one another.

Cross-acting Levers

As stated previously, when the chronograph is running, the split-seconds wheel is carried by the central arbor through the medium of the heart piece. There are two grip levers, situated one on each side of the split-seconds wheel, which cross over one another and are held in place by a shouldered screw. At the opposite ends to the grips, each lever is engaged on a crown, usually a four-post crown. This is turned in the same way as the chronograph crown, and normally has a separate push-piece.

The two levers rest on a post on each side of the crown when the split-seconds wheel is running. When the crown is turned one tooth, the ends of the lever fall into the space and the grips at the other end are closed down and hold the split-seconds wheel firmly. The chronograph runs on and the two hands part company. As soon as the crown is advanced another tooth, the grips move away from the split-seconds wheel and release it. Then by the action of the heart piece and pawl, the wheel is advanced rapidly and its hand catches up with the other hand, with which it proceeds. The split-seconds wheel can be held indefinitely as the action is so light that it does not interfere with the chronograph or the going of the watch.

Types of Split-Seconds Mechanism

There are different forms of split-seconds mechanism. One popular design, instead of having a hollow central chronograph arbor, has the usual solid type, while the heart piece for the split-seconds is on the front plate and is pressed on the front pivot of the central wheel arbor. With this arrangement, the arbor pivot acts as a stud for the split-seconds wheel-pipe and the chronograph hand is above the split-seconds hand.

A split-seconds chronograph must not be confused with an ordinary split-seconds watch. The split-seconds watch is a very old idea and was devised in various ways, which were usually very complicated. They are not made now, of course, and those that were in use have had the split-seconds mechanism removed and are used as ordinary watches.

One model had a barrel, similar to a mainspring barrel, fitted on to the seconds pivot and the mainspring was similar to a very thin hairspring. The inner eye was pinned to a steel collar which fitted the fourth or seconds pivot closely, and the outer end was pinned to a hole in the outside edge of the barrel.

They were not provided with a centre-seconds hand, but an additional hand was paired with the usual seconds hand at the side or bottom of the dial. One seconds hand fitted on the pipe of the barrel and the other on the pivot itself. A push-piece on the side of the case was used to split the seconds. The action was that the edge of the barrel was held by a lever and thus the hand fitted to it was stopped. As soon as the barrel was released, due to the power in the hairspring, the hand was advanced rapidly to catch up with the other hand.

Unfortunately, the seconds could be split for about 30 seconds only. If held any longer, the hairspring was wound fully and thus stopped the watch.

Chronograph Mechanism mounted on a Separate Plate

In very complicated watches, such as minute repeater chronographs or minute repeater and split-seconds chronograph perpetual calendar watches, the chronograph mechanism is mounted on a separate plate and screwed on to the movement.

This was often carried out with some Swiss watches. In conjunction with a standard model, the chronograph mechanism could be easily added at very little cost. It was only necessary to fit a new fourth pinion with a long pivot at each end to supply the motive power, and screw on the plate carrying the chronograph mechanism.

STOP WATCHES

Continuous-running stop watches are usually chronographs. The ordinary stop watch, however, is very different from a chronograph. There are stop watches recording one-hundredth and one-tenth seconds, as well as the usual fifths of a second. It is not impossible to have a chronograph giving these fractional seconds, but it is asking too much of an ordinary watch and also the wear would be too great.

A stop-watch dial, as a rule, has only a sweep-seconds hand and a minute-recording hand, and there is no provision for mean time hands. With stop watches recording hundredths or tenths of a second, the dials are marked as seconds on the usual minute-recording position.

Removing the Hands

There are, of course, the usual heart pieces but they are fitted directly on to the pivots or pinion arbors and kept friction tight by means of small springs which also keep them in position. The hands fit on the pipes of the heart pieces and are at times very difficult to remove. The best way is to take off the dials, with the hands and heart pieces still in place. The heart pieces can be eased off their arbors as the dial is being removed. The heart pieces can be pushed off the hands very easily. A tool used for knocking off platform 'scape pinions from the 'scape wheel will do the job satisfactorily.

The tool is held in a vice ; the thin jaws can be placed on the shoulder of the hand bosses. A light tap on a punch, or a joint pusher held on the top of the heart pipe will drive the heart piece off without any damage or marks. If any other method is attempted, it may mean a broken dial and broken heart pieces.

Stop-Watch Mechanism

The fourth pinion is usually planted in the centre of the movement and there is no actual centre wheel. There is no disconnection of wheels and pinions to stop and start. A lever with a springy pin rests on the rim of the balance and stops it. When the stop watch is started, the balance is flipped by the springy pin attached to the lever, which passes across the periphery of the balance.

The stop watch has the usual six-post crown and there are, of course, the usual fly-back jumpers to return the hands to zero.

Cause of Broken Hands

The stop watch is usually a more robust movement than the chronograph and will stand a certain amount of rough treatment. With some types, however, the hands are the weak point. When returned from, say, the half-way-round mark they are sent back so rapidly, owing to the strength of the jumper springs, that the ends of the hands often break off. When the hands break too frequently, the springs can be thinned or weakened to prevent the trouble.

There are split-seconds stop watches, in the same way as there are split-seconds chronographs, but, although they are less delicate, the action is exactly the same and therefore it need not be described again.

Separate Push-Piece for Fly-back Action

Another arrangement met with in some stop watches, usually of the larger type and also with some chronographs, is where a separate push-piece is used for the fly-back action.

When the starting push-piece is first pressed the chronograph starts running. The second push stops it. The third not only sets the train running again, but also places an intermediate wheel in gear between the transmission and the central wheel, and the sweep-seconds hand runs backwards or in reverse. When the push-piece is pressed again, the chronograph stops running. The next push reverses the hand and the chronograph runs normally. The hand can only be returned to zero by means of the separate push-piece when the chronograph is in the stopped position.

CALENDAR WATCHES AND CLOCKS

Calendars are divided into two different categories known respectively as " simple " and " perpetual ". We will deal first with the simple wrist-watch calendar in which the month and the day of the month have to be reset by hand at the end of a month having less than 31 days. The day of the week always changes automatically.

Simple Calendar Watches

The design of simple calendars varies considerably, but the action is generally carried out either by an arrangement of levers and springs, or by means of pins fitted to wheels which are planted in the path of star wheels and advance them one tooth every 24 hours.

The usual method is to have an additional wheel mounted on the hour-wheel pipe, which gears into a wheel, or two wheels arranged one on each side, of double the size and with, of course, double the number of teeth. This means that the two larger wheels, assuming that the latter arrangement is used, make one turn in 24 hours as against the 12 hours taken by the hour wheel.

Star Wheels and Jumper Springs

On each of these wheels is an upright pin. One engages with a star wheel of seven teeth corresponding to the days of the week, and the other with a wheel of thirty-one teeth corresponding to the days of the month or the date.

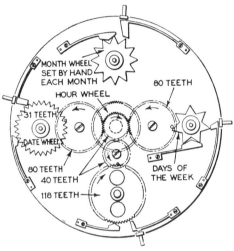

Each star wheel is held in place by a jumper spring and each has a setting spring which, when pressed into the star wheel by a push-piece, advances it by one tooth, enabling it to be reset.

The day-of-the-month star wheel is also fitted with a pin, or a small block, which acts on a 12-pointed star wheel and thus, at the end of 31 days, the month wheel is advanced one tooth corresponding to one month.

FIG. 269.—SIMPLE CALENDAR MECHANISM AS APPLIED TO BOTH WATCHES AND CLOCKS.

The moon star wheel is sometimes turned by a separate wheel (when the moon wheel must have 118 teeth as it is moved every 12 hours) or by the same pin which operates the day of the week star wheel. The moon wheel in a simple calendar, however, is usually provided with 59 teeth. It also has a jumper spring and a setting spring functioning in the same way as the other two.

Setting the Calendar

With simple calendar work, as mentioned previously, the mechanism has to be adjusted at the end of a month having less than 31 days.

The calendar work is sometimes mounted on a separate plate and the dial is snapped on to it. The push-pieces stand out beyond the dial and, with open-faced watches, the bezel often has to be lifted to set the calendar.

In a hunter watch the front cover only need be opened and the push-pieces are visible coming through the bezel.

Sometimes the star wheels, which move each day, are all operated together by means of one lever. The ends are supplied with a click-shaped piece which will give on the return journey. They must be resilient otherwise they will not clear, will hold up the motion work and may stop the watch or clock.

Dials and Hands

The day of the week, the day of the month and the month are shown on small dials by hands or pointers fitted to the pipes of the appropriate star wheels.

On opposite sides of the moon wheel are two representations of a full moon, usually engraved with a face and having a background enamelled in blue to represent a starry sky. As the wheel is provided with 59 teeth, it is possible to obtain $29\frac{1}{2}$ days for each lunation, which is not exactly correct, but is sufficiently accurate for a simple calendar. The mechanism is so arranged that the two " moons " appear alternately. Each in turn is advanced gradually day by day, from left to right, across an aperture in the dial, which is specially cut out and arched to display the appropriate lunar phase.

Sometimes the calendar is indicated by means of silvered and engraved discs, which are mounted on the star wheels and show through apertures in the dial. This method of displaying the information is usually employed with wrist watches, although it is met with in some of the very early watches and clocks.

An Ingenious Arrangement for Setting the Month

Some calendar watches have an ingenious arrangement for setting the month. When the winding button is pulled out into set hands, the day-of-the-week dial can be changed or set. When the button is in winding, the month dial can be set. Both operations are carried out by the same push-piece.

The day-of-the-month wheel is usually in the centre of the watch and runs on the pipe of the hour wheel. The figures are engraved on the dial just outside the minute circle, and the day of the month is shown by a long hand with an arrowhead usually painted red. The day of the month can only be set through the motion work, that is, by setting the hands forward. It is rather a strain on the cannon pinion, which should be tightened each time the watch is cleaned.

This arrangement has also been applied to ladies' wristlet watches.

Simple Calendar Clocks

The calendar work on some old clocks is quite simple. A large ring is supported on the outside edge on two grooved pulleys, and at the top is a small bridge to prevent it falling forward. Ratchet-shaped teeth are provided on the inside edge of the ring. These teeth engage with a pin on a date wheel, which is geared into a small wheel (or pinion) mounted on the hour wheel, usually between the snail and the hour wheel itself.

Sometimes the pin takes the form of a brass block mounted on the date wheel. The middle is filed away to give the block freedom from the highest point of the hour snail. Care must be taken to gear the hour wheel and the date wheel, otherwise, even with the cut-out, they can foul and stop the clock.

The Date Ring

The pin or block on the date wheel simply pushes a date ring round one tooth every 24 hours. It has to be reset most months. These date rings are often hand-cut and are not always accurate. At times, the pin or block in the date wheel will catch on the top of the ring teeth and stop the clock. If this happens, it is advisable to mark the faulty tooth and turn the ring round to find where it is fouling. The best way is to remove the minute hand and wedge up the lifting piece of the striking work, and then each tooth can be rapidly tested and adjusted where necessary. Neither a spring jumper nor any other means is provided to hold the ring in place ; it simply depends on friction.

The figures are engraved under the ring and show through an aperture in the dial, usually at the bottom and just above the chapter ring on the dial proper.

A large moon star wheel is pivoted on a stud and is usually held in position by a jumper spring. It is generally carried over by a pin fitted on top and near the centre of the snail on the hour wheel. Thus it is moved one tooth every 12 hours. The wheel is usually provided with 118 teeth. It has two representations of the moon which appear alternately and are displayed through a shaped aperture in the arch of the dial.

The Perpetual Calendar

The advantage of the perpetual calendar is that the mechanism does not require resetting at the beginning of a new month. The mechanism automatically adjusts for all months of less than 31 days, also for leap year when February has 29 days. There is no provision, however, for the centennial year when it is not a leap year and there is no extra day for February, but obviously this is considered unnecessary.

The dial is usually divided into four parts and shown as 1st, 2nd and 3rd years and leap year. Most perpetual calendar clocks do not show which particular year it is, but some have a separate disc which shows through an aperture in the dial. It is generally moved by the month wheel as it completes one revolution.

In a watch the months are all contained on one wheel which has 48 teeth. There are four sets of months and the wheel completes one revolution in four years.

Perpetual Calendar Watches

In most perpetual calendar work applied to watches, the hour-wheel pipe is fitted with an additional and smaller wheel which gears into a wheel having twice the number of teeth, and thus this larger wheel performs one revolution in 24 hours. Mounted on the pipe of the larger wheel is a cam held in position by a spring, which also holds the wheel in place on a stud. This cam is bevelled on one side to enable the hands to be set backwards, and also to allow for easy disengagement with the lifting lever. The active side of the cam is banked against a pin.

The cam lifts a lever on which are mounted resilient clicks, that is, clicks which can move away when moved in one direction, but bank solid when moved in the other. Sometimes there are three of these clicks and sometimes only one ; it depends on the layout of the movement. Where there are three, one is provided for the day of the week, another for the moon wheel, and a third for the day of the month. The tail of the lever is banked by the particular month, as will be seen later.

The lever, as it is moved across by the cam, first moves the day of the week, next the moon wheel and then the day of the month, after which the lever drops. Acting on the day-of-the-month wheel are two clicks or pieces. One click is shorter than the other and can move the wheel only one tooth at a time, whereas the other can advance it four teeth at once.

Mounted on the day-of-the-month wheel is a steel snail-shaped piece, that is, a steel disc in which a step has been cut. The longer click acts on this steel disc.

How the Mechanism is Reset Automatically

The lever tail, as stated before, banks on a particular month. These months are indicated on the four-year wheel by steps and raised pieces. The raised pieces give the 31-day months, and the lesser number of days required for the shorter months is obtained according to the depth of the steps. The lowest or deepest steps are for the three Februarys having 28 days. The step for the fourth February is not quite so deep, but is deeper than that for the 30-day months. These steps allow the lifting lever to drop back farther to enable it to pick up the step in the steel disc mounted on the day-of-the-month wheel.

At the end of each month this step comes into range of the long click, and the amount by which the lifting lever drops back determines whether the step is engaged earlier or later by the click. On a 31-day month it engages late and only carries over the same as usual, that is, one tooth.

At the end of a 30-day month, the tail drops back into a step on the four-year wheel, thus engaging the step one tooth earlier and advancing the day-of-the-month wheel by two teeth.

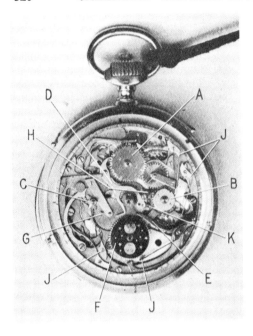

FIG. 270.—MODERN PER-
PETUAL CALENDAR
WITH MINUTE RE-
PEATER AND MINUTE-
RECORDING CHRONO-
GRAPH INCLUDED IN
THE SAME FRAME.

A. Four-year wheel and
   month wheel.
B. Date or day-of-the-
   month wheel.
C. Day-of-the-week star
   wheel.
D. Daily lifting arm or
   lever.
E. Arm to set all actions
   forward one day.
F. Moon wheel.
G. Lifting pallet acting on
   daily lifting arm.
H. Pallet acting only at
   end of month.
J. Jumpers for star
   wheels.
K. Daily lifting pallet.

Note that some of the
repeater mechanism can also
be seen.

*(Reproduced by courtesy of Mr.
R. John Low.)*

On a 29-day month, the tail drops lower into the four-year wheel and engages the step on the day-of-the-month wheel three teeth before the end of one turn of the wheel, thus advancing it three teeth. On the three deepest steps in the four-year wheel, the click engages four teeth before the day-of-the-month wheel has completed one turn, and four teeth are moved on the one movement of the lifting lever.

Adjusting for Wear

Any trouble experienced with a perpetual calendar is generally due to wear, so do not make the mistake of trimming the pieces. Usually the actions take place almost simultaneously and can be arranged to change just at midnight or a minute or two afterwards. This is carried out by adjustment of the hour wheel and the wheel with the lifting cam.

Sometimes the lifting cam becomes worn and fails to raise the lifting lever high enough. In this case, the end must be stretched and then filed again. The resilient clicks are also subject to wear and instead of gathering up the teeth may slip over the tops. It is advisable, therefore, to adjust them so that they lift just slightly more than is required, but make certain they do not lift too much. Also see that the long click cannot slip over the teeth of the day-of-the-month wheel and thus miss the step.

Perpetual-Calendar Work of Complicated Watches

Perpetual-calendar work is included in some complicated watch movements combining several features in one frame. The photograph reproduced in Fig. 270 shows part of a complicated watch comprising a minute repeater, minute-recording chronograph and perpetual calendar.

The calendar work differs very slightly from normal, as the wheel carrying the lifting cam has a steel pin to operate the day-of-the-week star wheel. Also the lifting cam moves the moon wheel just before it starts to lift, therefore the moon wheel is changed some hour or so before the rest of the calendar mechanism. The position of the pin on the cam wheel is so arranged that it carries the day of the week over about the same time as the other mechanism.

The four-year wheel is changed one space every month, and in the mechanism illustrated it is changed by means of a steel arm or cam very similar to the daily lifting lever. A separate wheel is provided for this action, which is usually carried out by the day-of-the-month wheel itself. In the normal way, one wheel tooth is longer than the others, and this long tooth is moved at the end of the month and carries the four-year wheel one tooth.

The design of perpetual calendars varies and few are identical ; something is generally a little different. In the majority of perpetual calendars a four-year dial is used, but some show only 12 months on the dial. The latter arrangement looks better but requires an extra wheel, which cannot always be arranged owing to the layout of the movement.

A wheel of 12 star teeth is used, interposed between the four-year wheel and the day-of-the-month wheel. As the rest of the mechanism is the same as usual, it does not warrant a detailed explanation.

Brocot's Perpetual Calendar Clock

Some clocks are provided with a very similar type of perpetual-calendar work as applied to watches, but more popular for clocks is the mechanism introduced by Brocot. Even with this type of perpetual calendar there are variations in design.

In one form the month wheel is in the centre of a separate movement. This wheel is stepped in the same way as a watch month wheel, except, of course, that there are only 12 months instead of 48. Underneath the month wheel is a brass cam ; this is mounted on a wheel of the same size as the month wheel (or year wheel as it completes one revolution in 12 months), but provided with a different number of teeth. Both wheels are geared into the day-of-the-month wheel pinion. Thus the year wheel moves progressively and not once a month, and there is no jumper.

The difference in numbers between the teeth is not a constant factor. Sometimes it is a day-of-the-month pinion of 10 and a

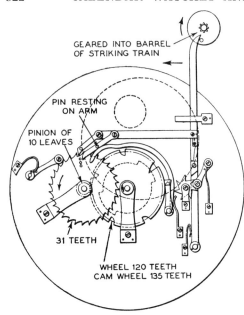

GEARED INTO BARREL
OF STRIKING TRAIN

PIN RESTING
ON ARM

PINION OF
10 LEAVES

31 TEETH

WHEEL 120 TEETH
CAM WHEEL 135 TEETH

FIG. 271.—ONE TYPE OF
BROCOT PERPETUAL-
CALENDAR WORK FOR
CLOCKS.

The central wheel has the
year wheel mounted on it.
On the same arbor is a cam
mounted on another wheel.
This cam controls the 29
days of February each
leap year. The day-of-the-
month wheel is mounted on
a pinion, which gears into
both wheels, the year wheel
and the cam wheel. The
day-of-the-week star wheel
is also mounted on a pinion
which is geared into the
moon wheel.

year wheel of 120 teeth, with a wheel underneath of 135 teeth.
In this number, the wheel underneath carrying the snail goes backwards in relation to the year wheel by 15 teeth.

For an ordinary year the lowest part of the cam is opposite the
step for February, but every leap year a higher part of the snail
coincides with the step for February, and the controlling lever does
not fall to the bottom of the cut out step in the year wheel.

Calendar Mechanism changed by Striking Train

The calendar is changed by the striking train and is so arranged
that as the clock is striking 12 o'clock all the calendar work is
changed, although the complete release does not take place until
1 o'clock is struck or even later.

Fitted between the frames is an arbor on which is mounted a
wheel, which gears into the striking barrel. On the opposite end of
the arbor is a brass snail-shaped cam, or a disc of brass with a pin.
The snail, or pin, engages and raises the lifting lever and thus
moves the calendar mechanism. This lever at one end engages
the day-of-the-week star wheel, and also has an arm which pivots
on a shouldered screw fixed into the lifting lever. Also on the
lifting lever is a piece like a striking-rack tail, which rests on the
steps of the year wheel. The pivoted or movable arm rests on a
stud screwed to the plate. The arm is so shaped that according
to its position in relation to the stud, the acting end is high or low.

On the day-of-the-month wheel are three pins, positioned one

above the other as shown in Fig. 271.   When the top pin is engaged
the wheel is advanced two days or two teeth.   Similarly, when
the centre and bottom pins are engaged, the wheel is advanced
three and four teeth respectively.   These actions are all controlled
by the tail of the lifter resting on the steps of the year wheel.   With
a 31-day month, the pins are not brought into action at all.

The moon wheel is geared into the pinion on which is mounted
the day-of-the-week star wheel.   This wheel and the day-of-the-
month wheel have jumpers and springs.   The jumpers are in the
form of arms, on which are mounted brass rollers which are free to
turn as distinct from the usual solid type jumpers with triangular-
shaped heads.

Equation Work

A feature sometimes added to the perpetual calendar is a device
indicating the equation of time, that is, the numerical difference
between mean time and solar time, which agrees only four times a
year, namely about 15th April, 14th June, 31st August and
25th December.

The usual arrangement is to have an arbor through the centre with
a wheel fitted at the back, into which a rack is geared.   The rack
rests on a kidney piece or cam fitted on to the annual wheel.   Thus,
as the annual wheel is turned, the kidney piece moves the rack
backwards and forwards.   A spring keeps the rack in position on
the kidney piece.   When the rack is moved either way it turns
the wheel which is geared into it and moves the hand on its arbor

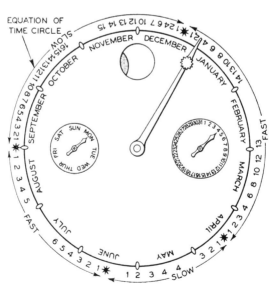

Fig. 272.—Dial of
   one   Type   of
   Brocot   Per-
   petual   Calen-
   dar Clock.

The circle on the
outside   dispenses
with the usual com-
plicated system to
give the equation of
time. Movement is
shown in Fig. 271.

over a graduated scale, thus indicating whether mean time is slow or fast of solar time, and by how much.

When assembling this form of perpetual calendar mechanism it is essential to place the wheels in correct mesh with each other. Some wheels are marked and here a warning must be added ; some are incorrectly marked, probably as a result of replacements having been made at some time or other, as most of these calendars are fairly old.

The same rigid rule applies to this type, do not trim the pieces, because it is generally a question of renewing worn parts if any trouble does arise.

Some of the very old calendar watches and clocks are extremely complicated and a separate book could be devoted to their description. If, however, the principles of the mechanism described in this chapter are fully understood, the craftsman should experience no great difficulty in their repair ; only great care and patience are required.

CHAPTER 15

CHRONOMETERS, TOURBILLONS AND KARRUSELS

A CHRONOMETER is a precision timekeeper fitted with a spring detent escapement. This form of escapement, known as the chronometer escapement, was at one time applied to pocket watches, but to-day it is employed mostly in marine chronometers. Used at sea for navigational purposes, this instrument is without question the finest example of horological craftsmanship, the development of which is due to the work of several highly-skilled horologists.

Marine Chronometers

The marine timekeeper, or chronometer as it was named, was invented by John Harrison in the middle of the eighteenth century, when he won a prize offered by the British Government for discovering a method of determining longitude at sea.

Further experimental work was carried out by Thomas Mudge, whose most notable contribution was his remontoire escapement. But it is due to the efforts of two famous horologists, Thomas Earnshaw and John Arnold, that the marine chronometer has been developed so successfully in this country. Both invented, at about the same time, an extremely accurate type of instrument. Not only were these instruments an improvement on earlier models, but were less complicated and could be produced at a lower cost.

FIG. 273.—A MODERN TWO-DAY CHRONO-METER MOVEMENT.

A. Balance.
B. Compensation weights.
C. Mean time screws.
D. Maintaining detent spring.
E. Maintaining detent.
F. Escapement or spring detent.

325

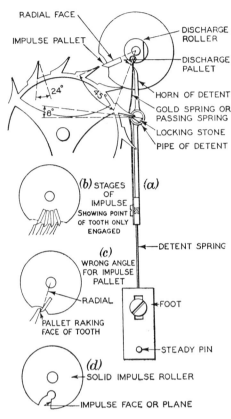

RADIAL FACE

IMPULSE PALLET

DISCHARGE ROLLER

DISCHARGE PALLET

24°

45°

18°

HORN OF DETENT

GOLD SPRING OR PASSING SPRING

LOCKING STONE

PIPE OF DETENT

(b) STAGES OF IMPULSE

SHOWING POINT OF TOOTH ONLY ENGAGED

(a)

(c) WRONG ANGLE FOR IMPULSE PALLET

DETENT SPRING

RADIAL

FOOT

PALLET RAKING FACE OF TOOTH

STEADY PIN

(d)

SOLID IMPULSE ROLLER

IMPULSE FACE OR PLANE

Fig. 274.—Earnshaw Spring Detent Chronometer Escapement invented by Arnold and Earnshaw.

(a) Theoretical drawing of escapement showing the acting parts. Note detent is below the 'scape wheel.
(b) Showing stages of impulse when impulse pallet is correctly fitted. Only tips of the teeth are in action.
(c) Showing action of impulse pallet when incorrectly fitted. The pallet cuts a hollow in the side of wheel tooth, greatly increases the friction and spoils the close rate. It acts like a pinion which is too large.
(d) Solid roller instead of jewel pallet. Gives a good performance until worn, but can be easily repolished.

In fact, the spring detent escapement devised by Earnshaw is used at the present day almost in its original form. Therefore we will deal first with the Earnshaw escapement, and then explain how it differs from the Arnold.

Chronometer Escapement

The escapement is highly detached and has a very small balance arc. It is also a single-beat escapement, receiving impulse only when the balance is travelling in one direction.

One of the greatest advantages is that the actual escapement *requires no oil*, and it is extremely detrimental if oil is used. It will cause damage to the 'scape-wheel teeth and will also result in the gold spring becoming badly worn. The only parts of a chronometer escapement which should be oiled are the balance staff and 'scape-pinion pivots.

The escapement, as shown in Fig. 274, consists of the impulse roller ; the discharging roller ; the detent, which carries a locking stone and is fitted with the gold spring ; and the 'scape-wheel. The 'scape wheel gives impulse direct to the impulse roller, which is mounted firmly on the balance staff. The 'scape wheel is locked by the locking stone on the detent. As the balance is turned, the discharging roller lifts the detent through the medium of the gold spring and releases the 'scape wheel.

The 'scape-wheel tooth drops on to the impulse roller, gives impulse, drops off the roller and is again locked by the detent locking stone.

The Impulse Roller

Most impulse rollers are slotted and are provided with a sapphire or ruby jewel pallet to receive the impulse from the wheel. The jewel takes a high polish and thus reduces friction, and, apart from this advantage, it seldom gets worn. Some are made of solid steel and, although sound and efficient, do get worn but can be very easily repolished. All the same, they will run for a very long time before wear is noticeable.

The jewelled pallet, however, has many other advantages, one being that the pallet can be twisted in position so that only the top or bottom of the tooth engages the pallet.

Likewise, the locking stone is often tilted in the opposite direction, so that the top part of the tooth engages the locking stone and the lower part the impulse pallet, as the jewel stone is called. The idea, of course, is to distribute the wear on the 'scape-wheel teeth.

Spring Detent

The gold spring is screwed lengthwise to the body of the detent, and is extended slightly beyond the horn of the detent.

The gold spring is acted upon by the discharging roller, which is a small roller fitted to the balance staff either above the impulse roller or below, according to the layout of the chronometer. The discharging roller also has a jewelled pallet fitted into it to reduce friction by the high polish.

The Discharging Roller

The function of the discharging roller is to lift the gold spring which is fitted to the detent.

As the balance moves in one direction the discharging roller lifts the gold spring and, as the spring is resting against the detent, raises the detent and releases the 'scape-wheel tooth which is locked there.

After releasing the wheel, the discharging roller drops or releases the gold spring and travels on. On its return the discharging roller again lifts the gold spring, but as it is only resting on one side of the detent it is free to move. Thus, after the discharging roller has travelled so far, it drops the gold spring, which promptly returns to the side of the detent and the discharging roller carries on to the end of the vibration.

On its return it again lifts the gold spring which pushes the detent, unlocks the 'scape wheel, and so on. Thus, the wheel is unlocked only when the discharging roller is travelling in one direction. That is the reason why the gold spring is referred to as the " passing spring ".

If the drawing of the escapement is studied these various actions will be more easily followed.

When a chronometer is brought in for repair always examine it very carefully. The balance staff and 'scape pinion pivot holes must be a very close fit and the endshakes of this pair must be close. In the ordinary way an easy fitting train hole, if not too bad, is left for attention at some later date. In a chronometer, however, the holes must be a good fit from start to finish. A wide hole, even in the barrel, will spoil its close rate.

Adjusting for Equal Power

Despite the fact that it is the most detached escapement, it is still affected by changes in motive power. Therefore, a fusee and chain mechanism is a necessity. The fusee, however, has to be adjusted, that is, the mainspring has to be set-up correctly to obtain the equality of power required. An adjusting rod is necessary for this purpose. The tool must be sound and strong, as the mainspring of a two-day chronometer is much stronger than that of an ordinary clock, also the mainspring of an eight-day chronometer is of a formidable strength and is difficult to handle.

The tool consists of a steel rod about 12 to 15 inches in length, with brass jaws at one end. The jaws are shaped to clamp on to the fusee square, and are tightened by means of a thumb nut and collet. A spiral spring rests on the rod between the two jaws, enabling them to be opened when the thumb nut is unscrewed.

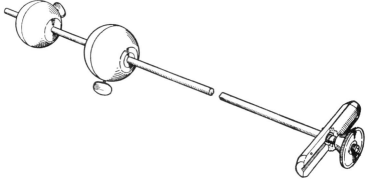

Fig. 275.—Adjusting Rod for Marine Chronometers.

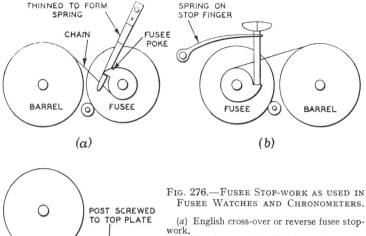

FIG. 276.—FUSEE STOP-WORK AS USED IN FUSEE WATCHES AND CHRONOMETERS.

(a) English cross-over or reverse fusee stop-work.
(b) Usual type of English fusee stop-work.
(c) Continental type fusee stop-work. This is not so strong as the English patterns (a) and (b).

Fitted on the rod are two, or sometimes three, adjustable sliding weights, and each is provided with a thumb screw to fix it in place.

Use of an Adjusting Rod

To use the adjusting rod the jaws are clamped tightly to the fusee square, so that there is no danger of it slipping off. The third wheel of the chronometer is removed in order to make the adjustment easier and to avoid the risk of breaking the 'scape pivots. The chronometer is then wound up by means of the rod. As it is wound, see that the chain settles into the grooves and that the spring does not jump or scrape. As it reaches the top, check the stop-work and make sure it is quite safe.

Hold the movement vertically and adjust the weights on the rod until the mainspring can only just carry the rod and weights from the bottom to the top. Be extremely careful when the weights pass the half-way mark, as the rod may fly over and give one a nasty rap on the knuckles, or a blow in the face. Also keep the fingers holding the movement well away from the barrel in case the chain should break.

Finally, try all the turns of the fusee and see that the weights are lifted by the same amount on each turn. If the pull is less at the bottom the mainspring is set up another tooth, and if the pull is too much, the mainspring is let down one tooth, and so on until the pull is equal.

Subsidiary Train of Eight-Day Marine Chronometer

With the eight-day chronometer, the third and fourth wheels and pinions, and escapement, etc., are on a separate unit which is screwed on to the main frame (Fig. 277).

The balance is mounted above the top plate of the frame and fitted round the balance is a semicircular brass guard. This guard is situated on the side nearest to the barrel and protects the balance and spring should the fusee chain break and fly round with the barrel, as it would do with terrific force. The guard is usually fixed to the top plate of the subsidiary frame by two screws.

When adjusting an eight-day, the subsidiary frame is taken off and only the fusee, barrel and centre wheel and pinion remain on the main plate, so the adjustment is simplified.

Dismantling a Chronometer

When a chronometer has to be taken to pieces, the important rule to bear in mind is that *before the balance is disturbed in any way whatsoever all power must be taken from the escapement.* If the balance is removed while there is any power on the escapement it

Fig. 277.—Eight-day Marine Chronometer Movement, showing Subsidiary Movement.

A. Fusee and fusee chain.
B. Subsidiary movement.
C. Helical balance-spring.
D. Barrel arbor ratchet.
E. Fusee cap. (Fusee cup on the square inside cap.)
F. Barrel.
G. Great wheel.
H. Maintaining ratchet wheel.

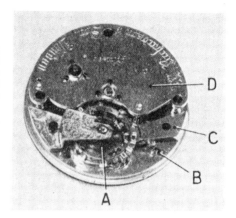

Fig. 278.—Fusee Pocket Chronometer Movement with Quadruple Overcoil Balance-spring instead of the usual Helical Type.

A. Quadruple overcoil balance-spring.
B. Detent.
C. Fourth cock.
D. Half plate.

is almost certain to run down with a rush. The 'scape wheel will break the locking stone and the detent, and the chances are that the 'scape wheel itself will be ruined. Do not take a chance, as however careful one may be this disaster can hardly be avoided.

To make absolutely certain of safety, thread a piece of soft iron binding wire through the arms of the fourth wheel and tie the wheel firmly to one of the pillars. A piece of cotton or silk will answer the purpose, but do tie up the fourth wheel. Do not wedge it ; the wedge may fall out or may not hold.

Pocket Chronometers

The same rule applies to pocket chronometers. A number are provided with a locking or safety screw. This screw is situated near the teeth of the 'scape wheel and can be easily recognized. Half the head is filed away, something like a dog screw. While the chronometer is running, the flat side of the screw faces the wheel teeth and the teeth can run freely. When the screw is moved a quarter of a turn it is in the path of the teeth and the wheel cannot run. The balance can be removed with safety only with the screw in the obstructing position.

Wedging the Train

If there is no safety screw, the first thing to do is to remove the detent and wedge the train with a thin steel wedge placed under one arm of the fourth wheel and pressed against the plate. A suitable wedge can be made from a fine pivot broach which is made almost dead soft and smoothed with a file and emery stick, so that it will not scratch or mark either the arms of the wheel or the plate.

If a chronometer is to be cleaned, or taken to pieces for any reason, take all power away by letting down the mainspring completely. Do not forget the maintaining detent. This must be

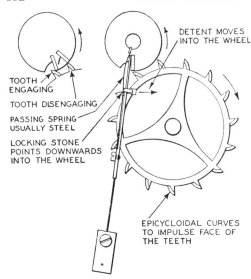

TOOTH
ENGAGING

TOOTH DISENGAGING

PASSING SPRING
USUALLY STEEL

LOCKING STONE
POINTS DOWNWARDS
INTO THE WHEEL

DETENT MOVES
INTO THE WHEEL

EPICYCLOIDAL CURVES
TO IMPULSE FACE OF
THE TEETH

FIG. 279. — ARNOLD SPRING DETENT CHRONOMETER ESCAPEMENT.

Note.—The detent is above the 'scape wheel and locks the root of the tooth ; also the detent is moved towards the centre of the wheel to unlock. Inset shows the action of impulse and why oil is necessary on the 'scape-wheel teeth.

released as well, as there is sufficient power in the maintaining spring to ruin the instrument.

Another important point is not to let the train run freely in order to run down the mainspring. A chronometer has a lot of power and it is sure to damage the 'scape pivot.

Earnshaw and Arnold Escapements Compared

The foregoing has dealt with the Earnshaw escapement, and we will now explain how the Arnold differs from it.

With the Earnshaw the detent unlocks by being moved away from the wheel, whereas with the Arnold the detent unlocks by moving towards the centre of the wheel (see Fig. 279).

The Earnshaw is locked on the outside ends of the teeth ; the Arnold is locked on the inside or roots of the teeth.

Again, with the Earnshaw only the tips of the teeth engage the impulse pallet. The Arnold, on the other hand, engages first with the bottom of the tooth and the whole length of the tooth is engaged. The Arnold tooth is in the form of an epicycloidal curve and, as a result, has to be oiled, which is its greatest disadvantage.

The layout of the Arnold is different. With the full plate Earnshaw chronometer the detent is underneath the top plate. With the Arnold it is invariably fitted in a cut-out slot in the top plate. In both cases, the detent is easily removed without disturbing the balance.

The Kullberg Auxiliary

The early Earnshaw chronometer has not been greatly improved upon. With modern chronometers, although the finish and workmanship are of the highest order and no better piece of mechanism has ever been made, the principle is still the same.

The greatest advance, however, in modern chronometer construction was brought about by the introduction of the Kullberg auxiliary compensation balance and palladium balance-spring.

Various auxiliaries were devised at different times in an effort to overcome the problem of middle-temperature error which has always confronted chronometer makers, but, as described in Chapter 11, the Kullberg auxiliary has been the most successful.

The great advantage is that the balance is solid, and no pieces are screwed on or riveted. Any piece of riveted mechanism is likely to give under changes of temperature and not remain firm, with the result that the rate suffers.

Pivoted Detent

There have been various forms of chronometer escapement. One type developed on the Continent uses what is termed the pivoted detent (see Fig. 280). The detent is mounted on an arbor and is pivoted between the plates or has a cock taking the top pivot.

A hairspring fitted to a collet is mounted on the arbor, and the stud, to which the outside end of the hairspring is attached, is screwed to the plate.

The strength of the detent can be adjusted by setting the hairspring " on ", or by easing it by twisting the collet on the arbor. The front, or acting part of the detent, is exactly the same as the spring detent, or solid detent.

The drawback to this type of detent is that the pivots have to be oiled, although some maintain that this is unnecessary. Admittedly the amount of movement is small, but it is also rapid and, unless oiled, the pivots may be worn off, especially if a 19,800 or 21,600 train.

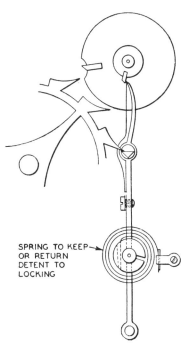

SPRING TO KEEP
OR RETURN
DETENT TO
LOCKING

Fig. 280.—Pivoted Detent Chronometer Escapement.

The detent is mounted on an arbor and is pivoted between a cock and the plate. The action is the same as the Earnshaw, but the pivots of the detent arbor have to be oiled, thus spoiling the qualities of the escapement. The spring used to return the detent to locking is similar to a balance-spring.

Duplex " Chronometer "

As stated at the beginning of this chapter, a chronometer is a precision timekeeper fitted with the spring detent escapement. On the Continent, however, the term " chronometer " is sometimes applied to a very accurate watch which may not be fitted with the spring detent, but with a good-quality lever escapement.

Another type is referred to as the duplex chronometer. It is provided with two wheels, one wheel locks on the detent and the other gives impulse. Naturally, it is a more expensive escapement.

Lever " Chronometers "

The type which is referred to as the lever chronometer has the impulse delivered in the same way as a spring detent chronometer. The locking and unlocking is carried out by means of a lever and pallets, but the pallets are not quite the same as those of a lever escapement. This type of escapement is made in many different

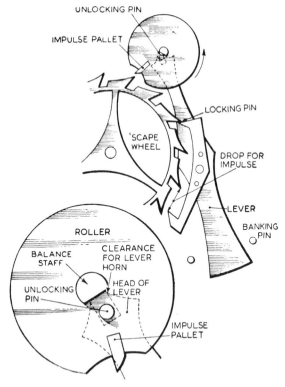

FIG. 281.—SINGLE-BEAT ESCAPEMENT.

forms, but, as the principle is the same, we will limit our description to one particular arrangement and another which is a slight modification.

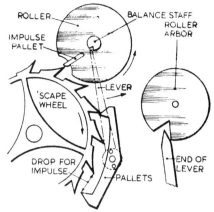

The 'scape wheel, impulse roller and impulse pallet are as usual, but the impulse roller is fitted with a ruby pin as near to the centre as safety will permit. A lever is acted upon by this ruby pin, but it does not receive impulse from the escapement. It is the unlocking pin. (See Fig. 281.)

FIG. 282.—ANOTHER FORM OF SINGLE-BEAT ESCAPEMENT.

The pallets are made in such a way that all the " drop " is either inside or outside, usually inside with very little drop outside. As the balance turns clockwise, it moves the lever and releases the tooth from the outside of the pallets, so that the tooth then rests on the inside of, what would be, the exit or hook pallet of a lever escapement. As the balance returns, the lever is again moved across and releases the tooth resting on the exit pallet.

As stated before, all the drop in the pallets is inside, or from the outside of the entrance pallet to the front of the exit pallet. Thus, as the tooth is released it gives impulse to the impulse roller and the actions are repeated, that is, the lever moves over, releases the tooth from the exit to the entrance pallet and no impulse is given ; as the balance returns, the tooth is released from the entrance pallet and impulse is given to the roller.

The horns of the lever and the notch are shaped like one section of the star wheel used in stop-work, and the balance staff is used as a banking or safety action to prevent the lever from getting on the wrong side of the pin. The front of the balance staff is filed flat to free the lever horns.

Sometimes the lever resembles a brass dart (Fig. 282). The balance staff is slotted like a duplex ruby or locking roller. The action is similar to a duplex escapement. The dart rests on one side of the balance staff. As the balance turns in an anti-clockwise direction, the dart is released from the slot and moves across. As it does so, the 'scape-wheel is released and gives impulse to the roller. The next tooth engages the pallets and pulls the dart back against the balance staff. As the balance returns, the dart again drops into the slot in the staff and is carried across until the tooth on the pallet is released. The dart then changes direction and banks on the balance staff ; no impulse is given. As the balance returns,

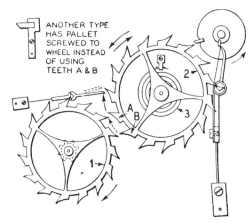

ANOTHER TYPE HAS PALLET SCREWED TO WHEEL INSTEAD OF USING TEETH A & B

Fig. 283.—A Type of Remontoire Chron-ometer Escapement.

1. Wheel driven by train which returns wheel 2 to its original position.
2. Wheel which gives im-pulse.
3. Motive power for im-pulse wheel can be adjusted by altering the setting of the collet on the arbor.
A. Tooth which releases secondary detent.
B. Tooth which is en-gaged when wheel 1 is released.

the dart drops into the slot, being released as the balance progresses and impulse is given.

Although these two escapements are sometimes referred to as chronometers, the only action they have in common with a chron-ometer is their method of impulse, and one is a modification of the other.

Remontoires

In remontoire chronometers a method is employed whereby the impulse is given by a means other than the mainspring and train. The whole idea is to obtain uniformity of power.

One type is provided with two 'scape wheels and two detents. The first wheel is mounted on the 'scape pinion, but the second has no direct connection. This second wheel has a hairspring mounted like a balance-spring on a collet, which is fitted on an arbor. This arbor is pivoted between the top plate and a cock screwed to the plate. The hairspring on the second wheel provides the motive power, which is passed to the balance in the usual way by means of the wheel teeth and the impulse pallet.

Mounted on the second wheel is a pallet which is usually jewelled. There is the usual type of detent on which the second wheel is locked and the whole escapement action is the same as the Earnshaw.

Action of the Remontoire Escapement

The discharging pallet thus unlocks the detent and the balance is given impulse by the wheel. As the 'scape wheel reaches the end of its impulse and is about to drop, the pallet fitted to it engages with another detent which is locking the first wheel, that is, the wheel fitted on the 'scape pinion. This detent is moved and unlocks the first wheel, which engages with the second wheel and pulls it back to its starting point, where it is promptly locked by the detent. The tooth on the first wheel is also locked on its detent and the action is thus repeated as before.

The amount or strength of impulse can be increased or decreased by adjusting the setting of the hairspring on the second wheel. The mainspring and train merely bring the second or impulse wheel back to its starting point, and as one tooth only of the wheel is engaged the wear is considerable. There is also the danger that the chronometer may trip because the actions are so quick.

Modifications of the Remontoire Principle

There are modifications of this same principle. In one case, instead of having two 'scape wheels, the second wheel is replaced by a pivoted steel arm or lever, but the action is almost identical.

Another type of remontoire bears some resemblance to the gravity escapement used in a clock.

The impulse is given either by a pivoted or sprung arm. Two wheels are mounted on the 'scape pinion, one above the other. Usually the one at the top is the locking wheel and locks on a detent in the usual way, while the lower one engages and lifts the sprung arm which imparts the impulse.

The action is that the discharging roller engages the detent and unlocks the top wheel, which immediately moves forward and allows the sprung arm to drop. The arm engages the impulse roller in the usual way and gives impulse. As soon as the arm drops, it is immediately gathered up by the teeth on the lower wheel mounted on the 'scape pinion and the top wheel is again locked on the detent.

In this case, the amount of impulse is adjusted, sometimes by means of a movable platform on which the arm is mounted, or by altering the setting of a secondary spring which is joined to the arm.

Here, again, the danger of tripping is always present owing to the speed of the various actions. It is, however, one of the best types of remontoire.

Chronometer Clocks

Some clocks are termed chronometer clocks because they are provided with a form of platform escapement in which the spring detent is used. These clocks are capable of a fine performance and give a very good rate, the reason being that the platform is mounted flat and on the top of the movement.

The contrate wheel and the 'scape pinion, however, present a certain amount of difficulty. At the best of times a contrate depth is not good. The trouble with a contrate wheel is the fact that with any thickness at all, the teeth are of varying size and pitch (see Fig. 284). The 'scape pinion, therefore, must never be large but should err on the small side.

The wheel teeth must be bevelled almost to a knife-edge where the engagement takes place in the 'scape pinion. The pinion leaves

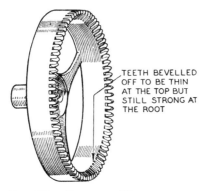

TEETH BEVELLED
OFF TO BE THIN
AT THE TOP BUT
STILL STRONG AT
THE ROOT

FIG. 284.—CONTRATE WHEEL AS USED
WITH PLATFORM ESCAPEMENT WHEN
THE PLATFORM IS PLANTED HORIZON-
TALLY.

and the wheel teeth should be of similar shape, that is, what is often termed "bishop's mitre", and both wheel and pinion should be high numbers.

Platform Escapement with Spring Detent

The escapement itself has a layout rather different from the marine chronometer. The best type has a circular 'scape cock, the main reason being to provide a support for the balance when the balance cock is removed. With any other form of 'scape cock, as soon as the balance cock is removed the balance may tip over and, owing to its weight, break the lower balance-staff pivot.

The 'scape wheel is mounted as high as possible. A sink is often turned in the 'scape cock in order to carry this out without making the 'scape cock too thin overall. The 'scape pivot at the wheel end is often below the top of the wheel teeth and, if the pivot does get worn, the only way to repair it is to dismount the 'scape wheel and remount it after the pivot has been repaired. The detent is mounted on the top of the platform and is under the 'scape wheel. The whole escapement, therefore, can be very easily examined.

The same rule applies, do not remove the balance while there is any power. If the clock is to be cleaned, wedge the contrate wheel and remove the platform complete. Again, it is inadvisable to let the train race to run down the power as these clocks usually have small train pivots.

These chronometer clocks are provided with a fusee and chain in the same way as a marine chronometer, and must be treated as such. The pivots must be polished and the holes must provide a good fit. The seconds hand must always be a good fit on the contrate or seconds pinion, otherwise the hand will work off.

Chronometer " Dead-Beat " Escapement for Regulators

The other type of chronometer clock or regulator is provided with, what is termed, the chronometer " dead-beat " escapement, as shown in Fig. 285. The action is similar to the usual type of chronometer, except, of course, that it has a pendulum.

These clocks either beat seconds or two seconds. That beating seconds has a half-seconds pendulum, and, thus, the other has a seconds pendulum which beats every two seconds. The reason, of course, is that every other vibration is a passing vibration with

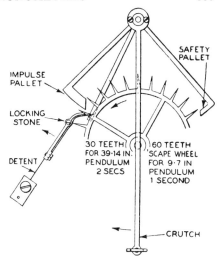

Fig. 285.—DENT'S CHRONO-
METER DEAD-BEAT ESCAPE-
MENT.

It is a single beat and thus
receives impulse only when the
pendulum is moving in one direction. As a result, with a half-
seconds pendulum, the seconds
hand will beat seconds.

no impulse being given and thus no movement of the 'scape wheel.
The pallets are made in the same way as in a Graham " dead-
beat ", but only one pallet is used to give impulse. Generally the
pallet not being used is filed very thin and acts only as a " safety "
in case the clock should trip. The 'scape wheel is usually provided
with 60 teeth, and true seconds are shown on the dial.

Mounted on the pendulum rod is a pallet which engages the gold
spring fitted on the detent. The detent is very similar to that used
in a marine chronometer ; it has a locking stone on which the 'scape-
wheel teeth are locked. The 'scape-wheel teeth are not quite the
same as in a marine chronometer, but some are the same as a
" dead-beat " 'scape wheel, or a ratchet-tooth 'scape wheel.

As the pendulum swings in one direction, the pallet on the
pendulum lifts and drops the gold spring and passes on. As the
pendulum makes the return swing, the pallet engages the gold
spring, unlocks the 'scape-wheel, the 'scape tooth drops on the
impulse plane of the pallet, usually the exit pallet, and the pendulum receives impulse. After impulse has been given, the wheel
is again locked on the detent· and the sequence of operations is
started again. It is an extremely good escapement and gives a
very fine performance.

Cheaper Form of Chronometer " Dead-Beat" Escapement

It has been applied in another form to a cheaper type of clock,
but does not reach chronometer or regulator standards (see Fig. 286).

The 'scape wheel is usually rather large and is mounted on the
front plate of the clock, being visible through a section of the dial
which is cut out.

The pendulum rod has a jewelled pallet fitted to it about a

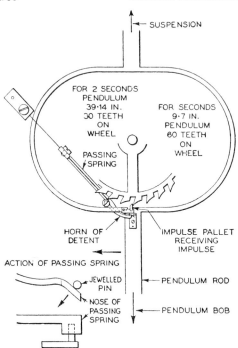

FIG. 286.—CHRONOMETER
DEAD-BEAT ESCAPE-
MENT.

The escapement is similar
in principle to that shown
in Fig. 284, but does not
employ a crutch. The
'scape wheel engages the
pendulum rod direct.

quarter of its length from the suspension. This pallet stands
upright and in the path of the 'scape wheel. Also fitted on the
pendulum rod is a jewelled pin which acts as the discharging pallet
and engages the gold spring.

There is the usual passing swing of the pendulum. On the return
swing, it unlocks the wheel and the wheel gives impulse direct
to the pallet fitted on the pendulum rod.

The idea is good and if a good-quality clock were fitted with this
escapement, it would give a satisfactory performance.

Faults with Chronometers

Although a chronometer is a fine piece of mechanism, faults do
sometimes arise and are mostly due to wear.

The 'scape-wheel teeth become worn, but, if not too badly,
adjustment can be effected by giving the wheel a little more drop.
This is carried out by moving round the discharging roller on the
staff in the direction which closes up the angle between the impulse
pallet and the discharging pallet.

Always alter the position of the discharging roller, when it is
possible, in preference to the impulse roller. The impulse roller
should be a very tight fit on the staff, but the discharging roller
should be tight yet capable of being moved to adjust the escapement.

Where the discharging roller is between the impulse roller and the balance, there is no alternative but to move the impulse roller to make the required adjustment.

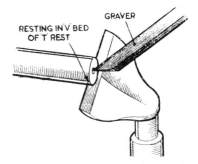

FIG. 287.—PIVOTING IN THE TURNS (1).

Method of cutting centre in the turns prior to drilling a balance staff or pinion.

Worn Pivots

Another common fault is worn pivots. If the wear is not excessive, the pivots can be repolished and new jewel-holes fitted, but the most satisfactory way is to replace the pivots. It is also advisable to renew the shoulder as well as the pivot, because this makes a cleaner job. It is easier if the operation is carried out in the turns (see Figs. 287 and 288), but it can be done in the lathe.

If the staff is to be pivoted, place it in the lathe and make certain that it runs perfectly true. Carefully turn the back slope behind the worn pivot and cut it away flush to the shoulder. With a very sharp-pointed graver mark the dead centre.

If, as is often the case, the staff whips away, use the attachment for the back centre (Fig. 289), which is a plate provided with deeply chamfered holes. This is placed so that the shoulder is supported and held truly in position. The centre is then carefully marked and tested for truth. Make sure it is perfectly true before proceeding any further.

Next make a spearhead drill about half the diameter of the arbor in size. Harden the drill in water. Clean off the fireskin. Grip the head of the drill in a pair of small pliers and then soften the rest of the drill. As soon as the thin part of the drill shows dark blue, plunge the whole drill into water. Sharpen the drill on an Arkansas stone and bevel the flat to bring the drill to a proper and central point. This should comfortably drill a chronometer balance staff.

Drill a hole in the staff of a depth of about one and a half times the length of the pivot and shoulder combined. Then harden and temper a piece of silver-steel rod to a dark blue colour. Choose a

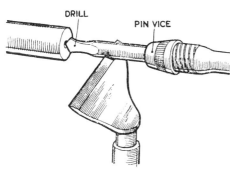

FIG. 288.—PIVOTING IN THE TURNS (2).

Method of drilling after centre has been cut.

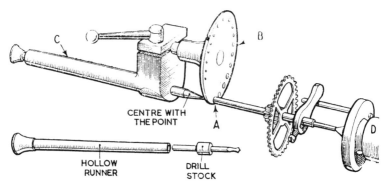

C

B

CENTRE WITH
THE POINT
A

HOLLOW
RUNNER

DRILL
STOCK

D

FIG. 289.—DRILLING A PINION, OR BALANCE STAFF IN THE LATHE USING
TAILSTOCK ATTACHMENT.

A. End of pinion to be drilled held in hollow cone centre.
B. Plate with graduated sizes of hollow cone centres.
C. Fits in tailstock of lathe and will take small runners.
D. Headstock of lathe.

piece of rod a little larger than the arbor which has been drilled.

Turning New Pivot and Shoulder

Turn a pivot on this hardened and tempered steel rod which will fit the drilled hole, and slightly taper the shoulder. This will form the back slope behind the pivot. Measure the depth of the drilled hole with a piece of sharpened pegwood. Then shorten the pivot until it is slightly shorter than the depth of the hole. (See Figs. 290 *a* and *b*.)

Partly cut through the hardened and tempered rod at a point where it is a little longer than required. It will be sufficient if the rod is cut about three-quarters of the way through.

Place the hole in the staff on the turned pivot and push it on *slowly* while turning the lathe. If the pivot is the right size it will suddenly " bite ", or fire in, and the rod will twist off where it has been partly cut through. A word of warning ; do not use commercial blue steel, it is not hard enough for a balance-staff pivot.

File a centre on the end of the plug and check that the balancy staff itself (not the plug) is running perfectly true. The best way to test it is between dead centres. The plug is almost certain to be out of truth, but this can be corrected later. Take the total length of the balance staff, as explained in Chapter 6, and shorten

FILE THIS CENTRE TO
BRING STAFF PERFECTLY
TRUE SHORTEN TO
LENGTH THEN TURN PIVOT

THIS MUST
RUN TRUE

FIG. 290a.—METHOD OF PUTTING
IN A NEW CONICAL PIVOT AND
SHOULDER TO A CHRONOMETER
BALANCE STAFF OR 'SCAPE
PINION.

the plug until it is exactly to length.

Place the staff between dead centres, turn the back slope and then polish it. After it has been polished, turn the pivot until it fits the jewel-hole tightly. Do not use a shaped oilstone slip, or a pivot file with a rounded corner, under any circumstances.

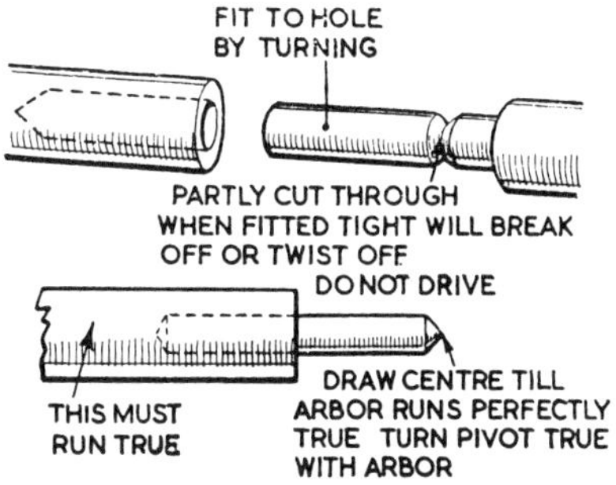

FIT TO HOLE BY TURNING

PARTLY CUT THROUGH WHEN FITTED TIGHT WILL BREAK OFF OR TWIST OFF

DO NOT DRIVE

THIS MUST RUN TRUE

DRAW CENTRE TILL ARBOR RUNS PERFECTLY TRUE TURN PIVOT TRUE WITH ARBOR

FIG. 290b.—METHOD OF PUTTING IN A NEW STRAIGHT PIVOT.

Finishing the Pivot

When the pivot fits the hole it can be polished. After polishing, give about one stroke with a shaped burnisher to obtain a good finish. If the pivot has been turned smoothly, polishing will take only a few seconds, the pivot will not be left small and it will have the correct freedom.

Finally, place the staff in a split collet and rub once with an Arkansas slip to remove the centre. Then a rub with a small flat burnisher will finish the end of the pivot. Do not shape it like half a ball, but just off the flat and slightly rounded. If the staff has been measured correctly the endshake and freedom should be correct

'Scape Pinion Pivot

Where the top 'scape pivot is badly worn, it is often necessary to dismount the 'scape wheel. There is no difficulty here, but care is required.

When remounting the wheel it is not riveted but is burnished on. The top pivot is held in a safety runner. A highly polished burnisher with a V-shaped end is placed against the pinion arbor, and, with just a trace of oil on it, is curved round the collet forcing the burr over the wheel. The pivot will withstand a lot of pressure, so there is no need to be afraid of breaking it. The wheel must run dead true and flat.

Locking Stone Setting

Another fault is the locking stone not being set at the correct angle to the wheel. The locking stone must be set to draw. If there is no draw, the wheel is likely to mislock. It may not stop the chronometer, but it will not give a good rate.

Testing Gold Spring Action

The action of the gold spring is sometimes faulty. Always make certain that the gold spring is lifted the same amount in both directions. To test the action, bring the balance to the point of rest. Turn it clockwise until the gold spring drops off and carefully notice the amount that the balance moves. Then bring the balance to rest. As the balance is leaving the point of rest it should be lifting the detent, and as it reaches the corresponding point on the opposite side it should drop the detent. If the detent is dropped before it reaches that point, the horn of the detent should be slightly bent to make the two actions equal.

Next test it with the 'scape wheel in place. Put a very small amount of power on, preferably one tooth of the maintaining power. Move the balance until the gold spring drops. Then lead the balance back until the wheel is unlocked and notice carefully how much the detent moves after the wheel has dropped.

If correct, the detent should unlock the wheel and then move half as much again before the detent is dropped. If it exceeds this amount, the gold spring action should be made shallower, either by pushing the gold spring back slightly or, if easier, by stoning the acting end of the spring. If less, then the gold spring must be pushed forward until it is correct.

Most detents have a screw to fit the gold spring, and, as the spring is usually slotted, it is not a difficult operation. Where the gold spring is not slotted and there is merely a hole, it can be elongated to the required size, using a small round file.

In addition, the maintaining detent sometimes becomes worn. This must be repaired and made sharp and smooth, otherwise it may not operate.

Cleaning a Chronometer

When cleaning a chronometer do not use an abrasive such as rottenstone, pumice powder or emery powder. Instead, use a soft soap and ammonia solution and be sure to wash out well in benzine and dry thoroughly in warm boxwood dust. The plates, bars and other parts are usually polished and spotted, and if this surface is spoiled it will have the appearance of a cheap clock.

Always handle the balance and balance-spring with care, as the adjustment can easily be upset and it is a long job to readjust a chronometer. The same applies to pocket chronometers. Always treat them with the utmost care.

Gymbal Screws and Replacing the Pivots

With the marine chronometer, the movement is fitted into a brass case called the bowl and is balanced in gymbals to ensure that the chronometer is kept in a " dial-up " position, irrespective of the ship's motion. Make certain that the pivots on the gymbal screws fit their holes well, otherwise, if there is any play, the chronometer will not keep a constant rate.

The screws can always be drilled to fit new pivots, if required, and the operation does not take a long time to carry out.

Another point, always see that the fusee square is fitted with a dust cup.

Adjusting Eight-Day Chronometer

The eight-day marine chronometer has a slightly different layout. On the main pillar plate are planted only the fusee and barrel, the maintaining detent and the centre wheel and pinion. The rest of the train and the escapement are mounted on a platform which is screwed to the main pillar plate. This makes it much easier to work on, as each section can be treated as a separate unit. It is easier to adjust the setting up of the mainspring ; also the platform can be cleaned, reassembled and tested before putting it into action with the main power.

The eight-day marine chronometer is always fitted with a smaller balance than the two-day. The fusee makes one turn every twelve hours, so there are sixteen turns on the fusee for the eight days.

Both eight-day and two-day marine chronometers, as well as most pocket chronometers, are provided with an " up-and-down " indicator on the dial. It is a very useful unit, and is of great assistance when a chronometer has to be adjusted.

Cutting a Chronometer 'Scape Wheel

These days it is often necessary to cut a chronometer 'scape wheel. For this purpose it is essential to use very good-quality hard rolled brass. A blank is turned to the right size and, as the dimension is very critical, it is advisable to use a gauge. The blank is shellacked firmly on to a wax chuck, or else it is mounted on an arbor with stout cheeks and a screwed nut holds the blank securely in position.

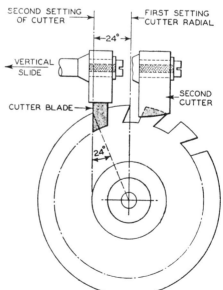

FIG. 291.—METHOD OF CUT-
TING CHRONOMETER 'SCAPE
WHEEL USING TWO CUT-
TERS.

Three cutters are sometimes used for this operation. A tool for polishing 'scape-wheel teeth is shown in Fig. 77 (*f*), page 95.

A fly cutter or a single-bladed cutter is used. Two cutters are normally employed. The space is cut first (see Fig. 291). The procedure is very similar to that used for cutting a ratchet-tooth wheel. For a 15-tooth wheel, we use six divisions of a 90-hole dividing plate, which equal 24°, or one-fifteenth of a circle.

First, with the point of the cutter upright, or radial, mark a line across the edge of the blank, of sufficient depth to be seen clearly. Next turn the division plate six divisions and alter the cutter to correspond with the line. This means that the cutter is high by 24° and will cut a tooth with an angle of 24° off the radial. Then cut a space which is deep enough to give the correct length of tooth, and advance the dividing plate by six holes each time, until the front of each of the 15 teeth has been cut. The next stage is to cut the backs. This can be carried out with the same cutter by advancing the blank by one hole or moving the front of the tooth one space away from the cutter. If a thin cutter has been used, it may be necessary to advance the plate by two divisions. Cut all the way round the blank until the backs have been cut.

The second cutter is provided with a rounded edge and is used to form the curved part of the tooth. Place the cutter in the

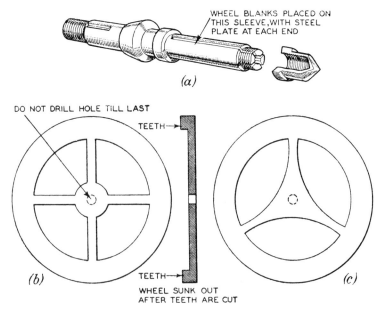

(a)

WHEEL BLANKS PLACED ON THIS SLEEVE, WITH STEEL PLATE AT EACH END

DO NOT DRILL HOLE TILL LAST

TEETH

(b)

TEETH

WHEEL SUNK OUT AFTER TEETH ARE CUT

(c)

Fig. 292.—Method of Cutting Chronometer 'Scape Wheels.

(a) Holder used when several wheels are cut together.
(b) Pressed-out wheel blank as used when several wheels are cut together.
(c) Usual type of blank used when cutting a single wheel. The three-arm crossing is filed out by hand.

correct position in relation to the wheel and rest the front against the tooth. By this means it will be easier to check that the cutter is adjusted properly. When the setting is correct, proceed to cut the teeth. Examine the teeth to see if they are " up " ; if not, put the cutter in deeper and go round again. It is far better to make two or three cuts rather than run the risk of spoiling the wheel.

Finishing the 'Scape Wheel

When the teeth have been cut, mount a plate in the mandrel and turn a sink which will fit the wheel exactly. Place the wheel in the sink and turn the hole out perfectly true. Make certain that the wheel is the right way up and fix it with shellac to the sink turned in the plate. Then sink out the wheel until the centre is about one-third of the total thickness. If a polished cutter is used the amount of finishing required will be reduced. After the wheel has been sunk, file the crossings and leave the wheel as light as possible without making it too delicate.

Polish the face of the teeth in a swing tool. The top and bottom of the wheel are best polished by hand, using a tin block coated with fairly dry diamantine. Place the wheel on a piece of flat cork and apply light pressure. After polishing has been carried out, the wheel is ready for mounting.

How to make an Impulse Roller

To make an impulse roller, choose a piece of silver steel which is slightly larger than required. Drill the hole and rough out the pipe in the lathe. Part off leaving it just slightly thicker than the height of the 'scape-wheel teeth. Then broach the hole to fit the balance staff tightly. True the edge by turning the roller on a true arbor and fit the roller on the balance staff. Place the staff and roller in the frame with the 'scape wheel to see if the roller is the right size.

With a marine chronometer there should be about five-thousandths of an inch total clearance from the teeth to the roller edge. With a pocket chronometer, the clearance should be about three-thousandths of an inch.

Take out the balance staff, remove the roller and cut the slot to take the impulse jewel. The slot must be cut so that it is radial and slightly out of square to prevent either the bottom or top of the teeth acting on the pallet. The cut must be made in the opposite direction to the locking stone. The idea is to reduce the wear on the wheel. The face of the pallet must be radial so that the points of the wheel teeth only are engaged.

There are a number of chronometers in which the pallet is set incorrectly, and acts like a pinion which is too large. As a result, the engaging friction is very high ; eventually the pallet corner wears a hollow in each tooth, considerably reducing the vibration and spoiling the rate.

If the diagram of the escapement is studied, it will be seen that where the first engagement takes place the pallet angle and the front face of the wheel form almost a straight line. This arrangement is ideal.

To slot the roller, it must be held in a holder and cut with a circular saw of the correct thickness so suit the pallet. Cut the slot to the correct depth, so that the tip of the impulse pallet coincides exactly with the roller edge.

Finishing the Impulse Roller

When the slot has been cut, file the crescent. The crescent should be central with the slot and of sufficient depth to allow the wheel teeth freedom when they are at their full intersection.

After these operations have been carried out, harden the roller and temper to a purple colour ; it should be no lower or softer. Then polish the roller edge. This can be carried out by using a special runner in the turns, as described in Chapter 8, or by using another roller (without a crescent in it) and mounting both on the same arbor. The solid roller will prevent the polisher from bumping into the crescent each time it passes. Use a flat zinc or bell metal polisher : the edge of the roller will take a high polish.

Polish the crescent in a roller crescent tool, as also described in Chapter 8.

The flat of the roller is polished on a zinc block. Hold the roller by means of a steel-pointed tool inserted in the hole, and then press on to the zinc block rubbing to and fro with a circular movement. Use wet diamantine at first and give the final finish with dry diamantine ; that is, diamantine which has been mixed wet but has been allowed to dry by keeping it unused for some time.

The impulse pallet is held in position with shellac. When fixing the jewelled pallet do not apply too much heat, otherwise the roller will be discoloured, the shellac will be burnt and will not hold the stone.

Making a Discharging Roller

It is not difficult to make a discharging roller. Choose a piece of steel rod which is just full for size. Drill the hole and part off the rod to length. Mount the rough roller on a true arbor and turn exactly to size with the ends dead square.

To make the slot for the jewel stone, a hole is drilled near the edge but quite sound. The hole must be perfectly upright and must not be broached. The front of the hole is then cut away with a thin file and a round-bottomed slot is made. File a flat on one side at 90° to the slot. Harden and temper the roller, leaving it a purple colour. It only remains to polish the exposed end of the roller and the edge, fit the jewel pallet and the roller is completed.

Making a Spring Detent

It has always been a job for the specialist to make a chronometer detent, but, owing to present-day conditions, the craftsman is often called upon to do this for himself. To make a detent for a marine chronometer the procedure is as follows.

First choose a piece of good-quality silver-steel rod of square section. Test it for flaws and for hardness, and see if any cracks or lines appear after it has been made red hot and allowed to cool slowly. After making certain that the piece of steel is good, proceed to file the foot, as it is called, and drill and tap the screw-hole (see Fig. 293). If the screw-thread cannot be matched, make a new screw; it will save time and trouble.

There is usually a rectangular hole in the plate, so the shoulder of the screw must fit across the width of the slot. Sometimes the hole is in the detent; it depends upon whether the screw fits into the detent itself or through the detent and into the plate. The rectangular shape is to allow a certain latitude in the original planting of the detent.

After the foot has been filed and the screw has been fitted, the blank is filed to the required thickness and height. Place the detent banking piece and the stop screw in position. The detent must pass just freely underneath the screw-thread and between the head of the screw and the banking, and must lie alongside the banking piece at the foot.

Next shorten the blank detent so that the end is just short of the balance-staff jewel-hole. Place the 'scape wheel in position and file a step underneath the detent so that the 'scape wheel just clears. Screw the detent in position, fit up the plate and put the balance staff and roller in place with the balance cock. If the discharging roller will not clear the end of the detent, shorten the detent accordingly or remove the roller.

Drilling Hole for the Locking Stone

Through the hole in the top plate can be seen the 'scape wheel, rollers and the part of the blank detent which is to be marked and drilled. Use a long and very small drill as a marker. Hold a tooth of the 'scape wheel with a piece of pegwood against the edge of the impulse roller, and make a mark with the drill on the blank detent where the tooth nearest but one to the roller lies, with the one nearest to the roller resting on the roller edge.

Then make another mark on the detent to indicate the new position of the tooth when the 'scape wheel is moved clockwise to bring this tooth away from the roller as far as it will go. Between these two marks is drilled the hole for the locking stone. Drill a hole just large enough for the locking stone to pass through. Be sure to drill the hole perfectly upright, otherwise it will be necessary to scrap the blank and start again.

350

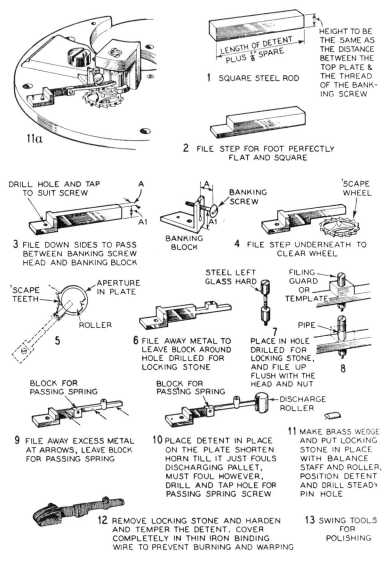

FIG. 293.—Method of making a Spring Detent for a Marine Chrono-meter, showing the Sequence of Operations.

After operation 12 has been completed the detent is ready for polishing. Swing tools for polishing the detent are shown in Fig. 77, page 95. Alternatively, if a grey detent, it is smoothed and not polished.

Filing Detent Pipe to Shape

The next operation is to file the detent pipe to shape. To file a perfectly round pipe by hand and without the assistance of a jig requires much skill and practice. A suitable tool can be made quite easily to simplify the operation. All that is necessary is a screw with a long head, such as a bar screw, and a perfectly round nut of exactly the same size as the screw-head. Alternatively, use a piece of steel with a pivot which fits the locking-stone hole exactly, together with a nut of suitable size which fits the pivot. Whether a screw or plain steel pivot is used, it must be hard and unable to be filed.

The pivot is then put through the hole in the detent block and the nut is pushed or screwed on tightly. This provides a form of filing jig. It is only necessary to file round it, and the resultant pipe will be perfectly round.

The horn of the detent can now be filed to the correct length and shape, but it should be left a little thicker than required. Also file the body of the detent leaving it slightly larger than required.

Fitting the Gold Spring

The next stage is to fit the gold spring. We will assume that the original spring is available.* The easiest way is to lay the gold spring along the detent on the correct side and slightly overlapping the end of the horn of the detent. Then mark with a drill where the slot of the spring lies and drill and tap the hole. Always hold the screw firmly as it is small and short with a proportionately large head, and may, therefore, easily flip away and be lost. In a marine chronometer the thread is usually about an 18 hole in a Swiss screw plate ; but in a pocket chronometer the thread is usually about 20 or 21 hole. Thus, great care is needed to tap the hole in the detent, especially as a broken tap may mean starting again.

Screw the gold spring tightly on to the detent. File away the excess metal so that the front or acting part of the detent coincides with the gold spring. Be careful that the gold spring does not move while working on the detent itself. Thin the back of the detent until the tail of the gold spring screw shows through on the other side. Keep the body of the detent square and central with the foot all the time. This is most important as there must be no twists or bends in a detent.

Planting the Detent

As the detent is now becoming thin and delicate, it can be planted permanently.

Fit the 'scape wheel in place between the frame, screw on the plate and put the balance staff and rollers in place with the balance cock screwed in position. Then fix the locking stone in the rough

* see page 360

detent in the position it will occupy when the detent is finished. Perhaps it will be advisable to explain how the locking stone is fitted at this stage.

To hold the detent the author has adapted an old pin vice. Both sides have been filed flat and left at a thickness of about ·02 inch. Through the sides are two holes of different sizes, one for marine chronometer pipes and the other for pocket chronometer pipes.

Fitting the Locking Stone

Place the locking stone in the pipe and make a D-shaped brass wedge which will fit the pipe with the locking stone in place. Do not fit it tightly as it may break the locking stone, but just tight enough to prevent it falling out. To make the wedge, a piece of brass wire, which will pass through the pipe, is filed flat on one side until it will pass into the pipe with the locking stone in place.

While it is in the pipe a scratch can be made with a sharp knife-blade to mark the total length of the wedge. It must be flush with the pipe at both ends. Then remove the wedge, shorten the top end and trim it smooth and flat, and cut the other end partly through, but still on the wire.

Again put the locking stone in place and insert the wedge. Turn the wedge and, at the same time, turn the locking stone until the stone is at the correct angle, then break off the wedge in the pipe. Hold the pipe in the adapted pin vice and fix the wedge and the locking stone in place with shellac. If the back of the pin vice is heated, the detent pipe will become quite hot enough to melt the shellac.

Freedom of Teeth from Roller Edge

After the locking stone has been fixed, place the detent in position in the frame. Ease the detent screw so that the detent can be pushed forward or pulled back stiffly. Then arrange the detent to hold the wheel in the correct place when the wheel is locked. With a piece of pegwood, lightly press the 'scape wheel until a tooth is resting on the locking stone. Examine the two wheel teeth positioned, one on each side of the roller, and see that they are equidistant to the edge.

If the tooth at the back is closer, push the detent forward by a small amount ; if the front one is closer, pull the detent away from the staff. When the shake or distances are equal, screw the detent home and check again to make sure that no movement has taken place.

Next notice if the bottom of the pipe is resting on the head of the stop or banking screw. It must rest firmly on this screw-head. Then drill the steady-pin hole in the foot of the detent ; it must be drilled perfectly upright. The plates may have to be parted to do this, but be careful not to move the detent. Then fit the steady pin and check the detent again to make certain that it has not moved.

Hardening the Detent

Remove the detent, take out the locking stone, remove the gold spring and screw, and harden and temper the detent. A simple method is to bind the detent completely with fine iron wire, covering it well at the horn end to prevent burning and warping. It should also be given a liberal coating of soft soap. Then heat to cherry-red colour if working by daylight; if not, it should appear a little brighter in colour when screened from a direct light. Then plunge it, horn end first, into a jar of water with oil floating on the top. Make certain that the detent goes in perfectly straight. Place the detent, still covered with the binding wire, into a blueing pan and cover well with brass filings. A piece of bright or polished steel should then be placed on top; an old roller or lever is quite suitable.

Heat over a spirit lamp until the piece of steel changes to a dark blue colour. Remove the lamp, and, when the steel lightens in colour slightly, take the bound detent out of the pan and cool it quickly. The detent must not reach a light blue colour, otherwise it may be too soft and, in action, will not return quickly enough to lock the wheel.

Polishing the Detent

The finishing stage which follows calls for the most delicate work. The first thing to do is to remove the iron binding wire and examine the detent to see if it has warped in any way; it is very unlikely, but if it has warped it should be straightened now. Clean the horn of the detent until it is bright and then soften to a very light blue colour, almost white; it must not be dead soft, however, but sufficiently soft to stand a small amount of bending for adjustment.

Fit the filing jig back in place on the detent pipe and polish the pipe with a zinc polisher. Place the detent in position in the frame and check that the horn is free of the impulse roller and not too low. It can be adjusted, if necessary, by stoning either the front of the foot or the back, whichever is required.

Next polish the horn of the detent, leaving the end where it joins the pipe, a little broader than the back. Where the horn engages the gold spring, it must be well polished with no sharp corners.

Polish the top of the detent, including the top end of the pipe. This can be carried out in a polishing tool shaped like a table with three legs. The detent can be fixed with shellac or screwed on, whichever way is easier. The three screws are adjusted to hold the detent flat while it is rubbed on a zinc block coated with diamantine, or the swing tool illustrated in Fig. 77 (a), page 95, can be used. The sides are rubbed down, using a flat polisher with oilstone dust and oil, leaving a square raised platform on which to rest the end of the gold spring.

Finishing the Foot

The next operation is to finish the foot. The side which rests on the plate is finished quite flat, using a flat steel polisher with oilstone dust and oil. The sides are polished in a swing tool shown in Fig. 77 (e), and can be grained or polished, whichever method is preferred. If polished, it is rubbed on a zinc block coated with diamantine. The visible flat side is polished by hand, employing a zinc polisher. If the edges are to be bevelled, the bevels must be made and polished before polishing the flat.

Thinning and Finishing the Spring

The final operation is to thin and finish the spring. The average thickness of the spring is ·0015 inch, and, obviously, is easily broken.

The spring must be ground or rubbed down with oilstone dust and oil, applied by means of a flat steel polisher, and it must be kept dead square and flat, otherwise it may be rubbed away on one side.

The best method is to cut a piece of good-quality cork slightly larger than the spring itself. Then rest the spring on the cork, which is held in a vice, and reduce first one side and then the other. When it is almost to size assemble the component parts of the detent and place in their permanent positions. Then fit the steady pin in position. A well-burnished pin with the ends nicely rounded and standing out on both sides is required. The end of the pin which does not enter the plate is very useful for handling the detent.

Place the detent in the frame and carry out all necessary adjustments. When all is in order, thin the spring to the correct thickness and polish. To polish the spring, another piece of cork must be cut as before, or a piece of willow wood can be used. The spring is polished, using a zinc polisher and diamantine.

Some makers grain the detent spring instead of polishing. This is carried out by means of a strip of ivory and triple-washed emery used dry. The ivory polisher is rubbed straight across the spring, is then lifted and rubbed across again, and so on. A backward stroke must not be given as it will spoil the effect.

The procedure for making a detent for a pocket size chronometer is basically the same, except that the construction often differs in regard to small details.

TOURBILLONS

It is appropriate to follow with a description of the tourbillon, which takes pride of place next to the chronometer as a precision timekeeper. The tourbillon is a form of revolving escapement which is directly driven by the train, as distinct from the karrusel which is only carried.

The Pivoted Carriage

The carriage of the tourbillon, on which the escapement is mounted, revolves on the fourth pinion. It is pivoted between the pillar plate and a steel bridge, which is mounted on steel pillars screwed to the plate. The fourth wheel is a fixture, being screwed to the pillar plate.

The fourth pinion is mounted on the bottom of the carriage and is driven as usual by the third wheel. The lower pivot of the carriage carries the seconds hand. The 'scape pinion is geared into the fixed fourth wheel. Thus, as the carriage is driven by the train, the 'scape pinion is driven round the fixed fourth wheel and is forced to revolve. The action is then the same as an ordinary escapement.

The pinion of the carriage is mounted on a steel collar, which is screwed to the bottom of the carriage. On the inner side of the collar is fitted the lower staff jewel-hole and endstone. The top pivot is fitted into a steel collar, which also carries the top staff jewelling and is screwed to the top of the carriage. The lever and pallets and the 'scape wheel and pinion are planted in a circle round the balance-staff hole. As the 'scape pinion is geared into the fixed fourth wheel, it is more convenient if the lever and roller are made to depth.

The 'scape wheel does not turn in the usual direction, the fixed fourth wheel causing the reversal. A tourbillon is normally provided with a double-roller escapement. Some have been fitted with a chronometer escapement, but these are extremely delicate.

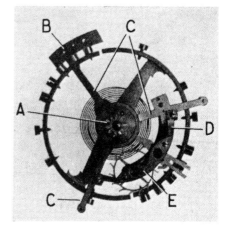

FIG. 294.—CARRIAGE OF A TOURBILLON MOVEMENT.

The tourbillon carriage completes one revolution per minute. Carriage is driven by third wheel as usual, but fourth wheel is a fixture. The carriage driven round transmits power to 'scape pinion.

A. Fourth pinion on which carriage is mounted.
B. Piece of gold to poise the carriage.
C. Three lower arms or lower plate of carriage.
D. Lower 'scape bridge.
E. Steel plate with lower 'scape and pallet endstones.

356

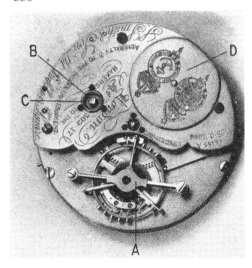

FIG. 295.—TYPICAL
ENGLISH   FUSEE
KEYLESS TOURBILLON
MOVEMENT AS SEEN
FROM THE BACK.

Carriage is shown separately in Fig. 294.

A. Steel bar supporting top pivot of the carriage.
B. Fusee square.
C. Gunmetal fusee piece.
D. Raised barrel.

Hardening and Tempering the Carriage

The greatest difficulty in making the tourbillon is hardening and tempering the carriage. Although it is hardened before it is filed down to size, warping is very difficult to overcome as well as being difficult to remedy.

FIG. 296.—TOURBILLON
MOVEMENT   WITH
CARRIAGE REMOVED,
SHOWING   FIXED
FOURTH WHEEL AND
PART OF THIRD
WHEEL WHICH DRIVES
THE CARRIAGE.

A. Fixed fourth wheel screwed to the plate.
B. Third wheel teeth just visible.
C. Third pinion cock supporting top third pivot.
D. Centre wheel.

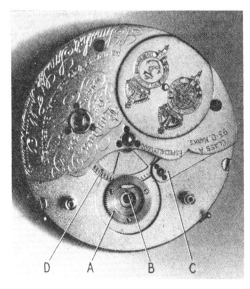

FIG. 297.—TOURBILLON MOVEMENT WITH DIAL REMOVED, AS SEEN FROM THE FRONT.

A. Crown type keyless wheel.
B. Main winding wheel screwed to fusee steel.
C. Up-and-down pinion.
D. Third and fourth bar supporting lower third and lower carriage pivot which is seconds pivot.
E. Barrel arbor ratchet.
F. Click.
G, G1, and G2. Idle wheels.
H. Third wheel.
J. Cannon pinion.

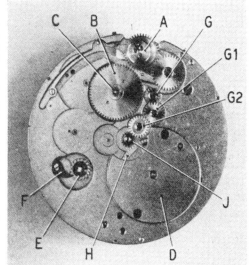

The carriage must be made of steel for lightness and strength. The dimensions and proportions must be correct, otherwise the advantages possessed by the tourbillon may be lost. It must have a minimum amount of drop in the wheel and pallets ; any excessive drop increases the jarring or jerking in the carriage each time a tooth is released.

Eliminating Positional Errors

The whole object of the tourbillon is to eliminate the errors occurring in the vertical positions, or, as it is often stated, to eliminate positional errors. This does not represent the whole case, however, because there are still three positions to contend with, namely, dial-up, dial-down, and hanging up or vertical. In a normal watch movement, all the errors can be placed on the pendant-down position. In a tourbillon this is impossible. The result is that a tourbillon must be isochronous and this can be achieved only by manipulation of the balance-spring terminal curves. If a tourbillon is not isochronous it will keep no better time than an ordinary watch.

Most tourbillons are provided with a fusee and are keyless. The fusee is a great help in timekeeping, but there are a number of tourbillons fitted with a going barrel. The proportions of the wheels and pinions are exactly the same as in a normal watch movement, beating the same number of vibrations per hour. The tourbillon usually has an 18,000 train.

KARRUSELS

The karrusel is also a revolving escapement, but is different in every way from the tourbillon. The carriage of a tourbillon revolves once per minute. The ordinary or open-faced karrusel takes 52½ minutes to perform one revolution, whereas the centre-seconds karrusel completes one revolution in 34 minutes. The carriage of a karrusel is not really driven by the third pinion, but rather it is carried. The fact of the carriage revolving, unlike the tourbillon, carries no power to the escapement. The fourth pinion receives power direct from the third wheel, and the fourth wheel revolves in the usual way driving the 'scape pinion.

Carriage Revolving on Large Brass Bearing

The carriage itself revolves on a large brass pivot or boss fitted into a large hole in the pillar plate. It is held in position by a flat wheel of 70 teeth screwed on to the brass pivot or boss of the carriage. Usually three screws are used. The brass pivot or boss must not be oiled under any circumstances whatsoever. This sounds strange, especially as there are two like metals rubbing together, but if this pivot is oiled, the performance of the watch will be completely spoiled even if the watch does not stop altogether.

The carriage is carried on the flat brass wheel and this wheel is geared into the third pinion, which is usually a pinion of 10 leaves. Therefore it requires seven turns of the third pinion for one revolution of the carriage. As the third wheel usually revolves once in 7½ minutes, the carriage completes one full turn in 7½ minutes less than one hour, that is, 52½ minutes.

The usual fault with a karrusel is a poor or indifferent fourth and 'scape depth. The 'scape pinion is generally large, and when it does cause trouble must be replaced. Trouble can also be caused by the top fourth jewel-hole becoming oval in shape due to the large amount of wear it receives. As the escapement has to be made to depth, that is to fixed distances, the lever and roller are sometimes out of proportion ; usually the roller is too large, with the result that the escapement has too much run. When we consider that these watches must be isochronous, these faults, which may be only very slight errors, become a serious matter. Like the tourbillon there are only three positions, dial-up, dial-down, and any one vertical position.

Sweep-Seconds Karrusel

The principle of the sweep-seconds or centre-seconds karrusel is the same, but the layout is different as the fourth or seconds pivot is in the centre of the frame. The carriage is similar, the difference being that a rim, provided with 136 teeth, is screwed on to the outside edge. This rim is geared into a steel wheel having 30 teeth

FIG. 298.—SWEEP-SECONDS KARRU-
SEL OR REVOLVING ESCAPEMENT.

The carriage makes one complete revolution in 34 minutes. The carriage is driven or carried by a pinion (or wheel) mounted on third pinion.

A. Pinion mounted on third pinion to carry carriage.
B. Teeth of carriage.
C. Fourth wheel and pinion which drives extra fourth wheel in the carriage.

which is mounted on the third pinion arbor, instead of being turned by the third pinion.

The fourth wheel is driven in the ordinary way and is geared into a wheel of the same number, having another wheel mounted on its arbor, which gears into the 'scape pinion on the carriage. The carriage is held in position in a similar way to the ordinary or open-face karrusel, but, instead of a toothed wheel, a disc of brass is simply used which is screwed to the pivot or boss of the carriage. Like the ordinary karrusel, the pivot or boss supporting the carriage must not be oiled.

Other Forms of Revolving Escapement

We have dealt with three different forms of revolving escapement, but there are others in which a very similar principle is involved. There is one where the carriage runs on a stud and revolves round a fixed fourth wheel. In this form the outside edge of the carriage is provided with teeth and is driven by a wheel on the fourth pinion ; there is no fourth wheel as is usually understood. The carriage completes one revolution in 5 or 6 minutes, depending on the proportion of the teeth on the carriage and the number of teeth in the small steel wheel mounted on the fourth pinion. If the carriage is provided with 100 teeth and the steel wheel with 20 teeth, the carriage will complete one revolution in 5 minutes ; if the carriage has 108 teeth and the steel wheel 18 teeth, the carriage will complete one revolution in 6 minutes.

Watches fitted with this form of revolving escapement are extremely good timekeepers and are not too troublesome to handle, although even these are sometimes pivoted between the frame and steel bridge in the same way as a tourbillon.

There is another form which is actually mounted on the third wheel, but it is very doubtful whether it possesses any added advantage, particularly when considering its delicate construction.

Fusee-Keyless Karrusels

A number of these watches are fusee keyless and give a very good performance owing to the equality of power transmitted to the train. The mainspring, of course, has to be set up correctly to adjust the pull of the fusee. This is carried out by means of an adjusting rod, as described earlier in this chapter. This same adjustment applies to all fusee watches, and particularly to marine and pocket chronometers.

Another important point with fusees is the maintaining power, that is, the power which keeps the train running while the chronometer or watch is being rewound. All fusees, when being wound, take all power from the train ; thus maintaining power is most important. Make certain, therefore, that the maintaining detent is free from wear and engages firmly with the maintaining wheel or ratchet. Make sure that the fusee is not pinned or screwed up too tightly, otherwise the maintaining spring will not act. See that the detent spring is arranged to act lightly on the detent. The detent should just be heard clicking over, not like a barrel ratchet click.

Finally, with fusee watches and chronometers always check that the stop-work is acting properly because the chain may be broken if it fails.

---

* A replacement gold spring is made from low carat (9 ct. or less) gold, part of an old gold balance is ideal. It should be annealed and then hammered on a hard smooth steel block, turning it over periodically, keeping it flat and straight until it is about .005 of an inch thick overall and slightly longer than required. It will then be quite hard. It should then be filed until it is no wider than the detent body and the slot, or hole as required should be made at one end for the holding screw. The spring is then thinned to about .002 inch by stoning with Water-of-Ayr-Stone kept damp with oil on a flat piece of willow wood leaving the slotted end full thickness. This is quite a delicate operation and it is only too easy to kink or break the spring. The final thinning and either straight-graining or polishing is left until the detent is finished when the final adjustments can be made.

CHAPTER 16

CLEANING CLOCKS AND WATCHES, AND PRACTICAL HINTS

CLOCKS and watches require cleaning and lubricating periodically if reliable and trouble-free service is to be expected. If proper attention is not given, the oil dries up, the power drops, the balance or pendulum just manages to keep going, and all the time damage is being done to a good instrument.

Whichever of the many satisfactory methods of cleaning is adopted, the work must still be carried out conscientiously in a careful and workmanlike manner. Therefore, a clock or watch must be completely dismantled ; it is not sufficient simply to put the piece into a pot of cleaning fluid, then dry out, re-oil and set going.

French Clock as a Practical Example

The proper procedure before taking a clock or watch to pieces is to examine it for faults. We will assume, for the purpose of a practical illustration, that we are handling a French pendulum hour and half-hour strike of the type without a visible escapement.

First remove the hands. Push the pin out of the centre arbor and remove the hand collet. Then remove the pins in the dial feet, and take the dial plate, bezel, etc., off altogether ; also remove the hammer.

Brocot Suspension

Next examine the suspension spring. It is usually a twin spring between brass cheeks (see Fig. 299 (A)). Replace the spring if it is buckled or broken. If buckled, the pendulum will oscillate and will not keep time. The spring must also fit closely into the slot or " chops " (B) in the block of the " Brocot ", as the whole unit is called. This is most important as any movement of the suspension in the block will result in loss of impulse, and the clock may stop. This block is fitted closely into another block (C), which is screwed to the pallet or back cock and is the main frame of the Brocot.

The block holding the suspension spring has three slots. The middle slot (1) holds the suspension. The outside slots (2) provide a means of adjustment for taking up any play between the inner and outer block ; these outer slots can be opened wider, if necessary.

This same or inner block (B) has a tapped hole at the back,

through which a threaded rod is fitted, having a wheel attached at one end, and a pivot on the other (*D*). A groove is turned in the pivot, and over it is fitted a forked spring (*E*). The wheel

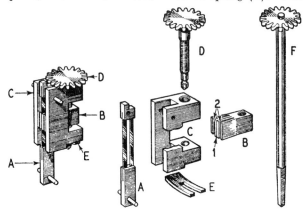

FIG. 299.—BROCOT PENDULUM SUSPENSION.

is positioned on top of the outer block, and the threaded rod passes through the inner block and through a hole at the bottom. The forked spring holds the pivot in place, allowing it to turn but preventing it from moving up or down. With this later form of Brocot, a right-hand thread is used. With the older pattern, however, a left-hand thread is provided. The principle in this case is slightly different (Fig. 300).

Older Pattern Brocot Suspension

The wheel has a large collet mounted on it, and the wheel and collet are often inside the block. The suspension spring itself is mounted on a small round block on which a left-hand thread is cut. The collet on the wheel is drilled and tapped with a corresponding thread. The collet and wheel are screwed on to the suspension block.

In the later form of Brocot, the inner block slides up or down when the wheel is moved, and, as it does so, it slides up or down the suspension spring, but the suspension remains a fixture. With the older pattern Brocot, the suspension spring itself is drawn up or down by the turning of the wheel. Thus in each case, if the clock is losing, the wheel is turned anti-clockwise to make it vibrate faster.

In the later form, the block slides downwards and shortens the acting length of the spring like index pins and the pendulum does not move up or down. In the older pattern the pendulum moves upwards, due to the suspension being drawn up into the wheel and collet. In this model, the suspension spring must be a good fit between the " chops " but must not be gripped.

The Regulating Rod

From the dial a square is visible, usually above the 12 o'clock. This square is at one end of a rod, which passes over the top of the movement and is pivoted into the back cock, or is inside the Brocot. It has a gear wheel riveted on the other end which gears into the threaded wheel and arbor (*D*). This is the regulating rod or arbor (*F*).

In order to regulate the clock, the square is turned clockwise to make the clock go faster, and, of course, anti-clockwise to make it go slower.

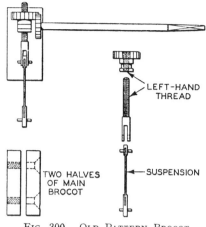

LEFT-HAND THREAD

SUSPENSION

TWO HALVES OF MAIN BROCOT

FIG. 300.—OLD PATTERN BROCOT SUSPENSION.

Silk Suspension

Sometimes, especially in the older French clocks, the rod is connected to a silk suspension. In this case, always make sure that the silk is wound on the rod in the correct way. The silk suspension is often troublesome, as it varies so much with temperature and barometric changes.

When a clock with a silk suspension is properly regulated and ready for delivery to the customer, do not take the pendulum off the suspension, but fix the pendulum by an elastic band or some other means so that it can be carried with safety. If the pendulum is removed, the silk will immediately become loose on the regulating rod. When the pendulum is replaced the silk will take up a different position, with the result that the clock will not keep time.

Sometimes the regulating rod is fitted at the back of the clock and is provided with a brass thumb nut. As the case is often very heavy, it is not an easy matter to regulate this type of clock.

The Crutch

The next operation is to remove all power from the mainsprings by carefully letting them down. The best way is to let them down two or three teeth of the ratchet each time. Then try the fit of the pendulum rod in the crutch. The rod must be a close fit in the crutch but must be definitely free. The sides of the crutch must be parallel to each other, and must be well rounded on the edges, where the pendulum rod is engaged ; also the sides must be smooth and burnished. Any wear must be remedied and the crutch closed.

To close the crutch and keep the sides parallel, place a piece of rod, very slightly smaller than the pendulum rod, in the crutch. Then give a sharp blow with a hammer on the back of the crutch, with the crutch resting on a stake. The sides can then be cleaned and finished with an oval burnisher rubbed from back to front. The burnishing hardens the metal.

Repairing the Pallets

The pallet-arbor holes must next be examined for wear. They are almost sure to be oval, and will need re-bushing. The hole in the back cock wears downwards, while the hole in the front plate wears upwards. When bushing a hole, always draw it back to the original position, or away from the direction in which it is worn.

Next examine the pallets. If a recoil escapement, notice if the inside and outside shakes are equal. Then examine the acting faces, or impulse planes as they are called. If worn, they must be repaired and repolished. The best way is to rub the worn surfaces with oilstone dust on a flat steel polisher until all signs of wear have been removed, and then polish with diamantine on a zinc polisher. Always make certain that the original angles of the impulse planes are maintained.

Inside and Outside Shakes

If the inside and outside shakes are unequal, they must be equalized. If the outside shake is excessive, the turntable on the front plate can be rotated to increase the depth, or intersection of the wheel and pallets. This will reduce the outside shake, but will not greatly reduce the inside shake although it will, of course, decrease both. If the inside shake is excessive, the outside of the exit pallet must be reduced to increase the outside shake so as to equalize with the inside. Then the turntable can be rotated to increase the depth, and this will decrease the shakes, but it will decrease the outside more than the inside shake, so the process may have to be repeated until they become equal.

There must be the minimum amount of shake as it is all loss. In the English type of recoil pallets, where the inside shake is excessive, the pallets can be closed to equalize the shakes, but with French clock pallets the construction is such that they cannot be bent or closed in any way.

Sometimes the pallets are fitted to a square on the pallet arbor. If the pallets are worn at the back, the square on the arbor can be very slightly reduced, and the pallets pushed a little farther up the arbor. This will bring a fresh part of the pallet faces into action. A word of warning here, do not drive the pallets up the arbor with a hammer, as the pallets are glass hard and will break.

If the pallets are so badly worn that they cannot be corrected by increasing the depth, a new pair of pallets will be necessary. The procedure for making a pair of pallets is described in Chapter 9.

Checking 'Scape-Wheel Teeth for Damage

Examine the 'scape-wheel teeth ; they are usually very thin and delicate and must be handled with care. Check for bent or damaged teeth, and put them in good order. If much worn they can be stoned up, and then made thin again by filing up the rounded parts of the teeth. Do not interfere with the radial face, as all question of equal division will be lost.

Motion Work and Striking Mechanism

Next check the motion work and striking mechanism. Try the rack teeth, also the rack tail. First set the snail at the 1 o'clock and notice if the gathering pallet engages cleanly into the rack teeth, not too close to the next tooth below. Sometimes, the gathering pallet will scrape or even foul this tooth. If so, it means the rack is not falling sufficiently, or is falling too far by nearly a tooth.

If the clock can strike two at 1 o'clock, the rack is falling too far. This may be due to the rack tail, or the rack itself, being loose on its collet, or the rack or tail may be bent or damaged.

When checking the striking mechanism, see that the appropriate number of blows is struck for each of the twelve hours. If only one particular hour is wrong, it may be that the snail is badly made. If it is, the snail can be stretched where it is low, or else recut all the way round and the rack tail altered accordingly.

Examine the rack-hook, and repair the nose if badly worn. Do not forget, however, that it must be stretched slightly, otherwise the striking train will lock too deeply and may fail to unlock.

The Lifting Piece

Notice how much the lifting piece is raised at the hour. If it is lifted too high, the warning piece will foul the top of the slot cut in the plate and the clock will be constantly stopping. Make certain also that the lifting piece raises the rack-hook properly. In the rack-hook is a brass pin, which is engaged and lifted by the lower half of the lifting piece. This pin can be bent nearer to the lifting piece to increase the lift, or away from it to decrease the lift. The half-hour lift is appreciably less than at the hour. The reason is that the rack is not dropped at the half-hour, but the striking train is released and the locking wheel just completes one turn and is again locked.

Always see that the various pieces are free on their respective studs, and do not have excessive endshake. The rack should not have much side shake, as it may foul other pieces or miss the rack-hook.

Examining Pivot Holes for Wear

Remove the complete striking mechanism, including the two springs which are screwed in through the front plate, and proceed to examine for oval or worn pivot holes. Points subject to most wear are the pinion end of the hammer wheel, the back centre pinion hole, and the locking-wheel pivot on which the gathering pallet is fixed.

The hammer-wheel pivot hole is in a small cock and is very easy to bush, but the hole must be drawn back to the original position, as it sometimes wears appreciably more in one direction.

The centre pivot is also in a cock. Very great care must be

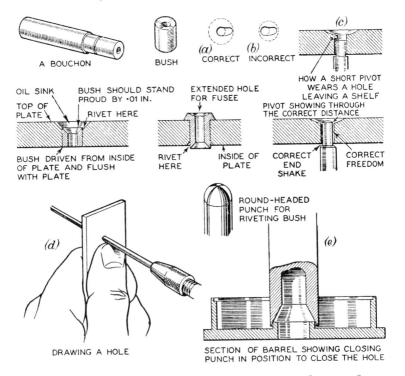

FIG. 301.—RENEWING HOLES OR BEARINGS WHEN WORN OVAL IN SHAPE.

Showing also extended bush for fusee arbor and the method of opening an old hole to bring it back to the original position.

(*a*) Position of new bush when drawn back correctly.
(*b*) Incorrect position, because it has followed direction of worn hole.
(*c*) Showing pivot too short. To correct, the oil sink is made deeper until pivot stands just above.
(*d*) Method of drawing hole from present position. Thumb nail is pressed against the broach in the required direction.
(*e*) Closing a barrel hole with a cone punch.

taken with this pivot and every effort must be made to keep it in the correct place, otherwise the centre pinion may not remain upright, with, of course, its attendant troubles. This can easily be checked by simply holding the plates, with, of course, the centre pinion in place, towards the daylight, and noticing the reflection of the centre arbor on the front plate. If the centre arbor and its reflection are in a perfectly straight line, then the centre pinion is upright. Do not check by artificial light, however, as this may give a misleading effect.

Another point which must always be remembered, is that the depth or intersection of a wheel and pinion must be correct. Some pinions will run either shallow or deep, but even with such a pinion the hole can wear sufficiently to cause trouble. If the clock has been running for a very long time, check the intermediate pinion pivots and holes for wear. In a French clock with a locking-plate striking mechanism, the wheel and pinion carrying the locking plate act as the intermediate wheel and pinion. Therefore, if the back hole is worn oval in shape, the locking-plate action will be chaotic.

The back hole of the locking lever should also be examined. With a rack striking mechanism this will stand being an easy fit, but if a locking plate it must be a good fit.

As the mainsprings have been let down, the ratchet and clicks can be removed for examination. Make certain that the click screws fit well and will not overturn. Examine the noses of the clicks for wear and renew if badly worn ; also see that the clicks drop to the bottom of the ratchet-wheel teeth.

Checking Ratchet-Wheel Teeth for Wear

Check the ratchet-wheel teeth for wear. Sometimes where the click is thinner than the ratchet, the teeth may wear, but it is not always obvious from a casual glance. Replace the ratchet wheels if there is any doubt ; it will save damaged wheel teeth and broken pinion leaves.

The ratchets are generally marked in some way, usually with a dot underneath one of the ratchets and a corresponding dot on its particular barrel arbor. Sometimes there is one dot on one ratchet and two dots on the other. This is unnecessary, as it is quite sufficient if one ratchet is marked. The small cocks holding the ratchets in place can easily be identified : the cock on the striking side usually has the corner filed off to clear the dial-plate pillar.

Parting the Plates

The next stage is to part the plates. Remove the pins, which are usually four in number. Use a pair of pliers with a good grip and endeavour not to slip, otherwise the pin will be spoilt and a replacement will have to be made, also the plate may be badly marked.   The grip marks on the pin can easily be removed in a few seconds.

When lifting the plate be sure to lift it perfectly straight, otherwise a bent or broken pivot may result.

Repairing Pivots

Take all the wheels and pinions out of their holes very carefully to avoid bending the pivots.   Then examine the pivots and polish if they are worn.   Do not leave a worn pivot, as it will cause trouble.

The pivots can be repaired in the lathe, but carry out the work between dead centres to keep them truly round.   If the pivots are very badly worn, they can be turned with a graver and left very smooth.   Then if about half-a-dozen strokes are given with a burnisher, the pivots will be brought up nice and bright.   Do not waste valuable time trying to file a pivot ; it is much quicker to turn them, and the result is far more satisfactory.   Some jobbers hold the pinions in a pair of pin tongs, and rub the pivot with a pivoting file on a filing block.   Such work is deplorable and should be discouraged.

When the pivots have been repaired and the holes renewed, we can attend to the barrels and mainsprings.

Repairing Winding Squares

Examine the winding squares ; if they are burred up, they will have to be repaired.   The best way to repair a square is to lay the side on a flat steel stake, carefully hammer the burrs down as much as possible, and then finish with a very smooth file.   Avoid removing too much metal, as it will make the square smaller.   If badly damaged and worn, the arbor can be drilled to fit a new top pivot and square.   However tightly it is fitted into the arbor, always put a pin through the arbor and the plug to make certain that the plug will not move.

When the pivot has been fitted into the frame, proceed to file the square.   It is always as well to place a brass collar over the pivot to avoid damage should the file slip.   The collar should be of the same length as the pivot.

Renewing Barrel Holes

The barrel holes often get badly worn and become wide, but can easily be renewed.   They can be closed with a cone punch placed over the boss inside the barrel.   Place the barrel on a flat steel block, with a piece of newspaper in between to prevent the bottom of the barrel from being badly marked.   A sharp blow on the punch with a medium-weight hammer will close and harden the hole.   The hole can then be broached open to fit the barrel-arbor pivot.

When broaching the hole, place a thin strip of wash leather through the hole with the broach. The leather will prevent the hole from becoming five sided. Always use a strip of wash leather round the broach when broaching any large hole.

Barrel Covers

Tighten the barrel covers if they can be removed easily, as they must snap tightly in place. It is worth while making a few levers of different sizes for lifting off barrel covers. Using a screwdriver is not good practice. The lever should be rounded slightly underneath, and the end which is tapered should be thin enough to be inserted between the mainspring and the underside of the cover. Obviously the levers must be hardened and tempered.

The cover can be removed by giving the opposite end of the barrel-arbor pivot a sharp tap on the bench ; but it may increase the endshake.

Removing Mainsprings for Cleaning

The mainsprings must be removed from the barrels for cleaning. To remove a mainspring, partly wind the spring by means of a mainspring winder so that it is possible to get at the hooking. Push the eye of the mainspring off the hook on the barrel. Then still holding the centre of the mainspring in the winder, carefully withdraw the spring so that it does not fly out from the barrel. It is always as well to place some identifying mark on the mainspring, if not already marked. Always mark the spring to correspond with the barrel and arbor to which it belongs. If the barrel has one dot, mark the spring with a corresponding dot. As the barrels are invariably marked, it is unnecessary to mark the going barrel with a " G " and the striking barrel with an " S ".

If the springs are badly set they should be replaced, although this is not always possible. A spring can, however, be pulled out straight (not bent) by placing a screwdriver blade through the outside eye of the mainspring, and then gripping the blade firmly in a vice with the handle uppermost, of course, so that the eye cannot slide off when the spring is pulled out. Hold the spring with an oily rag and pull out gradually, letting the coils slide through the rag. This will enable the spring to be cleaned at the same time. Do not let the spring sag or slip, otherwise it will be ruined. Pull the spring right out until the inner eye is reached, but do not open the centre turn ; just twist the oily rag inside to clean it. Then carefully let the spring run back, holding it taut and releasing it gradually. On no account must the spring be distorted, as it will be likely to break.

We have now dealt with the general run of repairs, but any other necessary adjustments must be completed at this stage before proceeding to clean the clock.

Cleaning Solution

It must be remembered that a clock is not cleaned primarily to make it look attractive, but to remove old and dry oil which has accumulated in the holes, and on the pivots, wheel teeth and pinion leaves, etc. Wheel teeth become charged with dust and dirt and tend to cut the pinion leaves, so all of this must be removed. The best way, without a doubt, is by using a soft soap and ammonia solution made up as described earlier in Chapter 2. The solution is best used hot or just cool enough to bear one's hands in it. Never boil it again once it has been made, and do not leave any pieces in the solution while warming it up on subsequent occasions. All pieces must also be completely covered, including steelwork, if left in the solution for any length of time.

The plates, barrels and other large pieces can be placed in the solution separately, but it is advisable to thread the smaller pieces together on a piece of wire. This will make it easier to remove the pieces and will save groping for small pieces at the bottom of the basin.

When the solution is fresh it will take only about 10 minutes to bring up all the brass work, as new.

When the pieces are taken out of the solution give a quick brushing with a soft brush across the wheel teeth and odd corners. Then wash out thoroughly in benzine or petrol and dry in boxwood dust. Each piece must be brushed up afterwards, using whiting or soft chalk on the brush, to impart the final polish. All holes must be pegged out, and pinion leaves rubbed with pegwood to remove any traces of boxdust, etc. After this process has been completed the clock can be re-assembled.

Re-assembling after Cleaning

The barrels are put together first. Wind the mainsprings back into their respective barrels, using a clock mainspring winder. If the ordinary type is used, the mainspring is wound with a suitable arbor in the winder, the arbor being of the same size as the barrel arbor in the clock.

The spring is wound almost fully, held in the hand, the barrel is slipped over the mainspring, and then released from the hand while pushing the barrel over the spring.

Replacing the Mainsprings

When the spring is in the barrel, wind it to get the spring to fit on to the barrel hook, and, of course, test to see that it holds properly. Then let the barrel run slowly through the thumb and fingers until right down and release it from the mainspring winder.

Always make certain that the eye at the outside end of the mainspring is quite sound, and is not split or torn. Re-make the hook if it is torn, otherwise it will be certain to slip later and will cause damage, especially if it breaks when the spring is fully wound. Examine the inner eye as well, of course.

When the mainsprings are in the barrels, put the arbors in place. Always apply a little oil to the shoulders of the barrel-arbor pivots. This will make certain that the oil will run through afterwards. Apply a reasonable amount of oil to the coils of the mainsprings and also to the bottoms of the barrels. Be careful not to swamp the barrels, otherwise the oil will seep out and spread over the plates. Suitable oilers are shown in Fig. 302. The barrel covers must now be replaced.

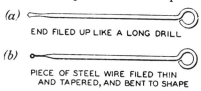

(a) END FILED UP LIKE A LONG DRILL

(b) PIECE OF STEEL WIRE FILED THIN AND TAPERED, AND BENT TO SHAPE

FIG. 302.—CLOCK OILERS.

(a) Convenient and robust type of oiler which can be made in different sizes and lengths for specific purposes.

(b) Type of oiler more suitable for small clocks.

Replacing Barrels and Barrel Covers

Push the cover home as far as possible with the thumb and hold it there. Then place the bottom of the barrel on the flat end of the bench, and strike the cover a sharp blow with the end of a brush handle to make it snap home.

When both covers have been replaced in this manner, fully oil the barrel-arbor holes. As they have already been slightly oiled, be careful to apply the right quantity. If the barrels have oil sinks, they should be half filled.

Next, fit the three little rectangular cocks in place on the plates. One carries the back centre pivot, another carries the back hammer pinion pivot, and a third is on the front plate carrying the front third pivot hole. The three are easily identified. The holes are usually of different sizes, and, another point, they will not interchange. In addition, they often carry makers' identification marks.

Fit the studs in place and see that all pins, which are a permanent fixture, are quite firm. Stand the pillar or front plate firmly on a box. This will make it easier to assemble, because of the winding squares, centre pinion arbor, etc., which stand beyond the plate.

Apply a little oil to the large or front centre pivot shoulder, and fit the centre pinion in place. Next fit the barrels in position, and then the two intermediate wheels and pinions. There is no danger of confusing these, as the striking intermediate wheel is smaller in diameter than the going. The hammer or pin wheel and the going third wheel and pinion can then be fitted in place. These are followed in turn by the hammer arbor, and the locking piece and arbor.

Fly Pinion and Spring

The locking wheel is then put in position, followed by the warning wheel, next the fly, and finally the 'scape wheel and pinion.

Do not forget to put a little oil on the groove in the fly pinion in which the friction spring rests, also in the holes in the fly itself through which the pinion arbor is fitted. Always make certain that the fly is on tension, and is not free to run round on the pinion. It must be friction held, but must be free to move when the train is suddenly locked. If not properly held by the spring, the train will race, and if tight on the pinion will bend some of the teeth owing to the momentum.

Assembling the Striking Train

The striking train can now be placed in mesh. Sometimes the top corner is filed off one of the pinion leaves and a dot is marked between two teeth on the wheel which gears into the pinion. Where the position is marked in this manner it is a help, but be careful as it is not always indicated correctly. Therefore, if any doubt exists, it is probably easier and safer to ignore the markings and assemble in the following way.

Position the locking pin to rest on the locking lever, and place the warning wheel with its pin half a turn from the cut-out slot where the warning piece will protrude. See that the lifting pin on the hammer arbor is equidistant between two pins in the hammer wheel. Then put the back or top plate in position, ease the centre and barrel arbor pivots in their holes and push just one pin in place, the one on the pillar between the two barrels.

Hold the frame in tissue paper to avoid finger marks, and apply very light pressure to hold the plates together. Fit the pivots in their holes, being careful not to bend them.

When the pivots are in place, fit all the pins in their pillar holes, check every wheel and pinion for endshakes and see that they all have just visible side shake. Press the barrel round with the thumb to see that the train runs freely. Then check the striking train and make sure that the setting up is correct.

Hammer and Locking Springs

Screw in the two springs, one for the locking lever and the other for the hammer arbor. These springs can be made by drilling screws, and driving blue steel wire into the holes and shortening to length. The hammer-arbor spring is slightly shorter than the locking-lever spring.

Push the barrel on the striking train, and let the train run slowly until the hammer pin drops ; it will be heard to click as it falls. Then notice if the locking pin has about an eighth of a turn to run to the locking ; if requiring adjustment, the little rectangular cock on the hammer wheel can be eased up and the hammer wheel taken out of gear with the locking wheel and altered accordingly. When this action is correct, place the locking pin on the locking lever and see that the warning pin is half a turn from the slot ; if it is not, the plates may have to be parted slightly in order to alter the mesh between the locking wheel and warning pinion. When this adjustment is correct, push the pillar pins in place and tap them home tightly.

Click Springs

Fit the ratchets on the barrel-arbor squares. Apply a small amount of oil to the barrel-arbor pivots ; they turn only when the clock is being wound, but must not be dry. Fit the cocks in place, positioning that with the corner removed near the dial pillar hole. The clicks and springs are usually interchangeable, but always make certain of this point as one may not be the original.

Oil the shoulder of the click screws, but apply only a small amount of oil. Then oil all pivot holes on the front plate, enough just to half fill the sinks, but no more, otherwise the oil will run away leaving the pivots dry. Do not forget to apply a small amount of oil to the click springs where they engage the clicks.

Tightening Motion Work

The lifting piece is next placed on its stud, with a little oil applied to the stud itself. Fit the cannon wheel, making sure that it is tight enough to carry the motion work ; also smear a little oil on the centre pinion arbor to prevent it from seizing up.

If the cannon is loose, it can be tightened by placing the pipe on a broach and closing the cut-away section of the pipe until it fits at the correct tension. The broach through the hole prevents the pipe from closing too much.

Assembling Motion Work and Striking Mechanism

Test the action of the lifting piece, and see that it is free in the cut-out slot. Oil the lower pivot hole of the minute-wheel pinion, and fit the minute wheel in place. The minute wheel and the cannon-wheel teeth are marked. Place the dot marked on a tooth of one wheel to coincide with the dot marked between two teeth on the other. Then put some oil on the stud on which the rack is pivoted, also apply a little oil to the cannon-wheel pipe, and fit the rack and the hour wheel together in their respective positions. Very often they cannot be fitted separately, as one part of the rack is under the hour wheel and the tail is above it.

The dots on the minute and cannon wheels, which have been arranged to coincide, should now be placed straight in line with the centre hole. There is a dot on the hour wheel, and this must be placed similarly in line and in gear with the minute pinion. Next, screw the minute-pinion cock in place. Turn the motion work until the snail, which is on the hour wheel, is in the correct position for 12 o'clock, and make certain that the rack tail drops freely to the bottom of the snail.

Turn the motion work for 1 o'clock. The rack tail must drop safely on the top of the snail, without the possibility of dropping off the corner. This is most important, because, if it does slip over the corner, it will stop the clock.

Fit the rack-hook with its collet, which is usually a collet with a square hole. Insert the pin from the top, leaving an equal amount of pin on each side of the square. Fit the rack collet next and pin it in place.

Note that all pins must be inserted from the top through to the bottom, should be almost straight and not carrot-shaped, must not be too long and, of course, must be quite firm.

Assembling the Pallet Cock

Put the pallet cock together, with the Brocot in place, not forgetting to place a little oil on the pivot of the wheel with its threaded rod ; also apply a little oil to the tongued spring, or, as is sometimes the case, to a pivoted screw which prevents the threaded rod from rising up. Then fit the pallets and arbor in place, and screw the pallet cock in position.

Oiling

After checking the escapement to see that everything is in order, proceed to carry out all the oiling with the exception, of course, of the back plate. Oil the hammer-wheel pins, the locking pin and the warning pin. Oil the gathering pallet, this will oil the rack teeth and the rack-hook. The lifting pins on the cannon wheel should be oiled, as well as the pin under the rack-hook which is engaged by the lifting piece. The top minute-pinion pivot hole can next be oiled, also the front pallet hole. Then fit the regulating rod in place and put a little oil on its pivot.

Where, as is often the case, a cock is screwed to the front plate to hold the front of the regulating rod, it should be fixed in place at this stage.

Fitting the Dial Plate

Put on the dial plate and pin it firmly, because there must be no play between the movement and the dial plate as it might stop the clock. Fit the hands in the correct places and see that the minute hand is on its correct square, also see that the minute-hand boss banks the hour wheel and prevents it from rising. Put on the hand collet and make a nicely burnished pin. Shorten the pin so that it projects by the same amount on each side of the centre pinion arbor, then put the pin in place and push it firmly home. Apply just a trace of oil, where the collet rubs the pin or the hand rubs the collet.

The suspension spring can then be fitted, after which all the holes in the back plate can be oiled. Do not forget to apply a trace of oil to the barrel-arbor pivots, also to the hammer-arbor pivot, as well as to the back pivot of the locking lever.

Hammer and Bell Standard

Fit the hammer in place, making sure that the head is quite tight. Do not solder the head if it is loose, as it will look bad, and, in any case, will not fix it permanently. Instead, as the rod is screwed into the head, re-tap the hole and screw in place again.

Screw the bell standard in position. If gongs are used there will be no bell standard, of course. The bell nut must not over-turn ; if it does, it must be replaced unless the hole can be properly closed and re-tapped.

Putting the Pendulum in Beat

The clock can now be placed on a suitable stand, after which the pendulum can be fixed in place. Apply a small amount of oil to the crutch where it engages the pendulum, then put the pendulum in beat. This is carried out by allowing the pendulum to come to rest and moving it first in one direction until the wheel tooth only just drops, then releasing it, when the clock should start off. Again bring the pendulum to rest and move it in the opposite direction until the wheel drops, when once more it should start off. When the clock will start in each case the pendulum is in beat. A check can also be made aurally. Rest a brush handle on the centre arbor and place the other end to the ear to amplify the sound of the beat.

Where this type of clock is provided with a Brocot pin-pallet escapement, it is not necessary to put the pendulum in beat in this way, as it is self-setting, and a good swing of the pendulum is all that is required. The crutch is not a fixture in this instance, but screws on to the pallet arbor.

Most French clocks are provided with a pendulum fitted with a regulating nut on the bottom of the rod or in the centre of the bob, but this is not necessary where the clock has a Brocot suspension. It is always better for the pendulum bob to be a fixture. A screw can be added to the bob to make it a fixture once it has been set to time, with the Brocot, of course, in the centre. In any case always make certain that the bob does not wobble on the pendulum rod, otherwise it will stop the clock.

As we have dealt with a French striking clock in some detail, it is unnecessary to go into further detail with other types of clock, as the general principle has been covered.

Methods of Cleaning Clocks

With regard to the method of cleaning, some older craftsmen still scrub the clock with rottenstone and oil. It certainly cleans a clock beautifully but takes longer. The rottenstone is washed off in benzine, or is placed into a box of whiting. Some use pumice powder, but this is scratchy, and although producing good results with some clocks makes others look drab.

It is not advisable to use ordinary domestic metal polish, as the clock tarnishes too quickly afterwards and the oil does not remain fresh for any length of time.

It is worth mentioning again that it is always as well to have two pots of soft soap and ammonia solution. The solution which has been in use for some time can be kept for the very dirty clocks, such as long case or English dial movements. When the worst of the dirt has been removed, the clock can be immersed in the fresher solution for final cleaning. Alternatively, if the clock is extremely dirty, use rottenstone and oil and brush vigorously, but, of course, this will take longer, as mentioned previously, although bringing up the clock like new.

With French carriage repeaters and grande sonnerie always remove the studs on the front plate. To avoid mixing the studs or losing them, cut a piece of thick cardboard of the same size as the plate. Then drill holes in the cardboard to correspond with the positions of the studs on the plate. As a stud is unscrewed, it can be fitted in the corresponding hole in the cardboard. The same applies to the springs and spring screws. This is a good plan to adopt with any exceptionally complicated clock.

One important point, do not place a clock in the solution unless it has been taken completely to pieces ; also do not put the barrels in the solution with the mainsprings in place. If a mainspring is extremely strong and it is unnecessary or inadvisable to remove the spring, clean the edge and the bottom of the barrel with rottenstone and oil, then clean in benzine and dry on a heated brass plate. Do not place the barrel complete into boxwood dust, as it will be almost impossible to remove it.

CLEANING WATCHES

When cleaning a watch the characteristic finish must be preserved, so one has to use discretion as to the best method to employ. The general tendency to-day is to clean a watch as quickly as possible. This may be good business, but is not necessarily good craftsmanship. Many watches are badly damaged and their appearance spoiled by quick and indifferent cleaning.

Hand-and-Brush Method

The best way with a very fine-quality watch is to use the old-fashioned and laborious method of cleaning in benzine and drying in boxdust, followed by a careful brushing with a good medium brush and using burnt bone with which to clean the brush. If, however, the 'scape wheel is made of brass or of gold it can be treated with a soft soap and ammonia solution.

Another way to clean brass 'scape wheels and good-quality

balances is to dip them quickly into a cyanide solution and then rinse immediately in water, and dry in boxdust. It is advisable to place the balances into lime afterwards to make certain that they are absolutely dry. Finally, a careful brushing with burnt bone will bring up the pieces like new. The great objection is that cyanide of potassium is a deadly poison and must be handled with extreme care to avoid accidents. Great care must also be taken to see that it is stored safely and that the jars are marked conspicuously with warning labels.

The use of a soft soap solution, however, is the better method and is certainly safer.

Cleaning Machines

The cleaning machine is a very useful adjunct to the equipment of a modern workshop, and, although many of the older craftsmen still prefer the hand-and-brush method, there is no doubt that it is efficient if properly used.

Various types are available, but the principle is the same, the parts being cleaned by fluid friction. One version consists of a small electric motor which rotates a wire basket containing the parts to be cleaned, three jars containing the solutions, and a fourth with a small heating element. The first jar contains the actual cleaning fluid and the rotation of the basket causes the fluid to enter all the crevices and remove the dirt. The basket is then raised and the solution spun off and then it is dipped into the first rinsing solution in the second jar. The third jar contains a further rinse and after this has been spun off the parts in the basket are dried in the fourth jar both by centrifugal force and heat. Care must be taken not to overheat during the drying cycle.

The earlier cleaning solutions were water based and could cause rust and tarnish unless the maker's instructions were carefully followed. It was advisable to strip the watch completely and be certain that no traces of cleaning-fluid were left behind to cause trouble later.

Waterless solutions are now available and it is not always necessary to strip a watch completely, though it is still advisable to clean the balance, lever and pallets, and escape wheel and pinion separately by hand. The pallet-stones and the impulse pin in the roller are fixed with shellac and the action of the cleaning fluid might loosen them and they could get lost, also the balance-spring could be weakened and/or distorted.

Later machines agitate the solution by setting up ultra-sonic vibrations instead of spinning the parts in a basket. Ultra-sonic tanks can be made large enough to deal with clock movements.

Solutions for use in cleaning-machines should be purchased ready made and the instructions for their use should be carefully followed. It must be emphasized that under no circumstances should benzine be used in a cleaning-machine. Benzine is highly rectified petroleum spirit and the vapour is very inflammable and explosive, a spark from the motor could well cause a disastrous explosion and/or fire. The soft soap and ammonia clock cleaning solution may smell and look the same as many water-based cleaning fluids but it should not be used in a cleaning-machine.

The larger horological material and tool vendors can either supply or recommend the correct machine and solutions to suit one's needs and pocket.

Examination of the Watch

We will take a typical movement as an example to explain the procedure involved when a watch is received for cleaning.

On receipt of the watch, examine the case for holes or gaps which permit the entry of dust and dirt. Then examine the glass and make sure there is sufficient freedom for the hands. If the glass is breathed upon and a circular scratch made by the minute hand shows up, this usually indicates that the glass is too low and it should, of course, be replaced. Another cause may be that the hands are too high, of course.

Make sure the hands do not foul each other, and also see that the hour hand does not ride up and down or is a bad fit. A foil washer placed between the hour wheel and the dial will often cure this trouble. In good-quality watches the boss of the minute hand banks the hour wheel to its correct endshake.

Inspection of Case and Fittings

Next, take off the hands without, if possible, removing the movement from the case. Where this is not possible, take the movement out of the case noticing whether it is a good fit, and rectify if necessary. Have the case repaired if the case screws have cut away part of the case. If the positioning pins are bent or worn, replace them before the watch is cleaned. Notice if the winding stem fits well and will not drop out ; also see

FIG. 303.—HAND-LIFTING LEVERS.

Levers are placed one on each side and under the boss of the hour hand. Both hands are removed together. If a silvered or metal dial, a piece of paper is placed between the levers and the dial to prevent scratches or marks.

that it fits snugly to the case, otherwise dirt and dust will enter. If a two-piece case, make sure that the two parts snap together tightly.

If a wrist watch, examine the strap and replace if badly worn. Likewise with bracelet watches, examine the springs and replace where necessary. The joint pins of a bracelet watch get very badly worn, and should be replaced. The knuckles at the end of the bracelet should also receive attention, because the watch may be lost if they become badly worn. Always inform the customer of the various points needing attention before the watch movement is cleaned, if the charge is likely to be large or more than usual.

Motion Work

When the case has been inspected and the necessary repairs effected, proceed with the examination of the movement itself. Remove the dial and examine the motion work for broken or damaged teeth. Take particular note of the hour- and the minute-wheel teeth. These teeth are sometimes bent and it is not always obvious from a casual inspection. The damage is caused by the cannon having been pushed in place with the minute wheel in position, with the result that a leaf of the cannon pinion just rests over the minute-wheel tooth, and, as the cannon is snapped home, it pushes the minute-wheel tooth downwards and bends it. The same sort of trouble occurs with the hour wheel. The dial is put on with the hour wheel resting on top of the minute nut or pinion, with the result that the hour wheel is pressed down and the tooth on the hour wheel is bent up. Damage of this nature is often the cause of a watch constantly stopping.

Make certain that the cannon pinion is tight enough to carry the motion work. In these days the snap-on type is mostly used, and, if necessary, the cannon pinion can be tightened as explained previously in Chapter 10.

Letting down the Mainspring

The next operation is to let down the mainspring and remove all power. Replace the winding stem and button. Lay the movement on the bench and hold it firmly with the last two fingers of one hand. Hold a piece of pegwood in the thumb and finger of the same hand. With the other thumb and finger turn the winding button, and, at the same time, use the pegwood to push the click out of action with the winding ratchet. Hold the click clear and let the button slide slowly through the thumb and finger until the spring is right down. Then take off the winding ratchet.

Examine each wheel in turn for endshakes, etc. Test the shake of the centre holes ; if the holes are wide, they must be renewed. Check for any obvious faults, such as broken teeth in the keyless wheels and broken screw-heads. Notice if the balance-spring is central. On some occasion it may have been pulled out with a pin, or otherwise damaged. Put a little power on the fourth wheel with a peg and try the escapement, making sure it locks ; also try the shake on the bankings.

When satisfied that the escapement is in order, ease the stud screw, and, if no turnboot is present, push the stud clear and ease the spring from the curb or index pins.

Removing Balance Cock

Unscrew the balance-cock screw and take off the balance cock.

If, on the other hand, a turnboot is fitted over the balance-spring, the balance cock must be removed with the balance and balance-spring in place. Take great care in this case not to catch the balance-spring in the teeth of the centre wheel as the cock is lifted ; also make sure that the balance can come out of the bottom hole freely, as the balance-spring must not be stretched.

When it is clear, turn the balance cock over carefully, and place it on the bench with the balance on top. Then move the turnboot, loosen the stud screw and remove the stud. The balance and cock will then separate. Be very careful not to bend the top balance-staff pivot. It is as well to try to keep the pivot outside the hole rather than in it.

Repairing Balance-Staff Pivots

Next examine the staff pivots for bends or other damage. The ends of the pivots become " mushroomed " due to slight blows received in wear, and this damage must be rectified.

The best way to repair pivots is in the turns. Use a screw ferrule of the type termed a " two screw ". This is a solid ferrule, which is easy to make. It is small enough in diameter to go inside the sunk-out part of the balance and is of sufficient thickness to

stand clear of the balance rim. On the flat side are fitted two large screws with thin heads. The balance is laid flat on the ferrule, with the arms under the heads of the two screws. The screws are then tightened sufficiently to hold the balance, but not so tightly as to cause damage.

The centre of the ferrule is turned out large enough to pass over the roller, so that it can be fixed on either side of the balance according to whichever pivot is to be repaired. The ferrule can be used without risk on the thinnest of balances. The front runner of the turns must be the eccentric.

Fig. 304.—
" Two Screw "
Ferrule.

On the back runner small beds are cut or filed to a depth of about ·002 inch.

A light bow is put on the ferrule, and, of course, the smaller the pivots, the lighter will be the bow. Use as small a burnisher as possible, as it will be easier to handle and will rest properly on the pivot. Use a fast backward and forward motion with the bow, and the reverse action with the burnisher, that is, as the bow is drawn down, the burnisher is pushed forward, and vice versa. The burnisher must be rolled at the same time to prevent the pivot from becoming ridged.

Never press very hard with the burnisher, which should also be slightly greasy, but not oily. A pivot polished in this manner will keep quite true and round, but if repaired in the lathe it is certain to become oval and will not be so highly polished.

Removing Burrs

To repair the ends of the pivots, replace the back runner by a lantern runner. As explained previously in Chapter 6 this runner is turned away to leave a thin face at the end through which small holes are drilled, just large enough to allow small pivots to pass through to the cone shoulder. Lantern runners can be made in various ways. A steel runner can be drilled with a hole about 1·5 mm. in diameter into which the lantern part can be fitted. This will make renewal easier.

The pivot is put through the hole, and is burnished with a thin, flat burnisher, which is rolled over the end of the pivot, as before, in the reverse direction to that of the bow. Do not round the ends of the pivots like half a ball, but just off the flat with no burrs on the edges. Test the pivots on the thumbnail and if the nail is scratched, a burr is present, which, although too small to be seen, must be removed.

The lantern runner is also useful to detect whether a pivot is very slightly bent. Put the pivot through the hole and rotate it slowly. If it is bent, however slightly, light will not be visible all the way round between the pivot and the side of the runner, as the pivot is turned, also the light on the side of the pivot will be deflected showing light and dark alternately as it revolves. Use a strong glass when carrying out this test.

Straightening Pivots

To straighten a pivot, use a pair of small, smooth-grip pliers. Make the pliers quite hot, hold the pivot for a few seconds to get it warm and then bend it. If the pivot is badly bent, do not attempt to straighten it with one sharp bend. It is far better to straighten it gradually and in stages, rather than risk a broken pivot. Each time, of course, try the pivot in the lantern runner. When the pivot has been straightened, repair in the usual way.

Lever Notch Repairs

Next examine the impulse pin in the roller. Make sure that the pin is tight ; also see that the guard roller edge is not damaged or marked in any way. Clean the edge if necessary, otherwise it will cause trouble.

Examine the lever notch and renew the sides if worn or pitted. This can be carried out by using a piece of very thin steel, stretched between a miniature saw frame. A piece of steel about ·001 inch thick is suitable, as it will pass between the dart and allow access to the smallest notch without the necessity for removing the dart. A little diamantine spread on the steel will give the notch a nice surface. Often a bad vibration in a watch can be traced to this source.

Polishing Pallets

Check the pallet-staff pivots for wear, and renew as necessary. As pallet-staff pivots invariably wear on one side, do not be deceived by a casual glance. If the pallet stones are worn on the locking or acting faces, they must be repolished or replaced. Replace if the pallets are of the visible or adjustable stone variety, and repolish if of the " invisible " type where adjustment is not possible.

The pallets should be polished on a revolving lap held in a collet in the lathe. The pallets are held in a holder, which fits on a plate fixed to the slide rest. The operation must be carried out on the slide rest to enable the angle to be brought coincident with the flat face of the lap. The tool holding the pallets must also be banked, otherwise when polishing the impulse plane, or the locking face of the hook pallet, the thin edge of the polishing lap may be damaged.

The finest diamond powder is used as the polishing medium or that which is termed the fourth washing. The diamond powder must be oily, otherwise the pallets will become hot and will move the stones. High speed is necessary. The speed of the lap should be about 6,000 revolutions per minute.

Checking Pivots and 'Scape-Wheel Teeth for Wear

The next stage is to take the watch completely to pieces for examination.

Examine all pivots for wear and repair where necessary, but replace the pivots if badly worn, or fit new pinions.

Inspect the 'scape-wheel teeth. In a club-tooth wheel, the heels of the teeth often get damaged. The only remedy in this case is to fit a new 'scape wheel, as there is no satisfactory way of repairing the teeth. If a ratchet-tooth wheel is damaged, it can often be repaired and touched up, especially if the locking on the pallets is on the heavy or safe side.

Correcting Depths

Always examine the leaves of the 'scape pinion ; if wear is present, notice how they are worn. If worn near the top, or the addendum of the pinion, it calls for closer examination.

Place the fourth and 'scape wheels and pinions in the frame together, and try the shake between the leaves of the pinion and

Fig. 305.—Worn Wheel Tooth and Pinion Leaf.

Illustrating normal wear met with in an old watch when the gearing is correct. If worn near the top, some inaccuracy is indicated.

the fourth-wheel teeth. If the shake is excessive, the depth is shallow and a new and larger fourth wheel is required.

If the fourth wheel is thick, it can sometimes be stretched and put through the topping machine and the teeth re-cut. Where there is any doubt, it is advisable to replace the fourth wheel, as it is a very important depth.

Polishing 'Scape Pinion to Size

If the wear on the 'scape pinion leaves is not constant there is some inaccuracy. If the depth is not shallow, the 'scape pinion may be proportionately too large. Where the pinion is only slightly too large, it can be polished down a little.

Use an old poising tool, that is, one having parallel steel jaws. File a slot in each jaw, both in a straight line with each other. Rest the 'scape pinion on its arbors in the slots. Close the jaws of the poising tool against the rivet on one end and the pinion head on the other. The pinion will withstand a reasonable amount of pressure this way.

Next choose a flat piece of soft solder and bend the end over at a right angle, about an eighth of an inch will be sufficient. Then hammer this part to make it very thin and wide. Now with wet oilstone dust on the piece of solder, proceed to rub it up and down the pinion leaves, keeping the wheel turning all the time. The soft solder will soon shape up to the pinion leaves and will start to grind them. Make certain that the wheel is kept turning in one direction only. The solder will be shaped like a rack and as it reaches the end, lift it up and start at the front again. As the end is reached each time, lift the solder and begin again. On no account turn the wheel and pinion backwards.

When the pinion is to size, clean off the oilstone dust, remove the teeth formed on the solder and thin it again. Then repeat the process, using diamantine instead of oilstone dust. This will polish the pinion, and will also remove all traces of wear.

If the pinion is much too large, the pinion and fourth wheel will have to be replaced. Examine all pinions for faults of this description.

Correcting Fault Caused by Third Pinion

The third pinion can cause trouble in some watches, owing to it being very short and the pivot shoulder being flush with the leaves of the pinion. The oil runs off the pivot into the pinion leaves, and is picked up and carried round by the centre-wheel teeth. The centre wheel runs over the balance-spring and when the watch receives a slight jar, the spring jumps up, gathers oil from the centre wheel and distributes it over the spring and index pins. As a result the watch gains rapidly, due to the coils sticking together.

The way to correct this fault is to turn a very deep undercut behind the third pivot shoulder, even if it means cutting the pinion head to form the undercut. Do not, of course, thin the pinion arbor at the top, otherwise if the mainspring breaks it may break the third pinion arbor. Use a long-pointed lozenge graver and it is easier if the operation is carried out in the turns, as very little power is required.

The Centre Wheel

Examine the centre wheel. Make sure that it is clear of the top of the barrel and also of the keyless work. Some large crown wheels have drop-down teeth and these always run close to the centre wheel.

Make certain also that the centre wheel is clear of the third wheel and of the sink turned in the centre bar or bridge.

Examining Barrel, Arbor and Mainspring

The barrel, arbor and mainspring should next be examined. Inspect the holes to see that they provide a close fit for the barrel arbor pivot. If the holes are wide they must be closed. It is almost impossible to re-bush the barrel holes in a small watch and, therefore, closing the holes is the only remedy.

Use a staking tool for this adjustment. Choose a cone punch which will pass over the tip of the boss of the barrel or cover, whichever is wide. Put just a trace of oil on the cone and place it in the staking tool. Turn the table of the tool to a part where there are no holes. Rest the barrel or cover on the table, with the boss uppermost. Place the cone over the boss. Hit the punch with a watch hammer, just hard enough to close the hole sufficiently. Then broach the hole to provide a close fit for the pivot.

Fit the barrel together without the mainspring and see that it runs true and flat with the minimum amount of endshake, but it must run perfectly free.

Fitting New Mainspring

Examine the mainspring and see that it is not set too much. It must open up when out of the barrel to at least three times the diameter of the barrel each side. If less than this, replace the mainspring. Fitting a new mainspring to a watch should be treated as a job of major importance, as the mainspring provides the whole of the motive power. The height of the spring must be the same as the distance between the bottom of the barrel and the groove for the cover. If the cover is not turned out, the spring must be just below the groove to be free. If the cover is turned out, the mainspring can reach the groove but must not be above it. The spring when resting in the barrel should occupy one-third of the space and the barrel arbor about one-third. This will give the maximum number of turns, irrespective of the strength of the spring.

The hooking attachment should take up as little room as possible. If the watch is fitted with stop-work, it is quite suitable for the hooking to be in the form of an eye, as shown in Fig. 306 (a). Where a watch is not provided with stop-work, a more resilient form is required, such as, a T-piece, or a riveted or loose piece hooking. Many fusee mainsprings are fitted with a square or round hook.

Making a Plain Hook

To make the eye in a mainspring, first drill a hole about a quarter of the width of the spring in diameter. Then broach the hole at an angle to produce a sharp hooking edge. Round the end so that the hole is the same distance from the end of the spring as it is from the sides. If too much metal is left at the end of the spring, it may force the eye off the hook as the watch is wound.

Finally remove all burrs and smooth with an emery buff.

Pivoted Brace Hook

The T-piece or pivoted brace hook is made from a piece of thin plate steel filed to the same width as the mainspring and with two pivots left standing, as illustrated. The pivots are rounded to work in holes drilled in the barrel and cover. The T-piece is riveted to the end of the mainspring in alignment and flush with sides of the spring.

The pivots must not protrude through the outside of the barrel or cover, otherwise they will be certain to foul. Do not shorten the pivots while in the barrel, or the barrel will be badly marked and scratched. Instead, remove the spring and shorten the pivots to the correct length.

Riveted Piece

In the form of hooking known as the riveted piece, a piece of spring is used, which is about $\frac{3}{32}$ inch long in a wristlet and about $\frac{1}{4}$ inch long in a pocket watch. A hole is drilled in the piece of spring, and a corresponding hole in the mainspring. A steel rivet is inserted to hold the piece of spring firmly to the mainspring proper.

The ends of the spring and piece are rounded and smoothed to prevent binding when the spring is fully wound. The end of the piece which goes on the barrel hook is filed back almost to a knife-edge to give it a lead on to the hook.

Loose-End Hooking

In the loose-end form of mainspring hooking, a loose piece is fitted between the bent end of the mainspring and the barrel. A piece of the mainspring is broken off and squared up. In length it should be about twice the width of the spring, or about $\frac{3}{32}$ inch long. The piece is bevelled at each end almost to a knife-edge and the corners are removed.

The end of the mainspring is heated gently to soften it and

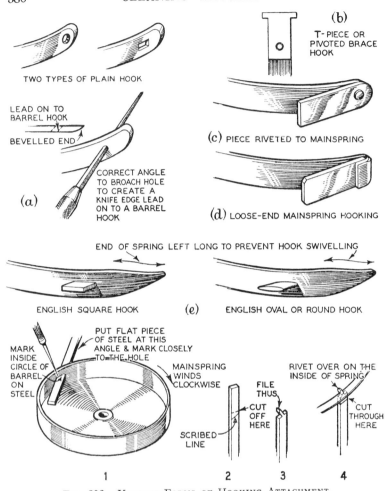

FIG. 306.—VARIOUS FORMS OF HOOKING ATTACHMENT.

(a) Two kinds of plain hook, with round and square eye respectively, and showing method of broaching hole to form a sharp hooking edge.

(b) T-piece or pivoted brace hook which is pivoted in the barrel and cover.

(c) Riveted piece on the end of the spring.

(d) Loose-end hooking. Sharp corners must be avoided, otherwise they will bind and stop the watch.

(e) Square and round hooks for an English fusee barrel, and showing four stages in the production of a square hook. The procedure is similar for an oval or round hook, except that a piece of round steel rod is used instead.

when red is bent to form a hook. Always bend while the spring is red, or it may break. More than required has to be bent over and shortened afterwards. The corners where the bend takes place must be rounded off to prevent any possibility of binding in the barrel. When the bend is completed, there must be sufficient to form a hook and no more ; also it must be open sufficiently to take the loose piece.

The mainspring is wound into the barrel, the loose piece is slipped in place, and the mainspring is wound up in the mainspring winder until the loose piece rests on the barrel hook.

As the loose piece must not be soft, it should be broken off the mainspring before it is softened. Some people bend the mainspring to form the loose piece solid with the mainspring, but as it is soft it buckles and collapses after the spring has been wound once or twice.

It is not essential to use a piece of the mainspring itself, providing the piece is not weaker or thinner.

Square and Round Hooks

The square hook in a fusee barrel is not so easy to make as the hookings just described. A piece of steel rod is filed to fit the square or rectangular hole in the side of the barrel. The steel rod is inserted through the hole at an angle, as shown in the diagram, and a mark is scratched on the steel corresponding with the inside edge of the barrel. The steel is then withdrawn from the barrel and placed in a vice, with the scratch parallel to the jaws. The surplus metal, which was inside the barrel, is now filed away, leaving a large pivot at the end.

A hole is then drilled in the mainspring, about a quarter of an inch from the end. The hole must fit the pivot closely ; also the hole must be chamfered on the *inside* of the spring. The steel rod is held firmly in the vice, and the *outside* of the mainspring is then put over the pivot.

The pivot is shortened until it stands about ·01 inch above the level of the spring, but no more, and is then riveted over until it is quite tight. The rivet is smoothed over, but not quite flush with the spring as it would weaken it. A saw is used to cut the rod, leaving a little more than the thickness of the barrel attached to the mainspring. This remaining part forms the hook. After any sharp corners have been removed from the hook, the mainspring is wound into the barrel. The attachment provided with the mainspring winder is used to hold the hook while the spring is being wound.

When the spring is in the barrel with the hook in place, the hook can, with great care, be filed to the level of the barrel edge. The mainspring should then be taken out of the barrel and the part of the hook which shows should be polished. The end of the spring beyond the hook should be filed to a taper, but not shortened in any way, and then smoothed or grained with an emery buff.

The reason for the surplus mainspring beyond the hook is to prevent the hook from swivelling when the mainspring is wound. The whole idea of this form of hooking is to prevent the barrel from being bulged when the mainspring breaks. It is a mistake to replace a square hook by an ordinary type of barrel hook. In any case, if this is carried out the square hole in the barrel must be filled in, otherwise the chain may turn over.

An oval or round hook in a fusee barrel is fitted in a similar way, except that a piece of round steel rod is used instead of square.

Replacing Barrel Hook

Another point with barrels is to check the barrel hook for wear. The punched type of hook is often used and frequently breaks off. Even the more satisfactory milled or screwed-in type becomes worn and unsafe, and has to be recut or replaced. Fitting a new barrel hook is a fairly simple operation, providing it is carried out in the right way. The procedure is shown diagrammatically in Fig. 307. It applies both to watch and clock barrels.

Drill a hole through the wall of the watch barrel. The hole must be central, of course, and should be about a fifth of the height of the inside wall in diameter. Tap the hole, but do not bring to a full thread.

File up a piece of steel rod to make a tapering pin, which will be small enough to allow about an eighth to a quarter of an inch to pass through the hole drilled in the barrel. Tap the steel pin to a full thread in the screw plate, and then cut the pin about ·03 inch above the thread as shown in the diagram. Do not cut the tapering part of the pin, but the larger part which has not entered the screw plate. Then file a well-shaped hook with an undercut, leaving it slightly higher than the thickness of the mainspring.

Hold the tapering end of the pin and unscrew it from the screw plate. Insert the thin tapering end through the hole in the wall of the barrel

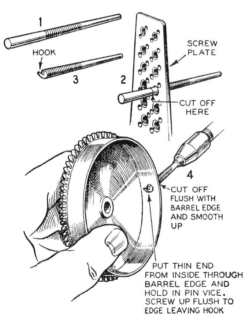

FIG. 307.—FITTING A NEW BARREL HOOK.

This type is sometimes known as the French hook. Silver steel rod is used and is not hardened.

from the inside. Hold the end firmly in a pin vice and screw the pin through the barrel wall until the hook is in the right place and is facing in the correct direction. When the hook is in position, cut off the surplus rod and smooth up flush with the barrel edge.

The barrel teeth should also be checked for wear. If the teeth are badly worn, find out the reason. Trouble may be caused by the barrel and centre pinion being badly matched, or by wrongly shaped teeth or leaves on the pinion.

Re-assembling and Oiling

Other parts of the watch have been dealt with in preceding chapters, so it only remains to clean the watch and re-assemble. After cleaning has been carried out, as described earlier in this chapter, assemble the barrel first. Do not forget to put oil on the coils of the mainspring and a little on the bottom of the barrel ; also apply a little oil to the shoulders of the barrel arbor. See that the barrel cover snaps on tightly. If the cover is loose, the barre can be closed to put this right. A small barrel can be closed sufficiently by gripping the barrel tightly in a lathe step chuck, but under no circumstances strain the chuck. If a large barrel, it can be closed by turning up a large cone in a piece of brass or steel plate, and forcing the barrel edge into the cone.

After the barrel has been replaced, fit the centre and third wheels and pinions in position. Do not forget to oil the shoulders of the centre-pinion pivots. With quite a number of watches, however, the fourth wheel and pinion has to be fitted first, so one cannot lay down a hard-and-fast rule. The craftsman must use his discretion in such cases.

Screw the centre bridge in position next. Do not forget that the lengths of the screws vary. At each stage of the assembly see that freedoms, endshakes, etc., are correct.

Fit the fourth and 'scape wheels and pinions, and place the cocks in position. Try the train to make certain it is quite free. Then put the trigger screw in place and screw the barrel bar in position with a trace of oil on the shoulder.

The Keyless Mechanism

Fit the keyless wheels in place, oil the top barrel arbor pivot hole, fit the click spring, and, should it be positioned underneath the winding ratchet, apply a small amount of oil where the spring engages the pin in the click. Then screw the ratchet wheel firmly in position.

Fit the large or idle crown, oil the steel collar and the sink where the screw holds it in place ; a smear of oil where the wheel rests on the plate is sufficient, and then screw it in position. If held by one screw, it will be a left-hand thread. Next fit the small crown and castle wheels. It is worth fitting the winding stem in place at this stage just to hold the crown and castle wheels in position.

Fitting the Set Hands and Motion Work

Fit the return lever and spring, also the trigger and spring, if a spring is provided, of course. Then put the small idle transmission wheel in place, applying a little oil to the stud, and screw the cover plate in position. If the cover plate carries the trigger lock spring, do not forget to apply a little oil where the action takes place, otherwise the spring is likely to be broken. Oil the lower or front centre hole, put a small amount of oil on the centre pinion arbor and then snap the cannon pinion in place.

Where the minute wheel is positioned under the keyless plate, fit the cannon pinion in place before setting the keyless mechanism. It is inadvisable to fit the cannon in place with the minute wheel, because the minute-wheel teeth may get damaged, if the cannon-pinion teeth foul them as the cannon pinion is snapped on.

Checking Crown and Castle Wheel Action

Pull the winding stem into set hands, and put a little oil on the ratchet teeth of the crown and castle wheels; also oil the winding stem slightly where it runs in the plate. Try the set hands, and see that the action is correct. Push the stem back and try the back, or reverse action to the winding, and see it is quite free to move and does not bind in the teeth of the crown and castle wheels.

Fitting Pallets and Pallet Cock

Fix the lever and pallets in place and screw the pallet cock in position. See that the pallet-cock screw does not stand above the pallet cock; also that the top pallet-staff pivot does not stand above the pallet cock when the pallets are raised up.

Oiling Pivot Holes on Front Plate

The pivot holes on the front plate must now be oiled. Apply a small amount of oil to the lower barrel-arbor pivot; it is turned

			Fig. 308.—WATCH OILER WITH PRICKER.
PRICKER, SHARP ENOUGH TO PASS THROUGH SMALL JEWEL HOLES	PIECE OF CLOCK PEGWOOD	OILER, DIMENSION ACCORDING TO SIZE OF WATCH. THIN END MAY BE USED AS A WEDGE	The pegwood handle prevents oiler and pricker from touching the bench and collecting dust and dirt.

only once a day but oil is necessary. Do not forget to oil the lower third pivot hole. Sometimes it is under the minute wheel and should be oiled before the minute wheel is fixed in position. Do not swamp the lower pallet-staff pivot hole with oil; only a little is required, but it must definitely be oiled.

Now apply a small amount of oil to the top pallet-staff pivot hole ; it must have oil, but as little as possible. Without oil this pivot would be worn off very quickly.

Oiling the Escapement

Wind the watch about half a turn of the winding ratchet. Then put oil on the impulse face of each pallet stone, and with a peg move the lever to release the teeth, until the wheel has completed a full turn so that each tooth is oiled by contact.

Oil the lower balance-staff hole, and be careful not to put oil on the lever notch. First put a little oil in the staff hole, and then let it through to the endstone. If it does not run through take off the endpiece and apply just a small amount of oil to the endstone ; then replace, being careful not to smear it. Finally, oil the top balance-staff pivot hole in the same way.

Replacing the Balance

The next stage is to replace the balance. First put the balance-spring in place. Place the balance on a stake, with a hole just large enough to allow the impulse pin to pass through easily with the small guard roller, and rest comfortably on the table roller. The collet is placed over the arbor on which it fits, and is pressed in place with a hollow flat punch. Do not use the sides of the tweezers, as the collet will be marked and it is a risky practice. If the tweezers slip, it may mean a ruined balance-spring, or a broken balance-staff pivot.

To remove a balance-spring collet, do not use a screwdriver blade or a knife blade to lever it off, but use a wedge, as described previously in Chapter 6. The wedge can also be used to turn the collet to put the watch in beat.

When the balance-spring is in place, ease the stud screw on the balance cock and put the stud through its hole. Then fit the balance-spring between the index pins and tighten the stud screw sufficiently to hold the stud. Next, carefully place the balance in position, making sure that the impulse pin enters the lever notch. Screw the balance cock carefully in place, making certain that the top balance-staff pivot enters the hole properly ; also be careful that the balance-spring does not get caught in the centre wheel and become buckled or bent.

The watch is wound up a little so that the balance can be kept swinging as the balance cock is being screwed in position. All screws must be screwed home firmly, but not viciously.

Putting in Beat

Test the movement to see that it is in beat. This is most important, especially in small watches, which should be perfectly in beat.

To test for beat, bring the balance to the point of rest. Then lead the balance round in one direction until the 'scape-wheel tooth drops and notice the distance the balance moves. Then bring the balance back to the point of rest again and lead it round in the opposite direction until the 'scape-wheel tooth drops. If the distance moved is the same in each case, the watch is in beat. If the balance sets on one side and not on the other, it is appreciably out of beat. It can, however, set on both sides and yet be a lot out of beat. If a watch will not set, it is nearly always in beat.

Checking Vibration of the Balance

When in beat, wind the watch a further half-turn of the winding ratchet and check the vibration of the balance. The balance should now vibrate half-a-turn each way, or a full turn altogether.

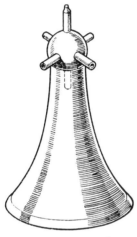

Next, wind the watch fully and carefully count the number of turns, not forgetting that it has already been wound one turn. The total should not be less than $5\frac{1}{2}$ turns ; a good-quality watch may require 6 or $6\frac{1}{2}$ turns. The vibration of the balance should now be $\frac{3}{4}$ of a turn each way or $1\frac{1}{2}$ turns altogether.

When the vibration is correct, oil all pivot holes not previously oiled. Remove the winding stem and put a trace of oil on the pivot, a smear on the sides of the square and a little where the crown wheel runs. Replace the stem and see that the keyless action is in order. Oil slightly where the return lever engages the groove in the castle wheel, and also where the hour wheel runs on the cannon pinion. Then put the hour wheel in place with a foil washer if necessary.

FIG. 309.—A USEFUL STAKE FOR PRESSING ON HANDS AND FOR SUNDRY OTHER PURPOSES.

Fit the dial and hands and see that the hands are free to run quite clear of each other. Hold the movement upside down over a small mirror to see that the vibration does not fall off ; also move it round on edge for the same purpose. Listen for any knocking or scraping. If everything is correct, case the movement, and it only remains to bring the watch to time.

Timing is dealt with in detail in Chapter 11.

PRACTICAL HINTS

Cleaning Jewel-Holes

English jewel-holes are cleaned by placing them in benzine and pegging them out on a piece of wash-leather. Always place them on a warm plate to make certain that there is no dampness in the settings. Peg off any hard dry oil on the curved backs or oil sinks.

Fusee Chains

Fusee chains are boiled in an oil pot, allowed to cool, and are then dipped in benzine and dried on tissue paper. It is advisable, in the case of ¾- or ½-plate watches, to hold the chain taut in two pairs of tweezers and pass it quickly through a spirit-lamp flame. This will destroy any small hairs caught up in the links, which may catch the balance screws and stop the watch.

Cleaning 'Scape-Wheel Teeth

Another point which applies to all watches, but particularly to the smaller movement, is that congealed or hard oil must be cleaned off the 'scape-wheel teeth.

The wheel must be held firmly, with a thumb or finger-nail placed against the teeth to prevent breakage, and then cleaned with pith or pegwood. These teeth are very delicate, but must be cleaned.

Watch Stop-Work

Do not remove the stop-work of a watch as it serves a definite purpose, which is to leave unused the weakest part of the spring and the strongest part in an endeavour to equalize the motive power. If the stop-work fails, it is not difficult to remedy even if a replacement has to be made. The stop-finger is easy to make as the old one can be used as a pattern and altered accordingly. The star wheel has to be cut on a wheel-cutting engine, but can be treated as an ordinary wheel of five teeth in the case of four-turn stop-work, and as a wheel of six in the case of five-turn stop-work. First cut the slots in the blank and then the curves.

One of the reasons why stop-work fails is that the star wheel has sharp corners which dig into the side of the stop-finger. To remedy this fault, round the corners very slightly and do not forget to smooth the damaged side of the stop-finger. (See Fig. 310.)

Another cause of failure is the corner of the stop-finger digging into the crescents of the star wheel where the finger itself moves clear of the slots. Again it is only necessary to round off the sharp corners, but carry out the alteration a little at a time and not to excess.

English Fusee Stop-Work

English fusee stop-work is different from the star-wheel form. It consists of an arm acted upon by a spring which keeps the arm towards the body of the fusee or away from the top plate. As the watch is wound, the chain raises the arm into the path of the fusee-poke and prevents the fusee from being turned any farther. If, as sometimes happens, it fails to hold the fusee-poke a broken chain or chain hook will result. This may be due to a wide top fusee hole or a bent stop-finger or arm. If the arm is bent, it can easily be corrected.

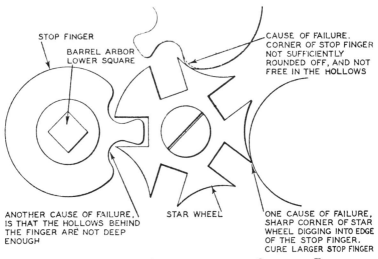

STOP FINGER

BARREL ARBOR
LOWER SQUARE

CAUSE OF FAILURE.
CORNER OF STOP FINGER
NOT SUFFICIENTLY
ROUNDED OFF, AND NOT
FREE IN THE HOLLOWS

ANOTHER CAUSE OF FAILURE,
IS THAT THE HOLLOWS BEHIND
THE FINGER ARE NOT DEEP
ENOUGH

STAR WHEEL

ONE CAUSE OF FAILURE,
SHARP CORNER OF STAR
WHEEL DIGGING INTO EDGE
OF THE STOP FINGER.
CURE LARGER STOP FINGER

FIG. 310a.—STAR WHEEL STOP-WORK SHOWING CAUSES OF FAILURE.

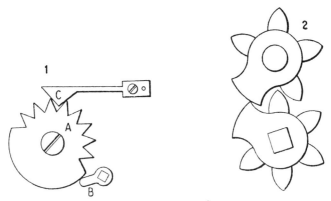

FIG. 310b.—CONTINENTAL STOP-WORK.

1. This form can be used for fusee as well as going-barrel stop-work.
   A.   Star wheel. This can be set for several different number of turns.
   B.   Finger piece.
   C.   Holding spring or jumper.
2. Geared stop-work. This type has to be correctly set up, otherwise it will fail. It is very seldom made now.

Straighten the arm until it is raised by the chain to a position where the fusee-poke will engage centrally with it. Always make certain that the poke is free of the stop-finger when the fusee has run down one turn.

Maintaining Power

Another important action in fusee watches and in chronometers

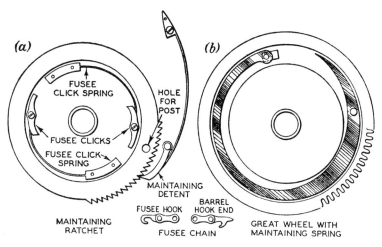

FIG. 311.—MAINTAINING POWER AND CLICK WORK OF FUSEE.

(a) Maintaining ratchet with clicks, etc.
(b) Great wheel with maintaining spring.

is the maintaining power. See that the nose of the maintaining detent is sharp and will engage properly with the maintaining-wheel teeth ; see, also, that it is clear of the fusee chain hook and the great-wheel teeth. The detent must have very little endshake.

The spring acting on the maintaining detent must not be strong, but it must keep the detent acting to the bottom of the ratchet on the maintaining wheel. The spring must also tend to lift the detent away from the pillar plate. This will help to take up the endshake. The fusee must be pinned up in such a way that there is no shake or wobble, yet the maintaining spring must act sharply.

Blueing Screws and Hands

Although in many Swiss watches of good quality nut-brown coloured screw-heads were used, the English have always favoured blue screws and steelwork.

The screws have first to be hardened and tempered to obtain a rich polish. Normally, when steel is polished, diamantine is used almost dry to obtain the required effect, but in blueing it should be used wet.

After the screws have been polished, they must be thoroughly cleaned to remove all traces of oil or grease. Then they are placed in a blueing pan and held over a spirit-lamp flame. The screws must be watched very closely as they change colour quickly, first to light straw and then in turn to dark straw, brown, purple and then dark blue. Always take the pan away from the flame as soon as the screws begin to change from purple to blue. The screws look better with just a trace of purple in the blue. With practice an attractive effect can be obtained.

Watch hands are blued in a similar way on a flat brass block with holes drilled to take the bosses of the hands, so that the hands can be laid flat to obtain an even film of blue.

Clock hands are blued similarly, but some clock-makers use an iron plate which is curved at the end. The hand is held in a pair of clean pliers and stroked on the plate which has previously been heated. Excellent results are obtained this way.

Sometimes the piece to be blued, especially if of an uneven shape, can be laid in brass filings in order to conduct the heat more evenly.

Jewelling

The fitting of jewels has been simplified in recent years by the introduction of the pressed-in type of jewel-hole. Many watches still in use, however, are jewelled in the old way, using either the brass set jewel-hole or the type which is retained by a burnished flange. The modern pressed-in type should present no difficulty, providing a suitable press is available, but it is the early type jewels which often present a problem.

Replacing a Broken Jewel

When a broken jewel set directly in the plate has to be replaced, always be very careful not to damage the setting when removing the old jewel. The setting is similar to the bezel holding the glass of a watch, the difference being that at first the setting is quite square and then, after the new jewel has been put in place, the bezel is burnished over the edge of the jewel to hold it securely in position.

The best method is to revolve the lathe slowly with the plate mounted in the mandrel, and with a pointed burnisher carefully open the bezel, or lift the " burr " as it is called. Then choose a suitable jewel-hole which will fit the bezel closely, and force the burr over until the bezel is closed and the jewel is retained firmly in place.

If a suitable jewel is not available, one which is slightly larger than required can be turned down to size and fitted. If the hole is too small it can be polished to size by means of an iron pin. This is a piece of thin, soft iron-wire which is filed down to pass through the hole. It is charged with fine diamond powder and lightly pressed into the hole while the lathe is turning at very high speed. Great care is required or the pin will bind and crack the jewel.

Brass Set Jewel-Hole

The English use the brass set jewel-hole and some Continentals use one of a similar principle. It is a very convenient method and

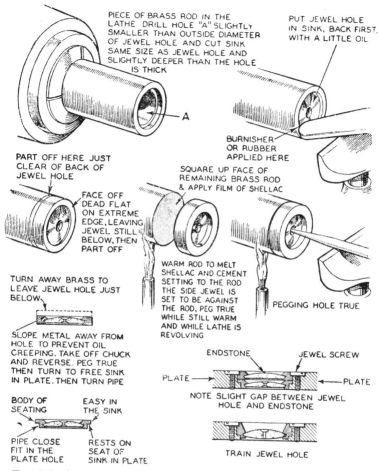

FIG. 312.—METHOD OF SETTING AND FITTING AN ENGLISH BRASS SET JEWEL-HOLE.

The jewel-hole and endstone are set in brass collets and held in place with two screws. This is a very convenient method, but it often gets mutilated.

the procedure is not difficult, but like all watch work requires practice.

Place a piece of brass rod in the lathe. The rod should be just larger than required. Drill a true hole slightly smaller than the outside diameter of the jewel-hole to be set. Turn a sink with a flat-ended cutter, which is about half as wide as the jewel. The sink should be turned to the same diameter as the jewel-hole and to a depth equivalent to twice the thickness of the jewel. The jewel must fit easily but not loosely in the sink. Put a little oil in the sink to hold the jewel while the metal is being burnished over the edge. The oil will also help to lubricate the burnisher and prevent it from tearing the brass.

When the jewel is secure, smooth the face with a polished graver and then turn the brass rod to fit the sink in the plate. With a parting-off tool cut the rod at the back of the jewel-hole, as shown in the diagram, leaving the sink quite sound. Square up the face of the remaining brass rod and warm the rod with a spirit lamp to apply a film of shellac.

Fix the jewel-hole with its brass setting to the rod, which is acting as a chuck. Place the side which has been burnished over against the face of the rod. Warm the rod and fix the jewel setting. Peg the setting true and flat with the jewel-hole by turning the lathe fairly quickly while the shellac is still soft.

Trim the outside edge of the setting true. Then turn away the excess metal to bring the back of the jewel itself flush with the back of the setting. Undercut the brass just to reach the jewel without removing any of the seat. Break any sharp corners on the setting and then take it off the rod. Reverse and peg true and flat with the jewel-hole. Turn the pipe, leaving the body of the setting at the correct thickness, otherwise endshakes will be altered. Boil out in methylated spirits to remove any trace of shellac from the setting. Finally, peg the hole clean and fit in place. This is, of course, an escapement hole or one having a conical pivot.

Train Holes

A similar procedure is used when fitting a train hole. The difference is that the back of the setting is not turned flush with the jewel-hole, but the setting is turned flush with the plate and the screw-heads are sunk into it.

When fitting a new train hole, it is better to turn these screw sinks or half-sinks in the mandrel. It is difficult if carried out with an ordinary sinking tool. A suitable sinker is made simply of steel rod, hardened and tempered and filed to the shape of a screw-

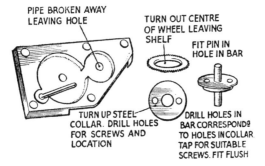

PIPE BROKEN AWAY LEAVING HOLE

TURN OUT CENTRE OF WHEEL LEAVING SHELF

FIT PIN IN HOLE IN BAR

TURN UP STEEL COLLAR. DRILL HOLES FOR SCREWS AND LOCATION

DRILL HOLES IN BAR CORRESPONDS TO HOLES IN COLLAR. TAP FOR SUITABLE SCREWS. FIT FLUSH

Fig. 313.—Method adopted to Effect Repair when Pipe of Large Crown Wheel is broken away.

As it is usually a left-hand screw-thread a steel collar is fitted with two screws.

driver blade, and fitted with a pin. The sinker can be used either in the lathe, or a ferrule can be fitted on it to work with a bow and runner held in the vice.

Repairing Broken Pipe of Large Crown Wheel

With some Swiss wristlet movements the pipe on which the large crown wheel is mounted, and through which a left-hand screw is fitted, becomes broken away. The remedy is to turn the centre of the wheel larger, leaving a shelf, and then to fit a collar to the hole and shelf and screw it to the bar with two screws. This makes a sound repair. (See Fig. 313.)

Adjusting Pallet Stones

Fitting and adjusting pallet stones is not such a simple operation as it sounds, and experience is needed to do it satisfactorily. Pallet stones chip very easily, so they must not be moved with tweezers. A thin, tapering piece of steel can be used as a wedge to push the stone outwards. The wedge is inserted behind the stone and is useful for making very fine adjustments. When pushing a stone back, there is less risk if a piece of pegwood or ivory is used.

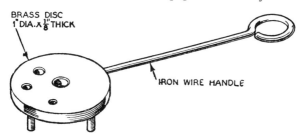

FIG. 314.—SIMPLE FORM OF PALLET-WARMER.
A similar tool is used for blueing hands, screw-heads, etc.

Fig. 314 shows a simple form of pallet-warmer, which is useful for holding the pallet while a stone is moved. The tool consists of a small brass plate mounted on four small feet to keep it off the bench and thus retain the heat longer, and a wire handle by which it is held while being heated and hung up when not in use. It is an advantage if the plate is drilled with one or two holes to take pallet staffs of different sizes, although one large hole is sufficient. In any case, one large hole is useful if it is wished to alter only one stone without interfering with the other.

The plate is heated until the shellac is softened sufficiently for the stone to be moved. The plate will retain the heat longer if the metal is about $\frac{1}{8}$ inch thick and 1 inch in diameter.

APPENDIX

CAUSES OF FAILURE AND BAD TIMEKEEPING IN WATCHES AND CLOCKS

WATCHES

Balance and Balance-Spring

1.—A watch " out of beat " is a common fault contributing to bad timekeeping. Bring the balance to the point of rest and move it first in one direction and then in the other. When " in beat ", the amount of movement to let the wheel drop is the same in each direction. Only the " duplex " and chronometer differ.

2.—Balance out of poise, causing positional errors.

3.—Balance-spring collet too thick, or not seating properly, and fouling underneath the balance cock when the watch is " dial-up ".

4.—Balance-spring out of flat and fouling the arm of the balance, or that part of the balance cock into which the stud is fitted.

5.—Balance-spring not tightly pinned into the collet or stud.

6.—Elbow of the overcoil fouling body of the balance-spring when the balance has a full vibration.

7.—Balance-spring out of truth in the centre, or not correctly pinned to the collet, " throwing " and causing second coil from the outside to foul the index pins in a flat-sprung watch.

8.—Balance-spring not at equal pressure from the index pins or, in a small watch, not playing evenly between the pins.

9.—Index pins not upright but embracing the balance-spring closely, thus tilting the body of the spring.

10.—Loose index pins causing isochronous errors ; very thin index pins have the same effect.

11.—Index pins too long, allowing the body of the spring to jump into them, in the case of a balance-spring with an overcoil.

12.—Index pins or turnboot too long and fouling the arm of the balance, in the case of a flat balance-spring.

13.—Loose index, moving as the balance-spring is wound or unwound.

14.—Oil or foreign matter on the balance-spring, causing the coils to stick together and the watch to gain. Often due to oil running down the third pinion leaves, being picked up by centre-wheel teeth and carried over the balance. At the slightest jar the balance-spring jumps and gathers oil from the centre wheel.

400

15.—Watch having become magnetized.

16.—Balance-spring slightly rusted. Always examine very carefully ; if the rust is very slight, boil balance-spring in oil, leave in hot oil until cold and then clean. This will prevent the rust from getting any worse.

17.—Balance-spring having been left in the cleaning solution too long, causing the watch to lose.

Lever, Guard Pin and Roller

18.—Horns of the lever fouling the pipe joining the two rollers of a double roller:

19.—Horns of the lever of unequal length, giving the false impression of the lever being out of angle.

20.—Guard or small roller fouling the lever. This is often due to excessive endshake in the balance staff, or wide holes for the pallet staff.

21.—Dart or guard pin too shallow, or guard roller too small, permitting impulse pin to butt on the ends of the lever horns or even to get behind the horns.

22.—Crescent in guard roller not coincident with the impulse pin, resulting in the guard pin or dart fouling the corner of the crescent on one side.

23.—Insufficient shake on the bankings, and guard pin resting on the edge of the roller.

24.—Impulse pin too long and fouling the dart, or the lever too high, or roller too low on the balance staff.

25.—Guard pin wedging against the roller edge in the case of a single roller. Either the roller is too large or the guard pin is too shallow.

26.—With both single and double rollers, the guard being too shallow and the lever passing across to the wrong side, resulting in the impulse pin coming to rest on the back of the lever and the watch being overbanked. The same applies if the pin or dart is missing.

27.—Balance vibrating too extensively, causing the impulse pin to foul the back of the lever and the watch to gain seriously owing to the rebound. This is known as striking the bankings or " rapping ". A weaker mainspring is the only remedy.

28.—Roller running out of true or out of flat, causing uncertain action. May foul the lever or cause balance to overbank.

29.—In some older Swiss watches of best quality the solid bankings having been scraped away, allowing the body of the dart to foul the 'scape-wheel teeth.

Impulse Pin

30.—The impulse pin in a small watch being tight in the lever notch and binding. A slightly tapering impulse pin is free when the endshake is up and tight when the endshake is down.

31.—Impulse pin fouling. Where small watches have a riveted dart, the dart itself is part of a round block. Sometimes this round block protrudes into the lever notch and the impulse pin may foul the block. A very thin notch file will clear it.

32.—Impulse pin fouling the horns of the lever.

33.—Impulse pin loose in the roller.

34.—Impulse pin too shallow, or banking pins too wide, allowing impulse pin to butt on the corner of the notch and horn instead of entering the notch cleanly.

35.—Oil on the impulse pin of a lever watch. A jewelled impulse pin should never be oiled.

36.—A steel impulse pin substituted for a jewelled pin, causing rust when working in a steel lever. Replace by a common gold pin if a jewelled pin is not available.

37.—A steel impulse pin working in a brass lever, not being very lightly greased. Do not oil in the ordinary way, however, as this will cause trouble.

Balance-Staff pivots

38.—Balance-staff pivots damaged and binding in the holes.

39.—Balance-staff pivots " mushroomed " or flattened and binding on the holes when the watch is either " dial-up " or " dial-down ".

40.—Pivots, whether balance, pallet staff or 'scape pinion, fitting too closely and stopping the watch in cold weather.

Banking Pins

41.—Banking pins not upright, the shake on the bankings being uncertain when endshake is up or down.

Jewel-Holes and Endstones

42.—Jewel-holes set some distance from the endstones and the pivots failing to reach the endstones. This applies to both the 'scape pinion and balance staff when they have conical pivots. Short pivots act the same.

43.—Jewel-holes set out of flat causing the pivots to bind in the holes under certain conditions and to be free at other times.

44.—Jewel-holes or endstones loose in their settings.

45.—Jewel-holes and endstones cracked or broken.

46.—Jewel screws or endpiece screws overturned.

47.—Endstones not set flat, thus increasing the friction against the side of the jewel-hole on one side, also increasing the friction on the end of the pivot.

48.—Endstone set too near the jewel-hole, resulting in the oil creeping away and leaving the pivot dry.

49.—Pits worn in the endstones, increasing the friction on the ends of the pivots and causing falling off of vibration.

Pallets

50.—'Scape-wheel teeth fouling the belly of the pallets.

51.—Exit pallet fouling underneath of pallet cock when the pallet staff is not quite upright.

52.—Top pallet-staff pivot too long, protruding above the pallet cock when the endshake is up and fouling the balance.

53.—Excessive " draw " or too little " draw " on the pallets.

54.—Lever and pallets out of angle.

55.—The locking corner of either a club-tooth or ratchet-tooth 'scape wheel dropping on the corner of the pallets or on the impulse plane, or, as it is commonly termed, " mislocking ".

56 —Wheel not properly free either inside or outside the pallets due to mismatching of the 'scape wheel and pallets, or damage.

57.—Pallet faces at the wrong angle, resulting in the lockings being unequal ; one only just safe and the other too heavy.

58.—Impulse angles on the pallets too high, causing the balance to set heavily with the 'scape-wheel teeth on the impulse planes.

59.—Loose pallet stones caused by the action of the cleaning solution. Always test pallet stones to see that they are quite secure.

60.—Chipped pallet stones or fragments of shellac left by careless fitting.

61.—Pallet-staff pivot, or 'scape-pinion pivots, being slightly bent.

62.—Worn pallet-staff pivots. An obscure cause of stoppage, usually the result of not oiling or greasing the pivots. Pallet-staff pivots wear on one side, not all the way round. In small watches, a new pallet staff is the only remedy.

63.—The 'scape wheel fouling the underside of the lever in a right-angled escapement. The lever is a separate unit and is pinned to the pallets. The 'scape wheel is too high or the pallets low.

Ratchet-Tooth 'Scape Wheel

64.—Front face of ratchet-tooth 'scape wheel being worn, and mislocking or failing to draw up sharply.

65.—Teeth of ratchet-tooth 'scape wheel too thick at the ends and providing insufficient clearance.

66.—In the case of a ratchet-tooth escapement with covered stones, the 'scape wheel working on the steels instead of on the jewels, through the wheel being planted too low or the pallets too high.

Club-Tooth 'Scape Wheel

67.—Heels of a club-tooth 'scape wheel worn or damaged with consequent loss of impulse.

68.—Pallet faces badly worn due to the jewels being soft. This is more apparent in the case of a steel club-tooth wheel.

69.—Tooth broken out of 'scape wheel, or wheel out of truth, or one tooth shorter or smaller in the impulse plane. These faults can cause serious trouble.

Chronometer and " Duplex "

70.—In a chronometer or " duplex ", the 'scape tooth missing the impulse pallet through insufficient " drop " or a worn wheel.

Pinion Depths

71.—'Scape pinion too large, causing fourth-wheel teeth to butt and stop the watch.

72.—'Scape pinion too small, causing leaves to butt on fourth-wheel teeth when 'scape wheel unlocks and recoils.

73.—Train pinions too large or pitched shallow, making frictional depths and resulting in uneven distribution and power losses.

74.—Wheels having the incorrect number of teeth, or pinions having the incorrect number of leaves.

75.—Wheels fouling each other, due to being out of flat or too thick.

76.—Centre pivots of a hollow centre pinion being burred or swollen as a result of using excessive force when fitting centre arbor and cannon pinion. The pivots bend in the holes ; sometimes the pivots are split.

77.—Centre pinion being bound by dust cap at one end and cannon pinion at the other, through short centre pivots or insufficient clearance in the top sink.

78.—Leaf cracked or broken in the centre pinion as a result of the mainspring breaking.

79.—Bent or damaged barrel and centre-wheel teeth, the result, as before, of the mainspring breaking. This can happen in wristlet as well as larger watches.

Holes

80.—Holes anywhere in the movement worn oval in shape. The pinion end in each instance is the most likely to be affected. Not only brass holes, but jewel-holes wear in the same way.

Train

81.—Lower fourth pivot being long and occasionally fouling 'scape-wheel teeth. This sometimes happens in small watches where the 'scape wheel is larger than the fourth wheel, and the fourth wheel is raised and the 'scape wheel runs underneath in a sunk-out space.

82.—Balance fouling the fourth wheel, sometimes occurring in hand-finished Swiss movements.

83.—The fourth wheel fouling the entrance nib of the pallets, where the fourth wheel is run near the bottom plate, and the pallets are above the wheel and the endshake of the fourth wheel brings them close.

84.—Balance sometimes fouling the third wheel in English centre-seconds watches where the fourth wheel is in the centre of the watch and the third wheel is above the level of the 'scape cock. The only remedy is a new balance staff with a slightly longer roller arbor. Do not bend the balance.

85.—In some flat English watches the centre wheel running very close to the fourth wheel and sometimes fouling. The wheels are too thick and should be thinned.

86.—The steady pins in some older watches have been bent or filed, permitting the cocks or bars to swivel. Remedy by making them firm in their proper positions.

87.—Endshakes too little or excessive, and insufficient freedom in the holes for the pivots.

Mainspring

88.—Mainspring hooks binding or scraping barrel or barrel cover. The ends of the mainspring must be rounded properly and burrs cleared.

89.—Mainspring too high for the barrel, causing the mainspring to bind in the barrel and stop the watch.

90.—Mainspring set and not giving maximum power.

91.—Mainspring too strong or not positioned correctly in the barrel, giving insufficient turns to drive the watch full time. A wrist watch requires 5 to $5\frac{1}{2}$ turns to run full time. The best quality give 6 to 7 turns and run for about 40 hours.

Stop-Work

92.—Stop-work action faulty, causing watch to stop. Correct but do not remove the stop-work, otherwise the quality of the timekeeping will be spoiled, as its function is to equalize the pull of the mainspring.

Motion Work

93.—Hands failing to carry through the cannon pinion being too easy or motion wheels not being free. Teeth being bent in the motion wheels. Steel idle transmission wheels not being free on their studs or being bound by caps or bars covering them.

94.—Hour wheel being caught by burr pushed up in slot of barrel cover, caused by lifting the cover carelessly, or due to barrel cover rising up when not pressed home properly.

95.—Hands fouling the glass or dial. Breathe on the inside of the glass and if a circular scratch made by the minute hand shows up, it usually indicates a low glass.

96.—Hour hand catching the seconds hand near the centre, or the point of the hour hand catching the seconds hand. This may not always stop the watch ; it may depend on the amount of freedom of the hour wheel. A foil washer may help to take up the shake.

97.—Centre or point of the minute or sweep-seconds hand fouling the glass. If an enamelled or polished dial, a finger placed over the glass will make a reflection on the dial of two or more hands. The distance between any pair in the reflection is the precise distance between the hand and the glass. If a silvered or dull dial, a piece of tissue paper placed over the centre and the bezel closed on it will show at once whether there is freedom. A good way to remove hands from small watches with silvered dials is to remove the minute hand only. The seconds hand will come off with it. The hour hand can be removed after the dial is taken off.

98.—Minute hand binding on hour hand.

99.—Hands not free in dial hole.

100.—Seconds hand too close to minute hand in centre.

101.—Pipe not free in pipe of cannon pinion.

Keyless Work

102.—Contrate teeth of the idle crown wheel fouling the barrel due to wide holes in the barrel or excessive endshake in the barrel and barrel arbor.

103.—Winding button too small or knurling much worn, causing difficulty in winding the watch fully. A mainspring which is too strong has the same effect.

104.—Pivot of winding stem in small watches left too long and fouling barrel teeth.

105.—The teeth of the castle wheel in some shaped watches, when in set hands, damaging the barrel teeth, resulting in dust filling the leaves of the centre pinion and stopping the watch.

Screws

106.—Case screws tightened excessively, sometimes causing plate distortion and lack of endshake, or even altering position of banking pins and stopping the watch.

107.—Long screws fitted incorrectly for short ones. Always check jewel screws or endpiece screws, especially with the very flat or thin watches.

108.—Screws not secured firmly in position. Always make sure that they are screwed home firmly, but not too tightly or the heads may break.

109.—Loose timing screws in a balance.

Burrs

110.—Small pieces of metal or burrs, left after machining, fouling the 'scape-wheel teeth.

111.—Burrs left in sinks, or fragments of metal left where two sinks meet and have not broken through cleanly. These foul wheel teeth or break off and catch in wheel teeth or pinions.

112.—Burrs left on pivots, after rounding the ends, binding in the holes.

Hairs and Obstructions

113.—Small bristles or hairs caught in the balance screws, acting like a brake when in contact with the 'scape cock.

114.—Hairs caught in the chain of a fusee $\frac{3}{4}$-plate watch, fouling the balance screws and possibly stopping the watch apart from other troubles. Always pass the chain through the spirit lamp after cleaning to lessen risk of this happening.

115.—Long dial keys working out and dropping in the train. Try to arrange for the keys to screw right home to secure the dial. Modern watches are provided with side screws.

CLOCKS

116.—Lack of firmness in the suspension spring, or a badly-fitting crutch, and the clock out of beat are the most common causes of failure.

Pendulum

117.—Pendulum bob loose on the rod, resulting in loss of impulse.

118.—Weights swinging with the pendulum and setting the case moving with them, when a grandfather clock is not fixed to a wall and the weights and lines become of the same length as the pendulum. The remedy, if the customer does not wish the case to be fixed, is to arrange for the weights to rest lightly against the door.

119.—Pendulum rod riding in the back of the crutch causing bad timekeeping, if not stopping the clock.

120.—Pendulum rod binding in the crutch due to crutch cheeks not being properly rounded, or not parallel.

121.—" Rise and fall " regulating mechanism floppy or easy in an English clock.

Suspension

122.—Pendulum bob oscillating or rolling when the suspension spring is buckled. A common fault in French clocks with a double suspension.

123.—Suspension spring not fitting the block in the " Brocot ".

Escapement

124.—Angles of the impulse planes of the pallets too high, especially in recoil escapements.

125.—Pallets worn and shallow with excessive " drop ", pallet arbor pivots worn on one side, and oval pallet holes.

126.—Small 'scape pinion in a recoil escapement stopping the clock, due to the pinion leaves butting on the teeth of the third wheel.

127.—Inaccuracy in the pallet pins of a Brocot pin-pallet escapement, causing a tendency for the clock to stop, or, at least, the timekeeping qualities to be impaired.

128.—Too much drop in the wheel and pallets, resulting in lack of impulse and causing poor vibration.

129.—In a dead-beat escapement the 'scape-wheel teeth dropping on the impulse plane of the pallets. Does not always stop the clock or regulator but will cause very bad timekeeping.

130.—Pallets loose on pallet arbor, or crutch loose on pallet arbor.

131.—'Scape-wheel teeth worn or damaged, and unequal freedom in the pallets. Straighten and repair teeth, or fit new wheel. A large 'scape wheel can be trimmed true and filed up again from the back, but not the radial sides of the teeth.

Train

132.—Bad 'scape- and contrate-wheel depth in a clock with a platform escapement and insufficient endshake to contrate-wheel pinion.

133.—Third-wheel teeth worn through working in a large 'scape pinion. The best remedy is to knock off and reverse the wheel. If the 'scape pinion is worn, move the third wheel lower on the collet before riveting back in position.

Motion Work

134.—Motion work not correctly geared where the snail is mounted on the hour wheel, and, as in French clocks, the pipe is not keyed, resulting in the rack dropping only half-way down at 12 hours and causing the clock to stop at a minute-or-two to one o'clock due to the step in the snail fouling the rack tail.

135.—Date wheel in a grandfather or long-case clock not correctly geared to clear the highest point of the hour snail.

136.—Date-ring teeth inaccurately cut and cam-wheel pin or post fouling the top of the tooth and holding up the hour hand or stopping the clock.

137.—Hour wheel bound by boss of minute hand, owing to friction spring on the cannon wheel flattening or losing tension, with the result that the cannon pinion is pushed lower down the centre pinion arbor.

138.—Cannon wheel fouling the bridge on which the hour wheel runs. Sometimes due to the pipe on the bridge being bent.

139.—Transmission wheel between hour wheel and alarm wheel in French grande sonnerie being too deeply meshed, causing occasional stoppage due to the wheels binding.

140.—Bent or damaged pins on the cannon wheel of a French clock, causing striking to be released too early or too late. Hand collet loose in the minute hand can give similar effect.

141.—Minute-hand collet binding inside hour-hand collet and holding up motion work, or stopping the clock.

142.—Failure to oil the pin securing the hands and collet on the centre arbor sometimes causing hand to be broken should the pin fire up when setting the hands.

Barrel and Mainspring

143.—Barrel teeth slightly bent, caused by a badly-fitting key, or careless winding, allowing the mainspring to jerk back and miss the teeth of the winding ratchet.

144.—Barrel arbor ratchet teeth worn or clicks worn, resulting in unsafe winding and risk of damage to barrel teeth.

145.—Winding squares too small or much worn. The squares must be replaced.

146.—Mainspring binding in the centre of the barrel when fully wound owing to boss being larger in diameter than the barrel arbor, or mainspring too high or barrel cover domed inwards.

147.—Insufficient endshake for the barrel arbor in the barrel. Too much endshake of barrel arbor between the frames causing barrel to foul intermediate wheel.

Fusee

148.—Fusee key screw too long in the head and fouling arm of centre wheel.

149.—Fusee-poke fouling the stop-arm on the first turn down after fully winding.

Striking Mechanism

150.—Failure to oil the warning pin in a striking clock, resulting in the clock stopping. The warning pin butting because it is badly engaged by the warning piece. Hands being knocked backwards in some older striking clocks because the cannon wheel friction spring is not strong enough.

151.—Quarter train failing to run after having released the hour rack and stopping the clock through hour rack tail fouling the snail.

152.—Flirt in French clocks not engaging correctly with the pin on the rack-hook, resulting in the clock failing to strike.

153. Warning wheel in a clock not correctly meshed, resulting in the clock failing to release, or the warning piece butting on the pin and stopping the clock.

154.—Studs replaced incorrectly in a French carriage clock causing binding in the various levers.

Dial Plate

155.—Movement not fixed firmly to the dial plate, allowing the movement to oscillate with the pendulum and causing the clock to stop.

Lines

156.—Lines of a long-case clock not clearing the clicks on the great wheel on the first turn down from fully wound.

INDEX

411